THE WORLD PHILOSOPHY MADE

THE WORLD PHILOSOPHY MADE

From Plato to the Digital Age

SCOTT SOAMES

PRINCETON UNIVERSITY PRESS

Princeton & Oxford

Published by Princeton University Press
41 William Street, Princeton, New Jersey 08540
6 Oxford Street, Woodstock, Oxfordshire OX20 1TR

press.princeton.edu

Library of Congress Cataloging-in-Publication Data
Names: Soames, Scott, author.
Title: The world philosophy made :
from Plato to the digital age / Scott Soames.
Description: Princeton, NJ : Princeton University Press, 2019. |
Includes bibliographical references and index.
Identifiers: LCCN 2019019545 | ISBN 9780691176925 (hardcover)
Subjects: LCSH: Philosophy and civilization. | Philosophy—History.
Classification: LCC B59 .S63 2019 | DDC 306.01—dc23
LC record available at https://lccn.loc.gov/2019019545

British Library Cataloging-in-Publication Data is available

Editorial: Rob Tempio & Matt Rohal
Production Editorial: Ali Parrington
Text and Jacket/Cover Design: Chris Ferrante
Production: Merli Guerra
Publicity: James Schneider, Katie Lewis & Alyssa Sanford

This book has been composed in Baskerville 10 Pro and Futura PT

Printed on acid-free paper. ∞

Printed in the United States of America

1 3 5 7 9 10 8 6 4 2

This book is dedicated to my dear wife Martha
without whom it could not have been written
and
to my friend Frank Price
the wisest man I know

CONTENTS

Introduction   ix

Timeline   xiv

1   The Dawn of Western Philosophy   1

2   A Truce between Faith and Reason   20

3   The Beginnings of Modern Science   40

4   Free Societies, Free Markets, and
    Free People   73

5   Modern Logic and the Foundations
    of Mathematics   92

6   Logic, Computation, and the Birth
    of the Digital Age   113

7   The Science of Language   133

8   The Science of Rational Choice   157

9   Mind, Body, and Cognitive Science   188

10 Philosophy and Physics   220

11 Liberty, Justice, and the Good Society   250

12 Laws, Constitutions, and the State   303

13 The Objectivity of Morality   341

14 Virtue, Happiness, and Meaning in the
    Face of Death   373

    Appendix: The Noble Deaths of Socrates
    and David Hume   386

    Bios of Leading Figures   397

    Acknowledgments   405

    Notes   407

    References   425

    Index   435

INTRODUCTION

In May of 2016 I published an article, "Philosophy's True Home," at the *New York Times Opinionator* blog. The article was written in response to an earlier piece, "When Philosophy Lost Its Way" by Robert Frodeman and Adam Briggle, which contended that western philosophy's institutionalization in the university in the late nineteenth century separated it from the study of humanity and nature, and diverted it from its central task of guiding us to live virtuous and meaningful lives. I responded that recent and contemporary philosophy in the west had not lost its way, but, on the contrary, was continuing its record of impressive success both in laying the conceptual foundations for advances in theoretical knowledge and in advancing the systematic study of ethics, political philosophy, and human well-being. After the article appeared, my editor, Rob Tempio, at Princeton University Press, suggested that I explore the topic in a book-length work, which I was initially not inclined to do.

Before long, however, I became intrigued by the idea and convinced that it might serve a larger purpose. Having spent my adult life trying to advance the areas in philosophy at which I am most adept, I had not given sufficient thought to the overall shape of the discipline and its place in the modern world. I knew that, in the aggregate, we philosophers have many productive, though rather specialized, professional contacts with mathematicians, physicists, biologists, psychologists, linguists, cognitive scientists, neuroscientists, economists, political scientists, law professors, historians, classicists, and others. As chairman of the Department of Philosophy at the University of Southern California, I was also aware of positive receptions our philosophy-led interdisciplinary undergraduate majors *Philosophy, Politics, and Law* and *Philosophy and Physics* have received, which I hope our new offering, *Philosophy, Politics, and Economics,* will too. But I had, I am afraid, tended to dismiss, as unalterable, the depth of ignorance about who we are and what we do among the general educated public, large swaths of academia, and, most importantly, among many of the young who might otherwise profit from what we have to offer.

Thinking more about it, however, I have become more optimistic. I now believe that the ignorance I previously deplored is due, in part, to our own failure as philosophers to seriously address a larger audience. This book is an attempt to correct that by explaining what western philosophy is, what it has been, and what, I am convinced, it will continue to be. Contrary to the opinion of many, the study of western philosophy today is not the study of a frozen historical canon from Socrates and Plato to Kant, Hegel, and Nietzsche, offering a smorgasbord of previous responses to unanswerable questions yielding no genuine knowledge. Although history remains an important part of the subject, today's philosophers generate new philosophical questions, while offering better answers to traditional questions than those given by earlier thinkers. As a result, philosophical knowledge is increasing and the canon in philosophy is always expanding.

Philosophers have been, and continue to be, deeply involved in all important areas of intellectual concern, including the arts, the sciences, and the humanities. Properly understood, philosophy is not an isolated discipline, but the partner of virtually all disciplines. Nor is western philosophy the whole story. Although this book is concerned with it alone, many of the remarkable advances in civilization that western philosophy has helped to bring about have become the common property of all cultures. As more works in different philosophical traditions are translated and new bodies of secondary literature grow up, new syntheses will become possible, sparking new philosophical departures.

In sum, this book is about the contributions philosophers have made, and continue to make, to our civilization. Of course, it wasn't philosophers alone, whether western or not, who made the civilized world we enjoy today. But the effects of their efforts have been more profound and far-reaching than is commonly realized. Our natural science, mathematics, and technology, our social science, political institutions, and economic life, our education, culture, religion, and our understanding of ourselves have been shaped by philosophy. This is no accident; it is due to the essential interconnection of philosophy with all foundational knowledge.

Philosophy never advances against a background of rank ignorance. It flourishes when enough is known about some domain to make great progress conceivable, even though it remains incompletely realized because new methods are needed. Philosophers help by giving us new concepts, reinterpreting old truths, and reconceptualizing questions to expand their solution spaces. Sometimes philosophers do this when sciences are born, but they also do it as disciplines mature. As science advances, there is more, not less, for philosophy to do. Our knowledge of the universe and ourselves grows like an expanding sphere of light from a point of illumination. As light travels in all directions away from the source, the volume of the sphere, representing our secure knowledge, grows exponentially. But so does the surface area of the sphere, representing the border where knowledge blurs into doubt, bringing back methodological uncertainty. Philosophy monitors the border, ready to help plot our next move.

The reader will, I hope, gain a sense of what this means when moving through the book. The first six chapters cover ancient Greece, the Middle Ages, the Renaissance, and the sixteenth through eighteenth centuries, followed by the late nineteenth and early twentieth centuries. There you will see remarkable advances by all manner of intermixtures of philosophical thought with mathematical, scientific, political, and religious thought—sometimes in single minds and sometimes in communicating minds. The focus will shift a bit when chapters 7 through 10 move you deeply into the twentieth century and beyond, examining the genesis of modern theories of rational decision and action, the efforts to advance our understanding of language and mind, and the struggle to make sense of what modern physics is telling us about the universe. Here the focus is less on the origins of easily recognizable tangible benefits we enjoy today (though there are some), and more on the role of philosophers, sometimes leading, sometimes merely supporting and supplementing, the work of specialists trying to bring order to natural phenomena that are difficult to conceptualize in both emerging and well-established sciences. The final chapters, 11–14, attack pressing legal, political, moral, and even existential questions. Here no problems are definitively solved. The contributions, if they are such, lie in articulating productive perspectives for attacking them.

I close with an invitation and a warning. Much in this book reports on the impact of philosophers and their work on broader areas of thought and action, as well as the impact of developments outside of philosophy on philosophy itself. But not all of the reasoning you will encounter is about philosophy. Some of it is philosophy itself—expositions of some leading ideas of the great philosophers, criticism and assessment of those ideas, and independent reflection on philosophical themes. In short, some of what you will encounter is philosophical reasoning and argument pure and simple. Thus, you are invited not only to review a picture of what philosophy has done up to now, but to engage with philosophy in the making, and, thereby, to do a bit of philosophy yourself by critically assessing the philosophical reasoning you find here.

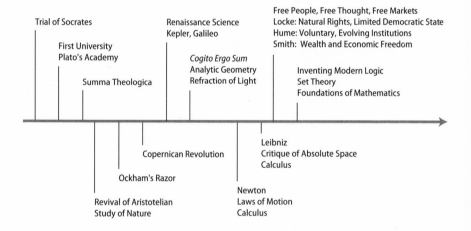

Trial of Socrates

First University
Plato's Academy

Summa Theologica

Renaissance Science
Kepler, Galileo

Cogito Ergo Sum
Analytic Geometry
Refraction of Light

Free People, Free Thought, Free Markets
Locke: Natural Rights, Limited Democratic State
Hume: Voluntary, Evolving Institutions
Smith: Wealth and Economic Freedom

Inventing Modern Logic
Set Theory
Foundations of Mathematics

Copernican Revolution

Ockham's Razor

Revival of Aristotelian
Study of Nature

Leibniz
Critique of Absolute Space
Calculus

Newton
Laws of Motion
Calculus

Understanding Modern Physics
Relativity and Quantum Mechanics

Rational Decision Theory
Subjective Probability
Agent Relative Utilities

Can Philosophy Reestablish
Moral Objectivity?

Death and the
Meaning of Life

The Study of Language and
Mind becomes Scientific

Mathematical Computability, the Birth of the Digital Age
Godel, Church, and Turing

The Struggle for a Principled
Theory of Law and Jurisprudence

Establishing the Scope and Limits of Logic
Completeness, Incompleteness
and Logical Consequence

New Approaches in
Political Philosophy

THE WORLD PHILOSOPHY MADE

CHAPTER 1

THE DAWN OF WESTERN PHILOSOPHY

The world-transforming goals of Socrates, Plato, and Aristotle; rational inquiry as the means to theoretical knowledge of the world and practical wisdom in the art of living; the intertwining of Greek science, mathematics, and philosophy; Plato's Academy; the later schools of Stoicism and Epicureanism.

There is no better expression of the spirit animating the birth of western philosophy than the first sentence of Book I of Aristotle's *Metaphysics*, "All men by nature desire to know."[1] What we desire to know includes not only particular facts, but also general truths that explain such facts in terms of features of the world that transcend the varying deliverances of our senses. It was a founding principle of western philosophy that such knowledge requires precisely delineated concepts—e.g., *number, element, point, line, angle, shape, circle, sphere, circumference, area, dimension, space, volume, matter, density, body, velocity, motion, direction, proportion, causation, change, permanence, quantity,* and *quality*—deployed according to the laws of logic, and used to formulate principles of mathematics, and universal laws of nature. In addition to knowledge of the world, what we seek also includes knowledge of ourselves, our common human nature, the good lives we aspire to live, and the good societies to which we hope to contribute. It was a further founding principle of western philosophy that knowledge of these normative matters can be objective, and so requires precise concepts of *goodness, happiness, virtue,* and *justice,* deployed with all appropriate rigor. It is to Socrates, Plato, and Aristotle, more than any others, that we owe these world-transforming ideas.

Of these, the central figure is Plato—in part because Aristotle was his student, and in part because what we know of Socrates is derived largely from the Socrates-figure of Plato's dialogues. Born in Athens in or about 427 BCE, Plato was raised in a culture in which one's knowledge of the world, one's place in it, and the models for one's conduct were derived largely from imaginative identification with the gods and heroes of orally performed epic poetry.[2] At the time of his birth, the poetry of Homer and Hesiod was still the primary vehicle of instruction in Athens. Such poetry was not only, or even primarily, a form of entertainment; it was, as Walter Burkert says, the glue that held Greek society and culture together.

> The authority to whom the Greeks appealed was the poetry of Hesiod and, above all, of Homer. The spiritual unity of the Greeks was founded and upheld by poetry—a poetry which could still draw on living oral tradition to produce a felicitous union of freedom and form, spontaneity and discipline. To be a Greek was to be educated, and the foundation of all education was Homer.[3]

Eric Havelock, whose pioneering work documented the transformation of ancient Greek culture from oral and narrative to written and rationally critical, saw epic poetry as a living encyclopedia for transmitting Greek history and culture to the young. The individual, he observed,

> is required as a civilised being to become acquainted with the history, the social organization, the technical

competence and the moral imperatives of his group. . . .
This over-all body of experience . . . is incorporated in
a rhythmic narrative . . . which he memorizes . . . something he accepts uncritically, or else it fails to survive in
his living memory. Its acceptance and retention are made
psychologically possible by a mechanism of . . . self-
identification with the situations and the stories related
in the performance. . . . "His is not to reason why."[4]

This was the mindset Plato set out to change. Deriving
inspiration from Socrates, he sought to transform his culture into a rationally critical one in which all knowledge—
normative and nonnormative alike—was objectively stateable, logically testable, and intellectually defensible. In
short, he attempted to change the culture from one based
on the oral story (narrative) to one based on the written
statement (objective description).[5]

The monumental change Plato sought, and largely
achieved, did not begin with him; it was already underway
in pre-Socratic philosophy, science, and mathematics.[6] The
pre-Socratic philosophers—Thales (624–547 BCE), Heraclitus (535–475), Parmenides (born circa 510), Democritus
(died circa 465), and others—mediated the transformation
from the narrative culture of the Homeric age to the rationally critical culture brought to fruition by Socrates,
Plato, and Aristotle. To take one telling example, prior
to the transition, the Greeks had no word for matter and
no abstract notion of motion applying equally to animate
and otherwise inert bodies. After the transition, they had
measurable conceptions of matter, motion, velocity, shape,
direction, and other abstract concepts that were used to
formulate and test explanatory hypotheses purporting
to be universal laws.[7]

The pre-Socratic philosophers, who set the stage for
the transition from an oral, narrative culture to a written,

rationally critical one, had a foot in both. Unlike the narrators of epic poetry, they were more teachers than entertainers. Still, they often performed their written compositions, and so expected more to be heard than read, which affected their texts, which weren't treatises in the style of Aristotle. Greek mathematicians, who were often philosophers and sometimes astronomers (investigating the trajectories of celestial bodies), were also crucial to the cultural transformation culminating in Plato and Aristotle. Their important pre-Socratic achievements included:

The observations (probably not proofs) of Thales (who famously held that water is the element out of which everything is constituted)
   a) that a circle is bisected by its diameter,
   b) that the angles at the base of a triangle with two equal sides are equal, and
   c) that triangles with an equal side and two equal angles are themselves equal.[8]
The proofs by followers of Pythagoras
   a) that the sum of the angles of a triangle are equal to two right angles (prior to 450 BCE),
   b) that the square of the hypotenuse of a right triangle is equal to the sum of the squares of the other sides (prior to 450),
   c) that the square root of 2 is irrational, i.e., a number that can't be expressed as a fraction (prior to 450), and
   d) that the square roots of 3, 5, 7, 11, 13, and 17 are (like that of 2) also irrational (Theodorus, pupil of Protagoras and teacher of Plato, circa 400).[9]
The discoveries by Democritus (who developed the classical metaphysical theory of atomism)
   a) that the volume of a cone is ⅓ that of a cylinder with the same base and height, and

b) that the volume of a pyramid is ⅓ that of a prism with the same base and height.[10]

The proof by Hippocrates (circa 440) that the ratio of the areas of two circles equals the ratios of the squares of their diameters.[11]

The astronomical observations and hypotheses

   a) that the earth is a sphere, conjectured by both Anaxagoras and Pythagoras, and

   b) that the Morning Star is the Evening Star.[12]

Summing up the scope of these and other advances, the distinguished historian of Greek mathematics Sir Thomas Heath estimates that

there is . . . probably little in the whole compass of the *Elements* of Euclid, except the new theory of proportions due to Eudoxus . . . , which was not in substance included in the recognized content of geometry and arithmetic by Plato's time.[13]

Eudoxus (born 395–390, died 342–337) knew of Plato's Academy, which opened in 387, as a young man, and, after first establishing his own distinguished school of mathematics elsewhere, he moved it to the Academy, where he is credited with solving the proportion problem mentioned by Heath, (probably) prior to Plato's death in 347. Thus Plato and the Academy had essentially all the results that would later be systematized in 300 BCE by Euclid's *Elements*, the most influential work in ancient mathematics.

In Plato's Academy philosophy and mathematics were seen not as independent disciplines, but as intimately related inquiries contributing to one another. The first European university, the Academy educated students in a curriculum that proceeded through arithmetic (number theory), geometry, stereometry (the measurement of solid bodies), and astronomy (the discovery of the mathematical properties of the heavens), before culminating in philosophy, or "dialectic" (reasoned philosophical argument). Thus, the words inscribed above its doors are reputed to have been "Let no one destitute of geometry enter my doors."[14] According to Heath, Plato was right to find the genius of the spectacular achievements of ancient Greek mathematics in their connection to philosophy. Speaking of those achievements, Heath asks, "How did this all come about? What special aptitude had the Greeks for mathematics?" He answers,

> The answer to this question is that their genius for mathematics was simply one aspect of their genius for philosophy. Their mathematics indeed constituted a large part of their philosophy down to Plato. Both had the same origin.[15]

Rigor and precision were the origins of Greek mathematics and Platonic philosophy. Nothing is more characteristic of that philosophy than the search for definition. When Socrates asks *What is goodness, beauty, truth, knowledge, virtue, piety, or happiness?*, he is asking for definitions of the Greek words we would roughly translate as 'good', 'beauty', 'truth', 'knowledge', 'piety', and 'happiness'. Let us use the term *concepts,* as it is often used in philosophy, for the *meanings* that abstract nouns and noun phrases like these share with their translations in other languages—the realities they are used to talk about.

Confessing not to know the proper definitions of these words/concepts, Socrates asks his interlocutors for help, and they typically offer examples—of good things, pious practices, and virtuous individuals. But Socrates doesn't want examples; he wants to know what goodness, piety, and virtue really are. To know this is to know the real properties we attribute to something when we call it good, pious, or virtuous. Consider another case. Suppose we ask *What is a circle?* and someone answers by showing us a single circular figure, saying *That's a circle.* We would respond: *We don't want an example of a circle; we want to know what it is for any conceivable thing to be a circle: what conditions it must satisfy to be a circle.* The answer we seek is a definition: *A circle is the set of all points in a plane equidistant from a single central point.*

The definitions Socrates sought were similar—definitions that give necessary and sufficient conditions for any person or thing to be good, pious, or happy, for any statement to be true or known to be true by someone, or for anything to be beautiful. The goal of the joint Socratic and Platonic enterprise was to extend the objectivity and precision of Greek mathematics to the study of all reality. Just as stunning mathematical discoveries required concepts that were precisely defined (like *circularity*) or rigorously governed by axioms (like *point*), so the advances in knowledge of the world, and of ourselves, that Socrates and Plato hoped to achieve required precise, well-regulated concepts.

For Plato, this quest for knowledge rested on *Platonic. forms,* which, he believed, were the precisely delineated concepts needed for knowledge in any domain. They include:

(i) the forms *goodness, justice, knowledge, virtue,* and *happiness* needed for general laws explaining human behavior, human nature, and human institutions;

(ii) forms for *identity* and *distinctness,* forms for different kinds and properties of natural numbers, forms for two-dimensional geometrical shapes (*circularity, triangularity,* etc.) and their properties (*area, circumference,* etc.), and forms for three-dimensional geometrical figures (*sphere, cone,* etc.) and their properties (*volume, surface area*, etc.), needed to state timeless mathematical truths;

(iii) forms for *body, space, velocity, motion, rest, proportion, weight, dimension*, etc. needed to describe aspects of the natural environment.

Plato's goal was to use these concepts to construct general, exceptionless laws about ourselves and the cosmos, the truth of which would be knowable, yet independent of the knower.

It is telling that the Greek word Plato used for these concepts is translatable as "shape," as well as "form," indicating the role in his thinking of geometry, which was well understood in the Academy. Just as there is such a thing as the precisely defined form/concept *circularity,* which is neither itself circular nor located at any distance from anything else, so there is such a thing as the precisely delimited form/concept *beauty,* which is neither itself beautiful nor perceptible through the senses. The same is true of the other forms. Although they are real—there are, after all, such things as circularity, truth, and beauty --to ask where they are in space and how long they have been there seems misplaced. Since Plato took them to be constituents of the objective truths about reality which, with proper study, we may come to know, they had to be independent of our minds. For him, this meant that they were real things existing outside of space and time, yet capable of being recognized by the intellect.

These abstract concepts needed to state general explanatory truths were half of the Platonic equation. Objective knowledge requires not only propositions to be known but also a mind capable of knowing them. What is this mind, or psyche, that it may know itself and the world? Havelock addresses the question, as it confronted Socrates and Plato.[16]

[T]owards the end of the fifth century before Christ [about the time of Plato's birth], it became possible for a few Greeks to talk about their 'souls' as though they had selves or personalities which were autonomous and not fragments . . . of a cosmic life force. . . . Scholarship has tended to connect this discovery with the life and teaching of Socrates and to identify it with a radical change which he introduced into the meaning of the Greek word *psyche*. . . . Instead of signifying a man's ghost or wraith . . . a thing devoid of sense and self-consciousness, it came to mean "the ghost that thinks," that is capable both of moral decision and of scientific cognition, and is the seat of moral responsibility, something infinitely precious, an essence unique in the whole realm of nature.[17]

Plato outlines his conception of the soul in Book IV of the *Republic*, where he distinguishes three of its aspects or parts—the appetites or desires, willpower or emotive force, and reason. Proper education trains the will to be the ally of reason. Reason then controls desire, the soul is unified, and the agent achieves self-mastery. Plato speaks of this condition of the soul, in which each of its parts plays its proper role, as one of *justice* between the parts, drawing an analogy with the ideal state in which the philosopher king (reason) makes decisions for the good of all that are enforced by guardians (the will) to ensure proper order among the self-interested citizens (the desires). In Book VII he describes the education of philosophers in which they acquire abstract theoretical knowledge, which requires understanding the concepts that make such knowledge possible. To achieve such understanding, they must turn their attention to the forms, which are innately available to everyone.

The aim of Plato's Academy was to provide the education that leads to this self-realization. It did this by taking students through a rigorous curriculum in logic, mathematics, and philosophy, designed to enable them "to define the aims of human life in scientific terms and to carry them out in a society which has been reorganized upon scientific lines."[18] In bringing this educational plan to fruition, Plato invented the idea of a liberal education and founded the first institution dedicated to providing it. ·

Plato's greatest student, Aristotle (384–322/1 BCE), moved to Athens from his home in Stagira (in Thrace) in 368/7, joining the Academy at age 17. He remained there for twenty years, first as Plato's student and then as his colleague, until Plato died in 347. At that point, Plato's nephew became the head of the Academy and Aristotle left to found a branch of the Academy in Assos. In 343/42, he relocated to Macedonia, where he took over the education of a thirteen-year-old later known as Alexander the Great. Leaving his post when Alexander ascended the throne in 336/35, Aristotle returned to Athens a year later, where he founded his own "Peripatetic" school, in competition with the Academy.[19] There he remained until two years before his death.

A prodigious worker, Aristotle produced an enormous volume of work that began in the Academy, continued in Assos, and reached its zenith at his Peripatetic School. His writings extended nearly every domain of human learning. They are organized around the following major topics: *Logic and Language* (including definitions of truth and falsity, their bearers, the nature of judgment, predication, generality, patterns of logically valid argument, and fallacies), *Epistemology* (including proof, knowledge, and deductive and inductive reasoning), *Metaphysics* (including substance, essence, accident, existence, and God), *Physics* (the natural world and the cosmos), *Biology* (including the history, generation, life, and death of animals), *Psychology* (including perception, memory, reasoning, sleeping, and dreaming), and *Ethics, Politics,* and *Aesthetics* (including rhetoric and poetics).

A close follower of Plato in his early days, Aristotle then believed in the immortality of the soul, its preexistence before birth when it was acquainted with Platonic forms, and the need in later life to recollect or rediscover the forms through philosophical argument.[20] In time, he gave up those views and modified the theory of the forms in a far-reaching way. He also produced the first systematic codification of principles of logically valid inference and developed theories of ethics and politics that were more realistic and widely applicable than Plato's. Finally, he began to make good on the implicit Platonic promise of advancing empirical knowledge of the physical world and our place in it. While it was Plato who, more than anyone else, provided the inspiration, conceptual foundations, and institutional framework to advance human knowledge, it was Aristotle who, more than anyone else, gave us the systematic beginnings of logic, physics, biology, and social science (including psychology and political science).

None of the steps that Aristotle took away from his teacher on fundamental philosophical matters was more important than his modification of Plato's theory of the forms. To paraphrase what I noted earlier, it is plausible to suppose that just as there is such a thing as the form/concept *humanity,* which is neither itself human nor something of any height or weight, so there is such a thing as the form/concept *redness,* which is neither itself red nor any other color. Although it is plausible that *humanity* and *redness* are real, it seems strange to ask where they are in space and how long they have been there. However, Plato's conclusion—that the forms exist outside of space and time, and so are eternal and unchanging, despite being accessible to the mind—isn't the only way to think about them. Perhaps it sounds strange to ask when and where they are because they don't exist at any single place or time, but do exist at many places and times—namely, at all and only the places and times at which humans and red things do. If so, they are contingent existents of our world just as we are. That is how Aristotle thought of them.[21]

This modification of Platonic doctrine brought with it a new metaphysics of form, matter, substance, essence, and accident, which Aristotle used in studying physical change. Consider an individual man, Socrates, and a particular mountain, Mount Vesuvius. Both came into being at a certain time, endured through many changes, and at some point ceased, or will cease, existing. As a baby Socrates was small, and couldn't walk, talk, or survive on his own. In time, he grew larger and learned to do these things, while acquiring many new properties and losing others. One property he never lost was *being human*, which was essential to his nature. In contrast to this property, which is an essential property of everything that has it, the properties Socrates once lacked but later acquired, as well as those he once had but later lost, were inessential, or "accidental." A similar story could be told about Mount Vesuvius. It, too, has essential properties, including *being a mountain*, that it can't exist without having, as well as accidental properties that can be acquired or lost without affecting its continued existence.

Aristotle called things like Socrates and Mount Vesuvius, which endure through changes of the sort just illustrated, "substances." But, since these substances themselves come into existence and pass away, there must also be changes in, or of, substance. How could there be? Aristotle's model presupposes that in order for there to be change, something must change. What can it be, if no substance endures the change? His answer is that what changes is prime, or first, matter, which is the stuff out of which substances like Socrates and Mount Vesuvius are constituted. And what is that? The answer, unfortunately, is that prime matter is undifferentiated stuff—an all-purpose *we-know-not-what* in which properties, like *humanity* or *mountainhood*, somehow inhere. It is no good to ask what the essential properties of prime matter are. To think of a bit of prime matter as having such properties—in addition to accidental properties like *making up Socrates*, which it had for a time and then lost—would be to take it to be a substance, which it can't be, if, as Aristotle demands, prime matter is to be part of the analysis of *substance*. For him, every natural substance—i.e., every physically enduring entity E—is some bit of prime matter M shaped by a substantial form F into the kind of thing that E essentially is by F's inhering in M.

So the man Socrates was a bit of prime matter shaped by the form *humanity*. Since that is true of every human being, there must have been something else essential to Socrates that differentiated him from everyone else.[22] It is not entirely clear, from Aristotelian texts, what this was. But there is reason to take it to be his individual essence, a *form unique to him* that Aristotle calls the immaterial *soul* inhering in and giving life to his body. Something similar is said about every living thing. Naturally, human souls are different from those of other living things. For Aristotle the souls of plants are responsible for their nutritive functions; those of animals and humans have a nutritive component plus a sensitive component responsible for sensation, movement, and memory, while human souls also have a purely rational component called "the active intellect."

To appreciate this one must remember that for Aristotle, (i) contingently existing substances are combinations of form and matter, (ii) their forms don't exist independently of the substances they inform, and thus, (iii) when Socrates ceased to exist any form unique to him, i.e., his soul, also ceased to exist. It follows that the soul of Socrates, which was really the form, or principle of organization, of his particular body neither pre- nor post-existed him. There was simply no room for human immortality in Aristotle's world.[23] He did believe in an eternal God of pure thought—which was the uncaused teleological cause, or reason, for the existence, of everything else. But his God didn't intervene in the world, wasn't the object of prayer or worship, and wasn't a being that could either love or be loved.[24] This contributed to the impression that Aristotle the philosopher and Aristotle the budding scientist were more or less one and the same. For him, the greatest human goal was not to conquer the fear of death, to find consolation in the face of life's tragedies and disappointments, or to discover ultimate purpose in a universe impervious to our concerns; it was to understand the universe and everything in it. Although he believed this was the highest human good, he didn't take it to be the only human good. He was well aware that other, less contemplative but more practical, forms of the good life were possible for a wider range of people.[25]

If, in looking at all this, we ask *What, in sum, did ancient Greek philosophy contribute to the world?*, we must include the following.

(i) It played a vital role in transforming an oral narrative tradition based on myth and poetry into a more critically reflective culture in which the chief means of expression was the written word.

(ii) In so doing, it demonstrated the superiority of basing beliefs on evidence, argument, and rational examination, rather than on authority.

(iii) It offered a naturalistic worldview in which observed facts are to be explained not by interventions of deities, but by interactions of fundamental elements according to universal laws.

(iv) It asked the questions and provided the concepts—*truth, proof, definition, matter, mind, motion, causation, generation,* etc.—that made it possible to think scientifically about the world and ourselves, and, in so doing, laid the basis of what we now know as logic, physics, biology, psychology, and political science.

(v) It founded the first university in the western world, giving birth to the idea of a liberal education, blending mathematical, scientific, and humanistic investigations in a curriculum designed to produce not only technical proficiency, but wisdom.

(vi) It transformed our idea of god from an anthropomorphic one in Homer's time to Aristotle's perfectly good, perfectly rational cause of the universe, uniting Plato's form of the Good with Aristotle's Active Intellect.

(vii) It elevated our idea of the soul from a ghostly breath of life to the subject of conscious experience, the source of decision and action, and the seat of moral responsibility.

Though long and impressive, the list is still incomplete. In addition to providing the foundations for rational thought and the pursuit of theoretical knowledge in virtually every domain, the Greek philosophers, especially Socrates and Plato, imbued the search for theoretical truth with the urgency of a personal quest for meaning. The special genius that made them so compelling was in placing the idea that objective knowledge in any domain requires precisely defined concepts at the center of their vision of the good life. In order to live such a life, they thought, one should strive to know the essential nature of human goodness and happiness. Although Socrates didn't claim to have such knowledge, he did claim to know that it could be acquired only by rigorous reasoning. He also thought that to know the good is to be sufficiently motivated to do it. Thus, he reasoned, one's best hope of living a good life was in acquiring as much knowledge of oneself, of one's nature, and of goodness as one could.

This idea, endorsed by Plato, can be elaborated as follows: To believe that a goal is good is to value it, and to believe that a course of action is good is to place some value on performing it. When one acts rationally, one always performs the action one believes to be best at the time. A reason for action typically includes *the end one seeks* and *the means to secure it*. Faced with a range of possible actions aimed at bringing about various outcomes, one assesses the values of the outcomes and judges how likely the actions are to achieve them. If one is rational, one selects the action with the greatest expected return—i.e., the greatest value discounted by the probability of achieving it.

On this picture, there are two ways you can go wrong— by choosing an end that is inferior to another end you could have pursued, or by assigning an unrealistic probability to an action's achieving your end. These are failures that, Plato would say, can be minimized by extending your knowledge. The more you know about the good, the less likely you are to pursue a lesser end over a more valuable end. Similarly, the more you know about yourself, others, and the world, the less likely you are to misjudge the probability that an action will, if you perform it, produce a certain result. In short, increasing your knowledge of the relevant evaluative and nonevaluative facts should increase your chance of achieving the best result (even though it may not guarantee that result, because your knowledge may remain incomplete). Since one who habitually performs the best actions has the greatest chance of getting the best results, one who is wise should have the best chance of obtaining what is genuinely valuable. So, it would seem, if you always aim at what is good for you (or at what is morally good), acquiring wisdom should maximize your chances of being happy (or being virtuous). If, as Socrates and Plato thought, there is no fundamental conflict between what is good for you, and what is good full stop, then the pursuit of wisdom may turn out to be the pursuit of both virtue and happiness.

Although there is much to be said for this view, it leaves the relationship between virtue and happiness unresolved. One worry concerns the premise that we always do what we judge to be best (e.g., for us) at the time. That's not obvious. Sometimes, one is inclined to think, we may believe, or even know, that a certain action is best, but not perform it because we are tempted by something else. Although Plato and Aristotle had much to say about this, they didn't settle the issue, which is still debated today.

Another worry concerns the extent to which doing what one takes to be good for oneself coincides with, or differs from, doing what one takes to be good for others. To get to the bottom of this, one would have to explore what we human beings naturally value most. This is the last item on my list of what ancient Greek philosophy contributed to all who followed.

(viii) It conceptualized the problem of achieving virtue and happiness as that of discovering, and coming to understand, the essential elements of human nature, the nature of our relationships with others, and the requirements of our common life with them.

In addition to wishing to understand ourselves and the world, Socrates, Plato, and Aristotle recognized the high value we place on our relationships with selected others, their welfare and good opinion of us, the success of our communities, and the example we set for those who follow in our footsteps. Socrates displayed these self-transcendent goals during his trial, conviction, and confinement before being executed for impiety and corrupting the youth of Athens. Refusing to avoid his fate by quitting philosophy, by accepting exile, or by escaping from prison, he chose to honor his conception of the good life, to inspire others, to respect the laws of Athens, and to protect his friends from punishment.[26] Because he valued these things more than he valued a few extra years of life, the virtue he achieved didn't conflict with his happiness. Not least of those who learned from his example was Plato, who provided the theoretical underpinning and institutional framework for continuing the Socratic search for wisdom. When his teacher gallantly succumbed, Plato had the inspiring exemplar he needed to invest the search for the highest theoretical knowledge with the urgency of a personal quest for meaning.

Unfortunately, the idea that the highest theoretical knowledge was closely tied to living a good life was not an easy one to keep going. After Aristotle's death, neither the Academy nor his Peripatetic School, both of which lasted for centuries, were focused on philosophy as a way of life (as opposed to abstract theoretical inquiry) in the way that Socrates was.[27] But two other schools were—the school of Epicurus founded in Athens and two other cities around 306 BCE, and the Stoic school, founded in Athens by Zeno shortly thereafter. The latter taught acceptance of everything outside of one's control and cultivation of a peaceful state of mind. It was, for centuries, more popular than the former, which took the development of refined tastes and the satisfaction of desire to be most important.[28]

The Stoics derived their conception of the good from a view of the universe as a vast material thing, a living animal with a mind directing worldly events. To be virtuous was, for them, to be guided by thoughts that agree with those of the World Mind. Since that mind determines every event, and everything it determines is good, whatever happens is for the best. A wise person will therefore accept things, even when they thwart his or her aims. However, this didn't require renouncing desire. Being parts of the World Mind, one's desires play a role in determining what happens. Still, since all is for the best, one shouldn't be too attached to one's desires, but rather should greet every result with equanimity.

This view lasted until late antiquity, when Christianity and Neo-Platonism reintroduced immortal human souls as spiritual centers of consciousness—a view against which it was hard to compete. That Stoicism lasted as long as it did is a testament not to its fantastic theory of the world, but to its ability to provide consolation to those in need. As such, it is hard to see it as a legitimate heir to the world-transforming thoughts of Plato and Aristotle, the return of which in the twelfth and thirteenth centuries was, paradoxically, due to the intellectual needs of the religion that, with Augustine, had temporarily displaced them.

CHAPTER 2

A TRUCE BETWEEN FAITH AND REASON

*The rebirth in Christian Europe of Greek philosophy
as the route to worldly knowledge at a time in which
religion provided the individual's guide to living; the
Thomistic synthesis of Aristotelian philosophy and
Christian theology; the influence of John Duns Scotus,
Roger Bacon, and William of Ockham in setting
philosophy on an independent, scientific course.*

By the time of Augustine (354–430 CE), the energy derived from one of the founding ideas of Greek philosophy was exhausted. The idea, originating in Socrates and Plato, was that the systematic, reason-based examination of fundamental features of the world that makes advances in theoretical knowledge possible would, when applied to ourselves, lead to our greatest happiness, virtue, and wisdom. The decline of this idea was inevitable. The quest for theoretical knowledge is a collective task incrementally pursued over millennia; the quest for purpose, happiness, and virtue is the urgently personal task of a single lifetime. The two quests aren't incompatible and the former can contribute to the latter. But they aren't the same. Thus it's not surprising that the most long-lasting of the Greek schools, Stoicism, was more successful in articulating ways of coping with life's disappointments than it was with advancing theoretical understanding of the world, or with grounding its art of living in an informed conception of reality.

The world Augustine confronted contained no robust Platonic Academy, Aristotelian Peripatetic School, or Stoic School. He was initially attracted to Manichaeism, which saw reality as a perpetual struggle between two warring principles, one for good and one for evil. Although Augustine credited his rejection of this view to Plato, his Platonism was derived from the Neo-Platonism of Plotinus (204/5–270 CE), which, by the beginning of the fifth century, had degenerated into a dizzyingly abstract combination of other-worldly metaphysics with mysticism and obscure religious rituals.[1] Lacking the personal God of Christianity, the story of Jesus of Nazareth, and the promise of personal salvation, it couldn't compete with the rising power of the Church.

In choosing Christianity over Neo-Platonism, Augustine felt free to borrow from the latter in developing his own influential version of the former. It was largely in this way that important elements of Platonism survived in the Christian theology of the next eight centuries. During this period, God was the purely spiritual source of all being, simultaneously identified with goodness, love, truth, and reason; Platonic forms were ideas in the mind of God; the human soul was an immortal spirit, temporarily inhabiting a material body generating illusions and temptations that had to be fought; the goal of life was to ascend, after death, to an ecstatic union with God, and the means to that end weren't reason and empirical observation, but acceptance of God's gift of illumination.[2] Although Aristotle was not unknown in the Christian Europe of this period, what was known was largely confined to his work on logic.[3] Thus, the autonomous, systematic search for objective knowledge of ourselves and the world that had been Greek philosophy was, from the fifth century through the end of the twelfth, all but dead.

The genius of the High Christian Middle Ages—its foremost contribution to the world philosophy made—was in finding a way to give Greek philosophy a second chance by temporarily relieving it of the onus of finding the meaning of life and charting a path to personal fulfillment. It was able to do this because, by the end of the twelfth century, Christianity was the most secure, well-organized institutional force in Europe, with a far-reaching network of ecclesiastical and educational institutions. The beginning of the thirteenth century saw the founding of the Dominican and Franciscan orders, and the papal charter for the University of Paris, with its faculties of theology, canon law, medicine, and the arts. These took on the task of providing Christianity with what it then lacked, which was the intellectual underpinning needed to establish its place in the system of human knowledge. Thus, it was natural for Christian thinkers to put aspects of Greek philosophy in the service of their religion. Although they had been borrowing from Neo-Platonism since the age of Augustine, Aristotle ultimately became the major force. Comprehensive translations of his work into Latin in the late twelfth and early thirteenth century expanded his theological audience, as had the brilliant expositions and critiques by the great Arab philosophers Avicenna (Persia, 980–1037) and Averroes (Spain and North Africa,1126–1198). By the mid-thirteenth century his influence in the Christian universities of Europe was growing, brought to fruition by Albertus Magnus (circa 1200–1280) and Thomas Aquinas (1225–1274).

In this period, Christian Europe had no system of natural philosophy comparable to Aristotle's, so its rediscovery sparked intellectual excitement in the Faculty of Arts at the University of Paris, and elsewhere. Seeming conflicts between Aristotelianism and Christian doctrine appeared, provoking various calls to reject the former, revise the latter, or reconcile the two.[4] A distinguished professor and intellectual leader of the Dominican order, Albert the

Great (Albertus Magnus) took the path of reconciliation. Like Aristotle, he was a student of nature, noted for his intellectual curiosity and belief in the superiority of careful and systematic observation for gaining knowledge of the natural world, as opposed to armchair deductions of what one imagines reality *must* be like.[5] Though he produced explications of, and commentaries on, Aristotle, his most lasting contribution was his influence on his brilliant student Thomas Aquinas. As Copleston colorfully puts it, "St. Albert was Thomas's Socrates."[6]

As a philosopher, Aquinas tried to derive as much knowledge as possible from observation and reason. As a theologian, he took some Christian tenets—such as the personal relationship between believers and their creator and the eternal life they were to enjoy—to be truths knowable only by revelation. Since *truths* can't contradict one another, he had to make sure that what he believed to have been revealed was compatible with what he derived by reason and observation. It is to his credit that he carried out this task as conscientiously as he did.

Aristotle provided his framework for understanding the world. Like him, Aquinas took all natural living and nonliving things to be fusions of prime matter with immanent (rather than independently existing Platonic) forms. These things, called individual substances, had essential properties (e.g., *being a mountain, being canine,* or *being a rose)* that made them the kinds of things they were, which they retained as long as they existed. The changes through which they endured were additions or losses of accidental properties, which an object was capable of having, but could, in principle, do without.

Like Aristotle, Aquinas also believed that whenever any natural substance comes into existence, gains or loses accidental properties, or ceases to exist, there must be a reason the change occurred. Sometimes it occurred because

another natural change did, which in turn must have occurred for a reason. The two philosophers also believed that
no natural change is a reason for itself, that circular chains
of reasons—in which C is the reason for B, B for A, and A
for C—are impossible, and that an infinite regress of reasons is also impossible. Thus, they concluded, there must be
an ultimate, nonnatural reason for every natural change.
For Aristotle it was the unmoved mover.[7] For Aquinas it
was God.[8]

Aquinas gives this argument in three forms. In one, reasons for changes are purposes they fulfill. In another, they
are (efficient) causes of changes. In the third, they are things
on which the existence of the changing item depends. For
him, no form of the argument establishes that the universe
was created at an earlier time. Although Christian doctrine
told him it was, he didn't think reason alone could rule out
the possibility that the universe is eternal.[9] What then did
he think he proved? What was the independent thing on
which all else depended? It had to be something that exists
and has many of its properties necessarily. Otherwise we
could keep the regress going by asking the same questions
about it that we ask about natural objects—*Why does it exist?*
and *Why does it have the properties it does rather than different
properties?* For Aquinas, it doesn't make sense to ask of anything that couldn't have failed to exist, why it exists, or of
anything that couldn't have had different properties, why
it has the properties it does.[10]

Just as Aquinas deployed Aristotelian concepts in trying
to prove the existence of a god different from Aristotle's unmoved mover, so he maintained that the human soul was a
kind of Aristotelian form of the body, while affirming an immortality for it that Aristotle couldn't. With the exception
of human beings, Aquinas agreed with Aristotle that the
soul of a living thing (which combines with matter to form
a living being) is the form of the body, and cannot exist

without the body. In the case of a human being, he agreed that one's *humanity* determines that (a) one is a human being with a body capable of digesting food, growing, and reproducing, (b) one has sense organs making perception possible, (c) one has the physical and mental capabilities required for physical action, and (d) one is (unlike animals) capable of rational thought, theoretical understanding, and self-governance. From this it might *seem* to follow that when a human body dies, or ceases to exist, the person's soul must, as an Aristotelian rather than a Platonic form, also cease to exist. Surely, *the soul of Socrates* doesn't, after death, inform a different body, say Zeno's. Rather, it ceases to inhere in any matter. Since an Aristotelian form can't exist without inhering in anything, either Socrates's soul must also cease to exist, or it must have something that distinguishes it from classic Aristotelian forms. In taking the second path, Aquinas modified Aristotelianism.

Following Aristotle, he held that things, living and non-living alike, have substantial forms that make them the kinds of things they are (e.g., stones, plants, animals, humans), while also distinguishing different things of the kind.[11] However, different categories of things have forms of different kinds. The forms of living things—plants, animals, and humans—are souls. Aquinas says:

> In order to inquire into the nature of the soul, we have to presuppose that 'soul' [*anima*] is what we call the first principle of life in things that live among us; for we call living things 'animate' [or 'ensouled'], but things devoid of life 'inanimate' [or 'not ensouled'].[12]

The souls of plants endow them with nutritive abilities, the souls of animals add the abilities to act and perceive, while human souls add rationality, making abstract thought and understanding possible. Except for human souls, the souls of all living things are Aristotelian forms, which, though immaterial and distinct from matter, cannot exist without informing it.[13] By contrast, the rational souls of human beings are immaterial in a second and stronger sense. As an Aristotelian, Aquinas believed that the nutritive functions performed by souls of all living things, and the sensitive functions (perceiving and acting) performed by souls of animals and humans, *are always operations of particular bodily organs*. Thus, he thought, those functions cannot survive without the bodies in which they are localized. But, Aquinas argued, the *rational functions* unique to humans are *not* localized in any bodily organ.[14]

His argument is based on two principles: (i) "Through intellect the human being can [in principle] have cognition of [i.e., understand] the natures of all bodies." (ii) "Any [faculty] that can have cognition of [i.e., understand] certain things cannot have any of those things in its own nature [i.e., it cannot have a bodily nature]."[15] For example, the bodily organ for sight, the pupil of the eye, isn't, and couldn't be, of any color, since, if it were, its color (like the color of blue spectacles) would distort the perception of colors, *making it impossible for us to distinguish some colors*. By parity of reasoning, if the rational human soul had a bodily nature, that nature would distort its understanding. Since our rational nature allows us to correctly understand the natures of all bodies, human rationality is independent of bodily processes.[16]

This argument is illuminatingly discussed by Norman Kretzmann in the following passage.

[According to Aquinas] to be a cognitive faculty is to be essentially in a state of receptive *potentiality* relative to certain types of things, the faculty's proper objects—such as sounds, for the faculty of hearing. So if the faculty itself has such a type of thing in it *actually* [i.e., as part of its nature]—such as ringing in the ears—it forfeits at least some of the natural receptive potentiality that made it a cognitive faculty in the first place. . . . "So if the *intellective* principle [our rationality] had in itself the nature of *any* body, it would not be capable of cognizing [understanding] *all bodies*. But *every* body has *some* determinate nature, and so it is impossible that the intellective principle be a body" (*Summa Theologica* Ia.75.2C).[17]

In short, the rational aspect of our soul isn't located in any bodily organ, and does not have to use any organ in order to think. Although the bodily sense organs do supply the human soul with data for thoughts about what is perceived, such data are not required for purely conceptual thought, which can occur without them.[18] Aquinas takes it for granted that if the rational soul isn't located in any *bodily organ*, then it isn't located in any material body at all. Thus, he concludes that the rational aspect of the soul of Socrates *can* exist after the death of Socrates.

But does it exist after death? Presumably it does. Since it was *never* the (Aristotelian) form of any body, its existence and rational operation was always independent of matter, in which case there is no reason it should cease to exist with the death or destruction of Socrates's body. Thus, According to Aquinas, the rational aspect of Socrates can still think after the body dies—it can have purely conceptual thoughts—even though it can't then perceive or remember anything.[19]

This remarkable argument threatens the Aristotelian metaphysics that Aquinas worked so hard to revive. Aristotelian forms can't, by definition, exist without informing one or more bodies. Thus the rational human soul that Aquinas postulates can't be an ordinary Aristotelian form. What, exactly, is it then? This worry is connected to an even more basic problem. *Was Socrates himself identical with—i.e., the very same entity as—his rational soul?* If so, then he and his soul were one and the same, and, since *his soul* was never a fusion of form and matter, *he* was never such a fusion, in violation of Aquinas's contention that every human being is a composite of body and soul. If, on the other hand, Socrates's rational soul was *not* identical with Socrates, then showing it to be immortal (if one could do so) wouldn't show Socrates to be immortal.

The basis of Aquinas's response to this dilemma is given in the following passage.

> [We] come to know the human soul's mode of existence, on the basis of its activity. For insofar as it has an activity [rational thought and understanding] that transcends material things, its existence, too, is raised above the body and does not depend on it. On the other hand, insofar as it is naturally suited to acquire immaterial cognition from what is material [e.g., sensory cognition], the fulfillment of its nature clearly cannot occur without union with the body; *for something is complete in its nature only if it has [in itself] the things that are required for the activity that is proper to its nature.* Therefore, since the human soul, insofar as it is united to the body as a form, also has its existence raised above the body and does not depend on it, it is clear that the soul is established on the borderline between corporeal and separate [i.e., purely spiritual] substances [such as angels].[20]

This puzzling statement of the borderline character of the human soul and its junction with the body may be the most important, but also most problematic, aspect of the attempted Thomistic synthesis of Christian theology with Aristotelian philosophy.

Following Aristotle, Aquinas took rationality to be the distinctive feature of humanity, which is also, he argued, the respect in which human beings are made in the image of God.[21] Echoing Aristotle's "All human beings desire to know," he took the human desire to know and understand to be an expression of our deepest nature, which is rooted in the soul. Also following Aristotle, he took human beings to be composites of souls (which were special types of forms) and matter. But since human beings had to turn out immortal for Aquinas (though their bodies aren't) he had to argue three things. First, as we have seen, he had to argue that human souls can, and do, exist without the body. Second, as we have also seen, he had to argue that they cannot completely fulfill their function (of achieving knowledge and understanding) without a body. Third, he had to argue that nothing can exist forever without fulfilling its proper function, as the souls of dead human beings would do if they were never reunited with their lost bodies.

Aquinas does this in the following passage from *Summa Contra Gentiles*.

> It is therefore contrary to the nature of the soul to be without the body. But nothing which is contrary to nature can be perpetual. Hence the soul will not for ever be without the body. Therefore since the soul remains for ever, it should be united again with the body, and this is what is meant by rising (from the dead). The immortality of souls seems then to demand the future resurrection of bodies.[22]

This argument, in addition to assuring Aquinas of the immortality of the man Socrates, expresses something important about his conception of the interdependence of human souls and human bodies. Since each is, in a certain sense, equally in need of the other, Aquinas regards individual human beings as genuine unities, rather than immaterial Platonic souls who, when inhabiting bodies, merely use them as tools.[23] Having come this far, Aquinas adds that the human desire for immortality must be fulfilled because God wouldn't give us a desire that can't be fulfilled. Since divine revelation promises the resurrection of the body, many regarded his argument for the immortality of the soul, and its eventual reunion with the body, as a contribution to his broader reconciliation of faith and reason.

This temporary reconciliation provided Christianity with the intellectual resources of Greek philosophy, which was still the most comprehensive synthesis of knowledge of the natural world. Moreover, it did so without threatening the religion's role as interpreter of the ultimate purpose of life and the individual's guide to salvation. Although Thomism had it rivals, the *modus vivendi* between faith and reason it prompted became one of the lasting achievements of western civilization. A religion based on a mystical interpretation of particular historical events, appealing to every social class, with an ethic of human behavior based on a vision of the meaning of life, had become linked to an epistemological system the goal of which was to use observation, precisely defined theoretical concepts, logic, and mathematics to acquire comprehensive knowledge of ourselves and the universe. The legacy of this display of open-mindedness would be felt for centuries.[24]

The truce between faith and reason was also a boon to philosophy. By relieving philosophy of the responsibility for discovering the meaning of life and charting a path to personal fulfillment, it allowed philosophy to reclaim its role of advancing evidence-based knowledge in every domain (outside of revealed religion). As Copleston puts it:

Since historically speaking, Aristotelianism . . . was a production of reason unaided by revelation, it naturally brought home to the mediaevals the potentialities of the natural reason: it was the greatest intellectual achievement they knew. This meant that any theologian who accepted and utilized the Aristotelian philosophy . . . was compelled to recognize the theoretical autonomy of philosophy. . . . Looking back . . . we can see that acceptance of a great system of philosophy . . . was almost certain sooner or later to lead to philosophy going her own way independent of theology.[25]

This rebirth of classical philosophy—which would gradually become autonomous, self-critical, and focused on advancing scientific knowledge—was the great gift of Aquinas and other philosophically minded theologians who followed him.

One of these was the thirteenth-century British monk Roger Bacon (circa 1212–1292), whose belief in empirical observation, mathematics, and science coexisted with a conservative, even mystical, theology. In his chief work, *Opus Maius,* he declares it to be philosophy's purpose to interpret the scriptures and, in all other ways, to lead us to God. Reason, philosophy's tool, is identified with God, and so must never be despised. Since the function of truth is to lead humanity to God, no particle of truth should be neglected. These ideas led Bacon to science and mathematics, the latter essential to sciences like astronomy. A man of many interests, Bacon took the earth to be spherical and very small compared to the heavens. He also wrote about light, eclipses, tides, the structure of the eye, and the principles of vision. His work on reflection and refraction was devoted to learning how we could make small things appear large, and distant things near. Although he didn't invent the telescope, he did discover principles that others would use to do so.

Opus Maius also contains a sophisticated discussion of scientific methodology in which reason's role is to frame hypotheses and deduce observational consequences from

them. He took a hypothesis to be refuted if those consequences are false, and he insisted that no hypothesis can be
accepted without such testing. Like Aquinas, he used Aristotelian categories in his natural philosophy. But his major
contribution to the Thomistic synthesis of faith and reason
was his genuinely scientific spirit, not unlike Aristotle's,
which was reflected in the wide range of his empirical interests, the vigor of his investigations of natural phenomena,
the clarity of his experimental method, and the practical
value he hoped ultimately to be derivable from it.

If we pause at this point to ask *What did philosophy contribute to mid-thirteenth-century Christian Europe?* we see its
contributions in the thought of Albertus Magnus, Thomas
Aquinas, and Roger Bacon.

(i) It contributed, through Aquinas, to a view of faith
and reason as allies rather than antagonists, thereby
introducing a strain of rational theology into Christian thought that had already incorporated Platonic
elements from Augustine, now championed by Saint
Bonaventure.

(ii) It contributed, again through Aquinas, to a conception of God as a purely rational necessary being, who,
by making human beings in the image of God, made
them natural seekers of knowledge of what was assumed to be a rational, well-ordered universe.

(iii) It thereby contributed to a reawakening of the scientific spirit of Aristotle, which found expression in
the empirical investigations of the natural world by
Albertus Magnus and Roger Bacon.

As we move into the second half of the thirteenth century
and beyond, we find increasing philosophical ferment,
accompanied by a growing intellectual focus on the natural world. One of Aquinas's immediate successors was the

Franciscan theologian John Duns Scotus (1266–1308). Building on, and criticizing, the Thomistic synthesis of Aristotelianism with Christianity, he developed an independent following, while paving the way for more far-reaching departures from Thomism. One of his most consequential departures involved Aquinas's argument for the soul's immortality, which presupposed not only that Socrates and Plato were different persons, but also that their souls—the forms of their respective bodies—were different. Since Plato and Socrates were humans, those forms couldn't have been the single human nature common to all humans. How then did Socrates's individual human nature differ from Plato's? According to Aquinas, they differed *numerically* because they were forms of different quantities of prime matter, but they didn't differ *qualitatively*, because no qualities can be attributed prime matter. This thesis was generalized: *Matter is the principle of individuation that distinguishes different members of the same natural kind.*

Scotus argued that this doctrine, plus the Thomistic thesis that the different souls of Socrates and Plato exist after their deaths, entails that the two souls/forms contain prime matter that individuates them *even when they are not the forms of any body*. Since this was an Aristotelian absurdity, Scotus rejected the doctrine that matter individuates individual forms. He could have gone further. If Socrates's soul were the Aristotelian form of his body, but not of anything else, then it *couldn't* exist when the body dies or ceases to exist. Although this might seem to threaten the project of reconciling Aristotelian natural philosophy with Christian theology, Scotus didn't take that step. Christianity was secure because revelation assured him of the immortality of human souls and the eternal lives of persons after the resurrection of their bodies. Consequently, he seemed to suggest, it ought to be possible to construct a synthesis of Christianity and Greek philosophy in another way. Indeed, his philosophy is sometimes taken to be the last such medieval synthesis.[26]

The critique developed by William of Ockham (1287–1349) was more far-reaching. Though he was a theologian and philosopher, his emphasis on God's absolute freedom and omnipotence left little room for Greek notions of essence and necessity. Displaying strong logical, analytical, and empirical elements, his highly original philosophy offered no independent confirmation of God's existence or nature. Nor did it offer independent support for the spirituality of the soul, or human immortality. In part because of this, Ockham's thought was judged heretical by some in the Church. Among other things, he engaged in Church politics, including a dispute between the pope and the emperor of Bavaria. Despite being excommunicated in 1328, he remained an active intellectual influence until he died of the Black Death in 1349, after which his followers, advancing as advocates of the *via moderna*, continued their struggle against the *via antiqua* of Thomism, Scotism, and Augustinianism.

The heart of his critique of Greek metaphysics in Christian philosophy was his denial of *universals*—common natures of things of the same type, thought of as Platonic or Aristotelian forms. For Ockham, there is no such thing *humanity* that is common to all and only humans, and no such thing *redness* common to just red things. There are, of course, individual humans and particular red things plus the words 'human' and 'red' (and others with the same meanings) that are used to designate them. But there is nothing beyond being so designated that is common to those things—or so it seems until one asks *What is the meaning of a general term T used in a predicate 'is (or is a) T'?* The traditional answer is that it is *a way that individual things can be*. Since it is possible for some things to be human, some to be red, and some to be round, being human, being red, and being round are *ways things can be.* These ways, it had been supposed, are the meanings of 'human', 'red', and 'round'. When one uses a subject-predicate sentence, one represents the thing designated by the subject expression to be the way one's use of the predicate represents it.

This picture of linguistic meaning presupposes that there are *ways things could be.* What are they? Denying the existence of Platonic or Aristotelian forms, Ockham says that the meaning of a general term T is a *concept C* existing only in the mind.[27] He adds that when C is the meaning of T, the latter designates all and only things that are *similar to* each other in *the way* given by C. But how does this help? If one is puzzled by *ways individual things are or could be,* one should be equally puzzled by *ways pairs of things are or could be similar.* Either both really exist or neither does. If you doubt (or accept) that there are ways individual things can be—e.g., *being red* and *being green*—you should also doubt (or accept) that there are ways pairs of things can be—e.g., *being similar in color to this* (said of a fire engine) and *being similar in color to that* (said of a patch of well-watered grass). Ockham seems to miss this.

He also seems to equivocate. Although he often claims that only individuals exist, he sometimes adds the qualifier "outside the mind." For example, he denies that relations (presumably including *similarity*) exist outside the mind. He bases his denial on the claim that *all real existing things (outside the mind) are, in principle, independent of all other such things,* in the sense that God could have created them independently of whatever else he created. So, Ockham argues, if relations existed outside the mind, God could have created them without creating any objects they relate. Regarding this as absurd, he concludes that relations exist *only in the mind.*

The claim on which he relies is questionable. Consider the relation *originating from* in which a giant redwood stands to the seed from which it originated, and in which I stand to the particular zygote from which I originated. Is it clear that the first members of those pairs (the redwood and me)—not qualitative duplicates but those very things—could have existed without the second? For that matter, is it also clear that I could have existed even if my biological mother never did, and hence even if I didn't stand in the relation *being her child* to her? If these things aren't obvious, then Ockham's argument that relations don't exist "outside the mind" relies on a questionable premise.

Ockham gives another argument for the same conclusion. If, he says, there were relations *outside the mind*, then when I move my finger, I would change the spatial relation in which it stands to other things, and so change the properties of everything in the universe. He regards this as absurd, but doesn't say why, or indicate how the absurdity is supposed to be removed by saying the relation exists only *in the mind*. Surely, for each physically located object x in the universe, it ought to be possible to construct a spatial predicate relating x to my finger that is true of x before I move my finger, but not after, and another predicate that will be true of x after I move my finger, but not before. Since to say this is just to say that certain things are true of x before I move my finger that won't be true after, this should mean that x changed properties. Since this result doesn't depend on the awareness of any mind, it's not clear that Ockham's in-the-mind stipulation does any real work.

The alleged elimination of "real relations" is supposed to be an example of the use of Ockham's razor, *Don't postulate entities beyond necessity*, which may be paraphrased, *Don't posit entities beyond those needed to explain evident truths*. So understood, it can hardly be denied. One might be able to use it more directly to eliminate properties and relations, if the only truths one had to explain were particular truths like '*Scott Soames is a philosopher*' and '*Greg and Brian Soames are his sons'*, which logically entail the existence of Scott, Greg, and Brian, but don't logically entail the existence of the property *being a philosopher* or the relation *being a son of*. But if we also need explanations of truths about the meanings of general terms, or the cognitions of agents who believe the contents of the thoughts we express by using such sentences, then it's not clear that Ockham's razor can be used to eliminate properties and relations.[28]

Ockham put it to better use in understanding causation. He refuses to recognize any combination of features in a prior event A as the cause of a later event B, unless events with precisely that combination of features *never fail* to be followed by an event of the same type as B. He thus tends to identify causation with constant conjunction of items of the same sort, which, he argues, can be known only by empirical observation. In this way, he avoids positing an unobserved necessary connection between cause and effect. Since science is concerned with causes, this was rightly understood to be a blow against assuming in advance that the natural world *must* conform to any preconceived picture, and in favor of observation-based investigations.

Ockham was also parsimonious with traditional proofs of the existence of God. He rejected the final-cause (purpose) version of the first-cause argument as presupposing a divine purpose the existence of which it is supposed to prove. He rejected the efficient-cause version of the argument because we can't rule out an infinite sequence of prior causes. But he did accept an argument based on the idea that every contingent being—i.e., every being which, although it does exist, could have failed to exist—has, at each moment at which it exists, something that conserves its existence. Although the conserver could be another contingent being, the chain of conservers couldn't, he thought, be infinite, because that would require infinitely many conservers existing at one time, which he judged to be impossible. However, he didn't take his conclusion to establish the existence of a *single*, unconserved conserver of all things, or a conserver with any of the attributes usually attributed to God. For Ockham, the Christian belief in God and knowledge of his nature had to be founded on revelation.

His message about the human soul was similar.

> Understanding by intellectual soul an immaterial and incorruptible form . . . it cannot be known evidently either by arguments or experience that there is such a form in us or that the activity of understanding belongs to a substance of this kind in us, or that a soul of this kind is the form of the body. I do not care what Aristotle thought about this. . . . [T]hese three things we hold only by faith.[29]

In short, Ockham rejected Aristotelian metaphysics, the Aristotelian distinction between essence and accident, and the use of philosophy to prove central Christian doctrines. But he didn't reject either Christianity or philosophy itself; on the contrary, he was both a fervent believer and an ardent philosopher. He was also an innovator, whose non-metaphysical, "nominalist" theory of language formed the basis of detailed logical studies. He was followed in this in the last half of the fourteenth and the first half of the fifteenth century by a vigorous Ockhamist movement of Christian thinkers whose theology coexisted with a philosophical tendency to restrict necessary truths provable by unaided reason to those the negations of which could be shown to be logically contradictory—a tendency that led them to emphasize the importance of observation-based methods of acquiring worldly knowledge. This potent combination of theological conservatism with philosophically mandated empirical investigations won many adherents in European universities, encouraging the development of fourteenth- and fifteenth-century science.[30]

In sum, the period investigated here was one in which Greek philosophy was given a new start, relieved of the burden of discovering either the meaning of life or a practical path leading to the highest personal fulfillment. Its assigned task, to which it was so well suited, was simply to further the acquisition of knowledge of the world and ourselves. This new lease on life was granted by a religion that was, for a time, confident it could accommodate whatever was discovered by reason and empirical observation. At first, the accommodation took the form of a grand synthesis in which the doctrines of medieval philosophers—whether adapting, modifying, or superseding those of their Greek predecessors—complemented Christianity, while modifying it in the process. But as time wore on, philosophy asserted its natural critical autonomy, the synthesis eroded, and philosophers created the intellectual space they needed to begin laying the foundations for the spectacular growth of mathematics and natural science that was to come.

CHAPTER 3

THE BEGINNINGS OF MODERN SCIENCE

The interpenetration of philosophy, mathematics, and science in the late Renaissance and the early modern period; Copernicus, Kepler, Galileo, Descartes, Newton, Boyle, Locke, Leibniz, Berkeley, Hume, and Kant.

The remarkable development in western philosophy from the late sixteenth through the eighteenth century was intertwined with great advances in natural science and mathematics. Building on the contributions made by medieval and Renaissance thinkers in advancing observation-based knowledge independent of Aristotelian metaphysics, natural theology, and revealed religion, philosophers in the early modern period made notable contributions to the science and mathematics of their day. Two of those earlier thinkers, Roger Bacon in the thirteenth century and William of Ockham in the fourteenth, were notable for emphasizing the role of mathematics and logic in formulating and testing hypotheses about the natural world. The fourteenth century also saw the beginnings of sustained attacks on Aristotelian physics, which had separated terrestrial from celestial motion. Ockham decisively rejected the Aristotelian account of terrestrial projectiles, while the philosopher, physicist, and rector of the University of Paris John Buridan (died 1360) rejected Aristotelian physics as being incapable of explaining the motion of a spinning top. Nicholas Oresme (died 1382), who also taught at Paris, argued that the hy-

pothesis that the earth rotates can't be disproved by observation, and, although he didn't endorse the idea, he did
suggest that there are some grounds for taking it to be
true. He also questioned the geocentric conception of the
universe by taking seriously the idea that there might be
more than one world.

The independent study of nature continued in the fifteenth and sixteenth centuries, as physics became more
heavily mathematical and more focused on precise observation. The first major step was taken by the clergyman, physician, and astronomer Nicolaus Copernicus
(1473–1543). Recognizing that the Ptolemaic system had
evolved piecemeal—with predictions about one celestial
body's point of occlusion by another being calculated on
an individual planet-by-planet basis—he sought systematic
integration. In so doing, he addressed the so-called "retrograde" motions of certain planets, when they appear to
change direction and move backward in relation to the
fixed stars. To explain this, the geocentric system posited
bizarre planetary movements—halting, reversing, halting,

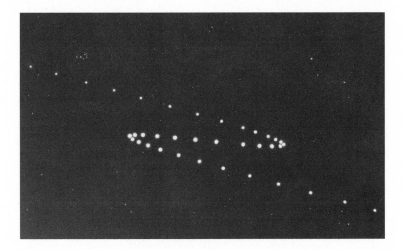

Retrograde motion. Courtesy of Tunç Tezel.

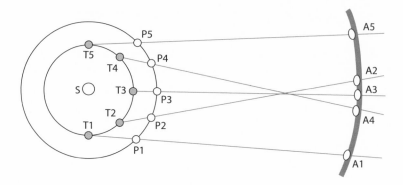

Heliocentric explanation.

and advancing again. By contrast, the heliocentric picture put us on a path to explaining why, if the earth moves around the sun, the position of its orbit in relation to those of other circling planets sometimes makes it appear that they change direction, when in fact they don't.[1]

The Copernican model in the second figure illustrates how an observer's position on an inner planet (the earth) in its orbit around the sun together with the position of a planet in an outer orbit will, at certain times, create the illusion that the outer planet has temporarily changed direction in relation to the fixed stars (A1–A5). However, in part because Copernicus didn't question the dogma that the planets moved in circles, he still needed some ad hoc epicycles to accommodate a few puzzling appearances. Thus, it wasn't until Kepler discovered the elliptical form of planetary orbits that the remaining observational illusions were explained and the need for epicycles was eliminated. Even then, the causes of celestial motion—about which Copernicus said nothing—remained to be identified and precisely measured. Partly for these reasons, Copernicus is better seen as the last great natural philosopher, charting the geometry of physical space, rather than the first modern celestial physicist offering causal explanations supported by mathematically precise observations.

That honor goes to Johannes Kepler (1571–1630), who, after eight years of precise and exhaustive observation of the orbit of Mars, announced in 1609 (i) that the planets move in elliptical, not circular, orbits, with the sun as one focus of each ellipse, and (ii) that the area covered by the sweep of the vector connecting the sun to a planet remains constant across equal units of time. Nine years later he announced his third law, that for any two planets, the ratio of the squares of the time taken to complete a single revolution is equal to the ratio of the cubes of their mean distances from the sun. With these discoveries, the epicycles of Copernicus were gone and the movements of the planets were seen as caused by an active force emanating from the sun.

At first Kepler analogized the sun to God the Father and the force emanating from it to the Holy Ghost. But he also observed something that eventually led him to think of this force in physical terms. Finding that the planets closest to the sun moved more quickly in their revolutions around it than those further away, he concluded that the sun's power to move the planets diminished with distance, and so the force it exerted must be something like light, which is emitted from a physical source. He described this force, gravity, as being one which, like light, is something that is emitted and somehow travels through empty space without having any substantial existence there, until it is received by a body which is then moved, in the case of gravity, or illuminated, in the case of light.

Although Kepler's dramatic findings about gravity were on the mark, he found himself in a quandary. As illustrated by the following remarks, he knew a lot about this universal force, including the fact that the force exerted by one thing on another is in proportion to its mass, while being inversely proportional to the distance between the two.

> Gravity is the mutual bodily tendency between cognate [material] bodies toward unity or contact . . . so that the earth draws a stone much more than the stone draws the earth.
>
> If the earth and the moon were not kept in their respective orbits by a spiritual or some equivalent force, the earth would ascend toward the moon $\frac{1}{54}$ of the distance, and the moon would descend the remaining 53 parts of the interval, and thus they would unite.
>
> If two stones were placed anywhere in space near to each other, and outside the reach of the force of a third cognate body, then they would come together, after the manner of magnetic bodies, at an intermediate point, each approaching the other in proportion to the other's mass.[2]

Nevertheless, he didn't know how to think about this mysterious force. How could a body A exert a force on a body B across (presumably) empty space, which provides no medium by which the force exerted by A might be transmitted to B? Astoundingly, his inability to answer this question led him to drop the notion of gravity in subsequent writings. Equally astoundingly, it led both Galileo and Descartes, who studied Kepler, also to reject the notion of force acting at a distance.[3]

Despite this puzzle about gravity, Kepler's advance swept aside the role of Aristotelian final causes (purposes) in explaining nature, the Aristotelian bifurcation of celestial and terrestrial physics, and the need to appeal to the active operation of a divine mind in understanding natural law. As Kepler wrote to a friend in 1605:

My aim is to show that the heavenly machine is not a kind of divine, live being, but a kind of clockwork . . . insofar as nearly all the manifold motions are caused by a most simple, magnetic, and material force, just as all motions of the clock are caused by a simple weight. And I also show how these physical causes are to be given numerical and geometrical expression.[4]

Despite this testament to what now seems to be commonplace scientific objectivity, Kepler was as much of a mystic as he was a scientist. In addition to being a believing Christian, he was a sometime astrologist and numerologist. He was also obsessed with ancient Pythagorean doctrine about what musical harmonies can tell us about planetary movements and what we can learn about the structure of the solar system from studying so-called perfect geometrical solids. Despite this, his commitment to careful, systematic empirical observation, and his belief in the power of mathematics as an essential scientific tool, allowed him to make great progress.

The Italian Galileo Galilei (1564–1642) was a contemporary of Kepler. A talented mathematician and professor of mathematics, first at Pisa and then at Padua, he was also an experimental physicist, a natural philosopher, and an astronomer whose technical improvements on the telescope (invented in Holland in the first decade of the seventeenth century) made possible his impressive observations of the sun, the moon, and the planets.[5] Well versed in the works of Aristotle, he was highly critical of Aristotelian physics, both terrestrial and celestial. For example, in defending the Archimedean view that it is the density of a body that determines whether it will float in water against the Aristotelian view that it is the shape of the body that matters, Galileo offered experimental evidence that the determining factor is the relative density of the body to the fluid in which it is placed that matters. He also provided experimental evidence confirming Simon Stevin's observation that bodies of different weight fall at the same rate, which refuted the Aristotelian view that the heavier the object, the faster it falls.[6] With this as his starting point, Galileo sought to empirically establish the law of uniform acceleration that the speed of a falling body increases at a constant rate over time (which had been anticipated by earlier investigators). He sought also to support the thesis that a moving body not acted upon by external forces— e.g., friction, wind resistance, etc.—will continue to move in the same direction at a uniform speed (again in opposition to Aristotle).

Galileo's contributions to astronomy stemmed in substantial part from observations made possible by his improved telescope, which he started using around 1610. With it, he could clearly observe the mountains on the moon, which led him to conclude that it is made out of material like the earth, contrary to Aristotle's dichotomy between celestial and terrestrial beings. He also observed sunspots—which a Jesuit priest, Christoph Scheiner, had observed slightly earlier using a telescope of his own construction that incorporated an improvement suggested by Kepler. Like the mountains on the moon, the existence of sunspots further disconfirmed Aristotelian celestial physics by suggesting that the sun (like everything else) consists of changeable matter. In addition, Galileo observed the satellites of Jupiter and the phases of Venus, both of which fit Copernicus and Kepler's heliocentric conception much better than the geocentric conception of the universe.

The phases of Venus were especially interesting. Like the moon, Venus, as seen from earth, presents a regular sequence of appearances—full, half, crescent, etc. Because it is closer to the sun than we are, its full orbit is visible to us.

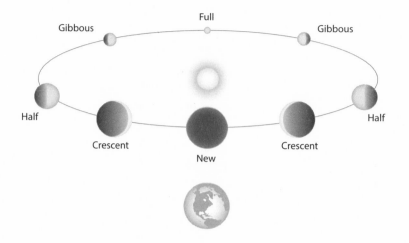

When it is on the side of the sun opposite us, it appears full, and small because it is far away. When it is at either end of its elliptical orbit its face is half visible. Because it orbits more quickly than we do, its orbital position gradually catches ours. Now on the same side of the sun as we are, it begins to approach the point at which it will be directly between us and the sun. As it moves closer and closer to this point, it is seen as a gradually thinning crescent—much larger because it is now so close to us. This continues until it disappears (because it is directly between us and the sun), after which it appears again, as a thin crescent on the other side that gradually thickens as the planet speeds ahead of us in its orbit. It is hard to imagine more convincing observational confirmation of the superiority of the heliocentric conception of the solar system over its geocentric competitor.[7]

Finally, it should be noted that Galileo's firmly grounded scientific results and observations existed side by side with his speculative philosophy of nature. A central part of that philosophy was his version of ancient metaphysical atomism—the belief, unconfirmed by experience or observation, that nature is nothing more than a grand system of some definite number of tiny bits of matter in motion, each with objective properties of having shape, size, position, and velocity in a certain direction. According to this picture, all change is the repositioning of atoms. Moreover, any change could, in principle, be predicted if one had a complete inventory of atoms, their sizes, shapes, positions, velocities, spatiotemporal coordinates, and the forces acting on them.

Since Galileo took the forces to be mechanical—basically the result of the movements and collisions of atoms—he could not accept the idea of force at a distance (with no intervening medium). Nor could he accept the idea that other, more familiar, properties of macroscopic things—e.g., the color of an object—are truly objective. Like many natural philosophers of the time, he took them to be subjective qualities in observers rather than objective qualities in things observed. His mathematical physics made this seem natural, since things like colors and sounds played no role in it. According to this doctrine—which found many adherents—insofar as the redness of a rose could be considered to be in the rose itself, it is merely the rose's disposition (due to its atomic structure) to cause certain (red) sensations in us.

But this isn't the end of the story. Because the doctrine seems to suggest implausible conclusions—e.g., that roses would have been colorless had there been no observers, and that they would change color if our sensory systems changed—this view, some versions of which are still advocated, is no longer as widely accepted as it once was. There is no need here to try to decide whether colors are, or are not, secondary qualities in Galileo's sense. The fact that the issue remains a live one in philosophy today illustrates the difficulty in drawing a clear line separating science from natural philosophy in the thought of Galileo and other great figures of the Renaissance and early modern period.[8] There was no sharp line because philosophy and science were closely intertwined. It is not so much that philosophy was *contributing* to an independent enterprise known as *science*, as that substantial parts of emerging natural science *were* philosophy, and substantial parts of philosophy *were*, if not exactly science, at least scientific speculation.

Whereas one might, looking back from our perspective today, say that Kepler and Galileo were *primarily* scientists and mathematicians, and *secondarily* natural philosophers, the British philosopher Francis Bacon (1561–1626) was decidedly a philosopher of science, rather than a scientist or mathematician himself. An early opponent of Aristotelian physics and metaphysics in a country in which Aristotle's influence on the philosophy of nature lasted longer than it did on the Continent, he emphasized the practical value of technological innovations such as printing, gunpowder, and the magnet, as well as their power to change the world. Advances of this sort were, he pointed out, more the product of looking directly at nature rather than of studying Aristotelian or scholastic metaphysics. A gifted writer, he favored some form of inductive process for studying it, without, it seems, being fully up to date on the blend of precise observation and mathematical sophistication of the best scientists of his day. Though one cannot credit him with original contributions to science or its methodology (his account of which was arguably less sophisticated than that of the thirteenth-century monk Roger Bacon [no relation] discussed in chapter 2), Francis Bacon did help create a climate of opinion favorable to those who made true scientific contributions.

Much more can be said about René Descartes (1596–1650), who was not only a renowned philosopher, but also a first-rate mathematician and a reasonably accomplished scientist. One of the period's most influential thinkers, he is best known for his arresting mind-body dualism, his attempt to establish a maximally secure philosophical starting point—*I think, therefore, I am*—and his goal of developing a sound method for advancing human knowledge. Together, these aspects of his thought set philosophy's agenda for the next two centuries. However, his intellectual achievements originated in mathematics and science.

Having received his degree from the Jesuit College of La Flèche in 1616, he shortly thereafter moved to the Netherlands, where he met and worked with the Dutch mathematician and natural philosopher Isaac Beeckman. During that time, he developed mathematical techniques for describing complex geometrical figures without resorting to compass and ruler constructions. In so doing, he laid the foundations of analytic geometry by inventing a way of using ratios between lengths to describe lines that allowed later mathematicians to replace geometrical figures with algebraic formulas in a coordinate system dubbed *Cartesian coordinates*. After finishing this work, he spent most of the 1620s in Paris. During that period, he discovered the sine law of refraction, which computes angles of incidence and refraction when light passes through different media, and he used this knowledge to explain why we see rainbows where we do. He also worked on optics, mathematically describing shapes of different lenses.

In 1629, he returned to the Netherlands, where he undertook two grand projects, one in metaphysical philosophy focusing on the existence of God and the nature of the human soul, and the other in systematic natural philosophy, in which he attempted to encompass "all the phenomena of nature, that is to say, the whole of physics."[9] His most famous work, *Meditations on First Philosophy*, which appeared in two editions, 1641 and 1642, grew out of the first, metaphysical, project.[10] The second project, in physics and natural philosophy, occupied several later works appearing between 1644 and 1650.[11] He described the relationship between the two projects as follows:

[T]he whole of philosophy is like a tree. The roots are metaphysics, the trunk is physics, and the branches emerging from the trunk are all the other sciences, which may be reduced to three principle ones, namely medicine, mechanics, and morals. By "morals" I understand the highest and most perfect moral system, which presupposes complete knowledge of the other sciences, and is the ultimate level of wisdom.[12]

It is notable that he uses the word 'philosophy' to stand for a comprehensive system incorporating all theoretical knowledge, 'physics' to stand for natural science, 'medicine' and 'mechanics' to stand for practical inquires based on science, and 'morals' to stand for the highest knowledge, which, though normative, rests on knowledge of all else. It is also noteworthy that he regarded philosophical metaphysics as the source of all systematic knowledge.

What Descartes called 'metaphysics' is really a combination of what we now call 'epistemology' (theory of knowledge) and 'metaphysics' or 'ontology' (an inquiry into the fundamental types of things that make up reality, and the relations holding among them). His central questions of metaphysics were *How can we acquire knowledge?*; *What is there to be known—i.e., what is the nature of reality?*; *What exactly are minds and bodies and how are they related?*; and *Does God exist?* In the first of his six meditations, he uses radical skepticism as a tool to establish a secure ground for all knowledge.

Stated in modern terms, his strategy of using radical skepticism to unearth absolute certainty goes something like this. We now know that the contents of our consciousness are determined by stimulations of neurons in our brain. Thus, we may think, it is theoretically possible for neurons of a brain preserved in a vat to be stimulated in a way that exactly stimulates the real-life experiences of a normal human being—even though the brain doesn't interact with anything in its environment in the way we interact with things in our environment. How then do we know that *we* aren't brains in vats? If we can't know we aren't, how can we know that other people or physical objects exist? After all, envatted brains don't know those things. Since their "perceptual" experience, which (we may assume) is identical with ours, doesn't provide them with such knowledge, it would seem that ours doesn't either. Having reached this point, we can drop the pretense about brains as so much unknowable baggage. Perhaps there are no brains, bodies, or physical objects at all, but only an evil demon feeding us sensations that make us think otherwise. If we can't rule this out, we can hardly be said to know the most ordinary things that we commonly take ourselves to know. Can we?

Descartes thinks we can. To show this, he must first arrest the slide into universal skepticism by identifying the absolute certainty, *I think, therefore I am.* Clearly, whenever I think *that such-and-such is so-and-so* I am thinking, whether or not *what I am thinking* (*that such-and-such is so-and-so*) is true. Thus, when I think *that I am thinking*, it must be *true* that I am thinking; I couldn't be wrong about that. But then, since I can think only if I exist, I *know that I exist.* In short, *I think, therefore I am.*

Next one wonders, *What sort of being is this thinker—a mind, a body, or a union of mind and body?* Descartes has an answer. Since one can conceive of oneself as existing without any body of one's own, or indeed without any bodies existing at all, he reasons that it must be *possible* for one to exist without the existence of any body.[13] But surely, *being a body* is essential to anything that is a body, and *having a bodily part* is essential to anything that is a union of mind and body. From this it follows that nothing that is a body, or a union of mind and body, could possibly exist if no bodies did. Thus, Descartes reasons, he, the agent employing his method of radical doubt, is neither a body nor a union of mind and body. Rather, he is a mind for which having the ability to think is essential. Repeating this process on our own, each of us may validly reach the conclusion "I am essentially a thinking being, distinct from my body."

The next step is to prove the existence of God. The purported proof relies on the observation that we have the idea of an infinite and perfect being, the existence of which is not dependent on anything else. Descartes takes it to be obvious not only that he is too limited and imperfect to be the source of this idea, but also that it must come from an infinite, perfect, and ontologically independent God. Since this God, being perfect, is no deceiver, Descartes concludes that he can put to rest the idea that he is systematically deceived by the appearances of his senses, and, with this, go on to put his knowledge of the world on a firm basis.

His argument for the existence of God is reminiscent of the ontological argument given by Saint Anselm in the eleventh century. Many versions of the argument, all of them widely regarded as suspect, have been given throughout the centuries. One version, called "the modal version," begins with the observation that we have the idea of an infinite, perfect, and completely self-sufficient being whose existence doesn't depend on anything else. Being self-sufficient, such a being must exist necessarily, if he exists at all. Since that idea isn't inconsistent, such a necessary being is *coherently conceivable*. To say this, the proponent of the argument continues, is to say *it's possible that God exists necessarily*—i.e., *there is a state the world could be in only if the claim God exists would be true no matter what state the world was in*. Since we can't now deny that there is such a possible state, it follows that God exists, no matter what state the universe is in. Either God exists, *no matter what possible state the universe is in*, or he couldn't possibly exist. Since we know it is possible that he exists, he must actually exist.[14]

For Descartes, the fact that God is no deceiver means that we are not systematically deceived, but it doesn't mean we are free from error. It is up to us to reason properly, to formulate hypotheses from which empirical predictions can be derived, and to accept those hypotheses only after their predictions have been confirmed by observational evidence. This was the essential point of contact connecting Descartes's "metaphysics" with his scientific endeavors and his mechanistic philosophy of nature. In the latter, he sketched a unified account of celestial and terrestrial physics based on laws of matter in motion, which, in conception, though not in empirical and mathematical execution, anticipated Newton.

The physics envisioned by Descartes was one in which matter is infinitely divisible, having only the properties of size, shape, position, and motion (the laws of which are decreed and sustained by God). As in ancient atomism, all physical change results from the movement, combination, and recombination of particles of matter. All apparent instances of action at a distance, including gravity and magnetism, are explained away as the result of the movements and collisions of particles. For Descartes, these principles apply as much to the animal world as to nonliving things. Unlike humans, animals are taken to be purely mechanistic systems, devoid of reason, will, and conscious experience. Only we are partial exceptions to the otherwise thoroughly mechanistic system of nature. Nevertheless, Descartes realized that our bodies function in much the same way that the bodies of animals do. For him, this meant that human respiration, heartbeat, nutrition, and many ordinary activities—including walking, running, and reflexively responding to external stimuli—are purely physiological processes having nothing to do with the reasoning of our non-corporeal minds. One of his more complex theories of this sort involved our visual perception of size, shape, and distance, of which he gave a non-mentalistic account. In addition to the subtle and fascinating details of Descartes's overall view, the point to notice is its comprehensiveness— science, mathematics, philosophy, and a bit of theology, pursued as a seamless whole.

Among the seventeenth- and eighteenth-century scientists and philosophers influenced by Descartes was the giant of the period, Isaac Newton (1642–1727). The preeminent scientist of his era, and one of the greatest of all time, his stunning scientific prowess included the philosophical ability to confront conceptual tangles and transform them into more tractable challenges. As an undergraduate at Cambridge, he studied Aristotle, logic, ethics, and physics. Prior to graduating in 1665, he read Descartes on philosophical method and naturalistic philosophy of nature, while also teaching himself mathematics and the astronomy of Kepler and Galileo. Newton spent the next two years away from Cambridge studying gravity and inventing the integral calculus. He returned in 1667 to Cambridge, where he shortly became professor of mathematics. Unable to find a publisher for his work on the calculus, he turned to optics, producing results that weren't published until 1704, in his *Treatise of the Reflections, Refractions, Inflections and Colours of Light*. He returned to orbital astronomy in 1679, giving a short paper to the Royal Society in December of 1684, which he expanded to *Philosophiae Naturalis Principia Mathematica* and published in 1687.[15]

His basic gravitational law holds that every mass of any size attracts every other mass with a force directly proportional to the product of the two masses and inversely proportional to the square of the distance between their centers. With this simple idea, plus a few others, he was able to explain a remarkably wide range of phenomena— including the behavior of projectiles, the orbits of comets, the size of planets, their orbits and moons, the motion of our moon and its effect on the tides, and certain very slow changes in the positions of stars due to a cyclic wobbling in the orientation of the earth's axis (the precession of the equinoxes).[16] The accuracy and precision of his results commanded assent and suggested that he had found genuine laws of nature, even though his treatment of gravity as a force acting at a distance was perplexing, and hard to accept for those who considered it not genuinely mechanical.

Even Newton found gravity hard to understand. In a letter written in 1692 he says:

> That . . . one body may act upon another at a distance through a vacuum without the mediation of anything else, by and through which their action and force may be conveyed from one another, is to me so great an absurdity that I believe no man who has in philosophic matters a competent faculty of thinking could ever fall into it.[17]

Still, it wasn't that Newton denied the existence of gravity, or the explanatory role it plays. On the contrary, he had been driven to this otherwise counterintuitive idea by the powerful explanatory role it played in so precisely accounting for the observed data. What he denied was that he had gotten to the bottom of what it is. In 1713, he wrote:

> I have not yet been able to discover the cause of these properties of gravity from phenomena and I feign no hypotheses. . . . It is enough that gravity does really exist and acts according to the laws I have explained, and that it abundantly serves to account for all the motions of celestial bodies.[18]

Newton's first law states that *every body not acted on by external forces will, if at rest, remain at rest, or, if not at rest, will continue its uniform motion in a straight line.* Motion is movement from one point in space to another. Space, for him, was a Euclidean structure infinite in three dimensions, consisting of eternally existing points (locations). The distance between two points, which can be numerically measured, is the length of the straight line connecting them. Uniform motion of a body is movement the speed and direction of which remain constant. For Newton, this talk of speed requires the elapsed time between two arbitrary moments to be, like the distance between any two points in space, constant and numerically measurable. In short, Newton presupposes absolute space and time.

This is highly intuitive, but also deeply puzzling. We observe objects moving relative to other objects. Since we have no way of observing absolute motions of these objects, we seem to have no way of determining the absolute motions in terms of which Newton's laws are stated. He recognized this.

> Absolute and relative spaces are the same in figure and magnitude; [both are 3-D Euclidean] but they do not remain always numerically the same. For if the earth, for instance, moves, a space of our air, which relatively and in respect of the earth, remains always the same, will at one time be one part of the absolute space into which the air passes; at another time it will be another part of the same, and so, absolutely understood, it will be continually changed [despite being relatively at rest].[19]

These thoughts give rise to a philosophical conundrum. How, if our observations of spatial locations and movements through space are always relative to the positions of other objects, including ourselves, can we draw conclusions about the direction, the velocity, and the positions of objects in absolute space? More pointedly, why, given the observational opacity of locations and movements in absolute space, did Newton formulate his physical laws in terms of it? The answer, in part, is that he found this conception of space intuitively plausible. But that's not all. He also identified an empirical phenomenon, a species of circular motion, that seemed to require it.

Newton's second law states that *the change made in motion of a body by a force exerted on it is inversely proportional to its mass and directly proportional to that force, along the straight line on which the force acts on the body.* His key experiment brilliantly connecting this law to absolute space involved water in a spinning bucket (suspended from the ceiling by a twisted rope that spins the bucket as it unwinds).

> [T]he surface of the water will at first be plain [flat] as before the vessel began to move, but after that the vessel, by gradually communicating its motion to the water, will make it begin sensibly to revolve, and recede . . . from the middle, and ascend to the sides of the vessel, forming itself into a concave figure. . . . [T]he swifter the motion becomes, the higher will the water rise, till at last, performing its revolutions in the same times with the vessel, it becomes relatively at rest in it. This ascent of the water shows its endeavor to recede from the axis of its motion; and the true and absolute circular motion of the water, which is here directly contrary to the relative, becomes known and may be measured.[20]

In this scenario the water recedes from the center and ascends the sides of the bucket because the water is spinning. But spinning relative to what? Not the bucket, since when the system reaches equilibrium, water and bucket spin at the same rate and so are at rest relative to each other. Yet the surface of the water remains concave, with

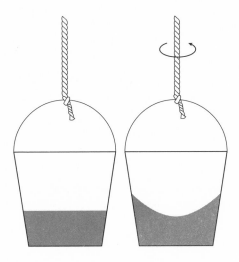

Bucket before and after spinning.

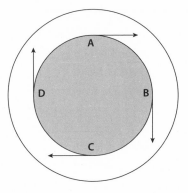

Forces acting on water in the spinning bucket.

some of it high on the sides of the bucket, while the center is depressed because a force is acting on the water, driving it from the center.

According to Newton's first law, this means the water must be moving and changing direction. Since its position relative to the spinning bucket isn't changing, its position

in absolute space must be changing.[21] Since, according to
Newton's laws, this change could only be the result of forces
causing quantities of water to climb the sides of the bucket,
stating physical laws in terms of absolute space and time
allowed him to explain an observed empirical phenomenon
that might otherwise have resisted explanation. So absolute
space and time are not gratuitous constructs in his system.

Newton was, of course, an inspiration to many of the scientists and philosophers of his day. One of them, Robert
Boyle (1627–1691), who discovered Boyle's law of gases, invented a barometer, and espoused a natural philosophy in
which physical phenomena are explained by laws of matter
in motion, saw himself as following Francis Bacon and Descartes. John Locke's scientific mentor at Oxford, Boyle was
a founding member of the Royal Society of London, which
published Newton's *Principia* and claimed both Locke and
the great physicist as members. Locke posthumously edited
and published Boyle's *The General History of the Air* in 1692.[22]

At Oxford, Locke (1632–1704), who was eventually to
become one of the greatest British philosophers of all time,
studied chemistry, physics, and medicine. Reading Boyle
led him to the natural philosophy of Descartes and the project of determining the scope of human knowledge and
understanding. Active in the tumultuous public life of his
day, Locke took nearly twenty years to complete his *Essay
Concerning Human Understanding*, which was published in
1689. Having read Newton and other scientists, he modestly
compares his work to theirs.

The commonwealth of learning is not at this time without master-builders, whose mighty designs, in advancing the sciences, will leave lasting monuments to the
admiration of posterity; but everyone must not hope
to be a Boyle or a Sydenham [with whom Locke studied medicine]; and in an age that produces such masters

as Huygens and the incomparable Mr. Newton . . . it is ambition enough to be employed as an under-labourer in clearing the ground a little, and in removing some of the rubbish that lies in the way to knowledge.[23]

Locke's *Essay* develops a simple empirical psychology and empiricist epistemology. For him, all our ideas arise from mental operations—association, comparison, combination, and abstraction—on simple ideas cognized in sense perception and introspection. Genuine knowledge comes from ideas that are properly grounded in these sources. Some ideas—of size, shape, mass, and motion—directly represent, or resemble, the *primary qualities* for which they stand, while others stand for *secondary qualities* like color and sweetness, which are powers of producing sensations in us. Physical substances, about which he took us to have knowledge, were combinations of qualities inhering a mysterious substratum, supposedly known to us by a cognitive process of abstraction. In short, the real properties of material things were those recognized by Newton, plus the powers of producing appearances—i.e., sensations—in us.

Although this satisfied Locke, the way he achieved his bifurcation of primary and secondary properties was suspect. So was his attempt to explain the empiricist origin of our idea of the underlying substratum of material objects, and his effort to ground our idea of causal power in the awareness of our own will. These became fair game for his empiricist successors, the philosophers George Berkeley and David Hume. Nevertheless, the lasting virtue of the *Essay* was its attempt to initiate a science and natural philosophy of the mind to complement the maturing science of the physical world that Locke and the philosophers of his day were both involved with and deeply impressed by.

Whereas Locke sought to extend Newtonian naturalism to the study of the mind, the German philosopher

G. W. Leibniz (1646–1716) sought to harmonize Newtonian physics with a speculative metaphysics purporting to describe reality at a more basic level. A mathematician who independently invented the calculus, he was also a historian and philosophical logician who was well versed in Aristotelian and scholastic philosophy, as well as the works of modern thinkers like Descartes, Kepler, and Galileo.

His metaphysical system featured a version of the ontological argument plus other purported proofs of a morally perfect, necessarily existing God as creator of a system of reality described by four theses of Leibniz's philosophical logic.

(i) All propositions are reducible to subject-predicate propositions, which are true just in case the subject has the property predicated of it.

(ii) An object x has a property just in case it is included in (the essence of) what x is.

(iii) Every property P that x has is included in its essence, because if x has P, then necessarily anything that doesn't have P isn't x. Since x can't fail to be x, it is impossible for x to lack P.[24]

(iv) For any object y and property P that y has, there is a relational property *P-similar*—of *being like y in possessing P*; there is also a relational property *P-different*—of *being unlike y in not possessing P*. If y were to come to lack P, then every object that now possesses *P-similar* would come to lack it and every object that now has *P-different* would come to lack it. So any change in the properties of one object would lead to a change in the properties of all objects.

It follows from (iv) that if we knew all the properties of any object, we would know every property of every object. It also follows that any change in the properties of one object would lead to corresponding changes in the properties of every object. Although this sounds pretty dramatic, it wouldn't be objectionable if it weren't combined with (iii). Combining it with (iii) gives us the result that any change in one object would result in the nonexistence of every object, and its replacement by another object. In short, reality is seen as a harmony of essentially interconnected objects any change in which would result in an entirely new system of different objects.[25]

Another consequence of the system is that every true proposition p is necessary and knowable *a priori* by one who completely understands it. The reason for this, according to Leibniz, is that p's subject already contains the property predicated of it—in the way that the concept *square* already contains *having equal sides* in the proposition *A square has equal sides*. But since complete analyses of propositions about existing things are always infinite, only God knows them *a priori*. For us, they are contingent truths knowable only by experience and observation.[26]

Leibniz applied this abstract scheme to an idealist version of metaphysical atomism in which the atoms are noncorporeal *monads*, which are simple, enduring substances without parts, shape, or spatial extension. They are spiritual because, for Leibniz, conceptions of matter in terms of spatial extension render it inert, and so incapable of explaining movement and change. It's not that there aren't things properly called bodies, which move and change in accord with Newtonian laws; there are. The point is that we can't explain the forces initiating motion and change unless such bodies are seen as vast complexes of more fundamental change agents. Since, for Leibniz, the ultimate forces of change are *perceptions* and *purposes*, this means that the ultimate agents of change, God and the created monads, must be spiritual. This combination of natural theology, putative logical analysis, and Aristotelian teleology was not an attempt to contribute to natural science. It was one of the last great systems of speculative metaphysics, which hoped to survive by interpreting natural science, without competing with it.

That said, Leibniz did reject the Newtonian conception of space as made up of infinitely many spatial points, taken to be fundamental constituents of reality in terms of which spatial relations between objects or events are defined. Reversing explanatory priorities, Leibniz took the relations to be fundamental, while regarding spatial points as constructions abstracted from them. To do otherwise, he thought, would only give rise to unanswerable questions: *Where is the earth, not in relation to the solar system (which we know), but in absolute space? Where is the solar system, not in relation to the Milky Way (which we also know), but in absolute space? Where is the universe as a whole?* Not only can we not answer these questions, we can't even formulate what answers might be possible. After all, points in absolute space don't come with their own unique addresses.

One can ask similar questions about the velocities of things—the earth, the sun, the galaxies, and the like. We can, of course, answer questions about their *relative* velocities; and we can even formulate *possible* answers, of the form, e.g., *n miles per minute,* some of which must be correct, if space really is absolute. We can do this despite the fact that we have no idea how to go about determining which of those possible answers is correct. In light of this, one can't help but wonder, "Does it really make sense to assume one such answer must be correct?"

Because he rejected as obviously nonsensical the unanswerable questions of precisely where the universe is located and how fast it is moving in the limitless Newtonian spatial domain, Leibniz rejected absolute space.[27] What he didn't make clear is how to think of the relative spatial relations between Newtonian bodies as somehow grounded in "perceptions" and "purposes" of nonspatial, spiritual monads. Nevertheless, this appeal to subjectivity did not go unnoticed, but rather became one of the chief influences on Kant's later subjective view of space and time.

Another philosopher who, for the most part, sought to interpret, rather than directly quarrel with, Newton was the Anglican bishop George Berkeley (1685–1753). Berkeley espoused a purified version of Locke's empiricism that led him to reject matter and to characterize the universe as consisting only of God, finite spirits, and their "ideas." The "matter" he reasonably rejected was Locke's imperceptible underlying substratum in which primary and secondary qualities supposedly inhered. With nothing to "support" them, these qualities disappeared in Berkeley's philosophy, leaving only "ideas" imprinted on our minds by God. Although Newton's laws remained (as descriptions of ideas God implants in us), Berkeley rejected Newton's natural philosophy, which spoke of what Berkeley took to be the "occult" force of gravitation as a "cause" of motion (despite its not being a genuine power). It seems not to have occurred to him that genuine causal explanation might not require anything beyond general regularities of the sort Newton provided.

Although his criticisms of Locke's conceptions of primary and secondary qualities, of causation, and of underlying matter as a kind of featureless glue holding bundles of properties together, revealed genuine problems with earlier philosophical systems, Berkeley's fantastic worldview found few adherents. Like Locke, he took the objects of immediate perception—vision, hearing, taste, and touch—to be sense impressions (ideas). This, arguably, was the fundamental mistake on which all empiricist attempts to construct a psychology of perception and representational cognitive states foundered. Our sense experiences are *not* mental things we see, hear, taste, touch, or otherwise cognize; rather they are mental things—cognitive processes really—by which, in normal cases, we see, hear, taste, and touch real, nonmental things—a view whose leading proponent at the time was an important figure in the Scottish Enlightenment, the philosopher Thomas Reid (1710–1796).

Berkeley's failure to see this didn't stop him from tackling real problems. For example, his theory of vision attempted to explain our judgments of the magnitude of objects and their distance from us. Noting that we don't see distance or magnitude themselves (in the way that we see trees and mountains), he rejected the Cartesian theory that we unconsciously judge distance by calculating the angle between an object and our eyes. Instead, he thought, we have kinesthetic sensations of focusing our eyes on the object, which increase as it comes closer, and which are associated with blurred vision when it is very close. For Berkeley, our judgments of distance and magnitude arise from these sensations plus the faintness or vividness of our perception. As with Locke and Descartes, the important point wasn't the correctness of the attempted cognitive theory, but the fact that it was offered at all.

Regarded by many to be the greatest British philosopher of all time, David Hume (1711–1776) was Britain's last great empiricist. His aim was, by observation and "the experimental method," to lay the foundations of "the science of human understanding." Being unable to derive any notion of substance—material or spiritual—from simple qualitative sense impressions, he rejected Lockean physical and mental substance. He also argued that neither the existence of physical objects—capable of existing unperceived—nor one's own existence—as one who thinks, perceives, and endures through connected experiences—can be validly derived from true premises about the sensory and introspective contents of our minds. He didn't, of course, cease to believe in physical objects and conscious beings. Like everyone else, he retained these beliefs, which he took to be true and justified in any reasonable sense in which empirical beliefs can be justified. But their justification didn't come from reason, as he conceived it; it came from habit and human nature, which were the centers of his natural philosophy.

His treatment of causation was similar. Arguing that we have no reason to believe in any *power* or *necessity* by which causes produce effects, he nevertheless tried to explain how causal claims can be known to be true, and why we are wrongly disposed to think that causes somehow make it impossible for their effects not to occur. For Hume, to say that event x causes event y is (very roughly) to say that for some event types A and B, x is of type A, y is of type B, and events of type A are always followed by those of type B. In short, causation is constant conjunction of events of specified types. But there is more to the story. After observing many cases of events of type A being followed by those of type B, *an idea of A* becomes mentally associated with *an idea of B*. Because of this, whenever we judge an event to be an A we immediately expect it to be followed by an event of type B. This associative principle was, for Hume, a fundamental law of our mental life—analogous to Newton's law of gravitation governing the physical world. Due to its operation, the expectation that an event, x, observed to be of type A, will be followed by an event, y, of type B, arises in us independently of our will, *being felt as an inevitable necessity*. This inevitable occurrence of the idea of B following the idea of A leads us, uncritically, to think of the *event y* as being made necessary by the *event x*.

It was, Hume thought, one of the chief virtues of his theory of mind that it dispelled this illusion. According to his deflationary analysis of causation, both physical events and mental events do standardly have causes; indeed the primary task of his *Treatise* was to discover the laws of mental causation. But there is never any *necessary connection* between cause and effect. Nor is the claim that all events have causes either a necessary truth or one that can be deduced from any principles of which we can be absolutely certain. For Hume, all necessary, *a priori* certainties express "relations of ideas" as opposed to "matters of fact." Taking the denials of these truths to be self-contradictory, he, in effect, assimilated them to tautologies—like *No unmarried man is married*—or those that can be reduced to tautologies by verbal definitions—like *No bachelor is unmarried*. Truths such as these, Hume believed, don't state facts, and so don't entail the existence of anything. Thus, he insisted that pure *a priori* reasoning alone, unaided by sensory observation, can *never* yield knowledge of the world. Empirical knowledge must always be grounded in observation and experiment.

Like Hume, the great German philosopher Immanuel Kant (1724–1804) saw philosophy as doing for the mind what Newton did for the physical world. Having been introduced to Newton's thought in college at the University of Königsberg, along with the work of the major British and European thinkers and philosophers of his era, Kant taught philosophy at Königsberg for four decades. He agreed with Hume that premises that merely describe contents of our ideas and sensations are insufficient to derive the conclusions that all events have causes, that physical space is Euclidean, or even that enduring objects "presented in space and time"—planets, animals, human bodies, and our own "egos"—really exist. However, unlike Hume, who believed that all genuine knowledge of matters of fact are based on the testimony of our senses, Kant looked to features of our minds to supply the extra ingredients he took to be needed for such knowledge. These, he thought, included space and time themselves, which, he maintained, our minds impose on perceptual experience, and causality, which he took us to impose on the world in attempting to understand it. Because these conceptual additions to the experienced world are knowable preconditions required by our own understanding, he took himself to have recovered our knowledge of many widely believed and seemingly fundamental truths—including the proposition that every empirical event has a cause, and the proposition that the space containing empirical objects we experience is Euclidean.

Despite this, he faced a dilemma. He had to hold either (i) that the planets, animals, mountains, and the like, about which we take ourselves to have knowledge, are independent of us, or (ii) that they are constituted in part by the mental categories our minds impose on experience. Neither option served his purpose. Since the skepticism he wished to refute concerned knowledge of independent things, taking them to be partially constituted by us threatened to drain his refutation of significance. Since there is no guarantee that independent things must conform to how we must think of them, even a successful explanation of why we (must?) think of them in certain ways would be open to skeptical challenge. In time, this dilemma was to be vividly illustrated by the inclusion of non-Euclidean elements in twentieth-century physical theories of space-time, contradicting the Kantian claim that we know *a priori* that physical space is Euclidian.

In sum, the philosophy of the early modern period was inextricably intertwined with the mathematics and natural science of the day. Scientists like Kepler, Galileo, Newton, and Boyle were themselves natural philosophers who studied other natural philosophers and incorporated what they recognized to be philosophical elements in their scientific theories. Natural philosophers like Copernicus, Descartes, Leibniz, and Berkeley attacked scientific and mathematical problems associated with their overall philosophical perspectives. Some made important advances in physics and mathematics, for example by inventing the infinitesimal calculus, by providing the conceptual basis for analytic geometry, by discovering the sine law of refraction, and by contributing to the science of optics. The philosophers Locke, Berkeley, Hume, Reid, and Kant also struggled to expand objective, scientific knowledge to encompass the mind. Although their theories of perception and cognition are primitive by today's standards, they succeeded in identifying problems and framing questions that were later dealt with more satisfactorily using descendants of the concepts they helped to articulate.

This quintessentially philosophical activity was also illustrated by Hume's anticipation of Darwin in his *Dialogues Concerning Natural Religion*. There Hume confronts the argument that just as we would conclude that a fine watch found on a beach was made by a skilled watchmaker, so we should conclude that the well-ordered natural world we observe is the work of a divine creator. Hume combats this argument by urging the possibility that, given enough time to operate, the laws of nature might explain this order on their own, without an intelligent creator.

> Strong and almost incontestable proofs may be traced . . . that every part of this globe has continued for many ages entirely covered with water. And though order were supposed inseparable from matter . . . yet may matter be susceptible of many and great revolutions, through the endless periods of eternal duration. The incessant changes, to which every part of it is subject, seem to intimate some such general transformations.[28]

For example, he suggests, the ingenious adaptation of plants and animals to their surroundings may result from their need to adapt to ever-changing environments.

It is in vain, therefore, to insist upon the uses of the parts in animals or vegetables, and their curious adjustment to each other. I would fain to know how an animal could subsist, unless its parts were so adjusted. Do we not find that it immediately perishes whenever this adjustment ceases, and that its matter corrupting tries some new form? . . . No form . . . can subsist, unless it possess those powers and organs requisite for its subsistence: some new order or economy must be tried . . . without intermission.[29]

He further obliquely suggests that the survival of the fittest may explain the adjustments undergone by all living things.

And why should man . . . pretend to an exemption from the lot of all other animals? . . . A perpetual war is kindled amongst all living creatures. . . . The stronger prey upon the weaker . . . the weaker too often prey upon the stronger. . . . Consider that innumerable race of insects, which either are bred on the body of each animal, or . . . infix their stings in him. . . . These insects have others . . . which torment them. And on each hand, before and behind, above and below, every animal is surrounded with enemies, which incessantly seek his misery and destruction.[30]

You ascribe . . . a purpose and intention to nature. But what . . . is the object of that curious artifice and machinery which she has displayed in all animals? The preservation alone of individuals, and propagation of the species.[31]

Darwin—whose records show him to have been an avid reader of Hume on the advice of his grandfather—was aware of these ideas. This is not to say that Hume's plausible speculation was responsible for Darwin's well-supported theory nearly 100 years later. It is to say that Hume did what philosophers congenitally do—suggest important ideas, some of which turn out to be scientifically productive. This was a recurring theme in the early modern period summarized here.

What, in sum, did philosophy contribute to the remarkable advances in natural science and mathematics during the period? No such advances were the work of philosophy alone. But philosophy did contribute to these advances in many ways: to the Copernican reconceptualization of the solar system needed to explain the apparent retrograde motion of the planets; to the reconceptualization of causation needed to accommodate the notion of a force, gravity, acting at a distance; to the beginnings of analytic geometry; to the invention of the calculus; to early advances in our understanding of light, optics, and vision; to the articulation of foundational questions about the conceptions of space and time needed in our theories; to the idea that the biological world, including the genesis and survival of species, might be explainable by natural causes; and to the project of developing a systematic empirical science of psychology. More important, however, than any of the individual achievements noted here was the fact that during this period science and philosophy were inseparable, overlapping contributors to one of the richest, most rapidly advancing intellectual cultures the world has ever seen.

CHAPTER 4

FREE SOCIETIES, FREE MARKETS, AND FREE PEOPLE

Philosophical conceptions of human nature and human societies; Hobbes on social organization and the justification of the state; Locke on natural rights and limited government; Hume's naturalistic conception of morality, social convention, and evolving social institutions; the influence of Locke, Hume and John Witherspoon on the American founding; Adam Smith's philosophy and economics; the contributions of Hume and Kant to morality.

The interpenetration of philosophy with science and mathematics in the early modern period was matched by its interpenetration with emerging descriptive and normative investigations of politics, economics, morality, and the relationship between the individual and the state. The first great political philosopher of the time was Thomas Hobbes (1588–1679), whose famous work, *Leviathan,* was published in 1651. An accomplished writer and scholar, he translated Thucydides and all of Homer, met Galileo, and submitted objections to Descartes concerning the *Mediations.* His pre-Newtonian philosophy of nature included a speculative physics of matter in motion, a philosophical psychology, and a theory of knowledge. But it was his political philosophy, resting on a theory of human nature, that was groundbreaking.

Hobbes believed the good to be what is desired. He also believed that each person seeks to maximize his or her own good. Hence, he thought, human life without the coercive power of the state would be a war of all against all, in which one must depend on oneself alone for everything, including survival.

In such condition there is no place for industry, because the fruit thereof is uncertain: and consequently no culture of the earth; no navigation . . . no knowledge of the face of the earth . . . no arts; no letters; no society; and, which is worst of all, continual fear and danger of violent death; and the life of man solitary, nasty, brutish, and short.[1]

This picture of life in a "state of nature" is used to tell two stories. The first is a causal explanation of how and why societies are formed. We form them because we realize we can't survive on our own. The second is a justification of the state. We should willingly submit to its authority because doing so is in our interest. Hobbes imagines a hypothetical social contract in which we mutually agree to give up our natural right to seek our own advantage as we wish, transferring authority to the state to forbid or permit actions as it sees fit. Because we benefit from the arrangement, we have a nearly unlimited obligation to obey the law, as long as it is rightly seen as preventing a war of all against all. Since functioning states do that, nearly all are justified.

This indiscriminate justification of states, no matter how authoritarian, is one reason why Hobbes was controversial. More to his credit, perhaps, he also provoked controversy at the time for challenging the divine right of kings. Despite taking monarchy to be the preferred form of government, he gave a naturalistic account of political institutions, which left plenty of room for empirical and philosophical argument. What he didn't do was recognize what we now know to be central aspects of human psychobiology.

Because cooperation promotes survival, human beings are social animals. In addition to needing help from others, we form attachments to them. Parents are genetically disposed to care for their young. Children bond with those on whom they depend, forming ties of affection and trust in which their self-conceptions are intertwined with others. They learn rules in games and collective activities, earning rewards proportional to the value of their efforts. They scrutinize each other for rule violations, and they punish violations of trust with social ostracism and worse. Because participants are socially connected, rule violations risk more than the loss of self-centered benefits. Violations are affronts to one's comrades, to one's friendship with them, to one's image in their eyes, and to the person one wants to be. In this way, rules obeyed to secure benefits of group action become principles honored for their own sake. Natural sentiment, social affiliation, recognition of mutual interest, and prudential rationality blend into a common morality. A number of the philosophers who followed Hobbes implicitly recognized much of this.

The first was the empiricist philosopher John Locke, discussed in the previous chapter. Like Hobbes, Locke's political philosophy was based on a hypothetical "state of nature" and social contract in which individuals cede authority to the state. But whereas Hobbes recognized no moral obligation independent of the state, Locke believed that moral law, discoverable by human reason, is the source of rights and obligations that don't derive from any political institution.

> The state of nature has a law of nature to govern it, which obliges everyone; and reason, which is that law, teaches

all mankind who will but consult it that, being all equal and independent, no one ought to harm another in his life, health, liberty, or possessions.[2]

Locke took these rights to be both natural and discoverable by reason, in the sense that they can be shown to be necessary in order for human beings living in close proximity with one another to secure the manifest benefits resulting from their cooperative involvement with one another. If we are to live with others, Lockean imperatives tell us, each of us must grant others certain rights or prerogatives. Among them are life, liberty, and possessions, including the right to acquire, produce, buy, sell, and exchange property.

Since for Locke, the family is the natural social unit, which fathers are obligated to support, they also have the right to bequeath property to their offspring. Property is initially gained by appropriating unowned natural resources, which one improves or puts to use. One can amass as much as one likes, provided one doesn't waste resources or let them spoil, and there is "enough and as good" available for others. Unfortunately, however, the moral law that *should* govern the state of nature will often be disobeyed unless it is backed by force. Thus a minimal state arising from the social contract is needed to preserve natural rights. In such a state, the citizens themselves or their representatives enact laws for the common good, which are published and known by all; they adopt a legal system for impartially adjudicating disputes that arise; and they develop and submit to a system of legal enforcement to ensure that their rights are protected.

How is the minimal state justified? One might argue that it is justified on the pragmatic grounds that it produces greater happiness and fewer violations of natural rights than other alternatives. Locke wouldn't disagree. However, he gave a different argument, based on consent.

Men being . . . by nature all free, equal, and independent, no one can be put out of this estate [of nature] and be subjected to the political power of another without his own consent. The only way whereby anyone divests himself of his natural liberty and puts on the bonds of civil society is by agreeing with other men to join and unite into a community for their comfortable, safe and peaceable living one amongst another, in secure enjoyment of their properties and a great security against any that are not of it.[3]

Since explicit consent to a social contract is rare, Locke needed a notion of *presumed* consent.

Although he left this notion somewhat undeveloped, it wasn't entirely without foundation. Recognizing that one must inevitably give up some freedom in order to enter society, he believed that certain rights cannot, without absurdity, be *presumed* to have been given up. An individual, he reasoned, enters society

only with the intention . . . the better to preserve himself and his Liberty and Property; (For no rational Creature can be supposed to change his condition with the intention to be worse) the power of the Society, or the Legislature constituted by them, can never be suppos'd to extend further than the common good; but is obliged to secure every one's Property by providing against [the] . . . defects . . . that made nature so unsafe and uneasy.[4]

In short, no one can rationally be presumed to entirely surrender life, liberty, and property to secure the benefits of organized society, for to do so would be to sacrifice more than would be gained.

Locke reiterates the idea a little later.

The Supreme Power [the state] cannot take from any Man any part of his Property without his own consent. For the preservation of Property being the end of Government, and that for which Men enter into Society . . . [to suppose it given up is] too gross an absurdity for any Man to own. . . . Hence it is a mistake to think, that the Supreme or Legislative power of any Commonwealth, can do what it will, and dispose of the Estates of the Subject *arbitrarily,* or take any part of them at pleasure.[5]

Though not without considerable force, this statement is less clear and compelling than one might expect. Locke hoped to establish a great deal from the observation that no one can rationally be presumed to surrender one's rights to life, liberty, and property to secure the benefits of organized society. However, it is unlikely that everything for which he hoped can be established by this route. One gains so much by entering society that merely prohibiting government from making one worse off than one would be in a state of nature, with no system of social cooperation to rely on, is to limit government very little. Consequently Locke's justification falls short of establishing the robust system of protected natural rights at which he was aiming.

At the very least, his heavy emphasis on hypothetical consent—*what one would consent to*—requires qualification. Mightn't a rational agent consent to *some diminution* of Lockean natural rights—some diminution of autonomy, some diminution of rights to acquire, retain, and dispose of property—well short of obliteration, to secure the benefits of social organization? Surely there is considerable room for a rational agent to do so. Mightn't one's willingness to make such trade-offs depend on the specifics of one's situation, and on the society one is joining? How could it not?

Instead of appealing to hypothetical consent to a social contract in the state of nature, one might do better simply to recognize that if, as virtually everyone desires, one is to live in society with others, one must demand certain rights for oneself while also extending them to others. One must grant all individuals the right to security from violent attack, and the right to a sphere of autonomy in which individuals are free to decide their most basic beliefs, to express themselves, and to follow their chosen way of life without harming or coercing others. Since this will typically involve the right to acquire, produce, buy, sell, and exchange property, some semblance of Lockean rights will be included.

Imagine choosing a form of government for ourselves now. Presumably the laws of human biology, psychology, sociology, and economics *constrain* successful forms of political and social organization. Suppose we know enough about these constraints to identify some presumptive rights and privileges that individuals are justified in expecting a morally just, and practically workable, government to respect. We don't have to think of the task as deciding everything at one time, for societies in all conditions, but as deciding for ourselves here and now.

Like Locke, we may want a democratic form of government. But we may also want some assurance that certain fundamental rights and principles will be respected. A reasonable way of increasing the probability that they will be respected is to put them beyond the reach of ordinary policy making by requiring *supermajorities* to change them. This doesn't have to happen all at once. Rather, we might see ourselves as starting modestly and incrementally building a structure that allows for constitutional adjustments, the need for which may become evident over time. At every stage the guiding idea should be to identify principles that, all other things being equal, the government must obey if its citizens are to have a reasonable chance of achieving the goals that voluntary collective action are designed to secure.

Although not all of this is in Locke, the basic picture is an elaboration of his ideas. For him, a democratically elected legislature is the supreme authority in making laws for the common good, applied uniformly to all. His separate executive enforces the law, but cannot enact it, while his separate judicial system settles disputes and tries violations of law. In short, he proposed limited constitutional government, with a clear separation of powers designed to avert tyranny and to secure natural rights, so that citizens can reap the benefits of peaceful, cooperative relationships with one another. Finally, he stipulated that if the government fails to enforce the natural rights of citizens, or exceeds its proper limits, rebellion is justified.

All of this should sound familiar to Americans. It is impossible to read the founding documents of the United States, and the arguments of those supporting them, without hearing echoes of Locke. As one influential commentator has noted,

> [T]here can be no doubt of his great influence on America. . . . In fine, the widespread and lasting effects of Locke's *Treatise of Civil Government* is a standing disproof of the notion that philosophers are ineffectual.[6]

David Hume, the great empiricist philosopher who was also a leading historian of England, added social, historical, and biological dimensions to Locke's conception of limited government. Hume's contributions began with his moral philosophy, the key to which fits his epistemology, discussed in the previous chapter. According to Hume, reason is capable of providing absolutely certain knowledge of necessary, *a priori* truths, but this is only because those truths are merely "relations of ideas," which, in themselves, tell us nothing about the world. Establishing any significant matter of fact involves not only reason but also observation. Action adds another dimension. Although reason and knowledge of the world allow us to calculate the means to our ends, they cannot provide those ends. Since action requires the motivating force of desire, Hume took it to be axiomatic that no statement that can be established by reason and observation alone is sufficient to fully guide or explain action. For that we need to include the values sought by the actor, which, in his words, were supplied by the passions.

Lessons for morality were close at hand. Since moral rules are intended to guide action, the passions, which motivate action, must be the source of morality. Since moral action requires moral ends, the values inherent in our nature must not be entirely self-centered, but rather must include other-regarding values that relate us to our fellows. To act morally, we must desire the well-being of others, especially, but not exclusively, the near and dear. For Hume, it was simply a psychobiological fact that we are prone to be benevolent and to approve of character traits, dubbed "natural sentiments," like honesty, industry, integrity, courage, loyalty, and kindness, while disapproving of their opposites. As he put it, "Morality is more properly felt than judged of."[7]

Hume's political philosophy adds a new element. Whereas his anti-rationalist ethics is anchored in natural sentiment, his anti-rationalist political philosophy is anchored in historically evolving institutions. Society, as he sees it, arises from our needs, from the scarcity of resources available to satisfy them, and from the absence, in the state of nature, of a system of property and division of labor to make productive use of those resources. Think of it this way. Rationality tells me I will benefit from cooperation with others, if they will cooperate with me. Past experience adds that they will cooperate with me only if I do my part. Because we all realize this, we tacitly agree on common rules to be obeyed by all, which will, in the end, benefit everyone.

I learn to keep my word, to do what I have promised, to respect your property, and not to interfere with your enjoyment of what you have earned; you learn the same. Continued interaction generates a social convention that, in Hume's words,

> is entered into by all members of society to bestow stability on the possession of . . . external goods, and to leave everyone in the peaceable enjoyment of what he may acquire by his fortune and industry. . . . I observe that it will be in my interest to leave another in possession of his goods, *provided* he will act in the same manner with regard to me.[8]

Hume regards the needed moral framework to be neither an explicit contract nor a hypothetical construct, but rather a social convention arising from historically evolving institutions that progress by trial and error.

> Nor is the rule concerning the stability of possession the less derived from human conventions, that it arises gradually, and acquires force by a slow progression, and by our repeated experience of the inconveniences of transgressing it. On the contrary, this experience assures us still more, that the sense of interest has become common to all our fellows, and gives us a confidence of future regularity. . . . In like manner are languages gradually established by human conventions without any promise [explicit agreement or contract]. In like manner do gold and silver become the common measures of exchange.[9]

In short, human societies are governed by moral rules that are social conventions that work. In this way, he arrives at rules governing property, its voluntary transfer, and the enforcement of promises.[10] Taking them to be scientific regularities found in political and economic institutions in communities of a certain size, he calls the rules "Laws of Nature."[11]

It may seem puzzling, given his distinction between fact and value, that Hume calls these principles of social and political morality *laws of nature*. According to him, no statement of value—of what should be, or of what one ought to do—follows logically from any factual statements. As he would put it, *one can't derive an ought from an is*. One can agree to any factual claims while disputing any moral claims without being guilty of logical inconsistency. How then can Hume call the social conventions governing property, promises, and other moral matters "Laws of Nature"? Surely, laws of nature, like Newton's laws, are facts. So, it would seem, Hume must think that the social conventions that make up morality are social facts.

He does, in fact. Nevertheless, he also takes these "laws" to be normative—i.e., to be rules we *should* follow. He says that *justice*—or *fairness*—is generally approved, and so is a virtue, because it is known to be in everyone's interest. He notices that this approval is freely granted, despite our awareness free riders—i.e., of people who pretend to cooperate but in fact don't. These people know that the general obedience to accepted social rules is in everyone's interest, including their own. Still, they secretly opt out and fail to do their part when they can get away with it. Hume thinks they ought not.[12]

Why do we recognize such narrowly self-interested behavior to be wrong? Hume hints at the answer when considering our reaction to injustice done to others but not ourselves. He says such action

> still displeases us; because we consider it as prejudicial to human society, and pernicious to every one that approaches the person guilty of it. We partake of their

uneasiness by *sympathy* . . . this is the reason why the sense of moral good and evil follows upon justice and injustice. And though this sense, in the present case, be derived only from contemplating the actions of others, yet we fail not to extend it even to our own actions [i.e., we come to think that we ought not to act in that way]. . . . Thus self-interest is the original motive to the establishment of justice: but a sympathy with public interest is the source of the moral approbation which attends that virtue.[13]

Hume takes free-riding—reaping the benefits of social cooperation while not doing one's part—to be immoral because it violates the social conventions that secure other-regarding values inherent in our human nature, and so common to us all.

From today's perspective, it is natural to think of these values as arising from our biological nature plus the commonalities of human culture derived from thousands of years of living in communities. The competitive advantages of social cooperation are so great that the degree to which various groups of our human and nonhuman ancestors mastered the dynamics of cooperation must have had important effects on which groups survived and which didn't. Survival of the fittest suggests that we carry the traits of the winners. Biologically we emerged as highly social animals who not only depend on, but also care about, others in our social group. In this way, unrenounceable other-regarding values became inherent to our nature. Because they are part of our biological makeup, these values provided the raw material for gradually evolving institutions of social cooperation that have become moral fixed points in most human societies.

These claims are both factual and normative. They are factual claims about the values arising in normal human beings from their biological inheritance, childhood experience, and the cultural institutions they are born into. They are normative principles because the values described are not erasable from our nature. The factual claims have normative power because the values they describe are ours, the ones we want to live by. Hume grouped them together under the headings *self-interest, justice,* and *sympathy.*

Imagine a species of rational creatures who didn't have social values—each of whom cared only for him or herself, and placed no value on the well-being of others. They might be as intelligent and rational as we are, but without any desire to form social attachments. They might cooperate when they believe it to be to their own individual advantage, but they would always be on the lookout for ways to cheat the system, and bend it to their own selfish interests. Hence, they wouldn't trust one another and they would have no socially inculcated morality. Being without Hume's natural sentiment, their systems of cooperation would be much more fragile and limited than ours. Because of this, their chances of evolutionary success might not be very great. Fortunately, they are not us.

Another aspect of Hume's social and political philosophy lies in its rejection of rationalistic schemes of social organization, its concern for liberty and innovation, and its focus on naturally arising institutions, participation in which wins general approval by proving to be in most people's long-term interest. Here Hume the historian of England meets Hume the philosophical critic of those who place too much faith in the power of reason. Unlike Rousseau, whose abstract conception of the *general will* encouraged authoritarianism, Hume's empiricism encouraged liberty. Thus, it's not surprising that, like Locke, he influenced the founders of the United States—as illustrated by James Madison's use, in Federalist Paper 10, of Hume's argument against Montesquieu to show how and why a representative republic governing a large and diverse society could safeguard liberty by combatting the dangers of faction.[14]

Hume was only one of several Scottish philosophers who influenced early America. Another Scotsman, though not a major philosopher himself, was the philosophically minded clergyman John Witherspoon (1723–1794). Witherspoon was president of Princeton from 1768 to 1794, where he was also head of its Philosophy, History, and English departments. A devotee of the school of commonsense realism of the Scottish philosopher Thomas Reid (1710–1796), Witherspoon may have done more than anyone else to spread the influence of the Scottish Philosophical Enlightenment in the new world. After his arrival in America, he became a staunch advocate of independence, and an important intellectual influence during and after the Revolution. A member of the Continental Congress and signer of the Declaration of Independence, he was the teacher of future president James Madison, and of four other representatives at the Constitutional Convention in 1787 as well. He also taught Aaron Burr, who became vice president of the United States, as well as three future Supreme Court justices, 28 future United States senators, and 49 former students who became members of the House of Representatives.

Another Scottish philosopher who influenced both Hume and Witherspoon was Francis Hutcheson (1694–1745). Hutcheson, who held the Chair in Moral Philosophy at the University of Glasgow from 1729 to until his death, was, like Hume, a moral-sense theorist who argued against Hobbes that human nature included social and benevolent elements. These theories of Hutcheson and Hume had a strong influence on Hutcheson's most famous student, Adam Smith (1723–1790). Smith studied philosophy first at Glasgow and later at Oxford, after which he lectured at Edinburgh, where he met Hume, who become his dear friend and philosophical mentor. As Arthur Herman notes:

As a philosopher and as a friend, Hume made a huge impact on Adam Smith. Smith read and understood him more thoroughly, perhaps, than any other contemporary. His own writings would be inconceivable without Hume's peculiar take on the "progress" of civil society, and on what an imperfect, trial-and-error process it truly is.[15]

In 1751 Smith was appointed professor of logic at Glasgow. In 1752, he was awarded the Chair of Moral Philosophy, which had been occupied for 16 years by Hutcheson. Smith himself occupied the chair for twelve years, teaching logic, moral philosophy, economics, and jurisprudence. His 1759 book *The Theory of the Moral Sentiments*—regarded by Smith at the end of his life as his best work—was a philosophical treatise on morality based on a theory of human nature along the lines of Hutcheson and Hume. But the book the world came to recognize as his masterpiece was *The Wealth of Nations*, published in 1776. The founding document of classical economics, it explained how individuals pursuing their own economic self-interest under conditions of fair and honest competition will, as if led by "an invisible hand," increase not only their own prosperity, but the prosperity of society as a whole. In the book, Smith emphasizes the efficiency and wealth-producing potential of free trade, free markets, and the division of labor, while warning against monopoly, unfair restraint of trade, and government protectionism of favored businesses. He also measured the wealth of a society not by its reserves of gold and silver, but by the value of all goods and services it produces.

The influence of *The Wealth of Nations* has, of course, been profound. But it wasn't anomalous. Taken together, the moral, political, legal, and social philosophy of seventeenth- and eighteenth-century philosophers from Hobbes and Locke to Hume and Smith gave us the theoretical foundations of limited government and modern economies, leading, as Smith seemed to foresee, to the greatest expansion of liberty and prosperity the world has ever known. Writing his masterpiece in the autumn of 1775, he says this about the society likely to result from the coming American Revolution:

> They are very weak who flatter themselves that . . . our colonies will be easily conquered by force alone. The persons who now govern the resolutions of what they call the Continental Congress feel in themselves at this moment a degree of importance which, perhaps, the greatest subjects in Europe scarcely feel. From shopkeepers, tradesmen, and attorneys, they are become statesmen and legislators, and are employed in contriving a new form of government for an extensive empire, which . . . seems very likely to become one of the greatest and most formidable that ever was in the world.[16]

Overall, the record of seventeenth- and eighteenth-century philosophical accomplishment in the social, political, and moral sphere is similar to that era's record of achievement in physics, mathematics, and natural philosophy. In the previous chapter we saw that Isaac Newton, the foremost physicist of his era, read philosophy and displayed a remarkably philosophical turn of mind in his thoroughly scientific work. The relation of Adam Smith, the first modern economist, to philosophy was even closer. In addition to studying Hobbes, Hume, and Hutcheson, Smith taught philosophy, he wrote some of the most important moral philosophy of his day, and he correctly took himself to be a philosopher.

There was, during this period, no sharp contrast between the multiple roles played by leading thinkers. As Newton, Boyle, Descartes, and Leibniz illustrated, there was no fundamental discontinuity between making contributions to physics and mathematics and making contributions to metaphysics and epistemology; nor, as Hume and Smith illustrated, was there a fundamental discontinuity between making contributions to history and economics, and making contributions to moral, political, or social philosophy. The world-transforming advances of the seventeenth and eighteenth centuries in politics, economics, and social organization could not have occurred without the philosophers of this era.

Philosophers were also responsible for a similar transformation in naturalizing moral thought, grounding it in human nature, rather than in natural or revealed theology. As we have seen, one of these approaches, championed by Hume, Hutcheson, and Smith, grounded it in our moral, other-regarding sentiments. The other major approach was championed by one of the philosophical giants of all time, Immanuel Kant. His most striking contribution to morality, the *categorical imperative*, identified our common rationality—*not* our benevolent sentiments (which Kant would have regarded as too variable and insecure)—as the source of morality. Anyone who asks "What if everybody did that?" in contemplating the permissibility or impermissibility of an act, is echoing Kant's imperative, which directs one to *act only on rules that one can rationally will to be universally followed, or perhaps be universally accepted*. Kant illustrated his idea with two paradigmatic examples. According to him, lying and promise-breaking are impermissible because they are, in a certain way, rationally inconsistent. If everyone routinely lied or broke promises, the social conventions of truth-telling and promise-fulfilling would not exist, thereby destroying the reservoir of trust that makes lying and promising possible. Since *universal lying or promise-breaking* is, therefore, *conceptually impossible*, no rational being can will, or intend, such behavior to be a universal law. Thus, Kant argues, it is never morally permissible to lie or break a promise.

Although this was a good thought, it was too extreme. There are occasions when it is permissible, and even morally required, to lie or break a promise. There are also things that everyone could do—acts that could, without contradiction, be willed to be done universally (e.g., rehearse secret fantasies of revenge every day)—that one shouldn't do. However, these defects in the strictly Kantian formulation might be addressed by more nuanced versions of the view. For example, one might hold (roughly) that *an act is morally impermissible if it is prohibited by rules the universal adoption of which as social conventions would produce the best system of social cooperation between free and equal parties; an act is morally required if it is mandated by rules the universal adoption of which as social conventions is a necessary feature of any effective system of social cooperation between free and equal parties; and all other actions are morally permissible.*

This view is Kantian in calling for the universal adoption of moral rules. But it is also consequentialist in assessing moral rules by the value of the consequences of adopting them, and also in taking the rules to be *social conventions* observed in normal cases, while allowing deviations in exceptional cases when justified by the need to avoid overwhelmingly bad consequences, or the opportunity to achieve overwhelmingly good ones. Such a rough-and-ready code would tell us, among other things, (i) that lying, promise-breaking, harming or coercing others, infringing on their natural liberty, or violating their rights to property are justified only in extreme or unusual cases, and (ii) that, except in such cases, one is required to support oneself (if possible), to provide for one's children, to contribute to needed public services, and to donate a portion of one's income, above a certain minimum, to care for those who are unable to care for themselves. Many difficult cases would, of course, remain to be adjudicated. But this doesn't detract from the usefulness of this amalgam of the moral and social philosophies of Hume and Kant.[17]

CHAPTER 5

MODERN LOGIC AND THE FOUNDATIONS OF MATHEMATICS

The philosophical origins of modern symbolic logic and its use in the philosophy of mathematics; the Frege-Russell attempt to explain what numbers are and what mathematical knowledge is; what was achieved, what was not, and how the program might still be advanced.

The invention of modern logic initiated by the German philosopher-mathematician Gottlob Frege, and continued by Bertrand Russell and other mathematically minded philosophers in the early twentieth century, is one of philosophy's greatest achievements.[1] Born in 1848, Frege earned a Ph.D. in mathematics from the University of Göttingen in 1873, followed by his Habilitation from the University of Jena in 1874, where he taught for his entire career. Now recognized as one of the greatest philosophical logicians and philosophers of mathematics of all time, his contributions initially went virtually unnoticed by his fellow mathematicians. He did, however, profoundly influence four young men who were to become philosophical giants of the early twentieth century—Bertrand Russell, Edmund Husserl, Rudolf Carnap, and Ludwig Wittgenstein.

Frege's goal was to ground the certainty and objectivity of mathematics in the fundamental laws of logic, thereby distinguishing logic and mathematics from empirical science in general, and from the psychology of human reasoning in particular. In 1879, his *Begriffsschrift* (*Concept Script*) presented the new system of symbolic logic now called "the predicate calculus," the expressive power of which vastly surpassed that of any previous system. The greatest advance in the history of the subject, its rigorous formulation rendered it capable of fully formalizing the notion of proof in mathematics.[2]

Frege's logic combined the simple truth-functional logic (governing reasoning involving 'and', 'or', 'not', and 'if, then'), known from the Stoics onward, with a powerful new account of reasoning involving 'all' and 'some', supplanting the far more limited syllogistic logic dating back to Aristotle. Whereas Aristotle's theory of logical syllogisms covered only a small number of simple inferences of the sort

(i) All human beings are mortal, Cleopatra is a human being, therefore Cleopatra is mortal.

and

(ii) Some philosophers are logicians, all logicians are mathematicians, therefore some philosophers are mathematicians.

Frege's logic vastly expanded the number of valid inference patterns, dwarfing those identified by earlier logicians.

A logic in his modern sense consists of precisely defined sets of sentences and formulas plus a proof procedure, typically consisting of axioms and rules of inference. Axioms are statements the truth of which is transparently obvious. Rules of inference—e.g., from *A* and *If A, then B* one may infer *B*—tell you what lines you may add to a proof-in-progress by inspecting earlier lines of the proof. A proof is, by definition, a finite sequence of lines, each of which is either an axiom or a formula obtainable from earlier lines by one of the rules of inference. A proof of Q from P is such a sequence of lines, starting with P and ending with Q. Whether or not something is a proof (in the sense of establishing that Q can't be false if P is true) is always decidable merely by inspecting the formula on each line, without worrying about which objects and properties its expressions stand for. Thus, the status of something as a proof can always be settled conclusively. As we shall see in chapter 6, this strict notion of proof was an early step leading to the mathematical theory of computation that made the digital age possible.

In addition to formalizing proof, Frege explained how to understand the sentences of his logical language. This is done by (i) identifying a domain of objects one is using the sentences to talk about, (ii) indicating which object in the domain each name refers to, and (iii) stating, for each predicate—e.g., 'is not identical with zero' or 'is an odd number'—the condition any object must satisfy in order for the predicate to correctly apply to it. A simple sentence in which a predicate is combined with names is true just in case the predicate correctly applies to (and hence is true of) the objects designated by the names. The negation of a sentence S is true just in case S isn't true. A conjunction of sentences is true just in case each conjunct is true; a disjunction is true just in case at least one is; while what is called "a material conditional," *If P, then Q*, is true if and only if it is not the case that the conjunction of P and the negation of Q is true. Finally, if *S(n)* is a sentence containing a name *n*, and the formula *S(x)* arises from *S(n)* by replacing one or more occurrences of *n* with a variable *x*, then *For all x S(x)* is true just in case *S(x)* is true no matter which object one chooses as (temporary) referent of *x*. *For some x S(x)* is true just in case there is at least one object in the domain that makes *S(x)* true when one assigns it as (temporary) referent of *x*. In this way, truth conditions of every sentence of the logical language are specified. Since there is no longest sentence, these rules are sufficient to interpret the *infinitely many* sentences of the Fregean language.

A sentence S is a *logical truth* if and only if it comes out true, when interpreted in this way, *no matter what domain of objects* one uses S to talk about, *no matter what referents* one assigns to its names, and *no matter what conditions* are used to define correct application of the predicates occurring in S. For example, *(If P&Q, then P)* is a logical truth. A sentence Q is a *logical consequence* of a sentence (or set of sentences) P if and only if *no matter what domain of objects* one uses both Q and the sentences in P to talk about, *no matter what referents* are assigned to their names (the same assignment when n occurs in both P and Q), and *no matter what conditions* are used to define correct application of their predicates (the same conditions when a predicate appears in both P and Q), Q will always be true when all the sentences in P are true. For example, *For some x (Fx & Gx)* is a logical consequence of *Fn* and *Gn*.

Today, these definitions are usually expressed using the notion of abstract *models* consisting of a domain D of objects, an assignment of objects in D as referents of names, plus an assignment, for each predicate, of conditions of correct application. A sentence is *logically true* just in case it is true in all models. The statement made by a use of such a truth couldn't possibly be false. When the truth of a sentence or set of sentences in an arbitrary model always guarantees the truth of another sentence (in that model), the latter is a logical consequence of the former; hence it is impossible for the latter to be false when the former sentence (or sentences) is (or are) true (or are) true. When two sentences are always either true together in any model or false together (in that model), they are logically equivalent. To Frege's credit, all and only the sentences *provable* in his basic system from a set of sentences are *logical consequences* of those sentences.[3]

Dismayed by the lack of attention initially paid to this momentous advance, Frege followed five years later with a clear statement of his philosophy of mathematics in *Die Grundlagen der Arithmetik* (*The Foundations of Arithmetic*).[4] In this now-classic work, he defends his vision of the objectivity of mathematics and the source of our certain knowledge of mathematical truths. He does so by (i) defining the natural numbers, (ii) outlining a strategy for proving the axioms of arithmetic from the axioms of logic plus logical definitions of arithmetical concepts, and (iii) offering the prospect of extending the strategy to higher mathematics through the definition and analysis of real and complex numbers.

In addition, starting in 1891, he laid the foundations of the scientific study of linguistic meaning by explaining, in a series of articles, the principles by which sentences—of natural languages like German and the invented languages of logic and mathematics—systematically encode information about the world. In 1893 and 1903, his grand project was brought to fruition in his two-volume work, *Grundgesetze der Arithmetik* (*Basic Laws of Arithmetic*), in which he gave detailed derivations of all arithmetical axioms from what he took to be the most fundamental laws of logic.[5]

Through it all, his aim was to answer two philosophical questions: *What are numbers?* and *What is the basis of mathematical knowledge?* Though, in conception, his answer was simple, his key notion of a *concept* requires some explanation. For Frege, simple predicates like 'is round' and 'is a ball' stand for concepts, which they contribute to the truth or falsity of sentences containing them. For our purposes, we can think of concepts as conditions objects must satisfy in order for predicates to be true of them. Thus the Fregean concepts designated by 'is round' and 'is a ball' assign respectively (i) truth to anything round and falsity to all else, and (ii) truth to anything that is a ball and falsity to all else. When we combine predicates—e.g., *x is round & x is a ball*—we form a complex predicate that stands for the concept that is true of all and only round balls.[6]

With this in mind, we return to Frege's answer to the questions *What are numbers?* and *What is the basis of mathematical knowledge?* In brief, he answered, *logic* is the source of mathematical knowledge; *zero* is the set of concepts true of nothing; *one* is the set of concepts each of which is true of something, and only that thing; *two* is the set of concepts each of which is true of some distinct x and y, and nothing else; etc. Since numbers are sets of concepts, *the successor* n of a number m is the set of concepts F each of which is such that for some object x of which F is true, the concept *being an F other than x* is a member of m. The natural numbers are members of every set that contains zero while also containing the successor of anything it contains. Multiplication is repeated addition, addition is defined in terms of counting, and counting is repeated moving from a number to its successor.

To understand Frege, one must understand his methodology. Prior to philosophical analysis we know many arithmetical truths, but we have no idea what numbers are and little understanding of how we know about them. His basic idea is that *numbers are whatever they have to be in order to explain our knowledge of them*. To discover what they are, we must give definitions of numbers that allow us to deduce what we pre-theoretically know. How, for example, should 2, 3, 5, and the operation of addition be defined so that Facts 2 and 3 can be logically deduced from the definitions plus our perceptual knowledge of Fact 1?

FACT 1

a. X is a black book on my desk and Y is a black book on my desk; X isn't the same object as Y; moreover, for any object whatsoever, if it is a black book on my desk, either it is X or it is Y.
b. U is a blue book on my desk and V is a blue book on my desk and W is a blue book on my desk; U isn't the same object as V and U isn't the same object as W and V isn't the same object as W; moreover, for any object whatsoever, if it is a blue book on my desk, then either it is U or it is V or it is W.
c. Nothing is both a black book on my desk and a blue book on my desk.

FACT 2

There are exactly two black books on my desk and exactly three blue books on my desk.

FACT 3

There are exactly five books on my desk.

Frege's chief objection to earlier philosophers of mathematics was that they didn't answer, or even really try to answer, questions like these.

He did. For him, the statement *there are four moons of Jupiter* is the statement that *the number of things falling under the concept* moon of Jupiter = *4*, or, more informally, *the number of moons of Jupiter = 4. For any concept F, the number of F's is the set of concepts C such that the things that are F and the things that are C can be exhaustively paired off one with another, without repeating any F or any C, until there are no more F's or C's to pair off.* Thus, the number of fingers on my right hand is the set of concepts C such that my thumb can be paired with a C, my index finger can be paired with a different C, and so on until each finger is paired with its own instance of C, and there are no more C's and no more fingers to pair off.

Having conceptualized statements about numbers in this way, Frege needed the following definitions to embark on his project of deriving arithmetic from logic.

> *Def:* Zero is the number of the concept *not identical with itself.*
>
> *Def:* n *immediately succeeds* m if and only if for some concept F, and some object x falling under F (i.e., some object of which the concept F is true), n is the number of F's, and m is the number of the concept *falling under F but not identical with x.*
>
> *Def:* x is a natural number if and only if x is a member of every set that contains zero and always contains the successor of anything it contains.

Since everything is identical with itself, it follows that zero is the set of concepts true of nothing, that 1 is the set of concepts true of some x and only x, that 2 is the set of concepts true of some distinct x and y, and only them, and so on. The principle of *mathematical induction* also follows: *For any concept F, if F is true of zero, and if F is always true of the successor of any natural number it is true of, then F is true of every natural number.* Definitions of multiplication as repeated addition, and addition as repeated ascent from a natural number to its successor, completed the set of needed definitions.

Convinced that the highest certainty belongs to self-evident principles of logic—without which thought itself might be impossible—Frege believed that by deriving arithmetic from logic he would show the certainty of arithmetic and higher mathematics to be based on logic itself. The most basic arithmetical truths—the axioms—were to be derived as logical consequences of his definitions plus self-evident logical axioms. All other arithmetical truths were to be derived from the arithmetical axioms. When, in similar fashion, results of higher mathematics were derived from arithmetic—a process already underway—Frege imagined that all classical mathematics could be so generated. Thus, he believed, all mathematical knowledge could be explained as logical knowledge.

This was the grand structure of his program in the philosophy of mathematics. The key step was to give proofs of all axioms of the arithmetical theory now known as Peano Arithmetic.[7] Relying on further reductions of higher mathematics to arithmetic, he concluded that mathematics (save geometry, for which he made an exception) is just an elaboration of logic. But there was a puzzle lurking in his plan that didn't become recognizable until later, when the nature of logic itself had been more fully investigated. If numbers are sets of concepts, and statements about numbers are logical consequences of logical axioms, then logic itself must make claims about what sets of concepts do, and don't, exist. But, how can it? How can a discipline devoted to specifying which inferences *in any domain of inquiry* are guaranteed to be truth-preserving, and which aren't, tell us which things of a special sort (sets) exist and which don't? Initially, this didn't concern Frege. He assumed that for each meaningful predicate expressing a condition applying to objects, there is a set—perhaps empty, perhaps not—of all and only the objects satisfying the condition. To build this principle into logic was, in effect, to assume that talk about x's *being so-and-so* is interchangeable with talk about x *being in the set of things that are so-and-so.*

In 1903 Bertrand Russell, who was then working on his own derivation of arithmetic from logic, showed this assumption to be false. Russell's system, while similar to Frege's, identified natural numbers with sets of sets, rather than sets of concepts. Like Frege, he had assumed that for every meaningful formula (predicate) in his logical language there is a set—possibly empty, possibly not—of precisely those things of which the formula is true. But he discovered that this assumption led to a contradiction.

Consider the formula *x isn't a member of x,* which says of any set that it isn't a member of itself. Since the formula is meaningful, Russell initially thought that there is a set, possibly empty, that contains all and only those sets of which the formula is true. Call that set Y. Now ask, *Is Y a member of itself?* If it is, then, by definition, it isn't a member of Y; equally, if it isn't a member of Y, then it is. Because of this, the assumptions built into Russell's and Frege's attempted derivations of arithmetic from logic turned out to be inconsistent.[8] Although Frege never succeeded in adequately revising the assumptions, Russell spent much of the next seven years doing so, resulting in a contradiction-free derivation of arithmetic presented in his and Alfred North Whitehead's *Principia Mathematica*.[9]

Unfortunately, Russell's way of avoiding contradiction raised questions about whether the underlying system really was logic. Whereas Frege dreamed of deriving mathematics from self-evident logical truths, some of the complications of Russell's system were neither obvious nor truths of logic. One, the axiom of infinity, simply assumed the existence of infinitely many non-sets.[10] Another, the axiom of reducibility, generated controversy from the start, while a related complication, the theory of types, imposed constraints that were difficult to justify.[11] Later reductions eliminated the worst complications, but the systems to which they reduced mathematics weren't *logical* systems governing reasoning on all subjects. Rather, they were *mathematical* systems.

The dominant theory of sets growing out of the early work of Frege and Russell is now known as *Zermelo-Fraenkel set theory.*[12] Rather than combining set theory with logic, ZF is an independent mathematical theory with its own axioms governing thought and talk about its own special objects. The reduction of arithmetic to ZF can be achieved in several ways. But there is no question of *justifying* arithmetic by reducing it to set theory, since our knowledge of the latter is no more secure, or philosophically explicable, than our knowledge of the former. The great utility of set theory lies in its role as a common base to which a great many mathematical theories can be reduced and thereby productively compared.

One wonders, in light of this, what to make of Frege's methodological principle *that numbers are whatever they have to be in order to explain our knowledge of them.* Now that logic has been distinguished from set theory, there are two reasons to think that natural numbers aren't sets. The first is that the problem of explaining our knowledge of sets—which are themselves mathematical objects—seems as daunting as that of explaining our knowledge of numbers. The second is that even if we could explain how we arrive at set-theoretic knowledge, there is no evident way of choosing among the many different ways of identifying natural numbers with sets. Although each reduction identifies individual numbers—1, 2, 3, etc.—with different sets than those provided by other reductions, the different systems do an equally good job of preserving all arithmetical truths. If this is the only criterion for justifying a reduction, we have no reason for thinking that any such reduction is uniquely correct. In fact, we may have reason to doubt that any reduction is; for surely, if the number 3 is identical with some set, there should be a reason for thinking it is one particular set rather than any other. No existing reduction of arithmetic to set theory has supplied it.[13]

Nevertheless, one should not reject Frege's maxim—*Numbers are whatever they have to be to explain our knowledge of them*. In *The Foundations of Arithmetic,* he rightly says that nothing we can picture or imagine seems to be an apt candidate for being the number 4. But he isn't deterred. Although we can, in his words, *form no idea of the content of a number term,* we can investigate which assignment of meanings and referents to number terms best enables us to explain our knowledge of arithmetical statements.

By "our knowledge," I mean everyone's knowledge—children who know only a little, adults who know more, and mathematicians who know much more. The first challenge is to explain how we achieve *any* of the knowledge of numbers that is common to us all. The second is to explain how instruction enables us to acquire more such knowledge. If we can meet these challenges, we may have a realistic starting point for explaining the rest of our mathematical knowledge.

One component of the needed starting point is what Frege called "Hume's Principle," which specifies that *the number of X's* is the same as *the number of Y's* if and only if the X's and Y's can be exhaustively paired off (without remainder). As it happens, *the number of universities* at which I have been a regular faculty member—Yale, Princeton, and USC—can be exhaustively paired off (without remainder) with the number of books now on my desk. So, the number of *universities* at which I have served is the same number as the number of books in front of me. Both the books and the universities are three (in number). What is this property, *being three (in number),* true of? It's not true of any of my past faculty homes; neither Yale, Princeton, nor USC is three (in number). It is also not true of the set that contains them (and only them); since the set is a single thing, it's not three either. Like the property *being scattered,* the property *being three (in number)* is irreducibly plural;

it applies, not to any *single* instance of any type of thing, but to *multiple things* taken together. My former Ph.D. students are scattered around the world, even though no one of them is scattered, and the set containing them, which isn't in space and time, isn't scattered either.

With this in mind, consider the hypothesis that each natural number N greater than or equal to 2 is the plural property *being N (in number),* and that the number 1 is a property applying to each individual thing considered on its own.[14] Zero is a property that doesn't apply to anything. Each of these properties is, like other properties, *a way that a thing or things can be.* Suppose then that natural numbers are *cardinality properties* of individuals and multiples of the kind just illustrated. How do we gain knowledge of them? In the beginning, we do so by counting. Imagine a child inferring that I am holding up three fingers from her perceptual knowledge that x, y, and z are different fingers. When counting, she pairs off, without remainder, the fingers I am holding up with the English words 'one', 'two, and 'three', thereby ensuring that the fingers and the numerals "have the same number" in Frege's sense. The number they share is designated by the numeral, "three," that ends the count; it is the property *being three (in number).*

With this, we have the germ of an idea that combines the best of the attempted Frege-Russell reductions with a striking but flawed and incompletely developed insight in section 1 of Ludwig Wittgenstein's *Philosophical Investigations.* The book begins with a quotation from Augustine.

When they (my elders) named some object, and accordingly moved toward something, I saw this and I grasped that the thing was called by the sound they uttered when they meant to point it out. Their intention was shown by their bodily movements, as it were the natural language of all peoples: the expression of the face, the play of the eyes, the movement of other parts of the body, and the tone of voice, which expresses our state of mind in seeking, having, rejecting, or avoiding something. Thus, as I heard the words repeatedly used in their proper places in various sentences, I gradually learnt to understand what objects they signified.[15]

Wittgenstein uses the passage to illustrate a conception of language he rejects—one according to which all meaning is naming. One reason he rejects this conception involves an imagined priority in introducing words into a language, and in learning a language once the words have been introduced. The priority is one in which our awareness of things in the world always comes first, followed our decision to introduce certain words to talk about them. In language learning, we first focus on candidates for what our elders use a word to name, and then, having done so, we converge on the single candidate that best makes sense of the sentences they use containing the word we are trying to learn.

Having set up the picture he wants to reject, he immediately jumps to a use of language that, he thinks, doesn't conform to it. He says,

> Now think of the following use of language: I send someone shopping. I give him a slip marked "five red apples". . . . [On finding the apple drawer the shopkeeper] says the series of cardinal numbers—I assume that he knows them by heart—up to the word "five" and for each number he takes an apple of the same color as the sample out of the drawer. It is in this and similar ways that one operates with words. . . . "But how does he know . . . what he is to do with the word 'five'?" . . . [W]hat is the meaning of the word "five"?—- No such thing was in question here, only how the word "five" is used.[16]

This emphasis on the use of the numeral 'five', rather than its referent, is illuminating. But the lesson *isn't* that its meaning is its use; the meaning of the numeral 'five', which is also its referent, is the *property being five in number*, which isn't a use of anything. The proper lesson is that *our use of the numeral in counting makes us aware of the property*, which, as a result, becomes cognitively associated with the numeral, rather than our antecedent nonlinguistic recognition of the property making it available for naming. *First the use, leading to the awareness of something to be named; not first the mystical awareness of number, and then the decision to name it.*

The importance of counting is in establishing an epistemic foothold on a vast domain that none of us, individually or collectively, will ever actually count. Most of us know what we would have to do to count to a trillion. But some of us don't know a verbal numeral in English for the number that comes after *nine hundred ninety-nine trillion, nine hundred ninety-nine billion, nine hundred ninety-nine million, nine hundred ninety-nine thousand, nine hundred and ninety-nine.* Fortunately, most people have mastered the system of Arabic numerals, in which each of the infinitely many natural numbers has a name.

Each of these distinct names can be taken as designating a distinct cardinality property, as long as we don't run out of multiples to bear those properties. That might seem problematic, since it seems likely that there are only finitely many electrons in the universe, and so only finitely many multiples of concrete things. But it's not a worry, since we aren't restricted to counting only concrete things. We can also count multiples consisting in whole, or in part, of properties, including cardinality properties (numbers) we have already encountered. Since this ensures there will be no end to larger and larger multiples, it also ensures the existence of infinitely many distinct cardinality properties.

As the philosopher Mario Gomez-Torrente has pointed out, this picture gives us an opportunity to explain our knowledge of numbers. Consider the child inferring from her perceptual knowledge that the number of fingers I am holding up is 3. In time, counting won't always be necessary, because she will recognize at a glance when she is perceiving trios of familiar types. At that point she has the concept, *being a trio of things,* which is the plural property *being three in number*—i.e., the number 3. The child learns a few other small numbers in the same way—initially by counting, but eventually by perceptual recognition, even though counting will remain the fallback method when in doubt, or when the multiples increase in size. In this way we come to have perceptual and other beliefs about numbers. Much of this counts as knowledge. In short, knowledge of natural numbers is knowledge of cardinality properties grounded initially in perception (visual and otherwise), in cognitive recognition of things being of various types, and in cognitive action—e.g., counting the items falling under a given concept by reciting the relevant numerals while focusing one's attention on different individuals of a given type falling under the concept.

In thinking of things in this way, it is important to realize that one doesn't *first* learn what numbers are, and *then* use them to count. On the contrary, one first learns the practice of articulating certain sequences of sounds (i.e., sequences of numerals) and pairing them off with sequences of things. That is the origin of counting. The point at which one *recognizes numbers* and *uses numerals to refer to them* is the point at which one has mastered this practice and integrated it into one's cognitive life. In saying things like, "There are four of these things but only three of those," one uses the numerals to attribute cardinality properties of multiples. The properties one attributes are the numbers, which exist independently of us and of our language, but which we cognize only in virtue of the linguistic (or other symbolic) routines we have mastered.[17]

At this point, a word about grammar may be helpful. One might think of the word 'three' on analogy with the word 'blue' as capable of performing three grammatical functions. First, both can be used to designate certain properties of which other properties are predicated, as in *Blue is the color of a cloudless sky at noon* and *Three is the number of singers in the group*. Second, they can combine with the copula to form predicates, as in *The sky is blue*, and *We are three*, said by Peter, Paul and Mary in answer to the question *How many are you?* Third, they can modify predicates, as in *There is a blue shirt in the closet* and *There are three singers on stage*. Here, the numeral 'three' designates a plural property that applies to Peter, Paul and Mary without applying to any one of them; the compound property *being three singers on the stage* applies to some individuals who are (collectively) three if and only if each is a singer on the stage.

The idea that properties, which are true of objects, might also be true of properties may cause worry about paradoxes analogous to those that plagued Frege and Russell. But it's not clear that paradoxes *must* result from plural cardinality properties. No such property, except the degenerate case of the number 1, is true of itself, for the simple reason that no natural number other than 1 is true of any single thing. That's not paradoxical. Is any N true of some things one of which is the property *being N in number*? Yes, each N (other than zero) is. But that's not obviously paradoxical either. Is there any plural cardinality property N such that for all pluralities F, N is true of all and only those Fs no one of which is the property *being N in number?* No, that condition isn't met by any plural cardinality property. Thus, we still have no paradox. There is, of course, no property that is true of any property p if and only if p isn't true of itself. That would be problematic if we needed properties satisfying *every intelligible condition* to arrive at our knowledge of basic arithmetic, but no such derivation is contemplated. Though one must be careful, even in our limited project encompassing only natural numbers, no clear threat is apparent.

What about another worry? While looking at Peter, Paul and Mary (a singing group) standing on the stage next to the Rolling Stones (another group), I may say, equally, the number of singing groups on the stage is 2 or the number of singers on the stage is 8. Indeed, I do see eight singers and I do see two singing groups. But in saying this, I am *not* saying that any of the things I see are both two and eight in number. You might suppose otherwise if you thought that each singing group was somehow identical with—i.e., the very same as—its members. But the groups and the members that make them up aren't the same. The singers were all much older than the groups, even though the groups weren't older than the groups. Since they had different properties, they weren't identical. In general, to *count* items—singers or groups—the items must already be individuated. The number 3 is the plural property applying to all and only those individuals x, y, and z, none of which is identical with any other. We can't begin counting until we have sorted the items being counted into distinct items of some common type. Nothing more is needed to predicate the plural properties.

So far we have examined only very early stages of our acquisition of knowledge of natural numbers. Some of this knowledge is perceptual. If one's knowledge of each of two things, x and y, that it is a finger, is perceptual, and one's knowledge that x isn't y is also perceptual, then one's knowledge that x and y are two in number is also perceptual. If the fingers had been painted *blue* one could truly say not only that *one sees that those fingers are blue,* but also that *one sees that they are two in number.* Indeed, if two people are standing at a distance from someone holding up two blue fingers, one of the observers, who has trouble making out precisely what is being displayed, might ask *Do you see the color of the fingers he is holding up?* or *Do you see the number of fingers he is holding up?* The one with better vision might reply, *Yes, I see the color of those fingers; they are blue* or *Yes, I see the number of those fingers; they are two.* So, it seems, there is a more or less ordinary sense of 'see' in which we can truly say that some color properties and some natural numbers, i.e., plural cardinality properties, can be seen.

Systematic knowledge of arithmetic—e.g., of the axioms and logical consequences of Peano Arithmetic—is, of course, more complicated. This knowledge can't all be *logical* knowledge of the sort Frege imagined. If natural numbers are *cardinality properties,* logic *alone* can't guarantee that there are any individuals, multiples, or distinct cardinality properties of multiples, let alone infinitely many. But we can use logic plus *updated versions of Frege's definitions* of *successor* and *natural number*—involving plural properties rather than sets—to derive systematic knowledge of natural numbers. The definition of *successor* tells us that the plural property *N is the successor of the plural property M if and only if there is some property F of individuals such that the things that are F, of which a given object o is one, are N in number, while the Fs excluding o are M in number.* Given definitions of *zero* and *successor,* we can define *natural numbers* in the normal way as *plural properties of which every property true of zero and of the successor of anything it is true of, is true.*[18]

From this plus our initial perceptually based knowledge, we can derive arithmetical truths. We can come to know that zero isn't the successor of anything by observing that if it were, then some property true of nothing would have to be true of something. We can come to know that no natural number M has two successors by observing that otherwise there would be properties F1 and F2 (where the F1s are

N1 in number and the F2s are N2 in number, N1 ≠ N2)
such that the F1s can't be exhaustively paired off with the
F2s without remainder, even though there are objects o_{F1}
and o_{F2} such that the *F1s excluding o_{F1}* and the *F2s excluding o_{F2}* are both M in number—and so can be paired off.
The impossibility of this is easy to see. Knowledge of the
companion axiom, *that different natural numbers N1 and N2
can't have the same successor,* is explained in the same way.
As for the axiom that every natural number has a successor,
this can be seen to be true when we realize that the plural
properties we arrive at by counting can themselves be included in later multiples we count. This ensures that we
can always add one of them to any multiple that has given
us a plural property M we have already reached. In this
way, plural cardinality properties can allow us to explain
not only the earliest knowledge of natural numbers we acquired as children, but also how systematic knowledge of
elementary number theory can be acquired.

There are, of course, other ways of expanding the mea-
ger knowledge of arithmetic acquired in grade school or
earlier. Most of us learned our arithmetic—addition, sub-
traction, multiplication, division, and exponentiation—in
the early grades, without being exposed to the Peano axioms. No matter. The efficient, user-friendly computational
routines we mastered are compatible with the philosophical perspective advocated here. Thus, it may turn out that
plural cardinality properties satisfy Frege's methodological
maxim by providing us with the best explanation of our
arithmetical knowledge, and so *should* be taken to be natural numbers.[19]

That said, we should not go away with the idea that this
way of reconceptualizing and following through on the
Frege-Russell attempt to explain our knowledge of arithmetic has been definitively established. On the contrary, it
remains a work in progress. However, one who has followed

the line of thought presented here should go away with some idea of what philosophers working on the foundations of logic and mathematics are, and have been, up to, and how they attempt to advance our understanding of aspects of cognitive lives that are, although simple and central to who we are, nevertheless not easy to comprehend.

Apart from this continuing line of philosophical inquiry, what were the most important and clear-cut achievements growing out of the Frege-Russell attempt to ground mathematics? Their most important advance was the invention of powerful new systems of logic that are vital to deductive reasoning in all scientific domains. Another was the impetus they provided for the development of set theory as the dominant foundational system for unifying mathematics. In the next two chapters I will explain how the contributions of Frege and Russell started us on the road to the formal notion of computation that sparked the digital age (and the development of contemporary cognitive science) and also laid the foundations of the still young science of linguistic meaning and the use of language to encode information about the world.

CHAPTER 6

LOGIC, COMPUTATION, AND THE BIRTH OF THE DIGITAL AGE

The fundamentals of modern logic; results about logical systems; how to logically demonstrate the limits of logic: the strategy behind Gödel's first incompleteness theorem; Gödel's original method; lower and higher-order logics; Gödel's second incompleteness theorem; proof, effective computability, and Turing machines as mathematical prototypes of real computers.

Invented by Frege in 1879 and put to philosophical use by Frege and Russell over the next four decades, modern symbolic logic emerged as an independent scientific discipline between 1929 and 1939, primarily through the unprecedented advances of four philosophically minded mathematical logicians—Kurt Gödel (1906–1978), Alfred Tarski (1901–1983), Alonzo Church (1903–1995), and Alan Turing (1912–1954). It was then that the now standard understanding of what logic is, what it is capable of achieving, and what is demonstrably beyond its limits were put in place. It was also then that the link between logic and computability, and ultimately digital computability, was forged, leading to the electronic processing of information that has transformed the age in which we live.

The transformation began with Frege's new system, the predicate calculus, which vastly expanded the expressive power of logical systems. This was accompanied by proof procedures that are *effectively decidable* in the sense that whether something offered as a proof really is a proof can always be uncontroversially decided by a purely mechanical procedure. In the decades following Frege, the form of guaranteed truth preservation known as *logical consequence*—which proofs are intended to verify—was defined in a way that allows mathematical investigation of proof procedures to determine whether (i) B is a logical consequence of A, *whenever* there is a proof of B from A, and whether (ii) there is a proof of B from A, *whenever* B is a logical consequence of A. These investigations established versions of the predicate calculus for which there are proof procedures satisfying both (i) and (ii), as well as versions, with greater expressive power, for which only (i) can be satisfied. Next, taking an arithmetical theory to include all logical consequences of an effectively decidable set of axioms, Gödel showed that it is *impossible* to construct a proof procedure that allows one to prove all and only the truths of elementary arithmetic; in fact, every such system that doesn't prove contradictions leaves infinitely many arithmetical truths unproven.

It was then that the connection between logic and computability became clear. Whenever membership in a set (or sequence) of natural numbers can be effectively decided, there is a formula (sometimes very complex) of the language, LA, of elementary arithmetic that is true of all and only the members of that set. There are also axiomatic theories T of arithmetic such that for every decidable set S of natural numbers (or sequences of such), there is a formula F of LA and theorem T_{yes} of T that says of F that it is *true of* a particular number n (or sequence of numbers), *whenever* n (or the sequence) really is a member of S; there is also a theorem T_{no} of T, that says of F that it *isn't true of* n (or a sequence), *whenever* n (or the sequence) isn't a member of S. *Given this, one can use systematic searches for theorems as effective decision procedures for membership in any decidable set of natural numbers (or sequences of such).* Since Gödel also showed how to use natural numbers to code things that aren't natural numbers, this result can be extended to decision procedures for any decidable set, as well as for any intuitively computable function.

Having come this far, we were now only one step away from the digital age. That step was taken by Turing, who articulated a new mathematical framework for formalizing the idea of *computable function.* Although the functions counted as Turing computable were the same as those counted computable by Gödel and Church, the means Turing used to compute them had far-reaching implications. What he gave us were logico-mathematical instructions for operating on sequences of 1's and 0's. Since the operations were digital, the 0's and 1's could be taken to model the two positions, open and closed, of an electric circuit, which meant that his instructions could be seen as encoding internal states of imagined machines. Despite the intervention of World War II, it was not long before these abstract models were turned into real machines.

What follows will add enough detail to this sketch to allow those who wish to get an idea of the main lines of argument, while leaving aside the most daunting technical refinements, of which there are many. Since the results achieved were among the greatest intellectual advances of the twentieth century, even the simplified story told here may include some elements that those new to the subject may find challenging. The goal is to provide interested readers with enough to deepen their knowledge. Asterisks (*) identify sections that deal with somewhat more technical material; those whose interests lie elsewhere can skip these without losing the thread.

FUNDAMENTALS OF MODERN LOGIC

The most important logical notions are *truth*, *proof*, and *guaranteed truth preservation*. If A is a *logical consequence* of B, then if A turns out to be true, its truth will *guarantee* that of B. In such a case, we may try to construct a proof of B from A—a sequence of obvious steps each of which is a *logical consequence* of earlier steps. While we may *hope* that there is a proof of B from A whenever B is a logical consequence of A, what we *demand* is that whenever there is a proof, B is, in fact, a logical consequence of A. Some logical systems justify our hope, because all logical consequences of a set of sentences are provable from that set. But, as indicated above, in other cases the expressive power of the system makes this impossible.

Making these ideas precise requires understanding the sense in which, when B is a logical consequence of A, A's truth *guarantees* B's truth. The intuitive idea is that if B is a logical consequence of A, it is *impossible* for A to be true without B being true. In addition, this impossibility mustn't depend on the special subject matter of A or B— e.g., on the essences of objects and properties designated by terms in A and B. Rather, the necessary connection must be due to the structures, or forms, of the sentences A and B alone. Finally, if one doesn't know B, but does know A, it should be possible to come to know B without appealing to information not contained in A or B, provided one can derive B from A by obvious steps, each of which is a logical consequence of earlier steps.

Although these ideas have always guided the construction of logical systems, Frege's invention of the modern predicate calculus brought them to a higher level. His system was the result of combining the truth-functional logic of the *propositional calculus*—familiar from the Stoics onward—with a new analysis of sentences containing

BIRTH OF THE DIGITAL AGE 117

'all' and 'some', used to make general claims. The key to Frege's achievement was his decision to trade the subject/predicate distinction of Aristotelian logic for a clarified and expanded version of the function/argument distinction from mathematics. This allowed him to assign functions—from (sequences of) objects to truth or falsity—to each of the infinitely many formulas of his logical language. When 'all' and 'some' were attached to a formula F, the resulting sentence was taken to be true if and only if the function designated by F assigned truth to all or some objects. In this way, infinitely many patterns of logically valid arguments were generated.[1]

A system of logic, in Frege's modern sense, always starts with a precisely specified language consisting of (i) an exhaustive inventory of names, simple predicate symbols, function signs, and the like, (ii) an unambiguous rule for combining them to form simple (atomic) sentences, and (iii) further rules for forming complex sentences out of simple ones. The result is a set of well-formed sentences and formulas leaving no room for doubt about whether a string of symbols is, or is not, a member of the set.

To this, one adds a proof procedure, which, in Frege's case, was a set of axioms drawn from the language, plus a fixed number of rules of inference. As explained in chapter 5, a proof in the system is a finite sequence of lines, each of which is an axiom or a formula obtainable from earlier lines by the inference rules. Whether or not something counts as a proof must, in principle, be decidable merely by inspecting the formula on each line, and determining (i) whether it is an axiom, and (ii) whether, if it isn't, it bears the required structural relation to earlier lines in order for it to be obtainable from those lines by the rules of inference. For this reason, the axioms themselves must be an effectively decidable set—that is, there must be a purely mechanical procedure capable of deciding, in every case, whether a formula is one of the axioms. Similarly, rules of inference must be stated so that whether or not a formula is obtainable from earlier ones is effectively decidable in the same sense. When these requirements are met, the question of whether or not something counts as a proof can always be resolved—thereby forestalling the need to prove that something is a proof.

Frege's method of interpreting formulas and sentences of his logical language, which was also set out in chapter 5, gives us an assignment of truth conditions to each sentence of the language. What were there called *models* are *interpretations of the language* that arise from selecting a domain D of objects and assigning objects in D as referents of names, assigning sets of objects in D (or of pairs, triples, etc. of those objects) as referents of predicates, and assigning n-place functions (e.g., the addition function) defined on objects in D (when D includes the natural numbers) as referents of n-place function signs (e.g., '+').

This allows us to define *truth in a model*, from which we define logical consequence. A sentence B is a logical consequence of a set S of sentences of the language if and only if B is true in every model (interpretation) of the language in which A is. One can now see the sense in which, when B is a logical consequence of a sentence or set S of sentences, the truth of S *guarantees* the truth of B. The truth of S is *sufficient* for the truth of B, no matter how the vocabulary—the names, predicates, and function signs—are interpreted, and no matter which, or how many, objects are under discussion. Because the guarantee is determined by the forms of the sentences themselves, it is independent of their subject matter. Thus, it is impossible for the claims S is used to make to be true without the claim B is used to make also being true. Finally, suppose one understands the sentences in S and knows the truths they express, while understanding B, but not knowing whether the claim it expresses is true. One can, in principle, come to know that claim by reasoning alone, without appealing to further information, if one can derive B from S via a proof each line of which is a logical consequence (in the sense we have defined) of earlier lines.

These ideas are central to understanding the tradition of modern logic initiated by Frege. It should be noted, however, that the concept *truth in a model,* in terms of which the modern concept *logical consequence* is now defined, wasn't explicit in Frege, and would not become so until those concepts were introduced by Tarski in two classic papers, "The Concept of Truth in Formalized Languages," published in 1935, and "On the Concept of Logical Consequence," published in 1936.[2] The importance of these papers was in making fully precise what had tacitly been understood for some time.[3]

THE SCOPE AND LIMITS OF LOGICAL SYSTEMS

Tarski's formalizations validated the idea that one could construct mathematical *metatheories* to investigate the logical properties of Frege-style systems of logic, and of broader theories incorporating them as parts. In particular, one can prove *metatheorems* about the relationship between the syntactically defined *provable sentences* of a given logical system and its semantically defined *logical truths.* One can also prove metatheorems about the relationship between the provable sentences of specific theories of arithmetic (which include both logical and strictly arithmetical axioms) and the *logical consequences* of those axioms. Some of these turned out to be surprising.

In 1930, Gödel proved an important metatheorem of the first kind.[4] He showed that it is possible to construct a *sound* proof procedure (which allows one to derive B from A *only* when B is a logical consequence of A) for the Fregean predicate calculus that is also *complete* in the sense that it *always* allows one to derive B from A, *whenever* B is a logical consequence of A. In such a system, the sentences of the logical language that are derivable from A are all and only the logical consequences of A. So, if B is a logical consequence of A, one can always find a proof of B if one looks long enough.

This result applies only to the *first-order* predicate calculus. A logical language is *first-order* if its only sentences that make general claims are those containing *all* and *some* in which these expressions (called 'quantifiers') combine with individual variables (*x, y, z*) that range over individual objects and that occupy the same position in formulas as proper names for those objects—e.g., *For all x (if x is a man, then x is mortal)*. By contrast, a *second-order* language also has sentences that make general claims in which *all* and *some* combine with *predicate and/or function variables*, which range over (i) arbitrary sets of individual objects (or sequences of such) and/or (ii) functions, and which (iii) occupy the same position in formulas as predicate constants or function signs—e.g., *For all P (if Socrates is P, then Socrates is P)*. Although Frege's original logical system allowed both first- and second-order quantification, the first-order fragment of it was *complete* in the sense of Gödel's 1930 theorem, which the latter proved 50 years after Frege presented his system. What Frege didn't know then was that for second-order systems, no complete proof procedure is possible, which, as we will see, is a corollary of another one of Gödel's revolutionary metatheorems.[5]

THE STRATEGY BEHIND GÖDEL'S FIRST INCOMPLETENESS THEOREM

Gödel's completeness proof for the first-order predicate calculus was first presented in his 1929 doctoral dissertation. Also in 1929, he was named, along with 13 other founding members of the Vienna Circle, in its founding document, "The Scientific Conception of the World," announcing logical empiricism as a new school of philosophy centered on logic and the philosophy of science.[6] In 1931, he proved two revolutionary theorems. One has come to be called *the Gödel-Tarski theorem that arithmetical truth is not arithmetically definable*.[7] This theorem is interesting because we know in advance that *every effectively decidable set S or relation R of natural numbers is arithmetically definable*—i.e., for every effectively decidable set S (or relation R) there is an arithmetical formula that is *true of* a natural number n (or a sequence of natural numbers n . . . m) if and only if n is a member of S (or n . . . m stand in relation R to one another). We also know that some sets of natural numbers are definable in arithmetic even though membership in those sets is not effectively decidable. The theorem tells us that the set of arithmetical truths isn't one of them.

The theorem uses "Gödel numbering" to assign numbers to expressions of the language of arithmetic, LA. The Gödel number of an expression is its numerical code. Using these codes allows us to treat formulas of LA (which are officially about the natural numbers 0, 1, 2, 3, . . .) as making claims about LA itself—e.g., claims that certain of its sentences are, or are not, provable. The indefinability theorem states that there is no formula of LA that is *true of* the set of numbers that code the true sentences of LA. In certain systems of Gödel numbering, the numerical code of a compound expression is the number denoted by the Arabic numeral that results from writing, one after another (in left-to-right order), the Arabic numerals that code the individual symbols that make up the expression. There is a decision procedure for determining the numerical code of any expression of LA, and for determining, given a natural number, the expression, if any, that it codes.

The Gödel-Tarski theorem is an application of the liar and heterologicality paradoxes. We begin by calling a formula with exactly one free variable a predicate.[8] We then stipulate that a predicate/formula of a language L is *heterological* if and only if it is not true of itself. For example, the ordinary English predicate 'x is a human being' isn't true of itself because the sentence *The predicate 'x is a human being' is a human being* isn't true; thus it is heterological. By contrast, the predicate 'x is a predicate' is *autological,* rather than heterological, because the sentence *The predicate 'x is a predicate' is a predicate* is true. What about the predicate 'x is heterological'? Whether or not it is a heterological predicate of ordinary English depends on whether or not it is a predicate of ordinary English at all, and hence on whether or not the sentence *The predicate 'x is heterological' is heterological* is a sentence of ordinary English. If it is, then it must either be true or not true. Since, by definition, it is true if and only if it's not true, it can't be either one. Thus, we must conclude that 'x is heterological' isn't a predicate of ordinary English. Instead, it is a predicate of a technical extension of ordinary English that we can use to talk about ordinary English. In general, a language can contain a predicate 'heterological' defined for languages of which 'heterological' isn't a part, but including it in the range of predicates for which it is defined leads to absurdities.

The Gödel-Tarski theorem of the arithmetical indefinability of arithmetical truth is an application of this result to the language, LA, of arithmetic. In proving it we take the predicates of LA to be formulas in which a single variable 'x' occurs free (not bound by any quantifier). If P is such a predicate, *a self-ascription* of P is a sentence we get by substituting the numeral that names the code (i.e., the Gödel number) of P for all free occurrences 'x' in P. Now consider the relation that holds between numbers n and m if and only if m is the code of a predicate P and n is the code of a *self-ascription* of P. Since this relation is effectively decidable, there is a formula *Self-Ascription x, y* of LA that is true of numbers n and m if and only if m is the code of a predicate *P*, and n is the code of its self-ascription, i.e., of the sentence that predicates *P* of its own code. Finally, suppose there is a formula *T(x)* of LA that is true of all and only the codes of true sentences of LA. Then, the formula *For some x (Self-Ascription x, y & ~ T(x))* is a heterologicality predicate of LA; it is true of m if and only if m is the code of a predicate of LA that isn't true of its own code. Let h* be the numeral that denotes the Gödel number of this heterologicality predicate. Then *For some x (Self-Ascription x, h* & ~T(x))* is a sentence of LA that says that some self-ascription of the heterologicality predicate isn't true. Since *this very sentence* is the self-ascription of the heterologicality predicate, *it says of itself that it isn't true.* In other words, it is a liar sentence that says *I'm not true*, and so is true if and only if it is not true. Thus, the supposition that there is a predicate of LA that is true of all and only the codes of its true sentences leads to the result that LA contains a sentence that is true if it is not true, and not true if it is true. Assuming that it must be one or the other, but not both, we conclude that there is no such sentence. Thus, the supposition that led to this result—namely that arithmetical truth is arithmetically definable—is false. This is the Gödel-Tarski proof that *arithmetical truth is not arithmetically definable.*

This theorem is an application of Gödel's first incompleteness theorem, which states that for every consistent proof procedure of first-order arithmetic, there are pairs of sentences S and ~ S that it can't prove. Since a proof is a finite sequence of formulas, we can assign a Gödel number to each proof. Now consider the proof relation that holds between numbers n and m if and only if n is the code of a proof of a sentence with code m. This relation is effectively decidable, since we can always decide, for any m and n, whether m is the code of a sentence S and n is the code of a sequence of formulas the last member of which is S, and given any such sequence, we can always determine whether each formula is an axiom or a consequence of earlier formulas via one of the rules of inference.

Since the proof relation is decidable, there is a formula, *Proof (x, y)*, of LA that is true of numbers n and m if and only if n is the numerical code of a proof of the sentence that m codes. Next consider the formula *For some y Proof (y, x)*—or *Prov x* (for short)—which is true of the codes of *provable sentences*. Since this set is definable in LA, but, as we have just seen, the set of arithmetical *truths* isn't definable in LA, the set of truths isn't the same as the set of provable sentences. So, *if* all provable sentences are true, some truths can't be proved in the system. This is the simplest version of Gödel's first incompleteness theorem.

GÖDEL'S ORIGINAL METHOD*

Gödel's own method of proving this result was a little different. The key predicate in his proof was G1, the self-ascription of which was G2.

> G1. For some x (x is a Self-Ascription of y & ~ for some z Proof (z, x))
>
> G2. For some x (x is a Self-Ascription of [k] & ~ for some z Proof (z, x))

G1 is true of all and only codes of predicates the self-ascriptions of which are not *provable*; in short, *G is true of predicates that aren't provable of themselves*. Let k be the code of G1 and '[k]' be the numeral denoting k. *G2 says that a self-ascription of G1 is not provable*. Since G2 is the self-ascription of G1, *G2 says that G2 isn't provable*. Thus, it is either true and unprovable, or false and provable. Assuming no falsehoods are provable, it must be true and not provable.

When we present Gödel's result this way, *we* prove— reasoning informally in a technical extension of ordinary English we use to speak about the language LA—that a sentence of LA saying of itself that it isn't provable (using a consistent proof theory T) isn't a theorem of T (i.e., isn't provable in T). Are there any *theorems* of T that themselves assert what we just asserted? Gödel showed that there are. He showed there are theorems of T—*G if and only if ~ Prov G (where G denotes the Gödel number of G)*—that assert that G is true if and only if G is unprovable in T. From this it follows that G isn't a theorem of T, for if it were, some natural number n would be the Gödel number of a proof of G in T, in which case *Proof (n*, G)* would be a theorem of T (where n* is the numeral denoting n), thereby guaranteeing that *For some x Proof (x, G)*—i.e., *Prove G*—was also a theorem of T. This is impossible, since if G were a theorem, it would mean that both *Prov G* and its negation *~ Prov G* were both theorems. *Thus, the simple logical consistency of T ensures that G isn't a theorem of T.*

Given this, we also know that *~Proof n, G* is a theorem of T for all natural numbers n. It might seem to follow directly that *~G* isn't a theorem, and hence that T is incomplete. But, due to certain complications, it doesn't follow unless one uses a notion of consistency slightly stronger than logical consistency, which Gödel did in 1931. Barkley Rosser, who was a student of Alonzo Church, showed in Rosser (1937) that simple logical consistency is enough by focusing on a slightly different class of unprovable sentences.[9]

THE DIFFERENCE BETWEEN THE FIRST- AND SECOND-ORDER PREDICATE CALCULUS*

At this point, it is worth saying a word about the difference between arithmetical theories formulated in first-order logic and those formulated in second-order logic. Recall, first-order logic has statements *For all x . . . x . . .* that make general claims about all individual objects in the domain of the model (interpretation) of the language of the theory—in this case the language, LA, of arithmetic. In addition to these, second-order logic also has statements *For all P . . . P . . .* that make claims about all sets of objects in the domain.[10] If that domain is the set of natural numbers, then sentences of the first-order predicate calculus can make statements about all of them, while sentences of the second-order predicate calculus can also make statements about all sets of natural numbers. A key difference between first- and second-order *theories of arithmetic* is that the most interesting first-order theories include the first-order *axiom schema* of mathematical induction, while the most interesting second-order theories include the second-order *axiom* of mathematical induction.

The former is expressed

$$[(F(0) \ \& \ \text{for all } x \ (F(x) \to F(S(x)))) \to \text{for all } x \ F(x)]$$

To include this *axiom schema* in a theory is to take its infinitely many instances as axioms of the theory. Each instance is formed by (i) replacing 'Fx' with a 1-place predicate of LA—i.e., with a formula of LA in which only the variable 'x' has free occurrences; (ii) replacing 'F(0)' with the result of replacing free occurrences of 'x' in that formula with occurrences of '0'; and (iii) treating 'S(x)' as designating the successor of the number 'x' designates. So understood, an instance of the schema (i.e., one of the infinitely many axioms the schema introduces) is true if and only if the predicate that replaces 'Fx' is true of *everything* in the domain, *whenever it is true of zero and also true of the successor of anything it is true of.* When the domain consists simply of the natural numbers, each of these axioms tells us that if zero is a member of the set of numbers of which the predicate is true, and if, whenever a number is in that set, its successor is too, then all natural numbers are in the set. By contrast, the *second-order* axiom of induction is expressed

For all P $[(P(0)$ & for all x $(P(x) \rightarrow P(S(x)))) \rightarrow$ for all x $P(x)]$

It is true if and only if *any set* of natural numbers that contains zero, and also contains the successor of anything it contains, contains every natural number.

The schema and the single axiom are different because there are vastly more sets of natural numbers than there are predicates of the first-order language of arithmetic. Hence, there are vastly more sets of natural numbers than there are sets of natural numbers designated by those predicates. Because of this, the set of logical consequences of second-order theories of arithmetic include many more statements about the natural numbers than the set of logical consequences of the corresponding first-order theories do. In fact, it is easy to show that all true first-order sentences of LA are logical consequences of certain arithmetical theories incorporating the second-order axiom schema of mathematical induction. This means that consistent second-order theories of arithmetic are complete in the sense in which Gödel's first incompleteness theorem shows that no consistent first-order theory can be.[11]

But this doesn't subvert the earlier theorem. Although all first-order truths of arithmetic are logical consequences of a certain second-order arithmetical theory, second-order logic is not complete in the sense in which first-order logic was proved complete by Gödel. In first-order logic, every logical truth is provable from a consistent set of logical axioms and rules of inference. Similarly, every logical consequence B of a first-order sentence A (or of a decidable set A* of first-order sentences) is provable from A (or from a finite subset of A*). By contrast, second-order logic is not complete in this sense. For any consistent system of proof for second-order logic, there will be second-order logical truths that are not provable in the system, and there will be logical consequences of second-order sentences that are not provable from those sentences in the system. So, although the relevant second-order arithmetic is a complete formal theory that, for each first-order arithmetical sentence S, has S or $\lceil \sim S \rceil$ as a logical consequence, the fact that no proof procedure in second-order logic is complete—in the sense in which some first-order proof procedures are complete—means that there is no effective positive test for first-order arithmetical truth. Thus, the central lesson of Gödel's first incompleteness proof is untouched.

GÖDEL'S SECOND INCOMPLETENESS THEOREM *

Gödel's second incompleteness theorem extended his incompleteness result by showing that strong, logically consistent, first-order theories of arithmetic like Peano Arithmetic can't prove their own consistency—i.e., although they don't prove contradictions, they can't *prove* theorems that say, relative to a system of Gödel numbering, *that they don't prove contradictions.*[12] Put simply, the idea is this. We know from Gödel's first incompleteness theorem that *if a sufficiently powerful arithmetical theory, e.g., Peano Arithmetic (PA), is consistent,* then *G isn't provable in PA, but G ↔ ~Prov G* is provable in PA. (In effect, G "asserts" its own unprovability.)

This is expressed in PA by the fact that $Con_{PA} \rightarrow \sim Prov\ G$ and $G \leftrightarrow \sim Prov\ G$ are both theorems of PA, where Con_{PA} "says," relative to the Gödel numbering, that PA is consistent—in the sense that we can establish, when reasoning about the system, *that Con_{PA} is a theorem of PA only if the set of theorems of PA is logically consistent.* If Con_{PA} were also provable in PA (and hence a theorem), then *~Prov G* and *G ↔ ~Prov*

G would both be theorems. Hence, G would be a theorem of PA, as would *Proof (n*, G)* (where n* is the numeral denoting a proof in PA of G). This would then guarantee that *For some x Proof (x, G))*—i.e., *Prov G*—is also a theorem. But then the theorems of PA would be inconsistent, since its theorems would include both *Prov G* and *~Prov G*. Since we know that Peano Arithmetic *is* consistent, this means that Con_{PA} isn't provable in Peano Arithmetic. In short, consistent first-order theories of arithmetic can't prove their own consistency (even though they are, in fact, consistent).[13]

PROOF AND EFFECTIVE COMPUTABILITY

One of the important lessons of Gödel's results is that there is an intimate connection between *effective computability* and *proof* in a formal system. Proof in these systems is an effectively decidable notion, and systematic searches for proofs can be used as decision procedures for determining membership in decidable sets of natural numbers. This close relationship between computability and logic was studied by the mathematician and philosopher Alonzo Church and his students Barkley Rosser, Stephen Kleene, and Alan Turing in the 1930s. In 1934, Gödel introduced a mathematical formalization of the notion of an effectively computable function; in 1936 Church proved his own formalization to be equivalent to Gödel's.[14] He also used Gödel's first incompleteness theorem, to prove that there is no effective procedure capable of always *deciding* whether or not a sentence of first-order logic is, or isn't, a logical truth (or a logical consequence of other first-order sentences).[15]

His proof is based on a Gödel-sentence G that "says," relative to the coding of sentences by Gödel numbers, that G is unprovable. G is the self-ascription of the predicate of

LA that is true of all and only the Gödel numbers of predicates of LA that are not provable of themselves. Since *Proof*
encodes a decidable relation, whenever two numbers stand
in that relation some theorem of our arithmetical theory
says they do, and whenever they don't stand in that relation
some theorem says they don't. With this in mind, consider
the 1-place predicate *For some x, Proof x,y*. Although it is
true of all and only numbers that encode provable sentences, this doesn't guarantee that whenever a sentence
isn't provable some theorem of PA says it isn't. If it did,
then, as Gödel showed, the fact that G is unprovable in
PA would guarantee that the negation of *[For some x, Proof
x,G]* was provable, from which it would follow that G was
provable after all. This means that when a sentence *isn't* a
logical consequence of the axioms of the theory, the theory
won't always tell us that it isn't.

This proves Church's undecidability theorem. For suppose first-order logical consequence were effectively decidable. Then the set of logical consequences of the axioms
of our theory would decidable. By the completeness of
first-order logic, the logical consequences of our theory
are its theorems. So, if logical consequence were decidable,
some theorem of our theory would tell us the G is unprovable in the theory. Since we have shown that no theorem
of the theory tells us this, we know that first-order logic is
undecidable.[16]

Church's future student Alan Turing independently
proved the same result by a different method using a new
mathematical model of the intuitive notion of a computable
function.[17] In his review of Turing's work, Church called
the model, which was provably equivalent to his own and
Gödel's formalizations, *a Turing machine*.[18] In reality, a Turing "machine" is a kind of abstract mathematical program
that a merely imagined machine could run. The imagined
machine operates on an infinite tape divided into squares,

each of which is either blank or imprinted with a single dot. It moves along the tape one square at a time, checking to see whether or not the square it is on is blank. It can also print a dot on a previously blank square or erase a dot on a square that had one. It has a finite number of internal states; its instructions tell it what to do—move left, move right, erase a dot, or print a dot—based on the state it is in at a given time.[19]

There are several key features of Turing machines. First, they are digital, operating on 0's and 1's (blank squares and squares with a dot) that model the two positions, open and closed, of an electrical circuit. Second, their instructions, which determine their operation at every moment, can be encoded by sentences of the first-order predicate calculus. Third, they are universal—i.e., Turing machines are capable of computing every function that can be shown to be computable by any means whatsoever. Fourth, there is no decision procedure for deciding in every case whether an arbitrary Turing machine will eventually halt (and provide an interpretable output) after having been started on an arbitrary input.

However, there would be such a procedure, if there were a decision procedure for determining whether any arbitrary sentence of first-order logic was a logical consequence of an arbitrary set of other first-order sentences. For each Turing machine T there is a set IT of sentences of the logic encoding its instructions, and for each input to T there is a sentence S that describes that input. There is also a sentence H of the logic that is true if and only if T ever halts. H will be a logical consequence of IT plus S, if and only if T ever halts. So, if we could *always* decide whether one thing was a logical consequence of something else, the halting problem for Turing machines would be solvable. Since we know it isn't solvable, there must be no decision procedure for deciding first-order logical consequence. That was Turing's version of Church's undecidability theorem.

Since Church's result narrowly preceded Turing's, the interest in Turing's proof lay not in what it proved, but in the brilliant model of computability he used to prove it. In addition to being conceptually transparent, it was technologically feasible, and so able to provide the mathematical basis for electronic computing, which began not long after his discovery. *This, in short, is how the turn to logic and language initiated by Frege, Russell, Tarski, Gödel, Church, and Turing ushered in the modern digital age that has contributed so much to the world we now inhabit.*

In addition to leading to stunning technological advances, digital computers also helped to launch what we now call *cognitive science,* which combines psychology, artificial intelligence, and computation theory. It soon became clear that digital computers could imitate, duplicate, or actually perform a range of demanding intellectual tasks that skilled human beings perform intelligently. This gave rise to questions: *What is the range of such tasks? Are there limits to it? Assuming, as seems natural, that computers could, in principle, at least imitate intelligent human performance, what, if anything, should stop us from recognizing them as intelligent thinkers?* Turing himself introduced fascinating philosophical speculation on these matters in "Computing Machinery and Intelligence," published in 1950. Whatever one might think of speculation along these lines, it now seems clear that studying the cognitive architectures of human beings and computing machines are complementary enterprises, each capable of positively influencing the other.

CHAPTER 7

THE SCIENCE OF
LANGUAGE

*The emergence of the scientific study of natural languages:
Chomsky's conception of linguistic theory and the role
of syntax in connecting sound with meaning; origins in
philosophical logic of the empirical science of meaning in
natural language; early models of linguistically encoded
information; the conception of meaning as truth conditions;
the cognitive breakthrough: information as types of
cognition; the current challenge: understanding how varying
contextual information mixes with fixed linguistic meaning
in communication; applications in legal interpretation.*

Nothing about human beings is more central to who we are
and how we differ from other animals than our extraordinary command of language. It is language that allows us to
communicate with those in the past, and in the future, as
well as with those with whom we are now in contact. Nor
is communication the whole story. Language is also the
vehicle for our most complex and wide-ranging thoughts.
Without it we would scarcely have any thoughts about
things we have never encountered. We would know little
history and have limited ability to project ourselves beyond
the present. Our mental universe would be tiny.

Human language is enormously complex, consisting of
interacting subsystems governing (i) the production and
perception of the finely discriminated sounds of spoken
language, (ii) the processes of word-formation, (iii) the

syntactic principles by which sequences of words are organized into sentences, (iv) the interpretation of sentences on
the basis of our understanding of their parts, and (v) the
dynamic flow of information carried by discourses consisting of many sentences. Each subsystem is the subject of an
advancing subdiscipline of the emerging science of natural
human language. The subdisciplines corresponding to (iv)
and (v)—the study of the principles governing the interpretation of sentences (used in various contexts) and of those
governing the flow of information in discourses made up
of many sentences—are the youngest subdisciplines of linguistics, and those most closely related to philosophical
developments in the last century.

The conception of an empirical theory of a natural language (such as English) as an integrated theory encompassing all these subsystems grew of the work of Noam Chomsky, who, between 1955 and 1965, laid down philosophical
foundations of the emerging science of language in *The
Logical Structure of Linguistic Theory, Syntactic Structures,* and
Aspects of a Theory of Syntax.[1] In these works he set out his
syntactic theory of sentence structure, his semantic theory
of how sentence structure relates to meaning, and his cognitive theory of internalized rule-following responsible for
our linguistic competence.

A syntactic theory of English—a.k.a. *a grammar*—was
taken to be a set of formal rules generating all and only the
strings of English words that are (well-formed) *sentences,*
and breaking each sentence into a hierarchical structure of
phrases capturing how the sentences are understood. Such
a theory *predicts* which strings are, or would be, recognized
and used as sentences by speakers, and which strings aren't,
or wouldn't be, so used and recognized. Since the number
of English sentences containing 20 words or less has been
estimated to be roughly 10^{30}—compare, for example, the

number, 3.15×10^9, of seconds in a century—the task of producing a predictively correct grammar is far from trivial.[2]

In *The Logical Structure of Linguistic Theory* and *Syntactic Structures,* Chomsky used two sets of rules: *context-free phrase structure rules,* which generated an initial set of word-sequences with hierarchical structures, and transformations that mapped such structures onto other such structures. In *Aspects of a Theory of Syntax,* he added constraints on their operation. First, the phrase structure rules generated grammatical *deep structures.* Then, obligatory and optional transformations were applied—the former that must applied to any hierarchical structures satisfying their application conditions, and the latter that could, but need not, be applied to such structures. The end result was to be the generation of all and only the sentences of the language.

The key point for our purposes is that each sentence was associated with a *surface structure,* the hierarchical structure representing the words as spoken, plus a *deep structure,* representing the meaning of the sentence. The former was the input of the *phonological component* of the grammar, which precisely described the sequence of sounds making up utterances of the sentence. The latter was the input to the *semantic component* of the grammar, the job of which was to specify the meanings to sentences. Hence, it was thought, a Chomskian generative grammar of a natural language would explain how produced and perceived sounds were connected to the meanings of sentences in speakers' minds.

Chomsky's mentalistic conception of these theories was both inspiring and contentious. Positing a rich system of *linguistic universals*—commonalities in the grammars of all languages of human communities—he took linguistics to be a nonexperimental branch of cognitive psychology describing not only syntactic, semantic, and phonological rules existing in the minds of speakers, but also a rich innate system allowing children to learn the highly complex systems that linguists were discovering natural languages to be. This was inspiring because it seemed be a new way to study one of the central aspects of human cognition. It was contentious because the ability to use a set of formal rules to produce outputs—sentences—that match or approximate those of ordinary speakers does not guarantee that the mechanisms used by speakers match or closely approximate those used by linguists. Although the issue remains contentious, there is little doubt that the formal and abstract study of language by today's linguists is capable of informing, and being informed by, genuinely experimental cognitive psychology.[3]

The Chomskian revolution in linguistics, which set the study of natural language on a new path, was the product of his deeply philosophical reconceptualization of the subject together with his technical and scientific prowess. This set the stage for more strictly philosophical contributions to the emerging science of language. As noted, an integrated theory of a natural language connects, via the syntax of a language, the sounds of spoken utterances with the meanings extracted from them by speakers. How theorists conceptualize this connection has evolved since Chomsky's 1965 discussion in *Aspects of a Theory of Syntax*. Typically, it still involves an input—often called the *logical form of the sentence*—to the semantic component of a theory, and an output representing its meaning, which combines with contextual factors to generate the assertive and other communicative content of the utterance. However, this raised a problem. The tradition in linguistics did not provide useful conceptions of what meaning is, or how it is possible to study it. Thus, linguists looked to philosophy. What they found was a logic-based approach to meaning, to which linguists and philosophers have been jointly contributing for the past half century.

The contemporary science of linguistic meaning, *linguistic semantics,* grew out of developments in logic starting with Frege's invention of modern logic in the late nineteenth century, and continuing through Russell's elaboration and application of that work in the early twentieth century. By the mid 1930s, Gödel, Tarski, Church, and Turing had established the scope, limits, and conceptual independence of the new logic as an independent discipline. As we have seen, one aspect of any modern system of logic is a technique for interpreting its sentences. That technique almost immediately became a template for studying meanings of declarative sentences of natural languages. Although imperatives and interrogatives received (and continue to receive) less attention, it has usually been assumed that their interpretations can be made to parallel correct accounts of declaratives.

The central interpretive idea is that language, like perception and thought generally, is representational. The things represented are whatever we are perceiving, thinking, or talking about. The ways they are represented are the properties our words, perceptions, or thoughts ascribe to them. Our visual experience represents things we see as having various characteristics—e.g., as being red, or round. Our nonlinguistic thoughts represent a greater range of things as having a wider variety of properties, while our linguistically expressed thoughts vastly expand our representational capacities. Whenever we represent anything as being any way, either the thing is the way it is represented to be, or it isn't. If it is, the representation—the thought, sentence, or perceptual experience—is *true* or *veridical.*

Perceptions and nonlinguistic thoughts are cognitions of a certain sort; linguistically encoded thoughts are a special kind of cognition, while sentences are cultural artifacts— cognitive tools created by communities. Because the same sequence of words or sounds could, in principle, mean different things in different communities, the meaning of a sentence in the language of a community is determined by the community's conventions governing its use. In the simplest case, there is a convention stipulating that a certain name 'N' is used to refer to a particular man, John, another convention stipulating that 'H' is used to represent individuals as being hungry, and a third convention from which it follows that 'N is H' is used to represent John as being hungry. To understand such a sentence is to know the properties it represents things as having, and so what they must be like for the sentence to be true. To know the meaning of a constituent of a sentence—e.g., a name, a predicate, or a clause—is to know what it contributes to the meanings of sentences in which it occurs.

But what are meanings? The meaning of our example 'N is H' represents John as being hungry, and so determines that the sentence is true if and only if John is hungry. In general, the meaning of a declarative sentence is a piece of information (or misinformation) about how things are. These pieces of information are called *propositions*. Since knowing the meaning of a sentence involves knowing the meanings of its parts, the proposition expressed by a use of a sentence must incorporate the meanings of its syntactic constituents, which, in our example, are the man John (which is the meaning of the name 'N') and the property *being hungry* (which is the meaning of the predicate 'H'). Finally, propositions are the things we assert, believe, deny, or doubt, as well as being the objects of a host of related cognitive attitudes. They are transmitted from one agent to another in the communicative exchange of information.

To convert these informal ideas into a framework for studying language, one must (a) identify meanings of subsentential expressions, (b) articulate how they combine to form meanings of complex expressions, (c) show that the resulting propositions expressed by sentences represent things as being certain ways, and are true if and only if those things are the ways they are represented to be, and (d) explain the cognitive attitudes—belief, knowledge, and the like—that agents bear to propositions, keeping in mind that knowledge and belief, though central to language use, are not restricted to language-using agents.

This last task—explaining how cognitive attitudes relate agents to propositions—highlights the magnitude of the challenge we face. The task is to explain and identify what thoughts are, to distinguish different kinds of thoughts (in humans and nonhumans alike), and to explain how thoughts are transmitted. We will never understand what human beings are, how we differ from other cognitive agents, or the relationship between mind and body, until we have met this challenge. We have only just begun to do so by developing real sciences of language, mind, and information.

Although great progress has been made, the tasks (a)–(d) sketched above have not yet been definitively completed for a single natural human language. In part, this is due to the complexity of natural language. But it is also due to the conceptual unclarity of central linguistic notions, most notably that of a proposition, or piece of information. Though Frege and Russell had reasonable ideas about how to identify meanings of sub-sentential expressions, and how to make progress in calculating the truth conditions of sentences on the basis of the meanings and referents of their parts, they had trouble with propositions.

Taking propositions to be abstract Platonic structures "grasped" or "entertained" by minds in a primitive and indefinable way, they couldn't explain what made propositions representational, or what was involved in believing them, or bringing them before one's mind.[4] In retrospect, one might charitably view their abstract structures as theoreticians' models or placeholders that would someday be traded for real things. Although that did eventually happen, Frege-Russell propositions weren't seen as mere models for much of the twentieth century, nor did Frege and Russell take them to be such. Their flawed proposals about propositions were early attempts to identify the real things.[5]

Their problem stemmed from an inversion of proper explanatory priorities. Instead of taking *minds* to be sources of representation—when they perceive, imagine, or think of things as being certain ways—and deriving representational propositions from them, Frege and the early Russell started from the other end. Taking purely abstract structures, assumed to be independently representational, they took minds to represent by passively perceiving those structures in the mind's eye. Having started this way, they could only fail.[6]

By 1910 Russell had changed his mind, grasping the basic truth that minds are the source of representation and that other things represent only by standing in the right relations to minds. Unfortunately, he didn't see that this insight could, in fact, be used to construct a new conception of propositions, eliminating the intractable problems of his earlier view.[7] Hence, he rejected the idea that any class of things could be what propositions had been purported to be—namely, meanings of sentences, bearers of truth and falsity, and things asserted, believed, known. Wittgenstein's *Tractatus Logico-Philosophicus*, published in 1922, seemed to put the final nail in that coffin.

Rejecting the Frege-Russell conception of propositions, Wittgenstein denied that any entities were sentence meanings. There were, of course, things that represented objects as being certain ways, and so were true when the objects were that way, and false otherwise. He even called them "propositions." But he took them to be meaningful sentences themselves—or, perhaps better, *uses of them*. After this, propositions—thought of as complex nonlinguistic entities expressed by meaningful sentences—came, for decades, to be regarded as creatures of darkness. As was the case with Russell, however, this blanket rejection was ironic, since we can now see how close Wittgenstein was to laying the foundation for a cognitively realistic conception of propositions that has finally won adherents in the first decade and a half of the twenty-first century.[8]

With propositions temporarily out of the way, the development of the scientific study of meaning was focused on the relationship between meaning and truth. Because meaningful declarative sentences represent things in the world as being certain ways, it was thought that we can study their meanings by studying what would make them true. This was done by constructing models of the world and checking to see which sentences were true in which models. The models were those descending from Tarski's notion *truth in a model,* discussed in chapter 6. Following his work, it had become commonplace to view an interpreted logical language as the result of adding an intended Tarskian model (interpretation) and theory of truth in a model to an uninterpreted logical calculus, thereby assigning truth conditions to every sentence. Using truth theories to *endow* uninterpreted sentences with truth conditions, and hence meaning, encouraged the idea that truth theories could also be used to *describe* the meanings of already meaningful English sentences, if we are clever enough to discern the logical scaffolding underlying those sentences. Thus began the attempt to build an empirical science of linguistic meaning in natural language by extending and applying the logical techniques of *formal* (or *logical*) *semantics.*[9]

By 1940, "classical logic" (descending from Frege) was beginning to inspire specialized extensions. One was *modal logic,* which introduced an operator *it is necessarily true that*—which when prefixed to a logically true sentence produces a truth. Since this operator was defined in terms of truth "at," "in," or "according to" *model-like elements*, logical models for modal calculi had to contain such elements, dubbed "possible world-states," thought of as *ways the world could be*. This strengthened the idea that for a (declarative) sentence S to be meaningful is for S to represent the world as being a certain way, which is to impose conditions the world must satisfy for S to be true. Henceforth meaning was to be studied by using the syntactic structure of sentences plus the representational contents of their parts to derive the truth conditions of sentences. For example, a semantic theory for Italian is expected to derive the statement *'Firenze è una bella città' is true at a possible world-state w if and only if at w, Florence is a beautiful city*—which is a technical way of stating *necessary and sufficient conditions* for the world to conform to the way the Italian sentence represents it to be.

Since to learn these conditions is to learn something approximating the meaning of the sentence, one who did so would acquire a rudimentary communicative competence in Italian. If one learned a theory that derived a similar statement of truth conditions for every Italian sentence, one would have acquired a more extensive competence—perhaps, it was thought, enough to be counted as understanding Italian. By 1960, theorists reasoning in this way thought they might come to understand what meaning is and how information is linguistically encoded.

Since then, philosophers and theoretical linguists have expanded the framework to cover large fragments of natural languages. Their research program started with the logical constructions recognized in classical logic, augmented by the operators *it is necessarily true that, it could have been true that*, and *if it had been true that such-and-such, then it would have been true that so-and-so*, plus similar operators involving time and tense. Gradually, more natural-language constructions, including comparatives, adverbial modifiers, adverbs of quantification ('usually', 'always'), intensional transitive verbs (like 'worship' and 'look for'), indexicals (like 'I', 'now', 'you', and 'today'), demonstrative words and phrases (like 'these', 'those', and 'that F'), and propositional attitude verbs (such as 'believe', 'expect', and 'know') were added to the language fragments under investigation. At each stage, a language fragment for which we already had a truth theory was expanded to include more features found in natural language. As the research program advanced, the fragments of which we had a good truth-theoretic grasp became more fully natural language–like. Although one may doubt that all aspects of natural language can be squeezed into this logic-based paradigm, the prospects of extending the results so far achieved justify optimism that we still have more to learn from pursuing this strategy.

Indeed, without the models provided by these truth-theoretic investigations plus philosophical theories of speech acts and philosophical accounts of conversational or communicative implications of our assertive utterances, today's thriving empirical sciences of linguistic meaning and language use—practiced by distinguished linguists including Barbara Partee, Angelika Kratzer, Irene Heim, Craige Roberts, Geoffrey Pullum, and Paul Elbourne—wouldn't exist. *Thus if we ask, "What did philosophers of language from Frege through the mid-twentieth century contribute to our understanding of language?" the answer is that they gave us the theoretical core of the scientific study of linguistic meaning as we know it today.*

Nevertheless, we now recognize certain limits to work done in that philosophically dominant paradigm. Because sentences that impose necessarily equivalent conditions that the world must satisfy in order to conform to how the sentences represent it to be can have substantially different meanings, sentence meanings can't be identified with such truth conditions. Nor can the things we assert, believe, and know be identified with sets of possible world-states satisfying the conditions. When it became clear in the mid-1980s that these problems couldn't be solved by swapping theories of truth at *possible world-states* for theories of truth at circumstances *of any sort*, there was a revival of interest in Frege-Russell propositions, as additions to (rather than wholesale replacements of) theories of truth at possible world-states.[10]

Nevertheless, the mere passage of time—more than a half century—didn't obliterate the problems that previously undermined Frege-Russell propositions. For Russell, propositions had been structured complexes of objects and properties combined in unexplained ways. For Frege, mysterious entities called "senses" were thought to somehow fit together like pieces in a jigsaw puzzle, despite being nonspatial. For both, the representational properties of propositions, in virtue of which they had truth conditions, were taken for granted rather than explained, while agents were said to represent things as being certain ways by virtue of bearing an unexplained relation to mysterious, ill-understood propositions. In short, Frege's and Russell's otherworldly conception of propositions as *sui generis* abstract objects (existing independently of us outside of time and space) made it impossible to explain how propositions manage to represent anything, how agents succeed in believing them, or why recognizing them at all should be needed for agents to represent things as being certain ways.

At this point it began to dawn on some philosophers and theoretical linguists that minds themselves might be the source of representation, and that the things asserted, believed, and known—which are also primary bearers of truth or falsity as well as being meanings of (some) declarative sentences—might be cognitive in nature. Although different theorists conceptualized this in different ways, the general idea was, and is, that propositions are cognitive acts, operations, states, products, or processes.[11]

According to one main development of this idea, agents represent things as being various ways when they perceive, visualize, imagine, or otherwise think of them as being those ways. *Propositions are then identified with repeatable, purely representational, cognitive act types or operations.* For example, when one perceives, imagines, or thinks of B as hot, one predicates *being hot* of B, and so represents B as hot. This cognitive *act* represents B as hot in a sense similar to the derivative senses in which various socially significant acts can be said to be *insulting* or *irresponsible*. Roughly put, an act is insulting when for one to perform it is for one to insult someone; it is irresponsible when to perform it is to neglect one's responsibilities. A similar derivative sense of *representing* can be used to assess the accuracy of cognitions. When to perceive or think of o as F is to represent o as it really is, we identify an entity, a particular cognition—a mental operation or doing—plus a property it has when it is accurate. The entity is a proposition, which is the mental act or operation type of representing o as F. The property is truth, which the act has if and only if for one to perform that representational act or operation is for one to represent o as o really is.

To *judge* that B is hot is to predicate *being hot* of B in an affirmative manner, which involves forming or reinforcing dispositions to act, cognitively and behaviorally, toward B in ways conditioned by one's reactions to hot things. To *believe* that B is hot is to be disposed to judge it to be hot. To *know* that B is hot is for B to be hot, to believe it is, and to be safe or justified in so believing. Since believing p doesn't require cognizing p, any organism that can perceive or think of the objects and properties in terms of which p is defined can believe p, whether or not the organism uses language or can predicate properties of propositions. Knowing things *about* propositions requires distinguishing one's cognitive acts or operations from one another. Self-conscious agents who can do this can ascribe attitudes to themselves and others, and predicate properties of propositions. Focusing on their own cognitions, they identify distinct propositions as different thoughts, which leads them to conceive of truth as a form of accuracy.[12]

In this way, we explain how an organism without the concept of a proposition, or the ability to cognize one, can know or believe one. We also explain how sophisticated agents acquire the concept, and come to know things about propositions. What about meaning? What is it for a proposition p to be *the meaning* of a sentence S? It is for speakers following the linguistic conventions of their community to use S to perform the representational cognitive act p; learning a language is learning how to use its sentences to perform the mental acts conventionally associated with them. For example, one who understands 'Plato was human' uses the name to pick out the man, the noun to pick out humanity, and the phrase 'was human' to predicate the property of the man, thereby performing the cognitive act—*predicating humanity of Plato*—that is the meaning, p, of the sentence.

Surprisingly, however, p isn't the only proposition the speaker thereby expresses. Because *using the sentence 'Plato was human' to predicate humanity of Plato* is itself a purely representational cognitive act, it also counts as a proposition p*, distinct from, but very closely related to, p. Since to perform p* is to perform p, but not conversely—just as to perform the act *driving to work* is to perform the act *traveling to work*, but not conversely—propositions p and p* are cognitively distinct, even though they represent the same thing as being the same way, and so are representationally identical.

The importance of *representationally identical but cognitively distinct propositions* is illustrated by sentences (1a–b), both of which express the proposition p that is the act predicating *being a planet* of Venus.

1 a. Hesperus is a planet.
   b. Phosphorus is a planet.

As with traveling to work, there are many ways of performing the predication, including (but not limited to) one that involves identifying the predication target (Venus) by using a name for it—e.g., 'Hesperus', 'Phosphorus', 'Venus'—or by seeing it and focusing one's attention on it. With this in mind, consider utterances of (1a) and (1b). In addition to the proposition p that consists in predicating *being a planet* of Venus (no matter how one identifies it), one who assertively utters (1a) also asserts the proposition p_H, which is the act predicating *being a planet* of Venus, *using 'Hesperus' to identify it*. In addition to p, one who assertively utters (1b) asserts the cognitively distinct but representationally identical proposition p_P, which is the act predicating *being a planet* of Venus *using 'Phosphorus' to identify it*. Since p_H and p_P are different, the pair of propositions—p_H and p— asserted and believed by someone sincerely uttering (1a) differs from the pair p_P and p asserted and believed by someone sincerely uttering (1b), despite the fact that the common member, p, of each pair is the meaning, or semantic content, of both sentences.

Examples like these illustrate another point: there is more to understanding a sentence than being able to use it with its linguistically determined semantic content. Understanding a sentence also involves the ability to use it in conformity with widely shared presuppositions in one's linguistic community. For example, even though those well enough informed to employ the names 'Hesperus' and

'Phosphorus' are *not* required to know that the two names designate the same thing, they *are* expected to know that those who use the names typically presuppose that 'Hesperus' stands for something visible in the evening sky, while 'Phosphorus' stands for something visible in the morning sky. One who mixed this up—taking 'Hesperus' to be the morning designation and 'Phosphorus' the evening designation—would misunderstand the names. Because of this, normal utterances of (1a) assert and convey the information that the body Hesperus *that is seen in the evening* is a planet, while normal utterances of (1b) assert and convey the information that the body Phosphorus *that is seen in the morning* is a planet.[13]

The treatment of uses of (1a–b) extends to all forms of cognition that give rise to representationally identical but cognitively distinct propositions, and to uses of sentences to express or report cognitive attitudes. Let p be the simple proposition the performance of which involves focusing on object o and predicating property F of it. Suppose in a particular case that the sub-act of focusing on o can be performed either by using a name of o, or by perceiving o (visually or aurally). Taking only this variation into account gives us several representationally identical but cognitively distinct propositions—the proposition p of predicating F of o in some way or other, the proposition p* of predicating F of o, cognizing o by using its name, and the proposition p**, cognizing o visually, and so on.

Next, suppose one predicates some property of oneself, cognizing oneself introspectively, which is different from any other way of cognizing oneself. Here again, a basic cognitive sub-act of a larger propositional act of predication is performed in a special way, with the result that the agent simultaneously performs both the general act of predicating F of someone or something, and the more specific act of doing so in a certain way, in this case by identifying the predication target introspectively. Because of this, one may fail to bear certain cognitive attitudes—e.g., belief or knowledge—to a proposition that predicates F of oneself, cognized introspectively, even though one does believe or know propositions that ascribe F to one, cognized in some other way. For example, if, after being stunned by a blow on the head, I forget my name—while continuing to believe that 'Scott Soames' names some professor or other—I may continue to believe *that Scott Soames is a professor*, while temporarily failing to believe *that I am Scott Soames* and wondering whether *I am a professor.*

Similar points can be made about propositions in which one predicates a property of the present moment, cognized as subjectively present, versus cognitively distinct but representationally identical propositions in which the property is predicated of the very same moment, cognized via some objective presentation, like a date (and time). Just as for each person p there is an introspective first-person way of cognizing p no one else can use to cognize p, so, for each time t there is an immediate "present-tense" way of cognizing t *at t* that can't be used at other times to cognize t. Suppose I plan to attend a meeting that will start at t—noon on March 31st. Not wanting to be late, I remind myself of this that morning. Nevertheless, as the morning wears on, I lose track of time. So, when I hear the clock strike noon, I say "The meeting starts now!" and change my behavior. Coming to believe of t *in the present-tense way* that the meeting starts then motivates me to hurry off. Had I not believed this, I wouldn't have done so, even though I would have continued to believe, of that very time t, that the meeting starts then. In this case, I believe something new by coming to believe something old in a new way. What makes it true for me to say, at t, *that I only just realized that the meeting starts now* is that the proposition to which I have only just come to bear the *realizing* relation requires *cognizing t in the immediate present-tense way.* By using considerations like these, investigators are beginning to make progress in solving problems heretofore often deemed intractable.[14]

A related development is the recognition that the linguistic meaning of (some) sentences is best thought of not as a single proposition that utterances of the sentence are typically used to assert, but as a set of constraints that determines a range of propositions that utterances in different circumstances may be taken as asserting. The simplest examples of this type have long been recognized. As the philosopher David Kaplan pointed out, to know the meanings of sentences containing indexicals—e.g., '*I* am hungry' and 'The meeting starts *now*'—is to know that one who uses the former asserts of oneself that one is hungry and that one who uses the latter at time t asserts of t that the meeting starts then—with different propositions asserted by different agents or at different times.[15] But as a few examples will show, the point generalizes much further. The old idea that contents of our assertions—i.e., *what we say or assert* in uttering a sentence—are usually fully determined by the linguistic meanings of the sentences we assertively utter has given way to the idea that they are determined by the complex interaction of austere linguistic meanings with contextual information and contextually mandated reasoning.

For example, sentences (2a–c) are grammatically but not semantically complete; (2a) requires the second argument of the finishing relation, (2b) requires an activity on which the semantic content of 'ready' must operate, and (2c) requires a reference point: *nearby what—our present location, Bill's present location, a location that he, or we, will be visiting next week?* It all depends on context.

2 a. Bill is finished.
   b. Bill is ready.
   c. Bill is going to a nearby restaurant.

When these sentences are used, the needed completion is sometimes provided by aspects of the context of utterance— e.g., the activity that Bill has been engaged in, the one he has been preparing for, or, in the case of (c), the location of the speaker, or the addressee. However, it can also be provided by activities and locations mentioned in the larger discourses of which utterances of (2a,b,c) are parts, or by the contents of shared presuppositions of speaker-hearers. Since there are indefinitely many possible completions of these utterances, this *isn't* a matter of *linguistic ambiguity* (which arises from multiple linguistic conventions governing particular words). It is simply one way in which linguistic meanings can be underspecified, and so require contextual completion in order to determine what proposition is asserted.[16]

Sentences containing bare numerical quantifiers *N Fs*, in which N is a numeral and F is a predicate nominal (*two children, three dogs, four bicycles*), are similar. Depending on the context of utterance, the quantifier can be interpreted as *at least N Fs, exactly N Fs, at most N Fs,* or *up to N Fs.* As before, this is not ambiguity; it is non-specificity. The meanings of these sentences leave open which of several possible completions may be dictated by the context.[17]

A different, but related, kind of under-specification concerns sentences containing ordinary *quantifiers*—e.g., phrases of the form *every/any/some/no so-and-so.* The linguistic meanings of these phrases determine their use in talking about so-and-so's, but the contributions these phrases make to what is asserted by uses of sentences containing them may be further restricted in specific contexts by the clearly discernible point of the speaker's remark. For example, parents whose children are holding a sleepover in the basement might utter (3a,b,c) to make the italicized assertions, which don't concern all people, or even all in the house, but merely the children downstairs.

3 a. Everyone is asleep. *Everyone downstairs is asleep.*
 b. Someone is lying on *Someone downstairs is lying on*
  the floor. *the floor.*
 c. No one wants to get *No one downstairs wants to get*
  up before 9 AM. *up before 9 AM.*

Similarly, a football coach wishing to keep the opposing team from learning his strategy for the big game might use (4):

4. No one may, without my permission, speak to any reporter.

to say to his players that no team member may, without his permission, speak to any reporter *about the upcoming game.* This doesn't restrict team members running for positions in student government from speaking to reporters about their candidacies.

It is just this kind of linguistic phenomenon that we find in the compact clause of Article I, Section 10 of the U.S. Constitution, "[N]o State shall, without the Consent of Congress . . . enter into any Agreement or Compact with another State," which asserts the more fully specified proposition that *No state shall, without the consent of Congress, enter into any agreement or compact with another state that diminishes federal supremacy, or undermines the federalist structure of this Constitution.* The fact that this is the proper interpretation of the compact clause—which doesn't prohibit all agreements between states—isn't news. What is news is that the interpretation is not, as prominent legal commentators have sometimes labeled it, a judge-made *constitutional construction,* which modifies original content of a clause in light of new facts or further judicial reflection prompted by litigation. Rather, the so-called construction is simply the mislabeled recognition of the original asserted content of the clause. The reason for the mislabeling is that the Supreme Court of the United States, when it ruled on this, didn't realize that it was merely recognizing original asserted content because it didn't have the sophisticated understanding of the relationship between linguistic meaning and asserted content that we do now.

Next consider possessive noun phrases *NP's N*. Interpreting them requires identifying the possession relation R holding between the referent of the possessor NP and the individual designated by the phrase. When N is a relational noun, it provides a default possession relation. The default designation of 'Tom's teacher' is someone who bears the teaching relation to Tom; the default designation of 'Tom's student' is one who bears the converse of that relation to Tom. Similar remarks apply to 'Tom's mother', 'Tom's boss', and 'Tom's birthplace'. Crucially, however, the default choice can be overridden. Imagine that two journalists, Tom and Bill, have each been assigned to interview a local student. When this is presupposed, one can use 'Tom's student' to refer to the student *interviewed by* Tom, and 'Bill's student' to refer to the one *interviewed by* Bill. In these cases what is asserted isn't fully determined by the linguistic meanings of the sentences used.

The lesson extends to uses of possessive noun phrases involving non-relational nouns, like 'car' and 'book', to which a potential possessor may bear many different relations. 'Tom's car' can be used to designate a car he owns, drives, is riding in, or has bet on in the Indianapolis 500; 'Pam's book' may be used to designate a book she wrote, plans to write, is reading, or has requested from the library. As before, this isn't ambiguity; it is non-specificity. The meaning of *NP's N* requires it to designate something to which N applies that stands in relation R to what NP designates. But the meaning of the sentence doesn't determine R;

the context of use does. Hence, linguistic meanings of sentences containing possessive noun phrases often aren't what they are used to assert.

Temporal modification can also be incomplete. Descriptive phrases like "the chair of the department," and "the owner of the Harrison Street house" lack any overt temporal specification. Depending on the context, the former can be understood as *the one who chairs, the one who chaired,* or *the one who will chair, the department.* The same is true of "the owner of the Harrison Street house." One who says "The owner of the Harrison Street house is temporarily away on business," shortly after the house has burned down, asserts that the person who *owned* the Harrison Street house is temporarily away. In other contexts, what one asserts by uttering the same sentence is that the person who *presently owns* the house is away. The linguistic meanings of the descriptive phrases lack temporal specifications, which must be contextually added before one has a candidate for assertion.

Tenseless descriptive phrases also occur in crucial legal contexts. Two prominent examples are found in the following fragment of the First Amendment to the U.S. Constitution: "Congress shall make no law . . . abridging *the freedom of speech,* or [*the freedom*] *of the press."* This statement promises that the government will never abridge two things—the freedom of speech and the freedom of the press. To understand the promise you must know that you can't abridge something that isn't already a reality. To abridge *War and Peace* is to truncate the original. So, to abridge the freedom of speech and of the press is to limit, restrict, truncate, or otherwise diminish the existing freedom to speak, write, communicate, and publish. The freedom to do these things when? At the time the Constitution was adopted, of course. What can't be abridged is the kind of freedom that existed to do these things then. Thus, the original asserted content of this fragment of the First Amendment is roughly as follows:

Congress shall not abridge (restrict, truncate, or diminish) freedoms enjoyed in America at the time (1788) to speak, write, communicate, publish, and disseminate information and opinion.

The new appreciation of the pervasive interpenetration of contextual and semantic information has opened a second new frontier in the study of linguistic meaning and the communicative use of language that supplements the one prompted by the recognition of a more realistic, cognitive, conception of propositions as pieces of information. This second new development has brought with it two important questions: *What normative principles govern the rational, efficient, and cooperative exchange of information that characterizes much linguistic communication?* and *What are the psychological processes involved in the extraction of asserted and conveyed information by normal human language users?* Both have been investigated since the mid-1960s, when the philosopher Paul Grice (1913–1988) showed how informal conversational principles guiding the rational and efficient exchange of information add extra content, beyond the linguistic meanings of the sentences uttered, to the messages communicated by ordinary uses of language.[18]

Building on this idea, contemporary philosophers of language are looking for more powerful tools to deepen and extend Grice's insights. How, they are asking, would ideally rational speaker-hearers converge on information asserted or conveyed by utterances of sentences the linguistic meanings of which merely constrain, without fully determining, the contents of communicated messages? Since modern decision and game theory provide mathematically sophisticated models of rational belief and action, these models are directly relevant to answering this question. For this reason, some linguistically and mathematically minded philosophers are now trying to figure out how to transform existing multi-person signaling games to incorporate conventionally meaningful linguistic signals—utterances of sentences of natural languages—in cooperative games in which players maximize benefits by communicating accurate information about the world. If, as seems likely, a productive new line of research emerges from this effort, it will be the latest fundamental contribution to the young sciences of language, mind, and information to which philosophers have already contributed so greatly.

CHAPTER 8

THE SCIENCE OF RATIONAL CHOICE

The rational assessment of actions as means to desired
ends performed under conditions of uncertainty; how
laws of probability constrain rational action; Ramsey's
philosophical foundations of general theory of rational
decision and action; subjective probability and agent-relative
utility; groundbreaking applications in recent social science.

Along with the world-transforming contributions of philosophy to the mathematical theory of computation leading to the digital age and the birth of the emerging sciences of language, mind, and information, few developments in the philosophy of the last 100 years have had as broad a social impact as the philosophical origins of subjectivist interpretations of probability and their use in modern decision theory. Starting with the Cambridge philosopher F. P. Ramsey in 1926 and continuing through the mid-century work of other important philosophers, the approach has grown exponentially, both in the social sciences and in the new philosophical sub-discipline, formal epistemology.

The model of rational action and belief resulting from this approach is based on the familiar idea that actions are, typically, the products of belief and desire. We do things to achieve desired ends by performing actions we think are best suited to do so. The propositions we believe represent the state we take the world to be in, while our desires express our preferences among different possible outcomes of the actions we are contemplating. Both are crucial when deliberating what to do. The aim of deliberation is to select the action that makes the best use of the limited information we have in bringing about the results we most desire. A theory of rational decision and action that spells this out is not an attempt to describe the psychological processes agents always, or even typically, undergo in making decisions. It is an idealized model of the rationally optimal thing to do; it aims to identify which action, from an array of possible actions, has the best chance of advancing one's interests, given one's information. In short, the theory is normative.

If it is successful, agents familiar with the theory may sometimes be able to use it as a tool to improve the decisions they would otherwise have made informally. Within limits, the theory can also be used descriptively. If it is true that many individuals and groups are reasonably well attuned to what will advance their interests—no matter what idiosyncratic decision processes they utilize—a normative theory of rational decision can help explain their general behavioral tendencies, over time, in responding to similar reward structures in similar situations. This is how leading social scientists often use decision theory.

To grasp this, we need to understand how the theory conceives of beliefs and desires as coming in degrees. In the case of desire, the idea is transparent. I want some things more than I want others, and when I want x more than I want y, and I want y more than I want z, I want x more than I want z. Right now, I would rather have two oranges than three bananas, and I would rather have one apple than two oranges; so, I would rather have one apple than three bananas. In the case of belief, we first put aside those propositions of which we are rationally certain—e.g., logical truths or tautologies—as well as their negations—logical falsehoods or contradictions. The remaining propositions—some of which we believe, some of which we neither believe nor disbelieve, and some of which we doubt (more or less strongly)—are all candidates for being true. None may be completely secure and none may be utterly insecure. Our degree of confidence in a proposition p—our credence in p (or, p's *credence* for us)—plays an important role in determining the actions we are rationally willing to take based on p. The higher the credence, the more sense it makes to base an action on p. The lower the credence, the less sense it makes to perform an act the effectiveness of which in producing a desirable result depends on the truth of p—unless the value of that result is high enough to compensate for our low credence in p.

Simple gambles illustrate the point. When rolling a pair of dice, we know in advance that there are 36 possible outcomes—one in which the two face-up sides total 12, two in which they total 11, three in which they total 10, four in which they total 9, five in which they total 8, six in which they total 7, five with a total of 6, and so on. If we know that the dice are fair, we will say the odds of rolling a 7 are 1 to 5, which means that the probability of rolling something other than 7 is five times that of rolling 7, and hence that the probability of 7 is ⅙. This suggests that, other things being equal, we should be willing to take either side of repeated gambles returning $500 on a roll of 7 versus losing $100 on a roll of anything other than 7.

The caveat, *other things being equal,* is important. When aren't they equal? When one has moral objections to gambling; when one is risk averse and so would never risk losing a substantial amount; when one regards gambling as thrilling entertainment for which one is willing to pay by accepting slightly lower odds of winning; or when one's marginal utility for dollars is nonlinear, so that dollars above (or below) a certain amount are worth more, or less, than dollars below (or above) that amount. For example, if you are $500 short of the money to finance an operation needed to save your child's life, it could be rational for you to wager more than $100 for the chance of winning $500 because ⅟₅₀₀ of the ultimate value you could purchase with those winnings (the life-saving operation) far exceeds the values of the individual dollars wagered attempting to win it. Similarly, if you can't afford to lose $50, lest you go to prison for defaulting on a loan, it could be rational not to wager that amount, even if offered what would otherwise be favorable odds. In these cases, the dollar amounts of one's gains or losses are poor measures of the real value of what one wins or loses.

These considerations highlight a limitation on models of rational decision illustrated by simple games of chance. Money alone isn't always a good measure of the values we place on possible results when deciding what actions to perform. Another limitation, which must be overcome in a general theory, is that the probabilities we assign to propositions needed to assure desired results are often less transparent than they are in simple games of chance. We must overcome these limitations if we are to transform uncontroversial observations about rational betting strategies in such games into general theories of rational decision under uncertainty. As we shall see, this was the locus of important philosophical contributions to modern decision theory.

First, however, more must be said about why the obvious strategies for simple games of chance are *rational*. One reason is merely an artifact of the range of possible outcomes defined by the games plus the determination of specific outcomes (e.g., the number showing on the dice) by a procedure that is *assumed* not to favor one outcome over another (because the dice are assumed to be fair). Within these parameters, we can read off the probabilities of simple propositions from the ratios of outcomes of a given sort (e.g., six ways of rolling a 7) to the totality of possible outcomes (36 configurations). The rationality of taking the probability that the dice will come up 7 to be ⅙ is then a trivial mathematical fact—made true by the rules of the game plus the *assumption* that the dice are fair.

But there is also another factor. What constraints does rationality impose on the relations between the probabilities assigned to one set of propositions and those assigned to another set? How must the probabilities of simple propositions be related to the probabilities of complex propositions— negations, conjunctions, disjunctions, universal or existential generalizations, etc.—in order for an overall assignment of probabilities of propositions to be rational? This question is analogous to a question about systems of deductive logic (deriving from Frege). Such systems never specify the truth or falsity of any of *simple sentences*; that is the job of observation, experience, and science. But modern logical systems do tell us which *complex sentences* must be true (logical truths or tautologies) and which must be false (logical falsehoods or contradictions). They also tell us when collections of sentences are inconsistent, and so can't be true because they *violate the laws of logic*. In telling us this, systems of deductive logic put constraints on rational beliefs. A similar point can be made about models that evaluate actions based on the desirability of their intended outcomes and the probability that performing them will result in those outcomes. *What constraints do they place on assignments of probabilities to propositions guiding action, and why are assignments violating those constraints irrational?*

To pursue this question, we begin by letting the assignment of probabilities to simple (logically independent) propositions be whatever one likes—so long as they are always between zero and 1.[1] Disallowing any proposition to have a probability exceeding 1, we next state general principles of probability theory deriving from the widely accepted formalization of Kolmogorov.[2]

WIDELY ACCEPTED LAWS OF PROBABILITY

The probability of the negation, ~p, of a proposition p is 1 minus the probability of p.

The probability of the disjunction *p or q* is the probability of p plus the probability of q minus the probability that p and q are both true.

If p and q are incompatible (and so can't both be true), then the probability of *p or q* is the probability of p plus the probability of q.

If neither p nor q entails the other, or its negation, then the conjunction *p and q* is the probability of p times the probability of q.

Let p be a proposition that can be true in either finitely, or infinitely but countably, many incompatible ways. The probability of p is the sum of the probabilities of those ways.[3]

The probability p = the probability of *p and q* plus the probability of *p and ~q*.

If p logically entails q, then the probability of p is less than or equal to the probability of q.

The probabilities of logically equivalent propositions are identical.

Another fundamental notion of the probability calculus is *the conditional probability of p given q*—e.g., the probability *that the dice come up 7, given that they come up odd*. This probability, represented *prob p/q*, is not the probability of a single proposition; it is a special measure of the relationship between a pair of propositions. It is the probability of *p and q* divided by the probability of q (provided that the probability of q isn't 0). In other words, it is the proportion of cases in which both p and q are true, from among all cases in which q is true. For example, the probability that *the dice come up 7 given that they come up odd* is the probability that the dice come up *both 7 and odd* (which is just the probability that they come up 7) divided by the probability that they come up odd. Since the probability of the former is ⅙ and the probability of the latter is ½, the probability that they come up 7 given that they come up odd is ⅓. This makes sense because 6 of the 18 combinations in which the dice come up odd are combinations adding to 7.

Conditional probabilities are intimately related to fair prices of conditional bets. Consider a bet made by purchasing a ticket that pays $6 if the dice come up 7, conditional on the dice coming up odd. Since the probability that the dice come up 7 is ⅙, $1 is the fair price of an *unconditional* ticket that pays $6 if they do (giving you a gain of $5). What about a ticket that pays $6 if 7 comes up, *conditional on an odd number coming up?* If you buy it and roll 7, you win $6 (from which you deduct the cost of the ticket). You lose the price of the ticket if you roll an odd number other than 7, but your purchase price is refunded if you roll an even number. Since the bet eliminates all the rolls in which the dice come up even, which make up half the total combinations, the conditional gamble is twice as valuable as the unconditional gamble. Hence the fair price for it is $2, and the conditional probability of *rolling 7 given that the dice come up odd* is ⅓ (meaning that a $4 net gain one time will compensate for a pair of $2 losses.) This illustrates the rule for conditional probability

$$\text{prob } p \mid q = \text{prob } (p \text{ and } q) / \text{prob } q$$

which is a consequence of what is sometimes called the product rule.

$$\text{prob (p and q)} = \text{prob (p | q)} \times \text{prob q}$$

Both are among the laws of the standard probability calculus.

All these laws are easily verified in simple games of chance of the kind here discussed. In that limited sense, the rationality of these laws is on par with the rationality of the calculations we have made concerning simple propositions about outcomes of individual rolls of the dice. Crucially, however, the laws also impose a more general constraint on rationality, independent of the probabilities we have taken for granted regarding simple cases like the proposition that the dice will come up 7. After all, the dice might not be fair; they might be constructed so as to systematically make some combinations come up more frequently than others. Since agents are aware of this possibility, we can imagine situations in which they accept hypotheses about the dice that result in probability assignments to simple propositions about rolls of the dice that conflict with one another and with the probabilities we have been assuming here. In some situations, their conflicting assignments may be rational. Each agent may have evidence based on his or her own experience plus testimony from normally reliable others for adopting a particular hypothesis about the dice. Thus, no agent may be irrational, in which case the probability assignments based on the evidence available to the different agents won't be irrational either.

The same can't be said for violations of *the laws of probability*. Assignments violating them can be shown to be irrational. Just as sets of propositions that are *inconsistent* with the laws of deductive logic can't all be *true,* no matter what possible state the world is in, so probability assignments inconsistent with the laws of probability generate sets of bets which, taken together, will *lose,* no matter what state the world is in, despite being acceptable to one who adopts those probabilities. In fact, the rational imperative to conform one's *degrees of belief* in propositions (assessments of their probabilities) to the laws of probability may well be stronger than the imperative to ensure that one's beliefs *tout court* don't form a logically inconsistent set—in the sense of *belief* in which for any agent A and proposition p, A either believes or does not believe p (no middle ground).

Though there may be something like a cost in believing any falsehood, that cost may sometimes be outweighed by the value of gaining other, true, beliefs. For example, it may be rational to believe, of each ticket in a heavily subscribed lottery, that it will lose, while also believing that one ticket will win, even though one's beliefs will then be logically inconsistent.[4] It may also be rational to retain one's belief in each of a series of propositions about ordinary matters about which one has formed an opinion, while also recognizing one's fallibility, and so coming to believe that at least one of those propositions is false, even though that renders one's belief set logically inconsistent. By contrast, it is not clear that there is anything to be said for adopting a set of credences (degrees of belief) which, if systematically acted upon, will guarantee that one's aims are frustrated. So, although optimal rationality *doesn't* require that one *never* believe all members of a set of logically inconsistent propositions, optimal rationality may require the credences on which one bases one's decisions and actions *always* to obey the laws of probability.

Optimal rationality of one's credences also involves conditional probability. Our assignments of probabilities to simple propositions—e.g., that the dice will come up 7—are often based on evidence. If we are in doubt about whether the dice are fair, we may gather evidence bearing on the question by rolling them two thousand times and calculating the ratio of times they come up 7 (or any other possible numerical outcome). If the observed proportion matches

or closely approximates the ideally expected proportion—
e.g., ⅙ in the case of coming up 7—then, all other things
being equal, we will naturally come to have that credence
in the proposition that the next roll will come up 7. More
generally, our post-test unconditional probability that the
next roll will come up 7 should equal (or perhaps closely
approximate) m/n if and only if the dice came up m/n in
our test, in which case our post-test conditional probability
that the dice will come up m times, conditional on its being
rolled n more times, is m/n. This, roughly put, is a further
constraint on our rational credences. In short, our unconditional probability for a proposition p should match our
conditional probability of *p given evidence e,* once we have
verified e and know it to be true. This holds for a wide range
of propositions p and e (including those in which p is a scientific theory and e is evidence for it). If one's credence in
a theory T that makes an important, but so far untested,
prediction p is x, then typically one's conditional credence
in T, given p, will be x plus some positive amount, while
one's conditional credence in T, given ~p, will typically be
x minus some amount. When one then finds out whether
p is true, or false, one's unconditional credence in T will be
the higher, or the lower, number. This, it is reasonable to
think, is how empirical confirmation works.

PHILOSOPHICAL FOUNDATIONS OF A GENERAL
THEORY OF RATIONAL DECISION AND ACTION

The norm of rationality—that one's credences obey the
laws of probability—was noticed by a founder of subjective
probability theory, F. P. Ramsey, in his seminal 1926 article
"Truth and Probability."[5] The subjective probability of a
proposition p for an agent A is the degree of confidence
that A has in the truth of p. In calling this probability "sub-

jective," we are in no way impugning, or endorsing, the accuracy or rationality of A's degree of confidence in p. There is no implied contrast with the "true" or "objective" probability that p is true (if such even makes sense in the situation in which A is considering p). We are simply measuring how strongly A believes, or is inclined to believe, p. After laying out the laws of probability, Ramsey notes that an agent whose probabilities are inconsistent with them is always subject to a "Dutch book"—i.e., a set of bets which, though acceptable (at odds based on the agent's subjective probabilities), guarantees that the agent ends up a net loser, no matter how the world turns out.[6] The idea is illustrated by the following simple example.

Suppose X's estimate of the probability for a disjunction, *A or B,* of *incompatible disjuncts* A, B, is *less than* the sum of X's probabilities for A and B, in violation of the law that such probabilities are additive. Imagine that X's probability for A is $\frac{1}{5}$, for B is $\frac{3}{10}$, and for *A or B* is $\frac{49}{100}$, even though the rule for *A or B* requires it to be $\frac{5}{10}$. To ensure X's loss, we can proceed as follows. First, we buy a bet (paying $100 if we win) from X on *A or B* for $49—i.e., we can, by giving him $49 now, obtain X's assurance to pay us $100 if the disjunction proves to be true. The price of this bet, $49, *is less than the sum of the price ($20) for a bet (paying $100) on A and the price ($30) of a bet (paying $100) on B.* So, after buying the bet on *A or B* from X, we next sell X individual bets on A and B, one for $20 and one for $30. We can do all this because, given X's credences on the disjunction and the two disjuncts, X is willing to take either side of each of the bets. But now, X will lose no matter whether A alone, B alone, or neither A nor B is true: (i) If neither is true, X loses $50 on his two bets, while gaining $49 on the one he sold us, leaving X with a net loss of $1. (ii) If only A is true, X has a gain of $80 on bet A, a loss of $30 on B, and a loss of $51 on the bet X sold us on *A or B,* again leaving X with a net loss of $1. (iii) If only B is true, X has a net loss of $11. The result generalizes. If your probabilities violate *any laws of probability*, a Dutch book against you can always be made.[7] If your assignments of probabilities are consistent with the laws, it's not possible to make a Dutch book against you.[8]

Having left the realm of games of chance conforming to the stipulation that the various alternatives are equally likely, we next need to find a general way of assigning agent-relative subjective probabilities to propositions. To do this we must face a challenging question: *What does it mean to say that an agent's degree of confidence in, or subjective probability for, p is n?* Ramsey's pathbreaking answer begins by identifying the aspect of belief he is trying to measure. For him, "the kind of measurement of belief with which probability is concerned is . . . a measurement of belief *qua* basis of action."[9] He proposes to measure this by finding the lowest odds the agent would accept for a bet on its truth. But he recognizes that the marginal utility of money renders monetary odds insufficiently general for calculating utilities. He also notes other factors—like enjoyment or aversion to gambling—that interfere with the idea that the monetary odds one is willing to take on gambles can be the basis of accurate measures of one's confidence in the truth of a given proposition. As we shall see, he believes that an accurate measure can be found.

This leads him to claim that "we act in the way we think most likely to realize the objects of our desires, so that a person's actions are entirely determined by his desires and opinions."[10] Assuming the value one seeks to be additive, Ramsey observes that one "will always choose the course of action which will lead in one's opinion to the greatest sum of good."[11] He then introduces the idea that we behave so as to maximize *expected utility (or value)*.

I suggest that we introduce as a law of psychology that [the] behavior [of an arbitrary agent] is governed by what is called mathematical expectation; that is to say that if p is a proposition about which he is doubtful, any goods or bads for whose realization p is in his view a necessary and sufficient condition enter into his calculations multiplied by the same fraction, which is called the 'degree of his belief in p'. We thus define degree of belief in a way that presupposes the use of the mathematical expectation. We may put this in a different way. Suppose his degree of belief in p is m/n; then his action is such as he would choose it to be if he had to repeat it exactly n times, in m of which p was true, and in the others false. (Here it may be necessary to presuppose that in each of the n times he had no memory of the previous ones.)[12]

Although this idea is arresting, it shouldn't be taken as identifying any definite psychological mechanism generating action. In particular, it shouldn't be taken to suggest that agents either consciously or unconsciously perform numerical calculations designed to identify utility-maximizing actions. Nor (I think) should it be taken as suggesting that agents always do maximize expected utility (value)—in the sense in which the latter arises from applying the laws of probability to their utilities plus their degrees of belief in simple propositions. Ramsey should be understood as allowing that agents sometimes violate those laws, and that, when they do, their actions will be out of line with what is rationally required by what they value plus their degrees of belief in simple propositions.

Still, in proposing his conception as a psychological law, he is, in effect, proposing it as a model that roughly tracks what we generally do. If, as we normally assume, most people are aware of what they want and are reasonably well attuned to what will advance their interests—no matter what actual decision processes they go through—then a normative theory of rational decision may model the general behavioral tendencies of individuals responding to common reward structures in similar situations. Indeed, it may be argued that had humans not been bred by natural selection to be reasonably good expected utility maximizers, the species would probably not have been so successful.

Ramsey illustrates his model by imagining a rational agent A on a journey to destination Z, coming to a fork in the road. A thinks the right fork is a more direct route to Z than the left. This makes a difference, since people are waiting at Z for A, and it is better for A to arrive early than late. Feeling a bit more confident in the right fork, A takes it, while looking for an opportunity to ask directions. Having gone a short distance, A sees a farmer working half a mile away in a field, causing A to deliberate whether to walk over and ask for directions. This is Ramsey's decision problem.

Suppose A is twice as confident that the right fork is the direct route—i.e., A's subjective probability *that the right fork is the direct route* is ⅔. Then the question of whether to ask for directions depends on the values of (i) arriving in Z at the *right* time R (taking the direct route), (ii) arriving at a worse time W (taking the other route), and (iii) the time D needed to consult the farmer. Given A's credence of ⅔ that the right fork is direct, we can evaluate A's options by imagining A confronted with the decision three times. The total value A would expect from deciding three times *not to ask* is (3 × ⅔ × the value of arriving at R) + (3 × ⅓ × the value of arriving at W). This equals *(2 × the value of arriving at R)* plus *the value of arriving at W.* By contrast, the value A would expect from three decisions *to ask* would be *3 × the value of arriving at R* minus *3 × the value of the time D spent to ask directions.* (We assume the farmer knows the right direction and would tell it to A if A asks.)

So for it to be rationally worthwhile for A to ask directions, the number associated with asking must be greater than the number associated with not asking. For this to be so, D (the cost of asking) must be less than (the value of arriving at R minus the value of arriving at W) × ⅓.

$$2R + W < 3R - 3D$$

$$3D < 3R - 2R - W$$

$$3D < R - W$$

$$D < (R - W) \times \tfrac{1}{3}$$

Noting that ⅓ is *1 minus A's subjective probability for proposition p* (that the right fork is the direct route), we see that this means that if the decision is to be consistent with A's credence in p, the cost D of asking must be less than *(the value of arriving at R minus the value of arriving at W) × (1 minus the probability of p)*. The result generalizes. For any m and n, if A's credence in p is m/n, the cost of asking for directions must be less than *(the value of arriving at R minus the value of arriving at W) × (1 minus the probability of p)* (i.e., *1 minus m/n*).

In working through this example, we started with A's subjective probability of being on the right road to A's destination. From this, we computed the maximum loss of time it would be rational for A to devote to asking for directions, as a function of the difference in value of arriving at the destination at one time rather than another. But the law-like relationship we found would also allow us to compute other variables given other information. For example, given a particular value of the maximum time D that A is willing to expend asking for information, we can calculate the subjective probability of p required for it to be rational to ask for directions. For the value of D to equal *(the value of arriving at R minus the value of arriving at W) × (1 minus the probability of p),* the value of D divided by *the value of arriving at R minus the value of arriving at W* must equal *1 minus the probability of p;* so the probability of p equals *1 minus the value of D divided by (the value of arriving at R minus the value of arriving at W).*

$$D = (R - W) \times (1 - \text{Prob}(p))$$

$$D / (R - W) = 1 - \text{Prob}(p)$$

$$\text{Prob}(p) = 1 - D / (R - W)$$

Here we simply assumed we could measure the agent's utilities. To further generalize the example, we need a way of explaining what this amounts to. What we need is not just a linear ordering of the agent's preferences over different outcomes, but a measure of *how much better* the agent takes certain outcomes to be than others. In short, we need a way of assigning numerical values to the agent's utilities. First let's see what we can do once we have such a measure. Then we can investigate what agent-relative utilities really are. (Since the discussion contains a bit more technicality than some readers may be comfortable with, those who wish may proceed to the final section of the chapter, "Social-Scientific Applications," without loss of continuity).

THE LAW-LIKE CONNECTIONS BETWEEN SUBJECTIVE PROBABILITY AND AGENT-RELATIVE UTILITY

Let p be a contingent proposition (which is true if the world is a certain way and false otherwise). Let A, B, and C be outcomes (representing states the world could be in) with utilities U(A), U(B), and U(C) for a particular agent. (In doing the calculation we assume we know what the outcomes are and can assign them numerical values.) The particular outcomes A, B, and C are chosen so that the agent is indifferent to *receiving U(A) for certain* versus *accepting U(B) if p is true, and U(C) if p is false.* In other words, U(A) is the value of the gamble *U(B) if p is true, and U(C) if p is false.* The subjective probability of p for this agent is then determined by the odds at which the agent would accept the gamble.

Suppose the agent would take either side of the bet on p at odds of 3 to 5, which means that if p turns out to be true, the agent gets an outcome at value 5 (which is U(B)), while if p is false the agent gets an outcome of value 3 (which is U(C)). This translates directly into a ⅜ subjective probability for p and a ⅝ subjective probability for ~p, which means that U(A) = (⅜ × 5) + (⅝ × 3) = ³⁰⁄₈. Given this as U(A), we see that [U(A) minus U(C)] / [U(B) minus U(C)] = (⁶⁄₈ × ½) = ⁶⁄₁₆ = ⅜.

That is how Ramsey defines the subjective probability of p for the agent—*provided, we set up the crucial gamble with U(B) greater than U(C), as we just did.* So, when the agent would take either side of a bet on p at odds of, say, 7 to 3, we do our computations on the equivalent bet with odds of 3 to 7 on the truth of ~p. Here we set U(B) at 7 and U(C) at 3. So, if ~p turns out to be true (and p is false), the agent gets value 7, while if ~p is false (and p is true), the agent gets value 3. This translates into a ³⁄₁₀ subjective probability for ~p and a ⁷⁄₁₀ subjective probability for p, which means that U(A) = (³⁄₁₀ × 7) + (⁷⁄₁₀ × 3) = ⁴²⁄₁₀. Given this as U(A), we see that [U(A) minus U(C)] / [U(B) minus U(C)] = ¹²⁄₁₀ × ¼ = ³⁄₁₀. Since this is the probability of ~p, the probability of p is ⁷⁄₁₀.

Similarly, if the agent would take either side of a bet on p at odds of, say, 5 to 4, we do our computations on the equivalent bet with odds of 4 to 5 on the truth of ~p. This gives us a ⁴⁄₉ subjective probability for ~p and a ⁵⁄₉ subjective probability for p, which means that U(A) = $(^4/_9 \times 5) + (^5/_9 \times 4) = {}^{40}/_9$. So $[U(A)$ minus $U(C)] / [U(B)$ minus $U(C)] = {}^4/_9$. Since this is the probability of ~p, the probability of p is $^5/_9$. *In short, given the utilities of A, B, C, we can always construct a bet that measures the agent's subjective probability of a proposition as* $[U(A)$ minus $U(C)] / [U(B)$ minus $U(C)]$.

DEFINING AGENT-RELATIVE UTILITIES

All of this will follow if we can assign numerical values to an agent's utilities. But how can we do this? Ramsey responds with a plan to propose options to the agent.

> Let us now discard the assumption that goods are additive and immediately measurable, and try to work out a system with as few assumptions as possible. To begin with we shall suppose . . . that our subject . . . will act so that what he believes to be the total consequences of his action will be the best possible. If we then had the power of the Almighty . . . we could, by offering him options, discover how he placed in order of merit all possible courses of the world. In this way all possible worlds would be put in an order of value, but we should [still] have no definite way of representing them by numbers. There would [still] be no meaning in the assertion that the difference in value between [outcomes] α and β was equal to that between γ and δ. . . . [W]e could test his degree of belief in different propositions by making him offers of the following kind. Would you rather have a world α in any event [i.e., for certain, without any contingency]; or a world β if p is true, and a world γ if p is false? If, then, he were certain that p is true, he would simply compare α and β and choose between them as if no conditions were attached.[13]

Now Ramsey imposes two restrictions on the proposition p in his proposed option: *α for certain vs. β if p is true, and γ if p is false*. First, to avoid confusions that may plague the agent's computations involving logically complex claims, Ramsey requires p to be a simple (atomic) proposition. Second, he requires p to be "ethically neutral," by which he means that the agent has no evaluative interest in the world being as p describes; no preference that p be true, or that it be false. For example, I am neutral on the proposition that in the first month of 1899 with an even number of days, and in which the odd-numbered days in which it rained in Seattle is not equal to the even-numbered days in which it rained, the odd-numbered rainy days exceeded the even-numbered rainy days. I am neutral about this proposition; I place no value on its truth or its falsity.

Next, Ramsey defines what it is to believe an ethically neutral proposition p to degree ½ (i.e., to assign it a subjective probability of ½). Let α and β be outcomes on which the agent places some value, and moreover prefers one to the other. An agent believes p to degree ½ if and only if the agent has no preference between the options *α if p is true, β is false* and *α if p is false, β if p is true*, despite preferring α, let's say, to β. The fact that the agent is indifferent to the two options despite preferring the first, provided that p is true, and the second, provided that p is false, reflects the fact—*or better, just is the fact*—that the agent's degree of belief in p is ½.

This is Ramsey's Archimedean point. Because p is ethically neutral, we can define what it is to have a credence of ½, *without having to first measure the agent's utilities*. Since we can't measure A's utilities entirely independent of A's credences, we need these special credences to give us a measure of A's utilities. Ramsey uses the definition of what it is to have a credence (degree of belief) of ½ to define what it means for *the difference in value between outcomes α and β to be equal to the difference between outcomes γ and δ*. Once we have this, we will be able to quantify agent-relative utilities by assigning them numerical values. When these numerical utilities are in place, we can then use the relationship already illustrated between an agent's subjective probabilities and the agent's utilities to assign the agent's subjective probabilities other than ½ to propositions. Thus, we have reached the final step in the conceptual task of providing precisely defined conceptions of probability and utility sufficient to ground modern theories of rational decision and action.

The following diagram tracks our journey. We have already taken the first two steps. We have also seen how, once we have taken the third and fourth, the fifth and sixth will follow from our previous discussion. The task now is to establish (3) and (4).

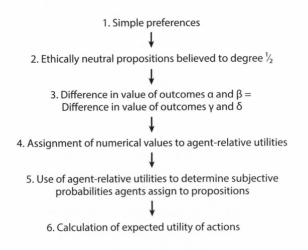

1. Simple preferences

↓

2. Ethically neutral propositions believed to degree ½

↓

3. Difference in value of outcomes α and β =
Difference in value of outcomes γ and δ

↓

4. Assignment of numerical values to agent-relative utilities

↓

5. Use of agent-relative utilities to determine subjective
probabilities agents assign to propositions

↓

6. Calculation of expected utility of actions

Ramsey's Conceptual Path

Step 3 is a variation on what we have already done. For Ramsey, to say that the difference, for an agent A, in value between α and β (the former preferred to the latter) to be equal to the difference in value between γ and δ (the former preferred to the latter) is to say that for any ethically neutral proposition p believed to degree ½, A has no preference between options (i) α *if p is true,* δ *if p is false* and (ii) β *if p is true,* γ *if p is false.* This tells us that the value to A of (i)—which is half [the value of α together with the value of δ]—is the same as the value to A of (ii)—which is half (the value of β together with the value of γ). So, *the value of α plus the value of δ* equals *the value of β plus the value of γ.* This can be so only if the loss to A of the difference in values between α and β—reflected in the first parts of the options (i) and (ii) (when p is true)—is exactly compensated by the gain to A of the difference between the values of γ and δ—reflected in the second parts of (i) and (ii) (when p is false). Otherwise put, *α minus β equals γ minus δ.* This, according to Ramsey's definition, is *what it means* for the value to A of the difference between α and β to be the same as the value to A of the difference between δ and γ. Although this doesn't, by itself, determine which numbers we assign to agent-relative utilities, it sharply constrains such assignments. For example, if α is assigned 9 and β is assigned 4, then the difference between numbers assigned to γ and δ will be 5, matching the difference between α and β.

Our final step is to further elaborate Ramsey's assignments of agent-relative utilities, using ethically neutral propositions p believed to degree ½, by showing how to numerically calibrate *the scale of the agent's values between any given outcome (state of the world) α that the agent prefers to another outcome (state of the world) β.* We start with the option (i) α *if p,* β *if not p.* We let W(½) be a state of the world in which, were the agent to take himself to be in it, he would be indifferent between buying or selling this option after it is described to him. Its value to the agent is defined to be whatever value is assigned to β plus half the difference between the values of α and β. (So W(½) is intermediate in value between α and β.) Next, we find a second ethically neutral proposition p* probabilistically independent of p for the agent, also believed to degree ½. We let W(¾) be a state of the world in which, were the agent to take himself to be in it, he would be indifferent between buying and selling option (ii) α *if p**, *W(½) if not p**. The value of this option is half the difference between the values assigned to α and W(½)—which is the utility of W(¾).

In the same fashion, we construct option (iii) β *if p#*, W(½) *if not p#*, evaluated at a world-state W(¼), the value to the agent of which is the value of β plus half the difference between the values of β and W(½). (As before, W(¼) is intermediate in value between W(½)and β.) Having divided the difference in values to A of the range between α and β, we could, if we wished, assign the five points we have identified the utilities 1, 2, 3, 4, and 5, or any multiple thereof. Moreover, the process could be repeated as long as we can continue to find ethically neutral, probabilistically independent propositions that are believed to degree ½. In this way, we can assign numerical values to all outcomes the agent prefers to β while also preferring α to them.

SOCIAL-SCIENTIFIC APPLICATIONS

This completes the account of the philosophical conception of subjective probabilities and agent-relative utilities growing out of ideas originally expressed by Frank Ramsey and later developed in various ways by philosophers and philosophically minded social scientists.[14] These ideas are now central to various different but related philosophical theories of rational decision and action. Versions of the ideas have also been used by social scientists to describe economically, politically, and socially significant behavior, and to critique political and economic institutions.

To understand these uses, one must remember that the goal of the formal model is not to directly describe, or to recommend, detailed processes by which agents do, or should, make decisions. The goal is to specify factors that determine the effectiveness of actions as means to desired ends, and to indicate how that effectiveness might be measured. The psychologically real processes by which we make decisions depend on our aptitudes, the time we have to deliberate, the nature and availability of relevant evidence, the cost—in time, effort, and foregone opportunities—to search for new evidence, and a host of other factors. These factors vary from agent to agent and case to case. But whatever process we employ in making a given decision, the question of how successful we are in tailoring our actions to achieve our ends is a measure of how well we choose. The more we learn about the determinants of this evaluation, the greater chance we have of better achieving our goals in the future. Finally, it must *not* be thought that optimally effective rational choice is optimally efficient selfish choice. Nearly everyone values the welfare of others, including the preeminent value we place on the welfare of certain selected others, even if it sometimes can be purchased only at our own expense. Rational choice is as valuable in achieving the aims of a saint as it is in achieving the aims of a sinner.

The theory of rational decision with agent-relative probabilities and utilities allows one to extend classical accounts of rational economic behavior, measured in dollars and cents, to utility-maximizing behavior in broader settings. Thus, it is natural that those leading this extension have been the Nobel Prize–winning economists Kenneth Arrow, James Buchanan, Gary Becker, and George Stigler, along with other leading economists such as Duncan Black, Anthony Downs, William Niskanen, Mancur Olson, and Gordon Tullock. Their applications of the decision-theoretic approach have been remarkably wide-ranging, including, especially in the case of Becker (1930–2014), the economic costs of social discrimination, the social utility of investments in education, the effect of certain kinds of negative incentives on deterring crime, and emerging trends in marriage and the family.[15]

The following passage from Becker's Nobel Prize lecture in 1992 underlines his recognition of how Ramsey's pluralistic model of agent-relative utilities makes it possible to extend traditional economic thinking far beyond its usual bounds.

[T]he economic approach I refer to does not assume that individuals are motivated solely by selfishness or gain. It is a method of analysis, not an assumption about particular motivations. Along with others, I have tried to pry economists away from narrow assumptions about self-interest. Behavior is driven by a much richer set of values and preferences. The analysis assumes that individuals maximize welfare as they conceive it, whether they be selfish, altruistic, loyal, spiteful, or masochistic. Their behavior is forward-looking, and it is also consistent over time. In particular, they try as best they can to anticipate the uncertain consequences of their actions.[16]

This passage is followed by a summary of Becker's contributions to (i) the causes and costs of discrimination plus the most promising ways of minimizing it, (ii) the effects on criminal behavior of changes in the probabilities of detection and conviction, and the utilities associated with different types and durations of punishment, (iii) the personal, social, and economic effects of various kinds of education and training, and (iv) the formation, structure, and dissolution of families.

Apart from Becker, most *public-choice* economists have focused their decision-theoretic methods on the interface between government, politics, and economics. Typically described as the application of *economic reasoning* to new domains, this new social science methodology is, at bottom, an ambitious application of the philosophical framework for evaluating means-end decisions created by Ramsey, who was himself a brilliant, though amateur, economist, in addition to being one of the leading philosophers of the early twentieth century.[17] This common terminological appropriation, describing a model for understanding all means-ends reasoning as *economic* reasoning, is illustrated by the following passage from *Public Choice: A Primer,* by the British economist Eamonn Butler.

> Will the view from the next hill be worth the effort of climbing it? How much time should we spend in finding exactly the right birthday card for a friend? No money is at stake, yet these are still economic decisions in the broad sense of the word. They involve us weighing up how much time or effort we think it worth spending to achieve our aims, and choosing between the different possibilities. *Economics is actually about how we choose to spend any available resources (such as our time or effort) in trying to achieve other things that we value more highly—it is not just about financial choices.*[18]

One can get a sense of public choice theory from the way in which it ties together the problem long known as *market failure* with the important, but previously under-conceptualized, problem of *government failure*. First, market failure. The beauty of free competitive markets is that typical transactions are voluntary exchanges of goods and services by parties each of whom exchanges something of value for something he or she takes to be of greater value. If, as is natural to think, each participant is, generally, the best judge of what in the situation is best for him or her, then the transaction will typically result in a net gain in utility for all participants. The assumption that this is the normal case is Adam Smith's *invisible hand*—which claims that agents maximizing their own utilities through voluntary transactions under conditions of fair competition end up maximizing the utility of society as a whole, despite not aiming at that.

Smith's idea is powerful, but the extent to which voluntary interactions that increase the utility of each party typically aggregate so as to increase total social utility is a matter of conjecture. What is not a matter of conjecture is that there are important cases in which they do not. These cases occur when voluntary transactions between parties impose costs (decrease utility) for those not party to the transaction—for example when they impose health and safety risks on others. When these costs, called *externalities,* exceed the gains generated by the original transaction, aggregate utility falls. The name for this is *market failure.* When recurring failures of this sort can be pinpointed, they often call for correction by government.

While the idea is familiar, its cousin, *government failure,* was not very familiar prior to public choice theory. Public choice theorists have made it familiar by observing that, like actors in *the private sector* (individuals, businesses, corporations, and unions), actors in *the public sector* (elected officials and their staffs, department and agency heads and their staffs, and members of regulatory bodies) are decision makers with utilities and subjective probability functions of their own. When one examines their actions as functions of their utilities and subjective probabilities, one finds situations in which these utility maximizers respond to incentives that sometimes reduce rather than increase social utility, and may even defeat the stated purposes for which the laws and regulations they enforce were enacted. The name for these cases is *government failure.* Identifying such failures, and attempting to alleviate the problems they create, have been the main focus of work in public choice theory.

One such failure, identified as *political rent seeking* in Tullock (1967), involves government restrictions—including
unnecessary licensing fees (e.g., for taxis, beauticians,
manicurists, etc.), extensive registration and reporting requirements, tariffs, quotas, and special subsidies. Since
these nearly always favor established enterprises, they tend
to make it more difficult for new firms to enter existing markets, thereby restricting competition, raising prices, and
imposing costs on the general public. Since the gains to
favored enterprises can be great, it often makes sense for
these enterprises to invest large sums in lobbying, in cam-
paign contributions, and in other forms of behind-the-
scenes politicking, thereby diverting resources that could
otherwise be used productively. Since the costs to the
public of the government's actions, in the form of higher
prices and reduced access to goods and services, are often
unavoidable to consumers, while their causes are invisible
to average voters, political and governmental actors often
have much to gain and little to lose from policies detrimen-
tal to the public welfare.

Similar results generated by a similar logic of interacting incentives have been found in studies of governmental
regulation of business and industry by other public choice
theorists, including the economist, George Stigler (1911–
1991). Suspecting that the same combination of concentrated benefits for the few with highly defused, and largely
invisible, costs for the many would generate perverse incentives for regulators, Stigler gathered empirical evidence that
much regulation ends up benefiting established players in
an industry at the expense of newcomers and the general
public. In 1962, he and his coauthor Claire Friedland found
that regulation of electricity prices had only a tiny effect on
holding down those prices, while in 1971, he argued that instead of reducing the harmful effects of targeted monopolies, government regulation tended to reinforce them by

curtailing competition.[19] In addition to being among the contributions for which Stigler won the Nobel Prize, these ideas influenced the deregulation of the airline, transportation, and natural gas industries in the United States in the 1970s. Stigler was also cited by the Nobel committee for pioneering the economics of obtaining, organizing, and disseminating information.

No project has received more attention from public choice theorists than the task of extracting defensible public choices from the preferences and subjective probabilities of individuals. Although some limited results have been achieved, the most important big questions remain unresolved. Ideally, one might hope to extract collective-relative utilities and subjective probabilities from agent-relative utilities of members of the collective. But no one seems to know exactly how to do that. The chief intellectual obstacle to be overcome arises from a result of another Nobel Prize winner, Kenneth Arrow, in his *Social Choice and Individual Values* (1951). There he demonstrated the impossibility of finding a general method for converting any realistic set of individual preferences over at least three options (without numerical utilities)—subject to seemingly necessary conditions for treating individual preference orderings fairly—into an acceptable social preference ordering. After decades of research into modifications of Arrow's original conditions, no general and widely accepted positive solution has emerged. Whether this might change if the inputs were individual *utilities* (preferences with numerical values) is doubtful, in part because we don't know how to objectively compare agent-relative utilities of different individuals. Thus, what might be called fully general *social decision theory* doesn't yet exist.[20]

Nevertheless, certain socially significant results involving voting behavior of individuals and of the actions of individual political actors have been achieved. One derives from Anthony Downs's *An Economic Theory of Democracy*. There he notes that because the probability that a single vote will decide an election in today's societies approaches zero, the rational utility of voting would seem to be tiny, and so, one might think, be easily outweighed by the inconvenience of casting a ballot. The idea is compelling, but it can't be the whole story. A substantial number of people do vote. Why? Are they irrational, or are there other utilities involved that don't depend on whether one's favored candidate wins or loses? Presumably the latter. These utilities may include the sense that it is one's moral obligation to vote, but they also may include the desirability of being able *to say one has voted*—and so to signal one's virtue, to maintain one's social relationships, and to solidify one's standing in a group with which one identifies—without the discomfort of lying, or the fear of being found to have lied.

Of course, accomplishing these goals by going to the polls is one thing; gathering information needed to cast an informed vote is another. Because the costs—in time and effort—of gathering and assessing the information needed to become informed are high, many votes will be cast in ignorance. This is why simplistic branding of parties and candidates, whether accurate or not, is so important in influencing low-information voters. It is also why candidates are tempted to insult and ridicule not only their political rivals, but also the supporters of their rivals, thereby reducing the agent-relative utility of identifying oneself as such a supporter.

Problems such as these are among the many defects inherent in modern democratic government. In order to combat them one needs, among other things, an objective and open-minded press and educational system with both the ability and the will to widely disseminate accurate information. As the founder of public choice theory Nobel laureate James Buchanan (1919–2013) insisted, one also needs a constitution encouraging consensus, limiting the scope of government and constraining the powers of majorities to impose their will on minorities. By a constitution, he meant a set of fundamental decision rules, intended to last for generations, guiding the procedures by which ordinary political matters are decided—e.g., rules governing elections, rules governing the operation of different branches of government, and rules preventing governments from doing certain things without authorization by supermajorities.[21]

In evaluating acceptable constitutional rules, he adopted what might be regarded as an analytical fiction. He insisted that such rules must be capable of being unanimously accepted in a hypothetical, idealized constitutional convention by rational, expected-utility-optimizing agents possessing knowledge of human nature and the world we inhabit, but not knowing what social and economic positions they would come to occupy over time. Realizing that no constitution would guarantee a political system that always maximized social utility while avoiding suppression of minorities, he believed that some constitutions could objectively be shown to be better than others. These are the ones he imagined ideally rational expected-utility-optimizing agents to be able to agree on. Historically existing constitutions were to be judged by their similarity to those that could be so adopted.

Although Buchanan regarded the identification of defensible constitutional rules to be a matter of highly idealized continuing inquiry, it is clear that his conception of such rules was importantly similar to that of America's founders. Thus, it is not surprising that he ended his 1986 Nobel Prize lecture with this paragraph.

In 1987, the United States celebrates the bicentennial anniversary of the constitutional convention that provided the basic rules for the American political order. This convention was one of the very few historical examples in which political rules were deliberately chosen. The vision of politics that informed the thinking of James Madison was not dissimilar, in its essentials, from that which informed Knut Wicksell's less comprehensive, but more focused, analysis of taxation and spending. Both [Madison and Wicksell] rejected any organic conception of the state as superior in wisdom to the individuals who are its members. Both sought to bring all available scientific analysis to bear in helping to resolve the continuing question of social order: How can we live together in peace, prosperity, and harmony, while retaining our liberties as autonomous individuals who can, and must, create our own values?[22]

Having laid the foundations of a subjectivist understanding of probability and incorporated it into a logical model of rational decision and action that can be applied to individual and institutional actors in any domain, twentieth-century philosophers gave their colleagues in the social sciences one of their most powerful tools, the applications of which have only just begun.

CHAPTER 9

MIND, BODY, AND COGNITIVE SCIENCE

The classic mind-body problem; new perspectives on mind, meaning, and representation, the new mind-body debate; understanding, naming, necessity and conceptual possibility; functionalism about the mind; a failed argument against identifying human pains with neurophysiological events; where we stand; computation, cognitive psychology, and the representational theory of mind.

THE CLASSIC MIND-BODY PROBLEM

Descartes famously imagined a scenario in which, despite having all his everyday thoughts, feelings, and sensations, he was really dreaming, or, worse, being deceived by an evil demon. He realized that if that were so, he wouldn't know most elementary things about himself and the world around him. He wouldn't even know there was a world around him; nor would he know that he had a physical body, or that anything outside his own thoughts and experiences existed. He would, nevertheless, know he existed, since the very fact that he was having thoughts and experiences would show that he did. So, he reasoned, it must be possible to know that one exists, without knowing that one's body, one's brain, or anything physical exists. From this he concluded that he, Descartes, wasn't identical with (i.e., the very same thing as) any body, any brain, or anything physical.

Although the argument is not entirely without appeal, the fantastic dreaming scenario may distract from what is really going on. This is easily fixed. Imagine waking up in the dark, unable to move or to see your body or anything else nearby. Your only sensations are of a tiny point of light and a faint sound of music. Although you are able to think perfectly well, you have no idea what happened. In such situation you might know little more than *that you must exist, since you have thoughts and experiences.* What is it that you know? Not simply that *there are thoughts and experiences* (of a certain type), or that *someone* is having them. You know something stronger and more specific than that.

What do you know? Consider the propositions associated with your use of the sentences "I exist" and "N exists" (Where 'N' is your name). These sentences predicate existence of the same person. Since there are no further predications, the propositions they express are representationally identical. Nevertheless, they are different, since you can take different cognitive attitudes toward them. In fact, your use of the two sentences puts three propositions in play—one that requires you to identify yourself in the first-person way that each agent uses to cognize him or herself, one that requires identification via the name 'N', and one that doesn't require one specific way with which you are identified.[1] Since the three propositions have the same truth conditions, it is impossible for one to be true without their all being true. But it is possible for some agent or other to believe or know one of the two more demanding propositions without believing or knowing the other one, and it is possible for some agent to believe or know the undemanding proposition without believing or knowing either demanding proposition.

One more step. Let 'B' name your brain, your entire nervous system, or your body—anything physical that might be taken to be a candidate for being you. Keeping B in mind, we return to the scenario in which you awake in the dark, aware only of your thoughts and sensations. You know you exist, but it is hard to say whether you know B exists. Although you don't know the proposition that requires identifying the putative existent via the name 'B', you might know the undemanding but representationally identical proposition that imposes no such requirement. Whether or not you do depends on whether or not you are B. If you are, then in knowing *that you exist* you predicate existence of yourself—i.e., B—and so know that B exists. If you aren't B, this isn't so. This observation is fatal to the Cartesian argument. Since one can't decide whether you know a proposition predicating existence of B without *first* deciding whether you are B, one can't use conclusions about what you do, or don't, know to decide whether you are a purely physical being.

The point can be made more general. No one would dream of arguing that Mark Twain wasn't Samuel Clemens just because there is a sense in which some people know (i) that Mark Twain wrote *The Adventures of Huckleberry Finn* without knowing (ii) that Samuel Clemens wrote *The Adventures of Huckleberry Finn*. If these two knowledge claims are correct, then the two propositions (i) and (ii)—one known and the other not—must differ, which, in turn, means that names must sometimes contribute more than their referents to propositions expressed by uses of sentences containing them. As we saw in chapter 7, there is a puzzle here to which philosophers have offered solutions, but it is one about thought and language, rather than minds and bodies.

This dismissal of Descartes's argument doesn't show that he was wrong to think that we are spiritual beings, distinct from our bodies. It only shows that his argument provides no reason to believe it. All the classical positions remain open—that we are purely physical, that we are purely nonphysical, or that we are part physical and part nonphysical.

NEW PERSPECTIVES ON MINDS, MEANING, AND REPRESENTATION

Although Descartes's argument for mind/body dualism was unsuccessful, his idea that thought, or—as we might more broadly put it—representation, is the essence of the mental has been taken to heart in the philosophy of the last few decades. Minds represent things in the world, including themselves, in thought and perception, which, in turn, make goal-directed action and linguistic communication possible. As seen in chapter 8, agents act on the basis of their beliefs, trying to bring about changes they desire. As seen in chapter 7, mental concepts like knowledge, belief, and assertion are relations between agents who know, believe, or assert and the things—propositions—known, believed, or asserted.

Conceiving of propositions as purely representational cognitive acts or operations, we see that minds are the source of both representation and meaning. Propositions—pieces of information or misinformation—represent because they are cognitive acts agents perform in representing things as being one way or another. They are also meanings, or semantic contents, of some sentences. For a sentence S of a language L to mean p (or for uses of S to have the semantic content p) is (roughly) for uses of S by speakers of L to be performances of p. Sentences are linguistic tools for performing representational acts and coordinating one's representations with others. Those who understand the sentence 'The earth is round' use the name to pick out the planet and the predicate to ascribe *being round* to it. To do this is *to perform* the act type that is the meaning (semantic content) of the sentence. Since no other cognition is needed, knowing what S means in L doesn't require having any thoughts *about* p or L, let alone knowing that S stands in a complicated theoretical relation R to p and L.

Because language is a social institution, it expands our cognitive horizons. It does so by making it possible for us to believe or disbelieve propositions our cognitive access to which depends on others. For example, I believe Uranus to be a distant planet, despite never having perceived it, seen pictures of it, or had any direct contact with it. I believe the proposition because I picked up the name from others, intending to use it to designate whatever they use it to designate. I have also been told it is a planet far from Earth. Because I both understand the sentence 'Uranus is a distant planet' and accept it, I count as believing the proposition it expresses in English. This doesn't require associating the name with an identifying description that could be substituted for it without changing meaning in sentences in which it occurs. In fact, the main identifying descriptions I have for the name are parasitic on uses of it by others on whom my uses depend. The name, as I use it, refers to *whatever they use it to designate*. Still, *what I believe* would have been true, even if the name 'Uranus' hadn't existed. Thus, my belief that Uranus is a distant planet isn't *about* the name; it simply predicates being a distant planet a certain object.

The same story can be told for many proper names of persons, places, and things, as well as for general terms that are, in effect, common names for natural kinds—e.g., *bauxite, tungsten, manatee, lemur,* and *sequoia*.[2] The propositions expressed by sentences containing such terms represent objects or kinds as having or lacking properties that many agents wouldn't be able to bring to mind were it not for the chains of communications in which the agents stand to other users of the terms. Since understanding and accepting sentences containing these terms counts as believing the propositions they express, it often turns out that when language is involved, even the solitary thought of an individual agent has a social dimension. Since, in

many such cases, we are not able to entertain the propositions sentences express prior to understanding the sentences themselves, it also turns out that understanding a
sentence isn't always a matter of searching through our
stock of antecedently entertainable propositions to find
which one others in our linguistic community use the sentence to express. It simply involves conforming our linguistic intentions to those of others, whose patterns of use
determine the governing linguistic conventions. In recent
years, the traditional philosophical mind-body debate has
been reformulated in a way that makes it sensitive to these
linguistic issues.[3]

THE NEW MIND-BODY DEBATE

In the 1950s and '60s a group of prominent philosophers
including U. T. Place, J.J.C. Smart, David Lewis, and
David Armstrong turned the mind-body debate in a new
direction. Instead of employing purely philosophical arguments, like Descartes, to try to establish the truth of
one position or another, or contenting themselves with
refuting the arguments of those who did, they argued that
whether mental states and processes could be identified
with physical states and processes was a scientific question. Observing the great progress that had been made in
physics, chemistry, and biology, they noted that surprising theoretical identities were already the order of the
day.[4] For example, they maintained that it had already
been discovered that heat is mean molecular kinetic energy, gold is the element with atomic number 79, biological genes are sequences of DNA, lightning is an electrical
discharge, the colors of objects are properties of reflecting light waves within precisely defined frequencies, and
water is H_2O. Because the explanatory power of these

advances was a product of the well-established physical-istic framework for investigating the natural world, there was, these philosophers thought, every reason to expect that advances in understanding the mind would be made within the same framework, identifying mental states and processes with physical states and processes. These early philosophical proponents of the psychophysical identity theory thought that pains, sensations, and consciousness itself could, in one way or another, be identified with neurological states and processes. They didn't specify which neurological states and processes were identical with pain states, sensation states, or consciousness. That was a job for neuroscientists. The philosophical job was to defeat conceptual objections to the possibility that any such identification could be correct, and to articulate the explanatory advantages of incorporating the mental into physical science.

According to these theorists, identifying a mental type, say pain, with a neurochemical type—call it "C-fiber stimulation"—is conceptually no more problematic than identifying lightning with a type of electrical discharge, heat with mean molecular kinetic energy, or water with H_2O. There was, it must be admitted, much to be said for this idea. However, there was also a catch. These philos-ophers took it for granted that, like all other theoretical identities in science, statements identifying mental states and processes with physical states and processes are both contingent and knowable only on the basis of empirical evidence. Indeed, the two points were connected. To say that scientific identities are knowable only on the basis of empirical evidence is to say that they can't be established by philosophical reasoning alone, because observation and evidence are needed *to rule out possibilities in which they are false.* Since this presupposes that there are such possibili-ties, it seemed to follow that the identities, though true, could have been false—and so are contingent rather than necessary truths. Although these ideas, which were applied to all science, seemed simple enough, they proved to be more difficult to defend than was initially expected.

UNDERSTANDING NAMING, NECESSITY, AND CONCEPTUAL POSSIBILITY

In January of 1970, a 29-year-old wunderkind, Saul Kripke (1941–), gave three lectures at Princeton University titled Naming and Necessity that changed the course of twentieth-century philosophy. At age 17, while still a high school student in Omaha, Nebraska, he had provided what was to become the first systematic and widely accepted semantics (theory of meaning) for formal systems of *the logic of necessity and possibility*—a problem that had been under investigation for nearly a quarter century starting with C. I. Lewis, C. H. Langford, Ruth Barcan Marcus, and Rudolf Carnap, among others.[5] Having received his bachelor's degree from Harvard in 1962, Kripke moved immediately to the Harvard Society of Fellows, spending alternate semesters lecturing first at Yale, and then at Princeton, before becoming a full-time research professor at Rockefeller University in New York.

The chief achievement of the Princeton lectures was the development of a realistic, world-based conception of necessity and possibility, different from conceptual necessity and possibility. His main points can be illustrated using a few simple examples.

1. Greg Soames ≠ Brian Soames (SS: Greg and Brian are my two sons.)
2. If Saul Kripke exists, then Saul Kripke is a human being.

3. This desk (pointing at the one in my office) was not originally made of metal.
4. If this desk exists, then it is made of molecules.

Since these propositions are true, they are, according to Kripke, necessarily true. Why? Well, Greg and Brian are two different people. Each could have existed without the other and each could have had different properties than he actually has. Greg could have been born in Princeton, New Jersey, rather than New Haven, Connecticut (where he was born). Brian could have been born in New Haven, rather than Princeton (where he was born). But the two of them couldn't have *both* existed while being one and the same individual. If there were a possible individual GB, identical with both (i.e., the very same individual as both), then, since Greg and Brian actually exist while being nonidentical, GB would actually exist while being nonidentical with himself, which is absurd. Hence the fact that Greg and Brian are not identical (i.e., not the very same individual) means they couldn't have been identical. It follows from this that the claim that they aren't identical is a necessary truth.

The point can be put by saying that nonidentity is an essential property of any pair of things that aren't identical. Similarly, Kripke argued, *being a human being* is an essential property of anything that is a human being, which means that if Kripke really is a human being, then he couldn't have existed without being a human being—in which case (2) is necessary, if true. So are (3) and (4). As it turns out, the desk in my office—this very one I am working on—is, and always was, made of wood, not metal. It is also composed of molecules. Like most things, it could have had some other properties it doesn't in fact have. But *being originally made of metal* and *not being composed of molecules* are not among them. No matter what possible state the universe were in, if it contained a desk originally made out of metal, or if it somehow contained something that looked like and functioned as a desk, but was *not* composed of molecules, it would *not* be this very desk which I am working on now. Hence (3) and (4) are also necessary truths, if they are true at all.

Although these points were, and are, elementary, they also were, and are, striking. Even though (1–4) are necessary truths, they are not true by definition, nor can they be known to be true by deducing them from self-evident truths (the negations of which are contradictory). On the contrary, they are knowable only on the basis of experience, observation, and empirical evidence. How can that be? How can a proposition that is necessary—and so would have been true no matter which state the world were in—require empirical evidence about the way that the world happens to be in order for it to be known?

Kripke's answer appeals to our knowledge of essential properties and relations. We know simply by understanding the terms 'human', 'not (originally) made of metal', and 'composed of molecules' that the properties they express— *being a human, being something not (originally) made out of metal*, and *being composed of molecules*—are essential properties of anything that has them. We also know, simply by understanding the nonidentity predicate, '≠', that the relation, *being nonidentical,* it expresses holds essentially of any pair that are actually so related. In other words, we have antecedent conceptual, *a priori* knowledge that if any objects actually have these properties, or stand in the relation *not being nonidentical to* one another, then they would have those properties, or stand in that relation, in any genuinely possible circumstance in which they existed. Because of this, we have conceptual, *a priori* knowledge that propositions (1–4) are *necessary, if true.* Still, discovering that they are, in fact, true requires gathering empirical evidence. This means that to discover certain things that would have been facts *no matter which possible state the world were in,* we sometimes must *first* empirically investigate *the state the world is in* to discover whether they are facts. Similarly, in order to discover what could, or could not, possibly be, one must sometimes *first* investigate what is.

This idea depends on a sharp distinction between conceptual and genuine possibility—i.e., between ways things could *conceivably* be versus ways things could *really* be (or have been). Following terminology adopted from Gottfried Leibniz, contemporary philosophers draw this distinction in terms of *possible worlds,* or better, *possible world-states.* For Kripke, possible world-states are maximally complete ways the real concrete universe could have been—maximally complete properties that the universe could have had. Conceptually possible world-states are maximally complete ways the universe can coherently be conceived to be—maximally complete properties the universe *can be conceived to have*— that one cannot know by reasoning alone (without empirical evidence) that it doesn't have.

These two sets of properties are different. Just as there are properties that ordinary objects could possibly have had and others they couldn't have had, so there are certain maximally complete properties the universe could have had—genuinely possible world-states—and others the universe couldn't have had—genuinely impossible world-states. Just as some of the properties that objects couldn't have had are properties that one can *conceive* them as having, and that one can't know *a priori* that they don't have, so some maximally complete properties that the universe couldn't have had—some impossible world-states— are properties one can *conceive* it as having that one can't know *a priori* it doesn't have. These states of the world are *conceptually possible.* Thus, empirical evidence required for knowledge of necessary truths like (1–4) is needed to rule out *genuinely impossible, but conceptually possible, world-states in which they are false.*

Here is Kripke's own formulation of the relationship between conceivability and genuine possibility.

[W]e sharply distinguish between the notions of a posteriori and a priori truth on the one hand, and contingent and necessary truth on the other hand, for although the statement that this table, if it exists at all, was not made of ice, is necessary, it certainly is not something that we know a priori. . . . This looks like wood. It does not feel cold and it probably would if it were made of ice. Therefore, I conclude, probably this is not made of ice. Here my entire judgment is a posteriori . . . given that it is in fact not made of ice, in fact is made of wood, one cannot imagine that under certain circumstances it could have been made of ice. So we have to say that though we cannot know a priori whether the table was made of ice or not, given that it is not made of ice, it is *necessarily* not made of ice. . . . [I]f P is the statement that the table is not made of ice, one knows by a priori philosophical analysis, some conditional of the form "if P, then necessarily P." If the table is not made of ice, it is necessarily not made of ice. On the other hand, then, we know by empirical investigation that P, the antecedent of the conditional is true—that this table is not made of ice. We can conclude by *modus ponens*:

P ⊃ Necessarily P
P
Necessarily P

The conclusion—'Necessarily P'—is that it is necessary that the table not be made of ice, and this conclusion is known a posteriori, since one of the premises on which it is based is a posteriori.[6]

In Kripke's argument, the fact that one can't know *a pri-ori* that P means that one can't know *a priori* that a world-state in which it is false that P isn't the state the world is actually in. Such states are coherently conceivable, and so conceptually possible. The fact that one knows *a priori* that *if P, then necessarily P* means one knows *a priori* that if a world-state in which it is true that P is actual, then no world-state in which it is false that P could have been actual. So, when one finds, empirically, that it is true that P, one learns that conceptually possible world-states in which it is false that P aren't genuinely possible.

With these clarifications in mind, we now return to the contention of proponents of the mind-body identity theory, who believed that widely accepted theoretical identities in physics, chemistry, and other sciences could serve as models for understanding empirically based statements identifying mental states and processes with physical states and processes. Remember, early proponents of mind-body identity believed that scientific identities are *contingent*, presumably because empirical evidence is needed to show them to be true. Not so, Kripke plausibly argued. Since gold is the very the same thing as the element with atomic number 79, gold couldn't have existed without having that atomic structure. Consequently, the identity statement is a *necessary truth*. So are the statements *that water is H_2O* and *that heat is mean molecular kinetic energy*. The former says that the substance water is the very same thing as the substance molecules of which contain two hydrogen atoms and one oxygen atom. Since this is a necessary truth, it follows that for any genuinely possible state, w, if the world had been in state w, then any quantity of water would have been a quantity of H_2O, and conversely. Similarly in the case of heat, the truth of the identity claim guarantees that for any genuinely possible state, w, of the world, and for any pair x and y existing at w, if the world had been in state w, then x would have been hotter than y if and only if the mean molecular kinetic energy of the molecules of x would have been greater than that of those of y.

When these lessons had been absorbed, Kripke and others concluded that *statements identifying the mental with the physical* must, like other scientific identity statements, be necessary, if true. This posed a problem because it was not clear that they could be so regarded.

FUNCTIONALISM ABOUT THE MIND

In order to determine the status of statements identifying mental states and processes with physical states and processes, we need to look more closely at mental concepts like *pain*. Since pains are conscious experiences, I am aware of my own pains in something like the way I am aware of my other conscious experiences (e.g., my visual or auditory experiences). I also know that my pains are caused by certain kinds of events, often injuries. Once caused, pains modify my thoughts, motivations, and actions in characteristic ways. Realizing all this about myself, I identify pain in others by observing their verbal and nonverbal responses to events similar to those that cause pain in me.

These ideas can be used to build sophisticated functionalist analyses of the mind according to which the mental states of an organism are internal states that causally interact with one another in systematic ways to mediate sensory inputs and behavioral outputs.[7] According to such analyses, sensory inputs interact with beliefs, desires, and preferences, often changing them and initiating action. Different mental states play different causal roles. Preferences assign high priority to certain outcomes. Believing that so-and-so typically leads to behavior that brings about highly valued outcomes in situations in which it is true that so-and-so.

Desiring that so-and-so—e.g., that one finds one's misplaced car keys—often leads to actions one believes will bring it about that so-and-so—e.g., that one finds the keys. Fitting pain into this picture means thinking of it as a kind of *internal perception of bodily injury* that an agent has a high preference for avoiding. Normally, this perception leads to actions intended to minimize the injury, and to intentions to avoid similar injury in the future.

Generalizing, we may say that a datable event or state of an organism is a pain if and only if it is an internal state of detecting injury, instances of which play a certain functional role in the life of an organism. In the interest of avoiding false precision, let us simply call this "the pain role." The state designated by 'pain' is then *the internal perceptual state of an organism o the function of which is to detect injury to o, instances of which typically play the pain role in o*. The predicate 'is a pain' is true of all and only instances of that state—i.e., of all and only the experiences of so perceiving and playing that role in an organism.

According to this analysis, it is highly probable that which physiological states count as pains varies from one kind of organism to the next. Presumably mammals, reptiles, fish, members of now extinct species, and members of species that may or could evolve in the future are capable of feeling pain. What they all have in common is an internal perceptual state the function of which is to detect bodily injury, to trigger changes in their motivational states that normally lead to actions intended to end or minimize the current injury, and to generate or reinforce desires and intentions to avoid similar injuries in the future.

This, I submit, fits our concept of pain pretty well. If this is what pain is, then something along the lines of the theoretical identity statement (5) is both true and necessary.

5. Pain in an organism o is the state in o that plays *the pain role.*

If it is also true that there are many organisms capable of feeling pain, despite having vastly different internal physiologies, then it is highly unlikely that there is a *single physiological state,* describable in the language of neuroscience, that can be identified with pain *in every creature capable of feeling pain.* It may turn out that *for each different type T* of creature, there is a physical state described by a phrase XXX in the language of neuroscience that makes (6) true, but *there is no single choice of XXX that makes* (6) true *for all types of creatures.*

6. For all individual organisms o of type T, and for all internal states y of o, y is a state of o's being in pain if and only if y is a neurophysiological state of type XXX.

If this is right, then pain is a functional state, *not* one particular kind of physical state. Still, you may ask, *Are pains in human beings purely physical events, or not?* To answer this question, we must look further.

A FAILED ARGUMENT AGAINST IDENTIFYING HUMAN PAINS WITH NEUROPHYSIOLOGICAL EVENTS

One of the best known arguments against the psychophysical identification of human pains with neurological C-fiber stimulation is based on Kripke's discussion of statements like (7) and (8a) in *Naming and Necessity.*

7. Human pain = C-fiber stimulation
8a. Heat = mean molecular kinetic energy

Noting that both initially *seem* to be contingently true, or contingently false, Kripke insisted that both must be *necessary*, if true. Although this was not, he thought, a problem for the genuine necessity of (8a), it was, he thought, a problem for the (alleged) necessity of (7).

The illusion that (8a) is contingent is, he speculated, rooted in the fact that we identify heat indirectly, by the sensations it causes in us. Because of this, he argued, we associate 'heat' with *the reference-fixing description* 'the cause of a certain sensation S'. Taking this sensation to be part of "our concept of heat," Kripke argued that we wrongly mistake the description for a *synonym* for 'heat', leading us to confuse the necessary truth (8a) with the contingent truth (8b).

8b. The cause of sensation S = mean molecular kinetic energy

Since many things could have been hot, even if there were no sentient beings capable of having sensations, (8b) could, genuinely, have been false. Thus, Kripke concluded, our confusion of (8a) with (8b) wrongly led us imagine that (8a) could, genuinely, have been false.[8] Once this error is pointed out, however, we can accept that (8a) must be necessary, if it is true at all.

Kripke argued that the same strategy can't be used to dismiss the impression that humans could, genuinely, have experienced C-fiber stimulations without pain. Unlike heat, we designate pain directly. We don't say, "*What a horrible sensation! Let's use 'pain' to refer to whatever causes it.*" Rather, we use 'pain' to designate the sensation itself. Since we don't use any description to fix the referent of the word 'pain', there is no such reference-fixing phrase to confuse with a synonym for 'pain', and no *contingent* truth to confuse with (7). Consequently, we *can't* dismiss the impression that *if*

(7) is true, it is contingent as an illusion. On the contrary, if (7) is true, it must be contingent. Since, in fact, Kripke thought he had shown that all theoretical identity statements of this general sort are necessary if true, he suggested that (7) is false.

This argument fails for two reasons. The first results from mischaracterizing the "illusion of contingency" carried by true theoretical identity statements that really are, as Kripke insists, necessary truths. The mischaracterization is applied to (7) and (8a) on the basis of a questionable contrast between how we identify heat versus how we identify pain. Although there is a contrast, it's not the one Kripke suggests. The most basic contrast is that whereas heat is something we perceive, pain is our perception of something. Our *sensation of heat* is our perception of heat; it is a special kind of experience that reliably, but fallibly, detects heat. Similarly, our *pain sensation* is our perception of injury; it is a special kind of perceptual experience that reliably, but fallibly, detects injury (think pain in phantom limbs). The reason there is no pain without "an experience of pain" is that pains are perceptual experiences.

Contra Kripke, we *don't* identify heat by first perceiving a sensation S, and then taking heat to be the *know-not-what* that causes S. The sensation *is* our perception of heat, just as a visual experience of my dog Lilly *is* a perception her. Lilly does cause my visual experience, but when I identify her I do so directly, not by making my visual experience the object of my attention, and defining her as its cause. If I ask myself, "To what do I use 'Lilly' to refer?" I look at her and say, "To her." If I ask myself, "To what do I use 'heat' to refer?," I move close to the fire, or the stove, and say, "To that." Since there is no "reference-fixing description," I don't take either term to be synonymous with a description. Nor do I confuse conceivable scenarios involving Lilly, or heat, with scenarios in which other things cause my experiences.

When I say I can conceive of heat not being molecular motion, or of Lilly not being an animal, I am *not* misdescribing *some other possibility* that I am *really* conceiving. I am *not really* thinking of sensation S being caused by something other than heat, or of my Lilly-perceptions being caused by a mechanical robot. I am simply thinking of heat, or Lilly, as lacking an essential property P. Because P is essential, the claim that x has P, if x exists, is necessary. Because I can't know, without empirical evidence, that x has P, knowledge of the necessary truth requires such evidence to rule out conceivable (but not genuinely possible) disconfirming scenarios that can't be eliminated in any other way.

The same is true of self-predications. Let P be a property I couldn't have existed without having—e.g., *having a body made up of molecules,* or *being a human being*—but which I can't know I do have without empirical evidence. My remark "If I exist, then I have P" will then express a necessary truth. Although this truth might wrongly *seem* contingent, the reason it does *isn't* that I wrongly take my use of 'I' to be synonymous with a reference-fixing description. There is no such description. When I use the pronoun, I don't identify myself as the creature, whoever it might be, designated by a privileged description. Thus, when I say that I am conceiving a scenario in which *I lack P*, I am *not* confusing myself with someone else, *Mistaken-Me,* who, in fact, is designated by my reference-fixing description—thereby misdescribing a different possibility in which *he* lacks P.

The lesson is the same in all genuine Kripke-cases—e.g., heat and *mean molecular kinetic energy*, Lilly and *being an animal,* and me and *being human*. In each case, the mistake of wrongly taking a proposition to be contingent that, in fact, must be necessary, if true, is due to the fact that establishing its truth requires empirical evidence ruling out scenarios in which it is false. It was surprising that these *empirical* discoveries turned out to be *necessary truths*. What was surprising was that the reason empirical evidence is needed to establish these statements *isn't* to rule out disconfirming *possibilities*; it is to rule out disconfirming *impossibilities* we can't know not to be actual by reason alone.

This is the core insight behind Kripke's groundbreaking distinction between genuine possibility and mere conceivability. Thus, *if the psychophysical identity statement (7) were really a necessary truth*, on par with (8a), the alleged illusion that it is contingent, if true, could be explained in the same way that the genuine illusion that (8a) is necessary, if true, is explained. This is enough to undermine Kripke's argument against the psychophysical identity theory. However, we are not finished. There is still an important question to be resolved. Must (7) really be necessary, if it is true?

THE ROLE OF NECESSITY AND POSSIBILITY

Up to now we have been reasoning as if (7) must be necessary, if true. But in so doing we have been ignoring the idea that our concept of pain is that of something that plays a certain functional role—of (i) perceiving certain kinds of bodily injury, (ii) triggering changes in an organism's current motivational structure that lead to actions intended to end or minimize the current injury, and (iii) forming or reinforcing desires and intentions to avoid similar injuries in the future. To see why this kind of functional characterization of pain makes a difference, imagine that scientific investigation had given us grounds for believing that every pain of each and every contemporary human being x is a stimulation of x's C-fibers, and every such stimulation is one of x's pains. We would then have reason to believe that (9) is true.

9. For all y, y is a human pain if and only if y is a stimulation of C-fibers.

But we wouldn't, thereby, have reason to believe that (9) was necessary. Perhaps earlier in our evolutionary history human pains were stimulations of a more primitive kind of neurological material, which then played the pain role that the stimulation of C-fibers plays today. If that were so, then (9) would be, at best, a contingent truth. The same conclusion would follow if there was reason to believe that under future evolutionary pressure D-fibers replaced C-fibers. In fact all that is needed to refute the claim that (9) must be necessary, if true, is the mere *possibility* that *human* evolution could have gone, or will go, differently enough to bring it about that something other than C-fiber stimulation plays the pain role in human beings.

In short, facts of the sort we have been considering about what is, and what is not, necessary, do *not* provide conclusive arguments against the claim that certain "mental" phenomena—pains in human beings—are identical with, and hence nothing more than, neurological events that play certain functional roles. A slight variation on these considerations would allow the continued existence of human C-fibers, even though stimulation of them wouldn't play the pain role, because, at the relevant possible state, w, of the world, C-fibers interact with other neural systems in humans not present in human brains in the actual state of the world here and now. Hence, for all we know, there may be genuinely possible states w at which particular C-fiber stimulations that are pains, because they now play the pain role, exist without being pains at w—in which case, *being a human pain* is not, contrary to Kripke, an essential property of any particular human pain. These "possibilities" are, of course, speculative. But since nothing in *Naming and Necessity* tells against them, it is fair to conclude that Kripke's objections to the version of mind-body identity thesis expressed by (9) don't succeed.

WHERE WE STAND

The discussion here has been favorable to the idea that not only pains, but also mental states and processes generally, might be physical states and processes that play functional roles in the lives of sentient agents. That had better be so, if the defense of the psychophysical story of pain in human beings sketched earlier is on the right track. However, defeating the most powerful contemporary philosophical objections to identifying human pains with neurological events doesn't establish the correctness of that identification. Having made free use of other mental concepts—*perception, belief, desire, intention,* and *motivation*—our story is hostage to the soundness of similar stories of these other mental states. Are C-fiber stimulations really *perceptions,* or are they merely physical events that accompany genuinely mental perceptions? It is worth noting that we apply these concepts—*perception, belief, desire,* and the like—only to conscious living things. I can't, for example, imagine any advanced robot constructed along the same lines as those produced by current technology doing more than simulating mental phenomena. Why? What is missing? Until we have convincing answers to these questions, we shouldn't be too quick to assert that the answers must be purely physicalist. Although we may have made some progress, we still haven't gotten to the bottom of the mind-body problem.

COMPUTATION, COGNITIVE PSYCHOLOGY, AND THE REPRESENTATIONAL THEORY OF MIND

The forgoing discussion tracks the transformation of traditional approaches of the mind-body problem into the scientific framework of post-behaviorist psychology. By the early 1960s, academic psychology was emerging from an earlier era dominated by the search for laws connecting environmental stimulus with behavioral response. Since events in the mind or brain had been taken to be beyond the range of scientific observation, postulation of internal causes and effects had been deemed unscientific, and learning had often been understood to be the acquisition of conditioned behavior shaped by rewards. In the emerging new paradigm, minds were coming to be seen as biologically based computers, understood on the model of Turing machines, with functional architectures of connected subsystems processing information, passing their outputs to the next subsystem, and generating a sequence of internal causes and effects mediating sensory input and behavioral output.

In the new framework, the mind is taken to perform computational operations on internal elements—e.g., maps, sketches, or sequences of other symbols—representing objects in the world, their properties, and possible states of affairs relating them to one another. Different cognitive systems—e.g., perception, memory, conscious reasoning—are, to varying degrees, able to interact, contributing informational output to, and receiving input from, other systems. Crucially, the computations connecting informational inputs and outputs don't require the *unexplained intelligence* of an internal interpreter. Rather, they *explain* the intelligence of the agent, whose cognitive architecture is a coordinated system of information-processing and action-generating subsystems. Just as Turing machines can—by performing a sequence of tiny tasks no one of which requires intelligence—solve all problems that can be solved using any intelligent method, so the intelligent mind is thought to be able to do the same sort of thing. Thus, it is hoped, intelligence will be explained, rather than presupposed.

At this point, three objections are likely to be heard. First, while it is all well and good to seek internal explanations of human thought and action, surely, one may assume, the internal causes we seek must be neurological brain processes; there is no cognitive science without neuroscience. To which we respond, "Yes and No." Of course, neurological processes play indispensable causal roles in enabling and shaping the actions we perform, and the thoughts we have. But the actions and thoughts for which we typically seek psychological explanations are those that relate us to realities outside our own skins. How do we acquire, store, and retrieve information about our environment, other people, other places, and other things? How do we learn to recognize people and things that are important to us, to understand and sometimes influence events that affect us, and to shape our actions to achieve our ends? Since the essential function of mind is to relate the individual to the world, the most fundamental question for cognitive psychology is *How does mind manage to represent the world and to devise ways of changing or adapting to it?* Although neuroscience has a role in answering this question, it is a supplement to, rather than replacement for, cognitive psychology.

The second natural objection to the search for internal computational/representational explanations of human cognitive abilities is that it is not obvious where, or how, consciousness fits into the picture. To this it must be conceded that consciousness does remain a mystery. Nevertheless, we shouldn't prejudge how much of our cognitive capacity is due to subconscious representation and computation, and how much isn't. So far the answer seems, from studies of, e.g., the perception of objects, faces, and speech, as well as the use and acquisition of language, "Quite a lot."

The third worry is that there is no way to observe or identify *unconscious* cognitive processes, and so no way to study them scientifically. But, that's not quite right. To take one easily imagined example, we know from the study of proof procedures in logic that it is possible to construct computationally very different procedures all of which recognize the same class of logical consequences. There are systems that economize on axioms, those that economize on rules of inference, those that economize on both, and those that economize on neither. There are even systems that simulate the generation of models that would make the premises true and the purported conclusion false, which when that turns out to be impossible—because the conclusion does logically follow from the premises—always terminate and tell us that. The fact that these systems are computationally very different means that, although they all eventually draw the same conclusions, some proofs that are short, quick, and easy in some systems are long, time-consuming, and laborious in others.

With this in mind, suppose we are confronted with a black box programmed to use one of the systems in drawing inferences. Even if we aren't given the program and can't look inside the box, we can measure the time it takes to reach various conclusions, thereby supporting some hypotheses, and eliminating others, about its internal computational routines. If, in addition, we are given a little information about the programming, and the internal structure of the machine, we may even be able to identify those routines. Think of this as cognitive science for a black box.

In *cognitive psychology* the subjects aren't opaque black boxes. Human biology, genetics, and neuroscience help guide psychologists in devising potentially informative tests in which subjects draw conclusions from information they are given. Imagine a test that asks them what statements follow logically from which others (explaining to them what we mean by this). By noting how long it takes them to decide; when they are right, when they are wrong, when they reach no conclusion; what factors interfere with their decisions; and when in their cognitive development they acquired the tested ability, psychologists can obtain evidence about the unconscious cognitive processes involved. One of the most interesting psychological theories of inference along these lines is presented by Philip Johnson-Laird, in *Mental Models* (1983), which supplements a wide-ranging 1977 state-of-the-art collection, *Thinking: Readings in Cognitive Science,* edited by Johnson-Laird and P. C. Watson.

The philosopher who has done more in the last 50 years than anyone else to initiate, conceptualize, systematize, and advance the representational conception of mind, and how to study it scientifically is Jerry A. Fodor (1935–). The following three of his many books provide a good introduction to his thought: *Psychological Explanation, An Introduction to the Philosophy of Psychology* (1968), *The Psychology of Language* (coauthored with T. G. Bever and M. F. Garrett, 1974), and *Representations* (1981). Here I will say a word about one of the articles, "Propositional Attitudes," that appears in *Representations*.

The article focuses on the "attitudes" belief and desire, in order to illustrate a paradigm for explaining behavior in cognitive psychology. Like nearly everyone else, Fodor assumes that much of our behavior results from our beliefs and desires. As he puts it, "John believes that it will rain if he washes his car. John wants it to rain. So John acts in a way intended to be car washing."[9] Here, the action John performs is attributed to a pair of internal cognitive causes—a belief and a desire, acting in concert. Many of the explanations Fodor seeks fit this picture, and so can be expressed along the lines of (10).

10. X performed action A because (i) X desired it to be the case that S, (ii) X believed that performing A would bring it about that S, and (iii) X believed X could perform A.

In order to provide interesting, scientifically grounded explanations of this sort, cognitive psychology must tell us what belief and desire are.

Like most philosophers, Fodor takes the verb 'believe' to stand for a relation holding between believers, like you and me, and things believed, like *the proposition that the earth is round*, the latter designated by the clause following 'believes' in the sentence 'John believes that the earth is round'. Since this proposition *represents* the earth as having a shape it really does have, it is true. Although it has long been a mystery what exactly propositions are, a new conception of them as representational cognitive acts or operations (sketched in chapter 7) provides something that may be of use to Fodorian cognitive psychology.

The best statement of his chief thesis in "Propositional Attitudes" is (roughly) that an agent *A believes a proposition P (at time) if and only if P is the content of (i.e., the proposition expressed by) a mental representation M in A's mind (at t) and A bears a certain relation—e.g., internally affirming or being disposed to affirm M.*[10] Thus, the relation between the believer and the thing believed is mediated by a cognitive relation to an internal mental representation, which presents the content of the belief in the guise of a formula, a sketch, or a sequence of symbols on which mental calculations are performed. The point of insisting on such a representation is to give cognitive computational processes enough structure to explain *different inferences* drawn from *different mental representations* in cases in which *the propositional contents* of the different internal formulas represent the same things as being the same way, and so are true or false in the same circumstances. Although the new *cognitive conception of propositions*, developed well after Fodor's paper, *reduces* the disparity between the cognitive requirements imposed by his explanations and those imposed by the proposition believed, the new conception may not eliminate the need for further symbolic structure of the sort he imagines, in which case his proposal can accommodate the new view of propositions. Fodor expresses essentially this point about the need for mental representations to mediate the belief relation between agents and propositions in the following passage.

A theory of propositional attitudes specifies a construal of the objects of the attitudes [the things desired, believed, known, etc.]. It tells for such a theory if it can be shown to mesh with an independently plausible story about the "cost accounting" for mental processes [how complex, time consuming, and difficult they are]. A cost accounting function is just a (partial) ordering of mental states by relative complexity. Such an ordering is, in turn, responsive to a variety of types of empirical data, both intuitive and experimental [which can be used to confirm or disconfirm hypotheses about conscious and unconscious mental functioning]. Roughly, one has a "mesh" between an empirically warranted cost accounting and a theory of the objects of propositional attitudes when one can predict the relative complexity of a mental state (or process) from whatever the theory assigns as its object [e.g., the proposition or a symbolic mental representation of it]. . . . [T]o require that the putative objects of propositional attitudes predict the cost accounting for the attitude is to impose empirical constraints on the *notation* of (canonical) belief-ascribing sentences [i.e., sentences which report an agent as believing something]. So, for example, we would clearly get different predictions about the relative complexity of beliefs if we take the object of a propositional attitude to be the . . . [complement] of the belief-ascribing sentence ["John believes *that S*"] than if we take it to be, e.g., . . . [a certain highly complex sentence S* that is a logically equivalent transformation of S].[11]

With this in mind, let us now ask how a psychological theory of the sort Fodor envisions might yield the kinds of explanations of behavior illustrated by (10).

10. X performed action A because (i) X desired it to be the case that S, (ii) X believed that performing A would bring it about that S, and (iii) X believed X could perform A.

It must, he suggests, do so by formulating and confirming general psychological laws of (roughly, and subject to various qualifications) the following form.[12]

11. If any individual x believes that A is an action that x can perform, and if x believes that performing A will bring it about that S, and if x wants it to be the case that S, then x will act in a fashion intended to be a performance of A.

Although there may be something important and correct about this, it is worth noting that claims of the form (11) cannot, in general, be expected to be true, exceptionless generalizations.

The reason for this is easy to see. One can believe that doing A will bring it about that S by affirming (or being disposed to affirm) the mental representation (12) in which *that S* is the propositional content of the mental representation M_1.

12. IF I DO A, THEN M_1

One can, simultaneously, desire *that S* in virtue of bearing an appropriate motivational relation to a mental representation M_2 that has the same propositional content as M_1, despite differing symbolically and computationally from M_1.

Since beliefs and desires relate agents to people and things in the world around them, the propositional contents of their beliefs and desires depend on environmental and other factors external to the agents themselves.[13] Because of this, it can, and sometimes does, happen that mental representations with the same propositional content aren't recognized as having the same content, and so are treated differently.[14] Thus, our agent may feel no motivation at all to do A, despite taking A to be doable and believing that doing it would bring it about *that S,* while at the same time intensely desiring it to be the case *that S.* Cases like this are violations of (11), which show that cognitive psychology cannot reasonably aspire to formulating true, exceptionless, universal laws of this general form.

This should not be cause for alarm. Generalizations like (11) require *all-other-things-being-equal* clauses in any case. Our example suggests that some of these clauses should specify that the agent apprehends the content *that S* in the same way (i.e., via the same mental representations) in the cognitive states that give rise to the relevant beliefs and desires. In addition, whatever questions may arise about the details of the more specific generalizations that are needed, they don't undermine the correctness of many explanations of particular actions caused by beliefs and desires. John may have done A because he wanted it to be the case that S, and he believed that doing A would bring that about, even if not everyone with those beliefs and desires would do A. This is no more mysterious than the fact that John may fall and break his leg because he steps on a banana peel, even though not everyone who steps on a banana peel suffers a similar fate. Thus, the burgeoning enterprise of cognitive psychology today, which owes so much to philosophers and psychologists like Jerry Fodor and Philip Johnson-Laird, will have little trouble surviving the partial breakdown of what some may once have seen as the preestablished harmony between internal representations—needed (Fodor believes) to track and explain the role played by computational processes in our thought and action—and the propositional contents of our beliefs and other cognitive attitudes, which reflect our cognitive relationships to things in the world.

COGNITIVE PSYCHOLOGY, NEUROSCIENCE, AND THE MIND-BODY PROBLEM

As I have emphasized, the contents of the laws and hypotheses of cognitive psychology are not the contents of the laws and hypotheses of neuroscience. The vocabularies used, as well as the concepts and propositions expressed, in the two sciences are different. The same can be said about the relationship between neuroscience and chemistry, and between chemistry and physics. One can think of these sciences as different, but hierarchically related. The objects talked about by each science are real, and the properties ascribed to them are, when all goes well, ones the objects really have. But it is plausible that objects and properties at higher levels of abstraction (somehow) are grounded in those at lower levels, and that all may ultimately be grounded in the kinds of objects and properties recognized by physics.

Sometimes we can discover what is grounded in what—for example, the biological concept of a gene is grounded in the chemical structure DNA. But that is unusual. The individual sciences are, though related, largely autonomous, with their own domains of productive theorizing. Cognitive psychology primarily studies the human mind. But the fact that the mind is an independent domain of study doesn't mean that the things it talks about—beliefs, desires, perceptions (to say nothing of pains)—are unrelated to, or fundamentally different from, those we freely call 'physical'. This is just another way of saying that we still have no final solution to the classical mind-body problem. The good news is that we don't need one in order to continue the progress currently being made by philosophers, psychologists, neuroscientists, and others.

CHAPTER 10

PHILOSOPHY
AND PHYSICS

*The continuity of physical categories over centuries;
the collaboration of philosophically minded physicists
with philosophers trained in physics; Einstein on the
importance of philosophy; the key question: What do the
unobservable parts of physical theories tell us about the
universe?; the eighteenth-century debate over absolute
space and the nineteenth-century statement of Newtonian
theory without it; the abandonment of absolute time in
special relativity; light, gravity, and general relativity;
puzzles and interpretations of quantum mechanics.*

Physics is our most fundamental science. Its task is to explain what the universe is like, including when, how, and
why macro- and microscopic events happen as they do.
Much of this task requires elucidating the central notions
needed for such explanations—time, space, matter, and motion. These were central to the physics of Aristotle, which
remained dominant until the sixteenth century. They remained central, with important modifications, in Newton's
Principia Mathematica at the end of the seventeenth century.
By the early twentieth century, they were still central, despite being radically rethought.

The philosophy of physics is about physics; it attempts
to explain what physics tells us. That may sound strange.
Why do we need a separate study to explain what another
study says? The question, though a good one, is somewhat

misguided. The philosophy of physics is not an area of study distinct from physics. It is a philosophically self-conscious way of doing physics itself. In one way or another, this has always been so. Recall the first sentence of Aristotle's metaphysics, "All men by nature desire to know." Among the things *Homo sapiens* have always most wanted to know is what the vast universe, of which we are such seemingly insignificant inhabitants, is really like, including what it was like before we were here, and will be like after we are gone.

Nearly 2400 years ago Aristotle systematized his thoughts on the subject in his *Physics*. He was followed centuries later by such men as Roger Bacon in the thirteenth century, William of Ockham, John Buridan, and Nicholas Oresme in the fourteenth century, Nicolaus Copernicus, Johannes Kepler, Galileo Galilei, and René Descartes in the sixteenth and seventeenth, and, of course, Isaac Newton in the late seventeenth and early eighteenth century. Some of these men were monks or theologians, some were mathematicians, some were astute observers or experimentalists, and some were all three. But, whatever else they were, all were, in part, philosophers, as the title of Newton's great work, *Philosophiae Naturalis Principia Mathematica,* reminds us. The same is true of Albert Einstein (1879–1955) and several other great physicists of our era. Hence the original name of the subject, *natural philosophy,* still fits.

There are of course very significant differences between professionals whose primary appointments today are in physics labs or departments and those whose primary appointments are in philosophy departments. But this doesn't erase the overlap between philosophically minded physicists and scientifically informed philosophers of physics. The philosophers use tools of conceptual clarification and rigorous evaluation of arguments to reveal potential flaws and presuppositions of important scientific reasoning that, if left unaddressed, may cloud our understanding of physical theories and inhibit their further development. That is why today's philosophers of physics are typically trained philosophers who are also physicists, and why some of the greatest physicists, like Einstein, were self-consciously philosophically minded.

Einstein himself always recognized this. Writing in his autobiography about the importance of his philosophical studies, he says:

> Today everyone knows, of course, that all attempts to clarify this paradox [involving the nature of light that lead to special relativity] satisfactorily were condemned to failure as long as the axiom of the absolute character of time, or of simultaneity, was rooted unrecognized in the unconscious. To recognize clearly this axiom and its arbitrary character already implies the essentials of the solution of the problem. The type of critical reasoning required for the discovery of this central point was decisively furthered, in my case, especially by the reading of David Hume's and Ernst Mach's philosophical writings.[1]

Much earlier, in 1915, Einstein had written something similar in a letter to the scientifically educated philosopher and founder of logical positivism, Moritz Schlick.

> Berlin, 14 December 1915
> I received your paper yesterday, and have studied it thoroughly. It's among the best yet of what's been written about relativity. Nothing nearly as clear has previously been written about its philosophical aspects. At the same time you have full command of the theory itself. . . . Truly masterful is your discussion of relativity theory's relationship to the philosophy of Kant and his

disciples. Their trust in the "incontrovertible certainty" of "a priori synthetic judgments" is badly shaken by the recognition that even a single one of those judgments is invalid. Your exposition is also quite right that positivism suggested relativity theory, without requiring it. Also you have correctly seen that this line of thought was of great influence on my efforts and indeed Mach and still much more Hume, whose Treatise on Human Nature I studied with eagerness and admiration shortly before finding relativity theory.[2]

What Einstein learned from Hume and Mach was not anything specifically about space, time, or motion (though both had many ideas about them, and Hume held that there is no notion of time separate from the motion of bodies). Rather, what Einstein found illuminating was a gap these thinkers made vivid to him—the gap between our habitual ways of thinking, directly but often uncritically derived from sense experience, and the proper concepts needed to truly describe reality. Einstein's debt to these philosophers was not to the contents of their doctrines, but to the inspiration provided by their willingness to rethink and revise even our most basic—seemingly rock-solid—commonsense notions, if doing so would increase our knowledge.[3]

In Einstein's case, the notions to be revised involved our pre-theoretic conceptions of space, time, and simultaneity. What the philosopher in him realized was that no matter how great their everyday utility to us, and no matter how deeply embedded they are in our biologically determined perceptual and cognitive architecture, there is no guarantee that these ordinary notions are well suited to understanding the fundamental structure of the universe. What the great scientist in him realized was that the universe *was* telling us that these notions had to be revised. It is a tribute to his genius that he saw how to do it.

The relationship between *physics* and *philosophy of physics* today is, if anything, closer than it was in Einstein's day. One can get a sense of why this should be so by thinking of physical theories as collections of abstract, mathematically sophisticated representations of reality which, when combined with attested observations, allow us to predict further observable events. When these events occur, the theory is partially confirmed (though not conclusively proved); when they don't occur, it is often necessary to modify the theory that led to false predictions. This way of thinking of theories—as prediction-generating representations of reality—raises three natural questions. Which aspects of the theoretical representation of reality are merely conventional devices adopted to smooth the calculations needed to make observational predictions? Which aspects of the theory are genuinely representational, and so make claims (beyond the directly observable) about the nature of reality? What (beyond the directly observable) do our best physical theories tell us about reality?

One view, formerly far more popular than it is today, dismissed the second and third of these questions by taking theoretical claims about non-observational matters to be mere calculating devices, with no representational content beyond the observational predictions to which they contribute. In the decades since this view has fallen from favor, philosophers of physics and philosophically minded physicists have struggled to answer questions about what our physical theories are telling us about the universe. Physicists themselves differ in the degree to which they are engaged in this enterprise. Some are understandably more concerned with using physical theories to calculate precise solutions to clear empirically stateable problems, while others place an equal priority on conceptualizing what, exactly, the non-directly verifiable aspects of their theories tell us about the world. These are the physicists who interact most deeply with today's philosophers of physics—not, of course, by looking to philosophers for new physical theories, but by working with philosophers of physics to clarify what their own physical theories are telling us (which in turn may spark further improvements).

To illustrate this, I will return for a moment to Newton. In chapter 3 we saw that he accepted absolute space and time in part because it was deeply intuitive and in part because stating physical laws in terms of them allowed him to explain the otherwise puzzling observed behavior of water in a spinning bucket. Thus absolute space and time were not empirically gratuitous constructs. They did, however, give him more structure than he needed, and so generated further puzzles. In Newton's 3-D Euclidean space, a distribution of matter in one portion of absolute space could (in principle) be relocated in a straight line to another location, preserving all relative spatial positions and sizes, without having any effect on the laws of physics. So the question *Where are we in absolute space?* seems to be inherently impossible to answer; similarly for questions about absolute velocities.

Newton realized this. He recognized that as long as we don't introduce new circular motions (like the spinning bucket), or eliminate such motions in the initial state, we can imagine the entire collection of matter moving in a straight line in one direction at a constant speed without changing any of the physical relationships between any of the bodies. This is puzzling because it suggests that no empirical evidence could be brought to bear on the question of which of these states our universe is in.

This was one of the scenarios that generated a spirited debate between the German philosopher and mathematician Gottfried Leibniz (1646–1716) and the British philosopher Samuel Clarke (1675–1729), a younger contemporary of Newton, and one of his defenders. Leibniz dismissed absolute space as an empirically empty fantasy, favoring his own relative conception. Although his system was metaphysical rather than scientific, and so not really a rival to Newton's, and although assuming absolute space helped Newton provide explanations of some observed events, Leibnitz had a point. If certain questions about position in absolute space, and about absolute velocities, can't be answered, or even supported by empirical data, then we might reasonably wonder whether it might be possible for us to replace absolute space in our theories, thereby avoiding unanswerable questions, without loss of explanatory power. If so, perhaps we should.

It is now known that Newton's laws can be translated into a theory that retains absolute time while giving up absolute space.[4] Absolute time is maintained by preserving Newton's linear, numerically measurable structure of moments of time, one following another at a constant rate. Although space remains 3-D Euclidean, there are no points of absolute space persisting through time. Rather, the universe through time is conceived of as a series of simultaneity slabs (one following another in time) each of which consists of a set of space-time moments or events (allowing for events at places in which nothing happens) occurring at a given moment. The space-time points on such a slab stand in measurable 3-D Euclidean relations to one another, even though those on one slab bear no spatial relation to those on other slabs. In other words, there are no common (absolute) spatial locations through time.

Nevertheless, one can trace relative spatial relations between distinct objects that persist through time. Changes in those relations can be visualized by imagining the slabs stacked vertically with lines connecting the occurrences of objects on lower slabs to the occurrences of those same objects on higher slabs (representing later times). The directions and distances between objects on a slab can be compared with those of the same objects on earlier and later slabs, indicating their relative movements over time. An object not subjected to external forces over a given period of time—i.e., a period in which the object, in Newton's original system, would either be at rest or in a state of uniform motion in a straight line—is represented in the new system as following a straight-line trajectory from lower to upper slabs (i.e., no distinction is made between rest and inertial motion over time).

In this framework, Newton's first law tells us that the trajectory (through time) of a body not acted on by external forces is a straight line. His second law says that when a force acts on a body, the trajectory of the body from lower to higher slabs is curved in the direction in which the force is applied, the amount of curvature being proportional to the amount of force applied and inversely proportional to the mass of the body. So, in a variant on the spinning bucket case, two globes connected by a cord and revolving around an axis running through the middle of the cord will remain at a constant distance from one another as they move from earlier to later simultaneity slabs, but their trajectories through space-time will be curved because of the constant force applied to them (as in the left side of the next figure). In this way, one accommodates the accelerated circular motions (rotations caused by the application of a constant force), without having to posit absolute space, thus avoiding the empirical conundrums to which it gives rise.

The next step toward the modern conception of space and time in physics was Albert Einstein's theory of special relativity, presented in his 1905 paper "On the Electrodynamics of Moving Bodies." The theory presented there describes a single inertial frame (where we don't have to consider the motions of any objects other than those within a limited physical system). It targets the notion of temporal

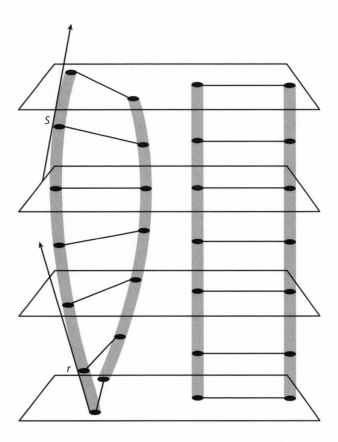

Diagram of rotating (*left*) vs. stationary globes (*right*).
From Maudlin (2012), p. 56.

simultaneity, giving up absolute time along with absolute space, thereby modifying our understanding of simultaneity.[5] One can get a sense of the change by considering how we normally establish the temporal simultaneity of two events occurring at a distance from one another. In daily life we judge two nearby events in our visual field to be simultaneous when we see them at the same time—when light emanating from one impacts our eyes at the same time as light emanating from the other. Since the distances are often short, this method works well for everyday purposes. But when we let the distances of the events from each other, and from the observer, vary, and become arbitrarily great, we need a method that takes into account the fact that the transmission of light from source to observer isn't instantaneous.

The idea can be illustrated by imagining synchronized (ideal) clocks present at the sites of two events A and B located at arbitrary distances from an observer. Each clock starts the moment its paired event occurs. The clocks are then transported to the observer through different paths at different speeds. If the speed of their transmission didn't affect their running, then an observer who knew the distance they traveled and their speeds could simply check their readings when they arrived. If one traveled twice as far but moved twice as fast, identical clock readings would register simultaneity of events.

According to relativity theory, however, the clocks' behavior is affected by their transmission through space.[6] If this sounds incoherent, it is probably because one is thinking of clocks as metaphysical know-not-what's that, by definition, track the passage of time, which, by definition, exists independently of any physical phenomenon. But that thought is unfounded. It's not true *a priori* that there must be such a thing as time conceived of in that way. Rather, the imagined clocks should be thought of as physical mechanisms, and so subject to physical laws. Because of this, it's not obvious that their behavior will be unaffected by their movement through space. Relativity theory maintains that their behavior is affected, thereby questioning the pre-theoretic idea of simultaneity.

Suppose we try to replace this idea with a physically defined notion of simultaneity applying to events at a distance. Let us say that for events at a distance to be physically simultaneous, and so not separated in time, is (essentially) for there to be no possible causal connection (e.g., by light from one reaching the other) between them. The argument of Einstein's 1905 paper shows that although physical simultaneity, so understood, is a symmetric relation (if x is simultaneous with y, then y is simultaneous with x), it's not transitive (x and z may fail to be simultaneous, even though x is simultaneous with y and y is simultaneous with z).

This result is illustrated by a sequence of events—A, B, C, and D—all occurring in that temporal order at point 1 in space, and another event Δ occurring at a spatially distant point 2. Event A is the emission of a ray of light at point 1 that travels to point 2. Its arrival there is event Δ, which, since it took time for the light to make the journey, occurs later than A. The ray is instantaneously reflected back to point 1; its arrival there is event D, which occurs later than Δ. Because the transmission of light is not instantaneous, events B and C, which occur at point 1 after A but before D, can't be connected by rays of light to the occurrence of Δ at point 2. (Since B follows A, light from B can reach point 2 only after Δ has occurred, and since C precedes D, light from Δ can't reach point 1 at the moment prior to D at which C occurs.) So there are no physical relations capable of causally connecting event Δ at point 2 with any events occurring at point 1 after A but before D.[7] This seems to suggest that events B and C at point 1, which occur after A but before D, are both physically simultaneous with Δ at point 2, even though B temporally precedes C.

But that seems impossible. Since we don't want one event to be simultaneous with two temporally nonoverlapping events, one of which is later than the other, we need to adjust our understanding of these relations. One way to do so is to let the relations simultaneous with, before, and after be undefined for pairs one of which is Δ and the other of which is any event in the temporal interval from A to D at point 1. If we do this, then these temporal relations will be physically grounded, but only partially defined. A different way out is to choose a unique event in the range of indeterminacy at point 1 and simply stipulate that it is to count as the event at point 1 that is simultaneous with Δ at point 2. The adoption of such a rule means that the simultaneity relation embedded in the theory will be partially a matter of convention or convenience, rather than a fully objective physical relation.[8] Einstein took the second option, offering a partially conventional synchronization rule for simultaneous events. This allowed him to assign a fixed numerical value to the speed of light, though different values could have been assigned had different conventions been stipulated.

Since, in special relativity, we give up absolute space and time, we must also modify our ordinary notions of motion, distance, and speed. When they are replaced with modified notions, the replacements don't have all the properties of the originals. Instead of independent time and 3-D Euclidean space, special relativity posits a 4-D space-time continuum, made up of points represented by coordinates <t, x, y, z>, each element of which represents an aspect, or dimension, of those points. Although t is called the temporal coordinate and the others are called spatial, the mathematical relations holding between the numerical quadruples that represent events reveal the physical interconnectedness of those dimensions, which is quite different from the independent variability of the dimensions in absolute space and time. This, in turn, yields surprising results involving motion, distance, and time.

One law of special relativity involved in generating these results is the experimentally validated hypothesis that the movement of light in a vacuum is independent of the physical state of its source. In particular, light from two sources moving in opposite directions in a vacuum, each emitting light when passing one another, will arrive at any point in the universe at the same time. This would not be true of two physical objects initially moving in opposite directions, each, at the moment of passing the other, subjected to the same external force in the same direction (i.e., in the direction of movement of one of the two bodies).

Einstein's realization that this is so was a crucial step in the development of special relativity. In "Fundamental Ideas and Methods in the Theory of Relativity, Presented in Their Development," he says, "The phenomenon of magnetico-electric induction caused me to postulate the (special) principle of relativity."[9] According to Maxwell, a magnet at (absolute) rest is surrounded by a magnetic field, but when it moves, the magnetic field changes and an "induced" electrical field comes into being. Since the presence or absence of electric current should, in principle be detectable, the presence or absence of the current should tell us whether the magnet is moving in absolute space. However, Einstein knew that it couldn't play this role, since whether the induced field could be detected depended on whether or not the observer was moving in absolute space in sync with the magnet—something that could not, in principle, be determined.

Einstein's solution was to relativize space and time, thereby making the presence or absence of the electrical field an objective and observable effect of movement of the magnet relative to potential observers, each with their own space-time trajectories. But this posed the further problem of reconciling Maxwell's electrodynamics of light, which Einstein accepted, with relativity. According to Maxwell, light consisted of waves in an electromagnetic field. How, then, should one conceptualize the velocity of light? In the Newtonian framework of the late nineteenth century, the velocity of light from a source moving in the same direction as the source should be the velocity of the source plus the constant velocity of light, which for Maxwell was 186,000 miles per second. (For light from a source moving in the opposite direction one would subtract the velocity of the source from the constant figure for light.) Call this "the emission theory of light." When Einstein gave this up—positing that the state of motion of the light source doesn't affect when light from a point will reach other points—he was able to incorporate Maxwell's theory into special relativity.[10]

Another law of special relativity states that the path of a light ray emitted from a source in a vacuum is a straight line. One can represent this visually in two dimensions with a vertical temporal axis t, a horizontal spatial axis x, and a light-emitting event e at space-time point p. Ignoring the y and z spatial dimensions (and thinking in terms of a flat spatial plane), we may draw two lines from p at right angles to each other, each climbing vertically at a 45-degree angle (so the values of x and t always change by the same increment along the line). Everything between the lines is called e's future light-cone.

The idea that nothing goes faster than light is given by a further law: that the path of a physical entity passing through the future light-cone of an event e never goes

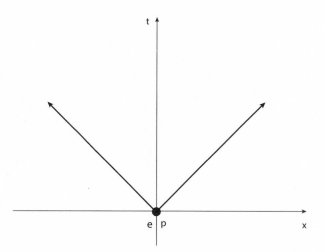

outside e's light-cone (which would require the x-value to change more rapidly than the t-value). To this we may add the relativistic law of inertia: The trajectory of any physical entity (light or a body with mass) not acted on by external forces is always a straight line.[11]

With all this in place, one can get an idea of how time is measured in special relativity theory. Movements are represented by lines, straight or otherwise, connecting space-time points through which something—physical objects or light—passes. The points are represented by four-dimensional numerical coordinates. The interval between two points is given by applying a mathematical formula to the pair of 4-D coordinates assigned to the two points. Given this, we can illustrate the hypothesized relation between time, space, and movement postulated by special relativity.

Suppose a pair of objects A and B are at rest relative to one another at a space-time point o, which, for simplicity, we will assign the temporal coordinate 0 and each spatial coordinate x, y, and z also 0. As explained by Tim Maudlin in *The Philosophy of Physics: Space and Time*, A and B are identical twins each in her own rocket ship.[12] B remains where she is throughout. A does not. By firing her rocket, she moves along the x spatial dimension only, arriving at point p, with temporal coordinate (t) 5, x coordi-

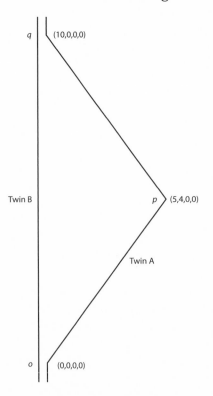

From Maudlin (2012), p. 78.

nate 4, and y and z remaining at 0 (reflecting the fact that she is moving in just one of the three spatial dimensions). A then returns in the opposite x-direction, arriving at point q, where B is located, the temporal coordinate of which is 10, the x, y, and z coordinates 0. (B hasn't moved in any spatial dimension). Visualizing this on a two-dimensional diagram, the line connecting space-time point o where A and B start out with the space-time point q where both end up (B by staying put and A by moving) is a straight vertical line.[13] A's movement from o to p is a straight diagonal line from one to the other; A's movement from p to q is similar, resulting in an isosceles triangle.

The sides of the triangle with vertices o, p, q represent intervals through space-time. The special relativity formula for measuring them is a simple arithmetical computation on the <t, x, y, z> coordinates of the endpoints of the three lines o to q, o to p, and p to q. For each line, the number we get, which measures its spatiotemporal trajectory, is the square root of n, where n is the square of the difference in the temporal coordinates of the endpoints, minus the square of the difference in their x coordinates, minus the square of the difference in their y coordinates, minus the square of the difference in their z coordinates.[14] Since the y and z coordinates are irrelevant in our example, the interval from point o to point q is assigned the square root of 10^2 minus 0, which is 10. The interval of A's journey from point o to point p is the square root—namely 3—of 5^2 minus 4^2 (where 5 is the difference in the t coordinates and 4 is the difference in the x coordinates). Not surprisingly, the interval of A's journey from point p to point q is the same. Thus the measure of A's entire journey from o to q is 6, while the measure of B's journey is 10.

So special relativity tells us that A's journey through space-time is shorter than B's—in fact it is 3/5 of B's. But, what, you may ask, is measured? Time is measured. The time A lived through by first moving away from B to p and the returning to B at q is less than the time B lived through by waiting for A to rejoin her.[15] Thus, although A and B were (we may imagine) exactly the same age when they were together at o, and although both are older at q than they were at o, A is now younger than B. Whatever amount of time B experienced in going from point <0,0,0,0> to point <10,0,0,0>, say 100 days, A experienced ⁶⁄₁₀ of that, or 60 days. If both had accurate clocks with them (whatever physical mechanisms might count as such), A's would register 30 days when reaching p and 60 days when reaching q, while B's would register 100 days while reaching q. In effect, A's clock would tick more slowly than B's. But it would not fail to keep correct time. According to special relativity, both clocks are correct. What the example shows is the essential interdependence, rather than independence, of space and time, and its consequences for our understanding of movement through space and time. This, special relativity tells us, is what space-time is really like, quite apart from how we are intuitively inclined to think of it.[16]

So far, we have simply assumed that clocks in our examples keep correct time. All that can be said at this point about what physical processes count as clocks is (i) that if they are on the same trajectory (moving neither nearer nor further from one another), they will, when synchronized, display the same time and "tick together," (ii) that if they are moving apart (like the clocks of A and B on A's journey away from B), each will seem to the other to be running slow, and (iii) that if they are moving toward one another (like the clocks of A and B on A's journey back to B), each will seem to the other to be running fast (even though overall, A will have expended less time in her journey than B will have expended standing still).[17] Ultimately, of course, these clocks have to be physical entities, which, one can demonstrate by experimental test, will perform as the theory predicts.

Although the experimental tests are difficult and complicated, there have been such demonstrations. The idea is often illustrated by imagining a pair of mirrors, between which a ray of light bounces—each round trip of the light between the mirrors counting as a "tick" of the clock.[18] In order for the mechanism to count as a clock, the intervals measured by each tick must be the same. As Maudlin explains, this condition will be violated unless, as Einstein proposed, the mirrors are connected by a rigid rod as they move through space-time. Without it, special relativity predicts that changes in velocity resulting from a force acting on the two mirrors would lengthen the intervals after the force is applied, destroying the system's ability to function as a clock accurately measuring time for the journey as a whole. According to relativity theory, the rigid rod connecting the mirrors prevents this by physically contracting as the force is applied, pulling the mirrors closer together in just the amount needed to keep the intervals traveled by the light back and forth between the mirrors the same.[19] In other words, the spatial distance between the two mirrors, as measured from the perspective of the original reference frame (before the force was applied), contracts in a way that preserves the length of the intervals traveled by the light. This is the sense in which the speed of light is constant in special relativity, even though there is no absolute space or time to objectively measure speed independent of any frame of reference.

Subjecting special relativity to empirical test is complicated by the fact that the temporal intervals of round trips between mirrors in a laboratory are too short to be reliably measured by ordinary clocks. But the fact that the speed of light is constant in the way predicted by relativity theory can be tested empirically. One such test involves a light source emitted from a spatial location p in line behind a pair of rapidly spinning discs (one behind and at some distance from the other) connected by a rapidly spinning rod. Each disc has a small slit in it through which light might pass. The light source shines on the rear disc, resulting in some light passing through its slit as it spins. If the light passing through reaches the space occupied by the slit in the rotating second disc, the light will pass through it and illuminate the screen behind the apparatus; otherwise it will be blocked by the second disc. By adjusting the speed of the discs, as well as the placement and the angle of the slits, it is possible to put the system into a state in which the light from p always gets through. Relativity theory predicts that this will remain true whether the source emitting light at p is at rest, or is moving toward or away from the apparatus. This has been verified.

A second experiment puts this apparatus on a floating platform that can be turned in any direction, e.g., facing north, south, east, or west. Because of the rotation of the earth and its revolution around the sun, these changes in orientation of the apparatus relative to the earth's rotation, as well as changes in the velocity of the earth's movement around the sun at different times, might—as far as one could know before putting it to the test—result in small changes in the speed of light passing through the slits of the apparatus. If so, the device would have to be recalibrated when its orientation in the laboratory is changed, or when it is used at different times of the year. Special relativity predicts this will never happen, and it doesn't.[20] One can also put the apparatus in motion in a straight line and determine whether the slits have to be adjusted for the light to pass through, depending on whether the light source moves with the apparatus or is stationary relative to it. As predicted by special relativity, they don't.

Einstein's theory of *general relativity*, which emerged ten years after he developed special relativity, introduced a new way of understanding gravity, which was accompanied by a new relativistic conception of the structure of space-time. In the new structure, the shortest distance between two points is a curved line, as it is on the surface of a sphere. In addition, parallel lines that intersect the same line at an angle of 90 degrees may, if extended far enough, intersect one another, just as the lines of longitude on the surface of the earth intersect one another at the poles, despite intersecting the equator at right angles. Nevertheless, Einstein didn't think of space-time as having the uniform geometry of the surface of a sphere. Rather, its curvature is variable. Unlike parallel lines on a sphere, parallel lines on a portion of space-time with a concave curvature can diverge from one another as they are extended. Space-time as a whole was not thought of as having a single type of curvature everywhere.

If the geometry of space-time is, as Einstein says, variable, what determines, or at any rate influences, that variability? The answer is, the distribution of matter in the universe. This is where gravity comes in. As we know, Newton thought of it as a force acting on bodies, proportional to their mass, which changes their trajectories through absolute space and time, pulling them closer together. By contrast, in developing general relativity, Einstein came to think of the mass of material bodies as bending the curvature of space-time itself, proportional to the mass of the bodies. Since light always follows the geometry of space-time, this means that the observed trajectory of light from a distant body will increase its curvature around a massive body in its path, seeming to an observer on the other side of the body to "bend" around it. This fact was experimentally confirmed in 1919 by Arthur Eddington, whose photographs of a solar eclipse demonstrated the bending effect.

Though this was rightly hailed as vindicating general relativity, talk of "bending" shouldn't be misunderstood. In following the locally curved path, light was doing what it always does: moving along the shortest physically possible path in space from one point to another.

More recent observations have provided further confirmation of general relativity. One involves a quasar 8 billion light-years from the earth, with a galaxy 400 million light-years away from us and intervening between us and the quasar. This galaxy, which is a massive collection of matter, bends the space-time through which the light passes, resulting in the appearance to us of a cluster of four images of the same star. In addition, the rotation of the earth has been shown to produce a disturbance in space-time around it, caused, according to general relativity, by rotation of a massive body. This was observed as the change in the axes of gyroscopes in a satellite—Gravity Probe B (GP-B)—in 2004. The principal investigator, Francis Everitt of Stanford University, explained the results this way.

Imagine the earth as if it were immersed in honey. As the planet rotates, the honey around it would swirl, and it's the same with space and time. GP-B confirmed two of the most profound predictions of Einstein's universe, having far-reaching implications across astrophysics research.[21]

One of the most fascinating discussions of the way in which gravity is understood in general relativity involves Richard Feynman's discussion of Galileo's famous experiment showing that the velocity with which bodies of varying masses (e.g., a bowling ball vs. a marble) dropped from a tower are not affected by their mass; except for air resistance, they fall at the same rate and so land together.[22] The reason for this in Newton's framework is that although the gravitational effect on a body by other bodies is proportional to its mass, the resistance of the body to the gravitational effects of other bodies is proportional, in exactly the same degree, to its mass. Hence, these two features of mass cancel each other out, and, Newton explains, the marble and bowling ball hit the ground at the same time.

By contrast, in general relativity the bowling ball and the marble are free of all forces after being dropped, and so follow straight (i.e., shortest) spatial trajectories, much like twin B in the earlier example, who, remaining at rest, was subjected to no forces during A's journey. *In Galileo's case, the tower and any clocks at the top or bottom of the tower continue to be moved by forces deriving from the earth's movement—rather like twin A was moved away from twin B when she fired her rockets.* With this in mind, suppose there are two synchronized clocks at the base of the tower. One, Clock A, remains there; the other, Clock B, is thrown upward precisely when Galileo drops the marble and bowling ball—thrown with just enough force so as to hit the ground the moment the marble and the bowling ball do. Just as twin A's accelerated motion relative to twin B resulted in more time elapsing for B than A between A's departure and return, so, Feynman observes, the account of gravity in general relativity predicts that the accelerated motion of Clock A (on the ground) throughout the flight of Clock B—which, in the second half of its trajectory, is free of forces and undergoes no acceleration—results in more time elapsing for (and being recorded by) Clock B than Clock A. (The same would be true if clocks were dropped along with the bowling ball and marble.) This, it has been reported, has been confirmed.[23]

Up to now, in speaking of Newton, Einstein, and others, I have mostly been concerned with macroscopic objects and events, which came to be understood much better in the twentieth century than they ever had been before. The twentieth century also saw stunning developments in our understanding of the universe at the microscopic level, including atomic and subatomic states and particles. The work of Max Planck and Albert Einstein on radiation and light early in the century was followed by Niels Bohr's theory of the atom, and the mathematical formalisms for describing the subatomic world developed by Max Born, Werner Heisenberg, Erwin Schrödinger, and Paul Dirac. The result was the spectacular success of quantum mechanics in precisely measuring and predicting subatomic events and processes. Paradoxically, this predictive success wasn't matched by a comparable advance in our ability to connect the micro-level of reality with the macro-level, or to even understand what micro-level facts generate the well-attested micro-level predictions we are able to make. Simply put, quantum physics is telling us something about the universe, but we don't yet know what it is.

The point can be illustrated with a simple abstract example. Suppose we arrange for particles of type P to traverse a region of space by one or the other of two possible routes, A and B, from which the particles emerge, continue on, and end up in places C or D. Having the ability to test whether a particle takes route A or B, we wish to know which of the two possible destinations it will arrive at when it takes those routes. So we set up an unobtrusive measuring device that displays 'A' or 'B' depending on which route the particle takes. When we run experiments, we find that 50% of the particles that take route A end up at place C and 50% end up at D. The same is true for route B. So, we are confident that we can turn off the monitor, knowing that running more particles through the region of space will always result in 50% ending at C and 50% ending at D. Surprisingly, however, we are wrong. With the monitor off, 100% of the particles arrive at place C and none arrive at D![24]

How can that be? Surely, one is inclined to think, either there must more than two routes or our measurements monitoring the routes are faulty. It turns out, however, that there aren't more routes and we aren't mismeasuring the particles going through them; every measuring device produces the same results. Thus, we are forced to conclude, measuring the particles somehow changes the reality we are trying to measure. But how? There is no consensus about this among quantum physicists or philosophers of physics.

There is, however, an accepted vocabulary for describing the situation and making probabilistic predictions. In quantum physics it is commonly said that certain properties of a particle don't exist until you measure them—or, at any rate, that it doesn't make sense to say that they have the properties, or fail to have them, until you measure them (at which point they definitely do or definitely don't have the properties). It is not clear what, if anything, is said to exist (prior to measurement), but it certainly *sounds* as if there is a *wave function* associated with the particle (or other entity)—a kind of smear of energy that can be represented by a mathematical function that contains information encoded in positive or negative numerical values.[25] Think of these numbers as measuring the amplitude—height (positive numbers) or trough (negative numbers)—of the wave. From these we calculate the *probability* that an entity has one or another property. The probability is the square of the measurement of the amplitude of the wave, so, in standard cases, the probability calculated from an assignment of a positive number n is the same as that resulting from its negative counterpart −n. As we will see, however, in special cases assignments of n and −n to the same possible outcome cancel out before the final probability is calculated. This is crucial to predicting differences between the behaviors of measured vs. unmeasured particles.

Proponents of the once standard Copenhagen interpretation of quantum physics sometimes seemed to want to say that an *unmeasured* particle (or other entity) has a certain probability of having a given property P, while refusing to say that it either does have P or doesn't have P prior to being measured, and suggesting that both the claim that it does and the claim that it doesn't are meaningless. This challenge to classical logic is troubling, in part because it isn't clear what it would mean to say that the statement "the probability *that x has P* is so-and-so" is true (and hence meaningful), if the claim *that x has P*—to which you have assigned a probability—is either meaningless, or a claim that couldn't possibly be true. It is one thing to assign a probability to a claim one doesn't, and perhaps can't, *know* to be true; it is another to assign a probability to a claim that one takes to be meaningless (or to a claim that one knows *could not possibly be true*).

Things are improved if we modestly revise the above, perhaps incautious, characterization, by saying simply that the claim that an *unmeasured* particle (or other entity) has a certain probability of *being measured as having property P* is true—while continuing to take the claim that it has a certain probability of *being P,* or of *not being P,* to be meaningless. Although this terminological revision doesn't remove the violation of classical logic, at least the claim it makes is not so obviously incoherent. Nor does the revision resolve the mystery of how mere measurement could *bring it about* that the wave function associated with a particle "collapses," and the particle *comes to have* the seemingly independent property of *being P,* or of *not being P.*[26]

With this in mind, let us return to our example of particles traversing different routes, A and B, to final positions C or D. When we measure the routes taken, we find that half the particles observed to travel through route A, and half those observed to travel through route B, end up at position C, while the rest end up at D. But when no measurement of the trajectories takes place, they all end up at C. Quantum physics has a way of accommodating this. Allowing wave functions associated with particles to take negative numbers among their values makes it possible to predict that certain possibilities will cancel each other out in a way that yields determinate results, even though in other cases no such canceling occurs and only probabilities can be predicted.

When, in our example, there is no measurement of particles passing through routes A or B, the wave function assigned to the particle generates a determinate outcome—arrival at position C. This result is reached in roughly the following way. First, the numerical value 0.7071 (which when squared would give us the probability 0.5) is assigned to arriving at C via route A; the same number is assigned to arriving at D via A. Second, 0.7071 is assigned to arriving at C via route B (no surprise), but the value assigned to arriving at D via route B is –0.7071. Because we have positive and negative values assigned to *the same outcome,* namely arriving at D, the rules of quantum mechanics tell us to sum these values before determining the final probabilities. Since their sum is 0, and since 0 squared is 0, we generate the prediction that the probability of arriving at D is 0. This, together with the reinforcing values for arriving at C, results in the prediction that the probability of arriving at C is 100%.[27]

What happens when we *measure* the particles moving through routes A and B? Since we know that measurement affects outcome, the relevant wave function is *not* associated simply with a particle; it is associated with *the pair* consisting of the particle and the measuring device, which, we may imagine, will be in one of two states, displaying 'A' or displaying 'B', immediately after measurement. As before, the wave function gives us numerical values for four states: (i) the value of the state consisting of the particle arriving at C after being correctly measured to follow path A is 0.7071, *0.7071 (particle at C, device measures 'A')* for short, (ii) the value of the state consisting of the particle arriving at D after being correctly measured to follow path A is also 0.7071, *0.7071 (particle at D, device measures 'A')* for short, (iii) the value of the state consisting of the particle arriving at C after being correctly measured to follow path B is 0.7071, *0.7071 (particle at C, device measures 'B')* for short, (iv) the value of the state consisting of the particle arriving at D after being correctly measured to follow path B is −0.7071, *−0.7071 (particle at D, device measures 'B')* for short.

Note the two italicized values involving arrival at D, one positive and one negative. Because the states assigned these amplitudes include *different states of the measuring device*, the states to which the positive and negative numbers are assigned are themselves *different*. Thus, the intrusion of measurement makes it impossible to sum or combine these values. This means that nothing sums to 0 and there is no cancellation, as there was when there was no measurement. As a result, a particle correctly measured as running through A has a probability of 50% of ending at C and a 50% probability of ending at D, and similarly for a particle correctly measured as running through B. This fits our observations: half the particles measured as running through A do end up at C and half end up at D; and half the particles measured as running through B do end up at C and half end up at D.

Getting the mathematics to work out this way was an achievement, which, once systematized and mastered, allowed physicists to make incredibly precise and surprising predictions. *But what reality is described by the assignment of probabilities to quantum states?* How and why does measurement prevent the cancellation of possible outcomes in our example? What physical reality is represented by cancellation vs. non-cancellation? Suppose we think of it this way. States of the particle (in the unmeasured case) and of the particle-measuring device pair (when we measure the routes taken) are physical situations that cannot causally interact with one another. The particle, when unmeasured and left to its own devices, always arrives at position C; physical laws determine this result. But when measurement is introduced we are left with two equally probable possibilities—arriving at C and arriving at D.

If we don't say that measurement changes the laws of physics—as it would seem we shouldn't—then we must say either that measurement introduces some real but previously unimagined element, or that measurement is somehow faulty. One possibility, espoused by the physicist David Bohm, is that some further hidden element, or variable, not caused by the measuring device, but somehow interacting with it, must be involved.[28] A different idea developed initially by Hugh Everett III in his 1957 doctoral dissertation in physics at Princeton has, after decades of neglect, now begun to attract more attention.[29]

Suppose, Everett imagined, that measurement (somehow) causes a single particle-plus-measuring device to split into a pair of such systems—particle p1 + measuring device 1 and particle p2 + measuring device 2. Suppose further that one of these particles reaches C, and is measured by its companion device as doing so, while the other reaches D, while being similarly measured. *We* don't observe the latter because, despite being just like p1, p2 is causally isolated from p1, and so incapable of interacting with p1 in any way at all, *including being observed by us to arrive at D when p1 arrives at C*. From the moment of its creation, p2 is in a part of the universe inaccessible to us and our measuring device. The laws of physics determine that whenever a particle of type P is *measured* passing through routes A or B, a duplicate is created that will arrive at D when the original arrives at C.

That, of course, is not all. Being incapable of interacting with p1, p2 is also incapable of interacting with anything causally related to p1, including us, our measuring device, anything causally interacting with us or our device, anything interacting with anything that interacts with us or our device, and so on without end. In short, certain quantum events, including (but not limited to) those that occur in actual, conscious measurement, open up new dimensions of reality, new "worlds" in Everett's sense, obeying the same deterministic laws as those in our dimension (world). These dimensions can be thought of as populated by "copies" of all entities in our dimension—including us, our measuring device, anything interacting with us or our measuring device, and so on without end. Despite traveling through different futures, these emerging entities share a common history with us and our dimension-mates.

In fact, we may not have to think of any of the elements in different dimensions ("worlds") as copies. Perhaps, after measurement, there is just one particle, just one measuring device, and just one observer, continuing on different futures in the different dimensions. Just as there is no contradiction between my being a young philosopher at t1 and my not being a young philosopher at t2, so there is no contradiction between (i) my observing p1 to arrive at C, and not D, *in dimension 1,* and (ii) my observing p1 to arrive at D, and not C, *in dimension 2.* According to this way of conceptualizing things, when *in dimension n,* I measure a particle going through either route A or route B, I come, *in dimension n,* to observe that particle as ending up at C or D, but not both, while coming, in *dimension n+1,* to observe it at the other of the two. Obviously, this can be iterated when further particles are observed passing through the routes. By contrast, if, in either dimension, I send a particle through without checking the route, I always see it ending up at C. In this way, my experience through the different dimensions will match the predictions derived from quantum mechanics.

This, in oversimplified form, is what is called the "many-worlds" conception of quantum mechanics. Though philosophically and mathematically brilliant, Everett's astounding idea was, understandably, too radical and too underdeveloped conceptually for the establishment physicists and philosophers of his day. However, his idea has been more fully fleshed out over time, and has now become one of the leading interpretations of quantum mechanics. Today, it is defended and elaborated by such luminaries as David Deutsch, professor of physics at Oxford University, David Wallace, professor of philosophy at University of Southern California, and Sean Carroll, professor of physics at California Institute of Technology (Caltech), as well as a number of others.[30] Its growing success appears to be attributable to the facts that (i) the reality it postulates bears a close relationship to the mathematical formalism of quantum theory, allowing it to be read as a straightforward description of the seen, and unseen, world, and (ii) it explains the probabilities predicted by the theory in a way that is consistent with deterministic physical laws. The same cannot be said for other leading interpretations.

Nevertheless, the many-worlds interpretation remains highly controversial, in part because of the profoundly perplexing philosophical issues it raises. For this reason it seems likely that the future debate over what our most advanced physical theory is telling us will be fought out on the common ground occupied by physics and philosophy. That much, at least, shouldn't be surprising. Twenty-four centuries after Aristotle's observation that human beings by nature desire to know, neither the desire, nor the need for philosophical clarification of perplexing possibilities encountered in trying to satisfy it, have lessened in the slightest.

CHAPTER 11

LIBERTY, JUSTICE, AND THE GOOD SOCIETY

Hayek's mid-twentieth-century revival in The Constitution of Liberty *of political and economic philosophy in the spirit of Hume and Smith; John Rawls's* Theory of Justice *and his contemporary Lockean critic Robert Nozick; Gerald Gaus's twenty-first-century proposal in* The Tyranny of the Ideal *for rethinking the central aims and methods of political philosophy; Karl Marx: a cautionary tale.*

Political philosophy today may be reaching a turning point comparable to one that faced the philosophy of science 50 years ago, when it was a single, abstract discipline concentrating on general issues common to the sciences—e.g., the relations between theory and observation, the logic of empirical confirmation, and the nature of explanation. Since then the philosophy of science has evolved into a cluster of specialized inquiries, including several centered on specific sciences—philosophy of physics, of biology, of psychology, etc. As illustrated in chapter 10, this change has brought philosophy closer to individual sciences, facilitating productive interactions between scientifically minded philosophers and philosophically minded natural and social scientists. One might expect, and even hope for, a similar evolution of political philosophy from what has traditionally been its focus on highly general and abstract conceptions of good and just societies into more tightly focused normative investigations of different aspects of societies—their legal systems, their economic and monetary systems, their systems of social stratification, their military and civilian establishments, and their divisions of governmental functions and jurisdictions. Although such an evolution hasn't gotten as far as it has in the natural and the most advanced social sciences, some movement has taken place.

In the next chapter I will separate out contemporary philosophy of law for special treatment. In this chapter, I will counterpose two great classics of twentieth-century political philosophy, *The Constitution of Liberty* by Friedrich Hayek (1899–1992) and *A Theory of Justice* by John Rawls (1921–2002), with a twenty-first-century work, *The Tyranny of the Ideal* by Gerald Gaus, which argues for a new and more empirically focused direction in political theorizing.[1] I will close by examining a historical approach, that of the nineteenth-century philosopher Karl Marx, which contrasts sharply with the twentieth- and twenty-first-century political philosophers with whom the chapter begins.

FRIEDRICH HAYEK: *THE CONSTITUTION OF LIBERTY*

The central concept in Hayek's political philosophy is liberty, by which he means the ability to act on one's own decisions, uncoerced by others. Because a person generally knows his or her own interests and the means of advancing them better than others do, Hayek maintains that a high degree of individual liberty tends to facilitate individual welfare. Since pursuing our goals requires us to make use of goods and services provided by others, it is vital that others be free to acquire, share, and benefit from the knowledge they have acquired. As Hayek observes, virtually everything one does in a civilized society depends on a vast quantity of knowledge that one doesn't possess; the higher the level of civilization, the greater the dependence.

We depend not only on theoretical knowledge acquired through formal education, but also on all manner of practical skills acquired through experience. Both sorts of knowledge often arise from trial and error, in which surprising success is preceded by disappointing failures. This constant experimentation requires the widest possible liberty, consistent with similar liberty for all, to inquire, to plan, and to act without coercing, or being coerced by, others.

Hayek insists that the enormous reservoir of knowledge supporting the continued innovation on which modern life depends is too vast and widely dispersed to be centralized in the hands of any small, ruling elite. Attempts to centralize it can only inhibit the production and sharing of knowledge, threatening future progress and current well-being. Just as the innovations that brought us from the dawn of the industrial age to our present level of civilization were unforeseeable to our forebearers, so the innovations on which our future depends are unforeseeable to us now. Being ignorant not only of what we will most need, but also of what our evolving conception of the good will demand, we must, Hayek thinks, be free to improvise without closing off what may prove to be viable options. For Hayek, all institutions, from family to government and everything in between, change both the conditions and the knowledge on which those institutions depend, and are in turn changed by those new conditions and that new knowledge. Since we can't predict what an ideally good and just society will look like, let alone plot a course to it, we must preserve maximum freedom to innovate.

Freedom to innovate means freedom to fail as well as to succeed. Because success is rewarded but failure isn't, liberty generates inequality. Though admittedly a problem to be dealt with, in part by the provision of a social minimum, Hayek takes inequality itself to be necessary to produce unprecedented benefits for all in the future.

[N]ew knowledge and its benefits can be spread only gradually. . . . It is misleading to think of those new possibilities as if they were, from the beginning, a common possession of society which its members could deliberately share. . . . [New knowledge] will have to pass through a long course of adaptation, selection, combination, and improvement before full use can be made of it. This means that there will always be people who already benefit from new achievements that have not yet reached others.[2]

What today may seem extravagance or even waste, because it is enjoyed by the few . . . , is payment for the experimentation with a style of living that will eventually be available to many. The range of what will be tried and later . . . become available to all, is greatly extended by the unequal distribution of present benefits. . . . If all had to wait for better things until they could be provided for all, that day would in many instances never come. Even the poorest today owe their relative material well-being to the results of past inequality.[3]

The empirical basis for his position is given by the graph and table on the next page illustrating the recent effectiveness of free market economics when compared to the rest of human history.

Although Hayek's concern with the elimination of *absolute poverty* is admirable, one might object that he neglects the unhappiness caused by *relative poverty*. He doesn't. Poverty, he notes, in the most advanced societies, has

become a relative, rather than an absolute, concept. This does not make it less bitter. Although in an advanced society the unsatisfied wants are usually no longer physical needs, but the results of civilization . . . at each stage some of the things most people desire can be provided

GDP/PER CAPITA IN 1990 U.S. DOLLARS

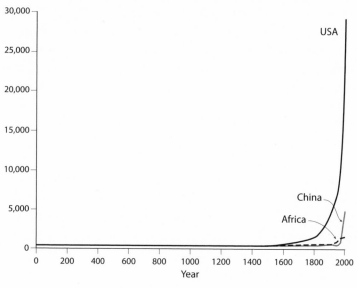

From Moller (2014), p. 97.

GROUP	LIFE EXPECTANCY AT BIRTH (AT 20)
Modern foragers	30s (40s)
Italian magistrates, 223 CE	25 (33)
England 1550–1599	38
Pre-industrial England 1750–1799	20 (34)
USA 1850	38
USA 1900	48
USA 1950	68
USA modern	77

From Moller (2014), p. 98.

only for a few. . . . Most of what we strive for are things we want because others already have them. Yet a progressive society . . . recognizes the desire it creates only as a spur to further effort. It disregards the pain of unfulfilled desire aroused by the example of others. It appears cruel because it increases the desire of all in proportion as it increases its gifts to some. Yet so long as it remains a progressive society, some must lead, and the rest follow.[4]

Sometimes we see others enjoying things we had no idea anyone might possess, and so come to desire them ourselves, simply for the pleasure or good they would bring us. At other times, however, our relative deprivation is infused with envy, resentment, and a strong desire to strip the relatively advantaged of their socioeconomic superiority. Insofar as the pain of relative poverty stems from an unfulfilled desire of the first sort, it is, as Hayek observes, the inevitable price to be paid for pursuing the quickest and most effective means of diminishing human misery and spreading previously unimagined benefits to more people. But insofar as this pain is the product of envy and a fiercely resented lack of social status, he suggests, it can never be eliminated, but only managed and minimized.

Unlike the desire for material advantages, the desire for status is a zero-sum game; A's increased status can't be had without B's loss. Since desire for status is among the most persistent human emotions, the best way to manage it is to encourage many status hierarchies based on a variety of human excellences, thereby increasing an individual's chances of being highly rated on some. An open, experimental society that prizes liberty while accommodating different, multifaceted but overlapping conceptions of the good, advanced by different social groups, is well positioned to do this.

With this variety in mind, we turn to Hayek's understanding of *equality, value,* and *merit*. For Hayek, *equality* includes *the equality of moral agents, equal respect for our common human dignity, equality before the law* in roughly the (ideal) sense of Anglo-Saxon jurisprudence, and a reasonable sense of *equal opportunity*. Equality before the law requires the objective, nondiscriminatory enforcement of laws made for the common good, the protection of natural liberties for all, and the equal freedom from coercion by others. Equal opportunity requires the freedom to compete for social and economic rewards without the imposition of artificial legal barriers by the state. If this is all one means by *equal opportunity,* then Hayek is a believer. But if *equal opportunity* is understood as requiring all to have an equal start in life and equal prospects of succeeding in whatever they choose, he isn't. On the contrary, he regards this conception of *equal opportunity* as incoherent, because there is no way to equalize genetic inheritance or environmental circumstance. Even worse, he argues, attempts to implement a utopian conception of equality of opportunity by penalizing the naturally advantaged while favoring the less advantaged (beyond the provision of a social minimum) will, by undermining liberty, diminish the intergenerational welfare of all.

The demand for *equality of result* is subjected to a similar critique. One strand of Hayek's critique holds that the plurality of different human goods renders the idea of using public policy to equalize them absurd. Hayek hints at this in saying that the idea would "mean that it is the responsibility of the government to see to it that nobody is healthier, or possesses a happier temperament, a better suited spouse, or more prospering children than anyone else."[5] The second strand of his critique is that equalizing prospects for all negates individual responsibility. Finally, he argues that a policy of equalizing results destroys liberty and so makes future progress impossible.

He also rejects the idea that justice requires that material rewards should be proportional to moral merit. On the contrary, he argues,

> in a free system it is neither desirable nor practicable that material rewards should be made generally to correspond to what men recognize as [moral] merit and . . . it is an essential characteristic of a free society that an individual's position should not necessarily depend on the views of his fellows about the merit he has acquired.[6]

> In our individual conduct we generally act on the assumption that it is the value of a person's performance and not his merit that determines our obligation to him. . . . In our dealings with other men we feel that we are doing justice if we recompense value rendered with equal value, without inquiring what it may have cost the individual [in time, money, effort] to supply us with these services. What determines our responsibility is the advantage we derive from what others offer us, not their merit in providing it.[7]

Hayek's distinction between the value we gain from our transactions with others and the moral merit of those who provide goods or services is well taken. Some with whom we interact have natural gifts—inherited intelligence, beauty, or athletic, musical, or artistic talent—for which they are not morally responsible. Others have benefited from a rich and nurturing environment not of their own making. Either way, the possession of their socially desirable traits may allow some to produce—without unusual effort, motivation, or sacrifice—goods and services of great enough value to others to be richly rewarded. By contrast, those with lesser gifts may exert themselves in a highly praiseworthy way, while failing to produce anything of comparable value. Individuals who have intimate knowledge of a few members of both groups may, of course, offer the latter friendship and respect they don't offer the former. Nevertheless, there is no systematic way for the social, political, and economic system to bring material rewards into line with moral merit.

We don't, of course, all agree about what moral worth is. But even if we did, we would lack the intimate knowledge needed to make economic success proportional to it. Hayek adds that the social cost of attempting to align the two more closely might prove to be psychologically devastating to those who don't rank highly on the coordinated scale.

A society in which it was generally presumed that a high income was proof of merit and a low income of the lack of it, in which it was universally believed that position and remuneration corresponded to [moral] merit, in which there was no other road to success than the approval of one's conduct by the majority of one's fellows, would probably be much more unbearable to the unsuccessful ones than one in which it was frankly recognized that there was no necessary connection between [moral] merit and success.[8]

Despite his objections to expansive interpretations of equality as a social norm, and his objections to attempting to link material rewards to moral worth, he sometimes seems to endorse the idea that material rewards earned by individuals in a free society are, and ought to be, closely correlated with *the value they produce for society*. Recognizing that society needs to motivate agents to do what produces the most social value, Hayek suggests that material rewards are, rightly, closely correlated with social value produced.

If the remuneration [for one's efforts] did not correspond to the value that the product of a man's efforts has for his fellows, he would have no basis for deciding whether the pursuit of a given object is worth the effort and risk.[9]

The market will generally offer for services of any kind the value they will have for those who benefit from them.[10]

It is not clear that this is defensible. In (relatively) free societies, income is correlated with the amount of money people (in the aggregate) are willing to pay those who provide goods and services they desire. Because of this, one imagines that if (i) the income needed to offer workers to produce social goods of equal value were always themselves equal, (ii) each individual were a reliable judge of what was truly valuable to him or her, and (iii) total social good were a simple aggregate of all individual good, then a general correlation between income and value to society might be both normatively desirable and roughly achievable in a free society. But (i) is likely to be false, (ii) is doubtful, and (iii) may be hard to establish.

To see the implausibility of (i), imagine two things, widgets and gidgets, the social value of which to a community are large but equal. Although individuals in the community need just one of each, many workers are capable of making widgets but very few are capable of making gidgets. Since it is necessary to offer a larger financial incentive to attract the needed gidget-makers away from other possible pursuits than it is to attract the needed widget-makers, the income of the former will exceed that of the latter, despite the fact that what each produces is of equal social value.[11]

In the case of (ii), it seems clear that most of us—myself included—are not terribly reliable judges about what is best for us. Many decisions we make turn out to be counterproductive. Sometimes this is so because we are ignorant of the means needed to achieve our ends. At other times it is so because of our misguided or insecure grasp of what our own most important ends really are—i.e., of what, ultimately, would be best for us. This all-too-human ignorance doesn't mean we should turn our decisions over to others. In most cases, no one else knows what, all things considered, is better for us than we do ourselves, and no one cares about maximizing our good as much as we do. Regarding (iii), it goes without saying that no philosopher-king knows this about any of us, let alone how to maximize the aggregate good for all. In light of this, it is hard to see how the proposition that *in a just society one's income, and other material rewards, should correspond to the amount of social good for which one is responsible* could ever be established.

The best conclusion for one who, like Hayek, prizes liberty is the one drawn by Robert Nozick (1938–2002): *there is no rule determining the just distribution of income or wealth to individuals based on their needs, their merit, the value of their contributions, their efforts, or on any combination of these, or similar, factors.*[12] There can be no such rule because liberty subverts patterns. In any society that values liberty—including the liberty to dispose of assets to which one is entitled, without harming or coercing others—there will be many ways of legitimately acquiring, losing, or transferring material advantages which, when allowed to operate, will subvert any distributive norm.

As Nozick observes, the total set of material holdings at any one time results from activities in which

> some persons receive their marginal products [the amount generated by the work they do], others win at gambling, others receive a share of their mate's income, others receive gifts from foundations, others receive interest on loans, others receive gifts from admirers [or inheritances from relatives], others receive returns on

investments, others make for themselves much of what they have, others find things, and so on.[13]

Because of this variety, there is no way to normatively correlate wealth and income with any foreseeable set of social characteristics. Suppose, for *reductio*, that some distributive norm DN is correct. Suppose the distribution of wealth and income satisfies DN at time t, and so is just; everyone is entitled to his or her material possessions at t. Being entitled, each is free to use or dispose of them—to devote them to oneself, to feed one's passion for gambling, to donate them to causes one supports, to give them to loved ones, or to invest for profit. Since each is entitled to act in these ways, those who gain from the transactions—whether oneself or others—are entitled to what they get. Although this may produce a new distribution that violates DN, the way the new distribution arose guarantees that it must be just, thereby falsifying DN. In short, no distributive norm can be accepted without rejecting either (a) that one is free to use or dispose of what one is entitled to in ways that don't harm or coerce anyone, or (b) that one who receives assets in this way from one entitled to them thereby becomes entitled to them. Since Hayek accepts (a) and (b), he should accept Nozick's conclusion.[14]

Nozick illustrates his point in the following famous passage of his book. He begins by assuming that some norm D1 of just distribution is correct.

> Now suppose that Wilt Chamberlain is greatly in demand by basketball teams. . . . He signs the following sort of contract with a team. In each home game, 25 cents from the price of each ticket of admission goes to him. . . . [P]eople cheerfully attend his team's games; they buy their tickets, each time dropping a separate 25 cents of their admission price into a special box with

Chamberlain's name on it. . . . [I]t is worth the price of admission to them. . . . [I]n one season one million persons attend his home games, and Wilt Chamberlain winds up with $250,000, a much larger sum than anyone else has. Is he entitled to this income? Is this new distribution D2 unjust? If so, why? There is *no* question about whether each of the people was entitled to the control over the resources they held in D1. . . . Each . . . *chose* to give 25 cents of their money to Chamberlain. . . . If D1 was a just distribution, and people voluntarily moved from it to D2, transferring parts of their shares they were given under D1 (what was it for if not to do something with), isn't D2 also just? . . . Can anyone else complain on grounds of justice?[15]

JOHN RAWLS: *A THEORY OF JUSTICE*

The reception of Rawls's 1971 classic in the social sciences and in analytic philosophy was far greater than that of Hayek's *The Constitution of Liberty*. In philosophy there was nothing to match it in the previous 100 years. Its enthusiastic reception was due in part to a decades-long eclipse of influential normative inquiry in analytic philosophy that Rawls helped bring to an end, and in part to the philosophical support he lent the dominant ideology of the liberal welfare state.[16] But mostly, the reception was due to the erudition and argumentative effort he marshaled to support that vision.

Rawls saw modern society as an intricate web of social cooperation from which we all benefit enormously, when measured against life outside society in a Hobbesian or Lockean state of nature. Since we are all moral equals and everyone depends on the cooperation of others, Rawls reasoned, each of us should have equal weight in establishing the fundamental rules allocating the burdens imposed by social cooperation and the benefits resulting from it. The most important of these were, he thought, rules governing the scope of individual liberties and the distribution of wealth. Because the rules must be backed by force, limiting one's liberty to act in one's own interest, they must be justified in ways agents would endorse. Thus, he searched for rules allocating benefits and burdens that would be unanimously adopted by rational, self-interested agents in a fair decision procedure.

The rules he arrived at are (i) and (ii), with (i) given priority over (ii).

(i) Each person is to have an equal right to the most extensive basic liberty compatible with a similar liberty for all.

(ii) Primary goods like wealth and income (which are advantageous no matter whatever else one may want) are to be distributed throughout the population to maximize the position of the least advantaged members of society, and to be derived from offices and positions filled by fair competition under conditions of equality of opportunity.

Rawls's attempt to derive (i) and (ii) rests on a conception of a *fair* procedure for deciding the terms of our shared social contract. It would, he thinks, be *unfair* for one to insist on terms favoring oneself due to anything one doesn't deserve. Since no one antecedently deserves one's biologically inherited traits (good or bad), or characteristics arising from one's (fortunate or unfortunate) childhood and adolescent environment, it would, Rawls thinks, be unfair for those who are ambitious, energetic, intelligent, creative, industrious, artistic, kind, honest, talented, or attractive in any socially desirable way, to bargain for a social contract rewarding these things. Why, after all, should others who are, through no fault of their own, ranked low on these dimensions agree to such a deal? Lacking the social capital needed to bargain with those who have more to bring to the deal, these less fortunately endowed agents would have little choice but to accept the terms dictated to them. Although this might lead to an agreement of sorts, it would not, Rawls thinks, arise from a *fair decision procedure,* and so would not yield *fair and neutral principles of justice* by which everyone could be expected to live.[17]

This conception of fairness leads him to pose the problem of justice as one in which agents in "the original position" deliberate the terms of a social contract behind *a veil of ignorance* without knowing any particular facts about themselves.

> We want to define the original position so that we get the desired solution. If a knowledge of particulars is allowed, then the outcome is *biased* by arbitrary contingencies. . . . If the original position is to yield agreements that are just, the parties must be *fairly* situated and treated equally as moral persons. The *arbitrariness* of the world [e.g., of biological and environmental factors that lead individuals to have different qualities] must be *corrected*.[18]

> Somehow we must nullify the effects of specific contingencies which put men at odds and tempt them to exploit social and natural circumstances to their own advantage. Now in order to do this I assume that the parties are situated behind a veil of ignorance. . . . [N]o one knows his place in society, his class position or social status; nor does he know his fortune in the distribution of natural assets and abilities, his intelligence and strength, and the like. Nor, again, does anyone know his

conception of the good, the particulars of his rational plan of life, or even the special features of his psychology such as his aversion to risk or liability to optimism or pessimism . . . I assume that the parties do not know the particulars of their own society. . . . [T]hey do not know its economic or political situation, or the level of culture it has been able to achieve. The persons in the original situation have no information as to which generation they belong. . . . [T]he only particular facts the parties know is that their society is subject to the circumstances of justice [e.g., that there are scarce resources and that social cooperation is needed to exploit them]. . . . [T]hey [also] know the general facts about human society . . . the principles of economic theory; they know the basis of social organization and the laws of human psychology.[19]

The obvious upshot is the exclusion of all characteristics that distinguish one person from another. This transforms Rawls's decision-making process from what is sometimes described as a *social task* in which real people try to find mutually acceptable terms of interaction into the *solitary task* of a rational, self-interested, genderless, Kantian cipher choosing a social future despite knowing nothing about itself except that it is member of a species described by certain scientific laws. Having purified the agent, Rawls believes that *whatever rules it chooses must be just because the decision procedure used to derive them is fair.*

Two further abstractions are imposed. Rawls requires his rational, self-interested agent, or agents, to be free of envy, and of any concern, positive or negative, for the welfare of others. Envy is excluded because agents in the original position are assumed to be rational, and rationality tells us that envy makes one worse off.[20] The exclusion of affection for others is more complex.

Once we consider the idea of a contract theory it is tempting to think that it will not yield the principles we want
unless the parties are to some degree at least moved by
benevolence. . . . [But] the combination of mutual dis-
interest and the veil of ignorance achieves the same purpose as benevolence. *For this combination of conditions
forces each person in the original position to take the good of
others into account.*[21]

This may seem puzzling. Although those in the original
position don't know what they will most value when they
enter society, they nevertheless seek to maximize their
acquisition of primary goods, which are assets that will
allow them to advance whatever their ultimate ends turn
out to be. This—apart from any concern for or against the
well-being of others—is the only concern guiding their
choice.

The assumption of mutually disinterested rationality,
then, comes to this: the persons in the original position try to acknowledge principles which advance their
system of ends as far as possible. They do this by attempting to win for themselves the highest index of primary social goods, since this enables them to promote
their conception of the good most effectively whatever
it turns out to be. The parties do not seek to confer benefits or to impose injuries on one another; they are not
moved by affection or rancor. Nor do they try to gain
relative to each other; they are not envious or vain. . . .
[T]hey strive for as high an absolute score as possible.[22]

How are agents in the original position *forced to take the
good of others into account?* There is one, almost trivial, sense
in which they must. Since they have no idea who they will
be once the veil of ignorance is lifted, they cannot afford to

ignore the good of anyone in the societies they are considering, lest they risk ignoring their own good. Still, I think Rawls has more in mind. He attaches great importance to the fact that those in the original position are *presumed* to be capable of *a sense of justice*.[23]

> [The presumption] means that the parties can rely on each other . . . to act in accordance with whatever principles are finally agreed to. Once principles are acknowledged the parties can depend on one another to conform to them . . . their capacity for a sense of justice insures that the principles chosen will be respected. . . . If a conception of justice is unlikely to generate its own support [i.e., if a society organized around it wouldn't win the allegiance of its citizens] . . . this fact must not be overlooked. . . . [The parties] are rational in that they will not enter into agreements they know they cannot keep, or can do so only with great difficulty. . . . Thus in assessing conceptions of justice the persons in the original position are to assume that the one they adopt will be strictly complied with.[24]

In short, Rawls assumes that agents in the original position would not choose any principles that would, if implemented, be widely rejected or disregarded by real self-interested people who know their interests and the social positions they occupy.

This constraint supplies two potential sources of support for the contention that those in the original position must take a robust interest in the good of others. First, *if Rawls is right that deliberation in the original position represents an ideally fair procedure*, then those in the original position will recognize the principles of justice they choose as fair. They will, for that very reason, believe that each citizen in a society organized around the principles will be able to see that his or her own good is protected to the maximum degree consistent with justice. Second, since those in the original position know the laws of human psychology, they know how zealously human beings promote their own interests, while also realizing how attached parents and children, husbands and wives, and friends and loved ones can be. Thus, those in the original position won't select rules obedience to which would require citizens to forswear vigorous attempts to advance themselves or to severely restrict their ability to benefit those who are near and dear in order to benefit unknown strangers.

Given all this, we now turn to Rawls's argument that his two principles would be chosen in the original position. The chief competitor to his principles ranks societies by average possession of primary goods; the more the better. This competitor can seem attractive if one judges the likelihood one will end up at or near the median to be greater than the likelihood one will be among the least advantaged. Nevertheless, Rawls believes agents in the original position won't opt for societies with greatest average utility. Knowing nothing about how likely they are to end up in any social category, and nothing about the wealth of the society they will enter, or the liberties it recognizes, they can't rule out the possibility that the least well off may be desperate, even if life at the median is comfortable. In addition to crippling poverty, those at the bottom might have no liberty.[25] They might also have descendants to worry about. Rawls remarks on "the desire to have one's decision [in the original position] appear responsible to one's descendants who will be affected by it."[26]

> We are more reluctant to take great risks for them than for ourselves; and we are willing to do so only when there is no way to avoid these uncertainties; or when the probable gains, as estimated by objective information, are

so large that it would appear to them irresponsible to have refused the chance offered even though accepting it should actually turn out badly.[27]

Thus, Rawls imagines, agents in the original position would seek to guarantee their liberty and maximize their welfare, even if they turn out to occupy the lowest levels of society.[28]

Finally, he returns to the idea that the principles adopted in the original position must be ones we could honor *no matter what social circumstances we find ourselves in.*

[The parties] cannot enter into agreements that may have consequences they cannot accept. . . . A person [in the original position] is choosing once and for all the standards which are to govern his life prospects . . . there is no second chance. Moreover, when we enter an agreement we must be able to honor it even should the worst possibilities prove to be the case.[29]

Since those in the original position could not in good faith agree to a social contract based on average utility, though they could agree to one based on his principles (i) and (ii), Rawls concludes that those principles would be chosen. He can't *demonstrate* this because the original position, which includes knowledge of the sciences, can't be stated precisely enough to provide proof. But the informal case he makes is plausible enough to be worth subjecting to closer scrutiny.

What makes principle (ii) seem reasonable is the vast ignorance of the parties in the original position. Since severe misery and extreme poverty for some aren't ruled out in societies under consideration, it may seem reasonable that those in the original position would try to minimize their plight if they turn out to find themselves at the bottom. Whether or not rationality *dictates* this risk-averse strategy is debatable; at least it isn't obviously unreasonable. But it's also not unreasonable to sacrifice principle (i), ensuring maximum individual liberty for all, if doing so would mitigate the misery one would suffer if one were badly enough off. Thus, it's hard to make the case that those in the original position would choose *both* (i) and (ii). Perhaps they would choose (ii) while swapping (i) for a principle that merely outlawed slavery. This would violate the priority that Rawls assigns to (i), but it is hard to see how the choice he sets up in the original position would exclude it.[30]

However, the worst problem with Rawls's discussion is his supposition that any principles chosen in the original position *must be just* because that process is *fair*. Rawls designed the process to reflect his unargued assumption that all socially desirable characteristics, including *"even the willingness to make an effort, to try, and so to be deserving in the ordinary sense,"* are ultimately undeserved, from which he concluded that there is no morally significant notion of *desert* or *entitlement* antecedent to an all-encompassing theory of political justice to which that theory must conform.[31] Instead, he took it for granted that our ordinary notions of entitlement and desert are conceptually dependent for their justification on a comprehensive and antecedently justified theory of political justice. This, I believe, is back to front.

Presumably, Rawls thought that all socially desirable characteristics are ultimately undeserved because he took their causal antecedents to include biological and environmental factors outside of one's control. *If to deserve x one must do something to bring x about*, then, of course, we don't deserve our genetic inheritance or our early environment, which together determine who we are. Since we did nothing to bring it about that our parents loved and supported us, we didn't, in the relevant sense, *deserve* their love and support, or anything else stemming from them, including their genes. But the trivial sense in which this is so has little, if any, moral significance.

Did our parents have a duty to love and support us, independent of their duties to society as a whole? Yes. Were they *entitled* to *give us* their love, time, energy, guidance, and some of what they had saved? Of course they were. Since they were entitled to do what they did, we are entitled to use what they gave—first to develop the socially desirable skills and traits they hoped to instill in us, and then to put those skills and traits to work to benefit ourselves and others without harming or coercing anyone. Because we live in a society with others with whom we are not acquainted, we may be morally constrained to devote some of our efforts to assist them. But this is a far cry from Rawls's claim that one's natural gifts and socially desirable traits are the common property of all.[32] They are parts of oneself to which one has a prior, though not unlimited, right to profit from as one sees fit.

Because Rawls misses the primacy of such pre-political entitlements, his argumentative strategy threatens to self-destruct. Fairness, his supreme evaluative notion, is far from our only way of valuing others. We also recognize a duty not to harm innocent others simply because they are human beings (whether members of our society or not). In many cases, we are prepared to go further—to assist strangers when doing so may be important to them without being onerous for us. In short, we recognize the presumptive moral value of innocent others, while presuming that their welfare deserves some respect. However, when we move beyond this broad but mild benevolence, the desirable or undesirable characteristics of other people, though ultimately "undeserved" in Rawls's extraordinary sense, *always matter* to our morally significant relationships with them.

Although real fairness is one component of our moral outlook, Rawlsian fairness isn't. As ordinarily understood, *fairness* involves cooperative activities, relationships, and agreements that give rise to reciprocal expectations, which, in turn, generate duties. Not all agreements do. Under certain conditions, implacable enemies—imagine human beings versus space invaders—could reach agreements that each would find advantageous, without in any way valuing the welfare of those on the other side. If such agreements were vigorously monitored, each side might have purely self-interested reasons to abide by them simply to avoid retaliation. But since genuine *moral duties* aren't generated, questions of fairness wouldn't arise.

They do arise when the parties are presumed to be moral equals in the modest sense I have sketched. Then, one is morally obligated to bargain in good faith, not to lie or mislead, not to agree to terms one is unwilling to honor, or to break agreements one has made, even if one's breach were to go undetected. Although Rawls recognizes this, his conception of fairness goes much further. Though it is part of his conception of fairness, it is no part of our normal conception that parties to a voluntary agreement *aren't* allowed, should they so choose, to condition their participation in a cooperative, rule-governed, activity or relationship on receiving benefits roughly proportional to the value they bring to it. Nor is it part of the ordinary conception of fairness, though it is part of his, that participants in such an activity or relationship should be committed to *maximizing* the advantages of some individuals, no matter how little they have, or are willing, to offer others.

In short, fairness is a pre-political social notion that must be understood before the basic principles for organizing the justice of a complex society can be established. To understand fairness, we need to understand how it is

connected to the value we place on others and our relationships with them. We don't interact with Kantian ciphers.
When we interact with people, the strength, the extent,
and the nature of our desire to be fair—indeed, our very
conception of what being fair, in the circumstance, consists
in—is conditioned by what we value, by those with whom
we are dealing, and by what each of us may reasonably expect from the other. What fairness requires in a given situation depends on the nature of the interaction, the social
connections of the parties, their needs, and the antecedent
entitlements generated by their assets and advantages. If
a more abstract notion of fairness is to be included in a
theory of justice for society, it must somehow incorporate
these features of ordinary instances of fair dealing; it must
factor them into the calculation of the overall justice of a
society. Since the original position was designed not to do
this, the Rawlsian decision procedure based on it is not
an ideally fair procedure for allocating social benefits and
burdens.

If this is right, then Rawls's principles (i) and (ii)
wouldn't be justified by showing that they would be chosen by agents in the original position (even if that could
be shown). What about the principles themselves? What,
independent of the original position, can be said for or
against them? Principle (i), which stipulates maximum
liberty for all, recognizes the fundamental value of liberty in human life, while implicitly incorporating the wisdom that wealth creation—along with medical, scientific,
technological, and intellectual advance—requires relatively
free markets, the rejection of a command economy, and the
broad freedom to inquire and experiment. Hayek could not
agree more. Though principle (ii) raises some problems, one
aspect of it—the idea that some sacrifices by the more advantaged are required to aid the less advantaged—is not
unreasonable, and indeed, if properly implemented, may

enhance social solidarity in a way that benefits the society as a whole. To this extent, there is a good deal to be said on behalf of Rawls's vision.

Nevertheless, it isn't the social or political ideal. The flawed conception of fairness that provides the rationale for principle (ii) is one which would, I think, be widely rejected by many who clearly understood it—thereby increasing discontent and instability in a society organized around it. Because of this, implementing it would be contentious, while also presenting daunting, and perhaps insoluble, practical and theoretical problems. How, for example, are the "least advantaged" to be identified? Are they those with the lowest *income* in a given period, the lowest *income plus wealth*, the lowest *income plus wealth corrected (somehow) for health, age, location, marital status, and other family obligations*, the lowest *income plus wealth, even further corrected by one's occupation (including its inherent danger, desirability, or opportunity for future advancement)*, the lowest *income plus wealth, still further corrected by available free time and free access to facilities provided by other private parties*, and so on? Since each of these criteria could be expected to gain its own political constituency, the practical problems posed by implementation of principle (ii) might well lead to social conflict.

There is also a theoretical problem: we don't know how to compare, weigh, and aggregate the different goods that make up total well-being. As we saw in chapter 8, we can measure not only what alternatives a *single individual* prefers to other alternatives, but also *how much more* the individual prefers them to others. But, as Rawls recognizes, there is no known solution to the problem of determining *how much more* I prefer A to B than you do.[33] Because of this, there is no precise way of measuring and comparing the total welfare (utility) of different individuals, and so of identifying the least well off. Although Rawls's use of interpersonal comparisons of access to primary goods (particularly wealth and income) is a defensible rule of thumb, it doesn't solve the justification problem. Because we know that much more than wealth and income go into happiness and well-being, we may resist taking wealth and income from some (who don't fare well on other dimensions) to give to others (who do fare well).

Finally, Rawls cannot escape Hayek's dilemma: any attempt to improve the material standard of living of the least well off by limiting the liberty of the most productive members of society is likely, in the long run, to lower the standard of living for everyone. To see this, first consider Society 1. It adopts Rawls's principles (i) and (ii), redistributing money from the most to the least well off, until the latter reach an income of X dollars, which cannot be increased because further redistribution would disincentivize those at higher levels enough to reduce the gross domestic product (GDP) below the level needed to ensure X dollars for those at the bottom. Society 2 is just like Society 1 in all respects except that its redistribution scheme provides an income of 90% of X dollars to the bottom group, allowing the more productive groups to keep slightly more income than their counterparts in Society 2. Being allowed to retain more, they spend a bit more, invest a bit more, and work a bit more, thereby increasing GDP by some percentage Z.

Imagine these policies continuing for decades. At the end of year 1 the GDP of Society 2 will be slightly greater than that of Society 1. Starting from a higher level in year 2, this increase will be compounded; at the end of year 2 the gap between the two GDPs will be a little greater than it was before. Since the compounding continues, the gap will continue to grow. At some point Society 2 will be more than twice as rich as Society 1, and the worst off in Society 2 will have nearly twice the material standard of living as their counterparts in Society 1. (A 1% increase in the wealth of Society 2 over that of Society 1, compounded annually, will lead in 70 years to Society 2 being twice as wealthy as Society 1.) Since health, longevity, education, and culture tend to increase with GDP, Society 2 is likely to provide a much better life for all than Society 1. It hardly seems *just* that those born into Society 1 should be deprived in this way of the better life they could have had.

The argument works no matter what nonzero amount X over any fixed period of time T is selected to implement Rawls's principle (ii). Surely, however, one is inclined to think that there must be some policy that would, over an indefinite future, maximize the position of the worst off. Hayek and Nozick would probably agree, setting X equal to 0. That is, they would say, a policy of *no redistribution for the purpose of reducing economic inequality* will, over time, redound to the advantage of the least well off. Nevertheless, they would, I think, find it reasonable to provide some social minimum. Crucially, however, their social minimum would not be defined in terms of its relation to the levels of wealth or income of those at higher levels. The proper principle would be one that provides the minimum needed for living a decent human life under contemporary circumstances, without requiring present citizens to make sacrifices below this level for the sake of future citizens. However, it would require beneficiaries to make reasonable contributions to the common good, consistent with their abilities to do so.

Although this is clearly not what Rawls had in mind, it is, I think, a reasonable blend of what he gets right with the indispensable insights of Hayek and Nozick. Whether or not it is the blueprint for an ideal society is a very different matter. Indeed, the presupposition that there is such a thing as an ideal society, which must follow some determinable blueprint, is not obviously correct. In recent years, the efficacy and feasibility of the philosophical quest for such a society have been subjected to critical scrutiny. The contemporary philosopher Gerald Gaus is one of the leading skeptics.

GERALD GAUS: *THE TYRANNY OF THE IDEAL*

Unlike Rawls, who used an imagined consensus on first principles to sketch an ideal system which, he hoped, might help us improve the societies in which we live, Gaus argues that there is no idealized consensus to be had, and that such ideal approaches should be replaced by more realistic models for extracting more limited agreements. Recognizing that complex societies are made up of many groups with different social and political ideals, he recognizes that improvements depend on substantial overlap of the beliefs and ideals of various groups, as well their willingness to converge on what all take to be better, even if none take it to be best. For Gaus, all social and political perspectives are partial. Because none comprehends the full potential for human social interaction, there is room for each to grow and change by interacting with others. When this leads to limited agreements between proponents of different conceptions of the good, new institutions arise. When these are seen to be beneficial, the resulting new knowledge may expand the original perspectives, making possible new agreements generating further progress. This process by which not consensus, but disagreement about the good (against a background of overlapping agreement about many things), leads to progress may, in principle, be unending. Thus, he suggests, there may be no realistic need to search for, and probably no realistic possibility of finding, a comprehensive political ideal to guide us.

His book examines how we ought to reason about sociopolitical norms. Like Rawls, Gaus uses the notion of a model consisting of (i) criteria for evaluating when one society is better than another, (ii) a description of the features of a society to which the evaluative criteria are to be applied, and (iii) the range of possible societies evaluated and the outcomes of the evaluations. For Rawls, (i) measured how desirable different societies were to self-interested rational agents in the original position, (ii) applied that criterion to the distribution of liberty and of primary goods (wealth and income) in the society, and (iii) measured how well any possible society fared in comparison with all the others.[34]

Unlike Rawls, Gaus doesn't favor one model above all others; nor does he demand that all possible societies be modeled. Since his goal is to understand the logic for using models to reason about social and political reality, he allows a model to use any evaluative standards it wishes to rank the total goodness of a society in terms of whatever social and political institutions it takes to be relevant to determining that ranking—e.g., a society's social, political, economic, educational, cultural, and religious institutions or practices, its taxation and national service policies, the extent of its debt and borrowing against the future, its uses of natural and other resources, etc. Applying the evaluative standards to the relevant social institutions and practices results in an "inherent justice score" (really an inherent goodness score) for each society. For simplicity, we may imagine extracting a partial linear ordering in which, for every pair of distinct societies modeled, either one is ranked higher than the other, or they are ranked as equal. If our society is among those modeled, we can use its position in the ordering to determine which possible changes would allow us to march upward in the ordering, only stopping if and when we reach the point at which further changes significantly reduce its score.

It is useful to begin by thinking about an actual society ⓐ, e.g., our own, about which we already know a great deal, identifying institutions and practices that have changed plus the characteristics of those changes we have found to be good or bad. These can be used to construct a simplified model that includes a description of @ along relevant dimensions, and a set of criteria for evaluating modifications that would result if so far unexperienced changes were to occur. The goal is to map possible futures of @—@1, @2, etc.—that we might use in our plans for improving @.

The model might be expanded by adding descriptions of actual societies other than our own, as well as possible variations on them, expanding the evaluative criteria in our model to apply to them. Models could then be tested against reality by noting and evaluating what happens to one of our real societies when it changes. To the extent that our model accurately evaluates the new change, we take it to be confirmed; to the extent that it doesn't, we revise it. This, very roughly put, is the kind of model-based investigation that Gaus presupposes.

These models measure the goodness of each society in terms of its inherent features, *without having to first locate its relation to an imagined ideal society,* which is not required to plot possible improvements. If the range of systems investigated is finite, one may end up ranked more highly than any other. But models needn't evaluate all conceivable systems. Even if we included infinitely many systems, there need be no maximum score, and so no ideal. But the key point is more basic: if the goodness of a society is wholly determined by its intrinsic features, there may be no need to locate *an ideal* to guide progress.

What would normative reality have to be like in order for this *not* to be so—i.e., for it to be *necessary* to *first* recognize an ideal system in order for us to improve our own society as much as possible? For this to be necessary, what we think of alternatives to our society when considering them as possible stepping stones on a path to improving it must sometimes depend not only on the intrinsic values of good-making features of our own and alternative systems, but also *on their overall similarity to the ideal*. The most obvious way for this to occur involves cases in which reducing *the intrinsic goodness* of a political system brings it *closer* to the ideal system.

How could this happen? Imagine you are Lenin or Stalin. You believe in an ideal Marxist future, but to achieve it you think you must make your present society initially much less good, in order to replace its institutions with new ones that will put it on the path to the ideal. Fortunately, few find this compelling today. Still, it illustrates the logic of sacrificing present goodness for greater goodness later. Put aside the grotesque historical features of this example. Isn't it conceivable that *the route to the political ideal might justify one in reducing the intrinsic goodness of a society now?* Gaus is skeptical; he argues that when we carefully trace the logic of such an attempt, we encounter severe constraints.

To understand why, imagine a scenario with eleven possible systems, the eleventh being ideal, the tenth being most similar to it, and so on ending with the first, which is least similar. Let the inherent goodness scores, $S(x)$, of the different systems be: $S(1) = 10$, $S(2) = 20$, $S(3) = 15$, $S(4) = 30$, $S(5) = 25$, $S(6) = 40$, $S(7) = 25$, $S(8) = 21$, $S(9) = 30$, $S(10) = 39$, and $S(11) = 45$. Distributions like this can arise if the goodness-relevant features of societies are institutions the values of which depend in crucial ways on its other institutions. Gaus agrees that changes that make one institution worse and *reduce the overall goodness of a society* might, when combined with other existing institutions, *reduce the distance to a better society*, putting us on a path to further changes which, if followed, would eventually raise the overall goodness of our society.[35] This is illustrated by the following figure, where the *goodness* of a society is represented by its height on the y axis (the higher the better) and the *similarity of the goodness-making features of two societies* is represented by the distance between them on the x axis (which means that the shorter the distance between two societies, the fewer significant changes are needed to transform the one into the other).

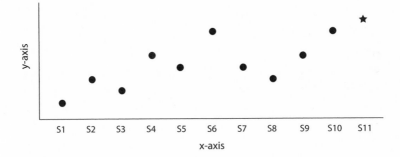

If normative reality looks like this, then the identification of the utopian ideal, S11, might, in principle, play a useful role in improving our own society. But, as Gaus emphasizes, the range of possible configurations in which the putative ideal can play this role is limited. In order for an ideal to help us plot a path to a better society, the overall goodness of a possible system must bear a reasonable relation to the goodness of those closest (i.e., most similar) to it; random or arbitrary correlations between goodness and closeness (similarity) must be ruled out. Otherwise *"there is no point in getting close to the ideal point . . . but not achieving it: [since] its near neighbors may not be at all just."*[36] We need a conception of a perfectly good society to orient changes we wish to make in actual societies, *only if* the range of possible states satisfies a daunting "fine-tuning condition." Gaus puts it this way:

If the problem of achieving justice is not sufficiently complex [if inherent justice is too closely correlated with similarity to the ideal] . . . all we need is to make the best pairwise choices we can, and we do not need to identify our long-term goal [making the political ideal superfluous]. If the problem is too complex [if justice isn't correlated closely enough with similarity to the ideal], the ideal will not help, because any move "working toward" it is essentially a leap in the dark.[37]

Even if this fine-tuning condition (allowing small changes to have just enough, but not too much, effect on the overall goodness of a society) is satisfied, there is another constraint limiting the potential utility of a philosophical identification of an ideally good society. Suppose our political philosophy tells us that normative reality is as illustrated by the previous graph. Suppose further that we know our society is S2. Because we live in S2, our knowledge of it is much greater than our knowledge of other systems—which are possibilities arising from imagined changes in goodness-making features our theory recognizes (changes in social and economic institutions). With this in mind, we ask, *How much faith can we put in the accuracy of our model?*

It would be nice to think that our evaluations of each of the eleven systems was as accurate as that of our own. But, Gauss argues, we shouldn't believe they are.

[O]ur current social world is in the domain [it is one of the systems in our model], and the evidential basis for judgments about the justice of the world we actually live in must be greater than the judgments about merely possible worlds [i.e., about the institutions and practices of societies, and their degrees of justice, that would exist if the descriptions of them in our model were realized]. For all nonexistent [merely possible] social worlds, we must rely for the most part . . . on predictive models to judge their social realizations; for our current world [our own society] we can employ our best model to understand it, but we also have masses of direct evidence as to its realization. Indeed, our models are often developed from our current data.[38]

In addition to knowing much more about our own society, it is reasonable to suppose that our knowledge of those closest to it—which would result from making relatively small changes to our present institutions and practices—is greater than our knowledge of other possible societies less similar to it. Since the imagined route from our society to one of those more distant societies is a series of unexperienced changes, the possibility of error in our representation and evaluation of them will increase as we move further away from our own society and its near neighbors.

This leads Gaus to his conception of *a neighborhood,* which he uses to challenge the defender of ideal theories in political philosophy.

A neighborhood delimits a set of nearby social worlds characterized by similar justice-relevant social structures. In this rough continuum of social worlds some are in the neighborhood of our own social world (and many are not); our understanding of the justice of alternative social worlds in the neighborhood of our own social world is far deeper than outside it. . . . *As we leave our neighborhood the precision and accuracy of our estimations of the justice of social worlds drops off sharply . . . and the reliability of . . . [our] models rapidly decreases as we move to increasingly unfamiliar worlds. In contrast, within our neighborhood there may be relatively obvious local optima, about which our judgments are reasonably reliable.*[39]

The Choice. In cases in which there is a clear optimum within our neighborhood that requires movement away from our understanding of the ideal, we must often choose between relative certain (perhaps large) local improvements in justice and pursuit of a considerably less certain ideal, which would yield optimal justice.[40]

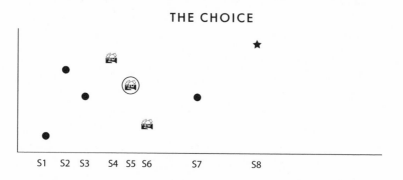

THE CHOICE

The kind of choice Gaus has in mind is illustrated in the figure, in which S5 is our actual system, S4 and S6 are in the neighborhood, S4 is a local optimum, S1, S2, S3, S7 and S8 are outside our neighborhood, and S8 is the imagined ideal system.

Suppose we are at S5, trying to become better. Our model tells us that moving up from S5 to S4 will do that, while moving down to S6 would make us much worse. Since both are in our neighborhood, we are justifiably confident that these predictions are correct. So we are inclined move to S4, despite the fact that doing so would *increase* our distance along the x axis to S8, and so take us *further away from our imagined ideal*, whereas moving to S6 would *decrease* our distance along the x axis to S8, and so would bring us *closer to the ideal*. It is rational for us to discount this fact because we *know* the path to S8 will (at least temporarily) make things worse by imposing potentially severe hardships on real people, *without knowing* that we will ever achieve the benefits we now attribute to S8. Since we realize that our calculation of those benefits is likely to be in error, we are, and ought to be, reluctant to sacrifice real people for what may turn out to be a theorist's illusion. Indeed, our very conception of the ideal may be changed by whatever we do in pursuing it.

Gaus's attitude toward this choice is expressed in the following passage.

> If the ideal is to be . . . a long-term goal, the ideal theorist must sometimes—one would think often—stress that we should pursue the ideal and so forgo possibilities to create a more just social world by moving away from the ideal to some near social arrangements. It is critical to stress that this *must* be the case: if the ideal theorist denies that such choices need ever be made, then . . . we can do very well without knowing anything about the Mount Everest of justice, and should simply climb the hills that confront us. But if we really do . . . [pursue the ideal] [t]hose who bear the cost of this pursuit will live in a less just world—their pleas must be discounted. . . . [F]or us to be under the sway of an ideal theory is for us to ignore relatively clear improvements in justice for the sake of a grander vision for the future. And yet this grand vision is ultimately a mirage, for as we move closer to it, we will see that it was not what we thought. . . . [F]or those who remember their twentieth-century political history, the position that such theorists have talked themselves into is far too reminiscent of less democratic idealists.[41]

The full force of Gaus's point requires thinking that the *only* way for a conception of the ideal society to be of use to us requires us to knowingly sacrifice ourselves and our fellows to pursue a possibility that we can't know to be an improvement over our present state. In cases of this sort, Gaus plausibly argues that we are well advised to moderate our search for the ideal. However, this Gausian lesson doesn't extend to all cases in which we might use a model of an ideal society to guide social change. On the contrary, it allows for the possibility that *sometimes* a plausible conception of the ideal would provide useful guidance. There are two kinds of case in which this might happen.

First consider a scenario in which there are two paths, A and B, for improving our society, the initial changes to each which involve equal improvements achievable within our societal neighborhood. After that, however, path A levels out, with no greater improvements, while path B continues upward to still further improvements. In such a situation, it would be reasonable to choose path B, since doing so would increase the magnitude of our possible gains, without sacrificing anyone's welfare in doing so.[42] Next, consider a scenario in which we could move toward the imagined ideal by making a change that would have little or no negative effect on *the inherent goodness* of a political system (when compared either with other possible changes or with doing nothing). The fact that our justified confidence in the accuracy of our model of the ideal might not be very high doesn't prevent us from justifiably taking it to be a guide in this sort of case. Thus, although Gaus's argument limits the utility of an ideal conception of social goodness, it doesn't render it irrelevant.

Still, if he is right, the task of constructing more modest models for making limited improvements in which we can be confident is probably the more pressing of the two theoretical tasks. In his eyes, this means committing ourselves to a conception of society that is diverse,[43] polycentric,[44] non-optimizing,[45] and open.[46] He sees complex societies as made up of different moral, political, economic, and religious points of view from which no all-encompassing perspective can be abstracted that is strong enough to yield authoritative resolutions of major issues. But, he maintains, a good, just, and open society doesn't require this. Collective agreements on moral, social, and political matters are, of course, needed, but foundational Rawlsian verdicts on ideal justice or goodness probably aren't. What is required is a stable fundamental framework of social rules, a kind of *moral constitution,* governing interactions between people with differing evaluative perspectives, allowing them to agree on solutions to problems that most find acceptable, and better than no solution at all, even if few, or none, find the solutions optimal.[47]

Ironically, Gaus argues, it is precisely by *not* insisting on optimal solutions that we may better approximate our never to be realized ideal.

> The optimizing stance is also self-defeating. . . . Our analysis . . . concluded that an individual perspective on justice will almost surely be unable to find its ideal; being confined to a neighborhood, the identification of its own ideal will be elusive. However . . . other perspectives can uncover parts of the landscape beyond one's neighborhood; revealing features of the social world that are not salient on one's own view, they can help bring one's own ideal into closer view. But this requires . . . a network of interconnected communities of inquiry. . . . It is precisely the framework for such interactions that the moral constitution of the Open Society provides. Adopting the optimizing stance toward the moral constitution [i.e., insisting that others interact with you only on terms that your particular perspective finds optimal] precludes one's own perspective participating in this framework for inquiry [because insisting on optimality blocks continuing inquiry and agreement]. . . . To wish to learn from other views, while insisting that only one's own view is correct and that all must live by it, is hardly a basis for a community of shared inquiry. By seeking to optimize in this way one forgoes optimizing in the sense of better understanding one's own commitments regarding justice.[48]

This paean to incrementalism, the open society, the incompleteness of our moral, political, and empirical perspectives, and the need for unrestrained inquiry and constant experimentation is very much in the spirit of Hayek. To a certain extent, even Rawls agreed by prioritizing his commitment to the most expansive basic liberty possible, consistent with equal liberty for all—which was not to be sacrificed to pursuit of greater egalitarianism in the distribution of wealth. Beyond this, however, Rawls retreated to a rigid, aprioristic conception of fairness, to which he was willing to subordinate ordinary normative perspectives on our social lives with others. Like Hayek, Gaus takes this to be a mistake. Respecting the moral and political wisdom that has arisen from the trial and error of historically evolving social institutions, they are not willing to sacrifice it to any purely abstract reasoning. But they also don't take it to be final. Like ordinary empirical knowledge, they take our moral and political knowledge to be capable of continued advance by successful social and institutional innovation. While humble about our present, they are optimistic about our ability to make moral and political progress in the future.

When one asks about the contributions made by Hayek, Rawls, and Gaus, not just to the world of political and philosophical theorizing, but to the wider world as we know it, the judgment is mixed. Hayek and Rawls were the most influential political philosophers of the twentieth century. Both valued liberty and understood the efficiency of the free market in producing wealth, while differing substantially in their conception of the role of government. Each has influenced political elites in the most economically advanced societies around the world. Although the work of Gaus is too new for that to have occurred, the empirical, microanalytic direction in political theorizing to which it points is a highly promising development that in time may come to be comparably influential.

KARL MARX: A CAUTIONARY TALE

Karl Marx (1818–1883) was, it must be admitted, the most influential political philosopher of all time. His thought played a major role in changing the map of the world, destroying social systems, and bringing about new ones that transformed countless lives and caused the deaths of tens of millions. Though Marx himself was not personally responsible for the grotesque crimes of despots invoking his name, the philosophical system he created could be interpreted, without gross or obvious misrepresentation, in ways that made the unjustifiable appear if not justified, at least excusable.[49] The idea that these events were excusable was an illusion. In order not to fall prey to it again, we must recognize the power of philosophical thought. Never a parlor game to be played in an ivory tower, philosophy, which struggles to understand the basic categories of our existence, knows no boundaries. Because it can affect every aspect of our lives, it should always be rigorously scrutinized. Up to now I have concentrated on the great positive contributions it has made. But the ledger contains debits as well as credits.

Marx began, and always remained, a German philosopher in the tradition of Kant, Fichte, and Hegel, all of whom were preoccupied with unusual conceptions of human freedom. Freedom was a problem for Kant because he believed both that our thoughts and actions must be free if morality is to make sense and that our decisions and actions, like everything else in time and space, can only be understood by us as being caused, and therefore must be unfree. His attempted resolution of this paradox invoked his distinction between our sensory *appearances* and the *realities*, of which they are appearances, about which we can, unfortunately, know nothing.

This distinction penetrated to our very selves. We are all aware of ourselves acting in time and space along with other items of "external appearance"—e.g., plants, animals, and inanimate objects. Perceiving ourselves in this way, as mere "empirical egos," we take our thoughts and actions to be caused. However, we, the perceivers, are also the real "transcendental egos" of which the empirical egos are merely appearances. Since our categories of perception, understanding, and knowledge are merely ways of organizing appearances, we can't know what we truly are, including whether or not we are free. Kant's solution is to preserve the possibility of morality by *postulating* that we are free.

Later German philosophers tried to do better. In "On the Dignity of Man" (1794), Johann Gottlieb Fichte undertook the emancipation of man, as spirit, from (seeming) determination by nature. Man, he proclaimed, should think of himself as "independent of everything outside him"; he "exists absolutely in and through himself . . . and by his own strength."[50] This hortatory statement was offered as a guide to action, rather than an objective description of independent reality, which post-Kantian German philosophy had convinced itself can't be meaningfully spoken about. Since unknowable Kantian things-in-themselves have no reality for us, they can be ignored. The pressing practical question was, *how should man use his freedom to fulfill himself by shaping his destiny through action?* Human history is, Fichte thought, the course of our attempts to do so.

Georg Wilhelm Friedrich Hegel (1770–1831) cut the Gordian knot, telling us, in effect, not to flee from, or struggle against, unknowable Kantian reality, but eliminate it by recognizing consciousness itself as the sole reality. But what, one wonders, does that mean? There is more to reality than the individual. Nor can humanity exhaust the whole of reality, can it? No, Hegel said, it can't. But Reality, the universe and all it contains, can be spiritual; it is a single, evolving divine mind of which human minds are integral parts. From this perspective, all history on earth, especially all human history, is the struggle of Reality itself—the World Mind of which we are parts—to perfect itself.

Although history appears chaotic and purposeless, in fact it follows a purposive rational dialectic—of progress, opposition, and overcoming of opposition in a higher, more encompassing, synthesis, followed by further cycles of the same sort. All aspects of this dialectic transcend the motives of individuals. Since this evolution results from Laws of Reality, it cannot be thwarted, hurried, or modified by human will. Human *freedom* comes, paradoxically, to be identified with understanding, and reconciling ourselves to, this *necessity*. As civilization progresses, human freedom expands as one adjusts one's own interests and aspirations to the *general will of all*, which is embodied by the laws, institutions, and directives of the governing state.

The state itself may be democratic, but it need not be, since Hegel never regarded the general will to be a mere sum of the wills of individuals. Rather, he took the general will to represent the highest level of perfection achievable by the World Mind at the time. Although this may sound like, and indeed may be, an excuse for tyranny, Hegel didn't think of it that way, because he imagined that the gradual replacement of individual wills by the general will would, in the end, be voluntary. He did not deny that coercion exists at early historical stages. Being the highest level of World Reason at any given time, the state must, at that time, be the final arbiter of any conflict between it and its subjects. This means that in immature states coercion might be widespread. Nevertheless, Hegel believed that it would gradually disappear as the state progressed to higher levels of perfection. This is the outline that Marx took over and modified.

Like Hegel, Marx believed that the laws of history would eventually bring about complete human freedom, when the general will becomes the will of each individual—thereby removing all sources of conflict and any need for coercion. Unlike Hegel, Marx didn't believe in the state as the repository of the general will, or in the individual's ultimate absorption by it. For Marx, the state always represents the interests of the dominant class, from which it follows that true emancipation will occur only when both the state and all social classes disappear, thereby eliminating all causes of conflict, domination, and coercion.

Like Hegel, Marx also believed that history moved by a recurring dialectic of progress, opposition, and overcoming of opposition by a new synthesis, bringing humankind closer to ultimate emancipation. Unlike Hegel, he didn't see the route to foreordained perfection as a gradual process of discernible improvement. Instead, he recognized that conflict, suffering, and violence were unavoidable, and he thought that the final step, needed to destroy rather than merely transform the state, would require increasing misery and culminate in a cataclysmic convulsion.

Marx also followed Hegel in recognizing that although human will can play an instrumental role in moving history forward, the general course of history was immutable. However, he differed from Hegel in taking conflict between social classes to be the chief instrument of historical change. For Marx the history of humankind is the history of our struggle to wrest what we need from nature, by means of our labor. The forces driving history are, therefore, economic, being concerned with how the products we require are produced and distributed. The struggle for power throughout history is the struggle for control over the processes of production and distribution of valued products. Different social classes, occupying different positions in the structure of production and distribution, at different periods, are the protagonists. Their interests, values, beliefs, and ways of life are fundamentally shaped by the economic positions they occupy.

Marx also rejected Hegel's conception of Reality. Whereas Hegel took it to be Pure Spirit advancing toward a state of perfect self-consciousness, Marx resisted taking any metaphysical view about *things in themselves*. Instead, he insisted that all our knowledge of nature and ourselves is ultimately practical, answering to our needs, to our social lives, and to our place in history. There was, he thought, no need for a transcendent standpoint, abstracted from our day-to-day struggles, from which we might view the world as it is in itself. In this respect, Marx was more naturalistic than Hegel.

However, his naturalism wasn't as empirical as it might at first seem. This can be seen in one his most important concepts, the *value* of useful products available for exchange in an economic system. To understand Marx on this subject, one must recognize that *price* and *value* were, for him, utterly distinct. The former is determined by supply and demand, which he saw as heavily influenced by the unjustified political and economic power of certain individuals and the dominance of certain classes. This he contrasted with the "real value" of a product in satisfying genuine human needs of free and equal individuals. According to Marx, the real value of an economic product is, as Kołakowski helpfully puts it, "the average amount of time necessary to produce a given article at a particular historical stage of human ability and technical progress."[51] According to Marx, products that have *the same labor value* in this sense have *the same real value*, no matter how different their uses, no matter how intensely the public wants or needs them, no matter how much knowledge or skill of various kinds the labor requires, no matter how scarce that knowledge or skill may be, no matter how hazardous or inherently disagreeable the work needed to produce the products, and no much how much capital is required for production and marketing.

Because of all this, products of different so-called "real labor value" in Marx's sense certainly can differ widely in price. What is problematic is whether his definition picks out any genuine type of *value* at all. Surely, there is no *all-encompassing value* of products that ignores everything Marx excludes. At most, his concept identifies one type of, or contributor to, total value. But even that is dubious. To be told simply that two unrelated products require the same average time to produce is to be told next to nothing about the real value of the products, unless we are also told about all the various factors Marx ignores. Finally, his innocent-sounding concept, *average labor time required to produce a product p,* is likely to be unmeasurable, when one considers all factors needed to come up with a number.

What would those factors be? In addition to (let us say) factory time in production proper, we would need to add (i) the labor time required to produce all tools used in p's production (plus tools for making those tools, and so on *ad infinitum*), (ii) the labor time required to provide training and education for those involved in planning and organizing the production and marketing of p (and for the education and training of those providing that education and training, and so on *ad infinitum*), (iii) the labor time required to construct all infrastructure necessary for transportation, storage, and sale of p, and (iv) the labor time required to secure necessary financing for every aspect of the production and marketing of p. Surely there is no way of measuring all of this, if, as Marx insists, we can't rely on *prices* in the computation of every item that goes into the production and marketing of a product. Thus, his concept, *average labor time required to produce a product p,* is useless in formulating empirically testable laws capable of explaining past events and predicting future ones, of the sort Marx claimed to provide.

His insistence that the real value of any economic product is its labor value was tied to his conviction that the *capital* involved in producing it adds nothing of value. From this, his desired conclusion—that return on capital is a form of theft, depriving workers of the fruits of their labors—followed by stipulative definition. But how, one may ask, can he have taken the definition to be justified? After all, he knew that the use of capital to improve the means of production increases worker productivity, thereby adding to social wealth. The answer is that *he took the role of capital to be parasitic*. Capitalist investment in machinery to increase the productivity of workers in a given industry is, he seemed to think, merely the purchase of the labor of those who made the machines. Thus, the resulting increase in wealth, though real, was, in his mind, entirely due to the workers involved, directly or indirectly, in producing the product.

This argument suffers from several flaws. First, the investment of capital is inherently risky, and so will rationally be undertaken only if there is a reasonable expectation of reward. Second, successful investing, which generates real social wealth, requires not only time and effort, but also unusual skill and highly specialized knowledge that must be compensated, if the value invested capital makes possible is to be realized. Third, although one can imagine a benevolent deity with the knowledge and good will needed to make wise investments for a society, no individual or human institution could possibly possess the vast knowledge, or the selfless benevolence, that would be required to match the performance of decentralized capital markets. In short, capitalist investment is, on the whole, not theft, but a major contributor to real value.

Marx didn't recognize this. For him, the return on capital was the appropriation by capitalists of *surplus value* from the workers—defined as the amount of value workers created in producing a product minus the amount of compensation required to sustain them in their present state. Although Marx recognized that capitalism greatly increased worker productivity, thereby making genuine social abundance possible for the first time in human history, he also believed that capitalism required ever larger appropriations of surplus value, increasing the relative impoverishment of workers (in relation to the value they produce) and exerting continuing pressure to keep their compensation near subsistence levels.[52] Because capitalist markets are ruled by competition, he reasoned, no level of investment or technology could ensure a permanent advantage for any enterprise. To stay afloat, new improvements, higher levels of investment, and further expropriation of surplus value from the workers must always be the order of the day.

In addition to leading to permanent poverty and ever greater inequality, the dynamic Marx thought he discerned could only result in an increasingly degraded and alienated working class. A few passages from *Capital* illustrate what he means.

The division of labor in manufacture . . . not only increases the social productive power of labor for the benefit of the capitalist . . . but does so by crippling individual labourers. It creates new conditions for the lordship of capital over labour.[53]

The lightening of labour [due to mechanization] . . . becomes a kind of torture, since the machine does not free the labourer, but deprives the work of all interest. . . . It is not the workman that employs the instruments of labour, but the instruments of labour that employ the workman.[54]

All methods for raising the social productiveness of labour . . . transform themselves into means of domination over, and exploitation of, the producers; they mutilate the labourer into a fragment of a man, degrade him to the level of an appendage of a machine, destroy any remnant of attraction in his work and turn it into a hated toil; they . . . subject him during the labour process to a despotism the more hateful for its meanness. . . . [A]ll methods for the production of surplus value are at the same time methods of accumulation; and every extension of accumulation becomes again a means for the development of those methods. It follows therefore that in proportion as capital accumulates, the lot of the labourer, be his payment high or low, must grow worse. The law that always equilibrates the industrial reserve army [of relatively impoverished potential workers] . . . establishes an accumulation of misery corresponding to an accumulation of capital. Accumulation of wealth at one pole is therefore at the same time accumulation of misery, agony, of toil slavery, ignorance, brutality and moral degradation at the opposite pole.[55]

These predictions, which proved spectacularly inaccurate, were central to Marx's conviction that capitalism would immanently collapse due to its internal contradictions, and be replaced, after a transitional period, by stateless society with no private ownership of the means of production, no enforced division of labor, no social classes, and no social conflicts. Capitalism's chief contradiction was alleged to arise from the fact that its central economic processes—which, for the first time in history, produced sufficient abundance to meet all genuine human needs—divided society into irreconcilable classes of capitalist exploiters versus proletarian workers. As the proletariat grew and its plight inevitably worsened, it would, Marx thought, finally become aware both of its class interests and of the cause of its misery, leading it to violently overthrow its oppressors.

Marx recognized that there would then be need for a dictatorship of the proletariat. Its role would be to eliminate the vestiges of capitalism, to do the social planning needed to ensure that production is governed by real social needs, and to guarantee that workers receive the true value of their products minus only legitimate deductions for essentials such as insurance against emergencies, schools, hospitals, and the care of those unable to work.[56] Later, Marx thought, when people have internalized the values of the new system and a level of production is reached sufficient for all, no enforced division of labor would be needed, the distinction between physical and intellectual work would be obliterated, and all but minimal activities of the state would wither away.[57]

Here Marx offers his own version of Hegel's idealized vision of ultimate human freedom as consisting in the adjustment of one's own interests and aspirations to the *general will of all*. Unlike Hegel, he imagines this occurring not within the authority of the state, but at a time in which state authority isn't needed. It is then that the new socialist citizen, seeing no conflict between his or her own deepest desires and interests and his or her role as a worker contributing to the good of all, is imagined to fully assent to the utopian slogan "From each according to one's ability, to each according to one's need."

This, in brief, is the dazzling, ingenious system of thought that helped to inspire so many horrors in the years since Marx's death. In light of that history, it takes some effort to understand how his intellectual creation could have had so great an influence. There were, I believe, three main factors involved. First, the Industrial Revolution and the rise of capitalism generated the most far-reaching changes in our individual and collective lives in the history of civilization. Although these changes were, for the most part, highly positive, they were accompanied not only by disorienting dislocations, but also by enormous increases in, and uses of, destructive power. Thus it is natural that the changes in the capitalist era were for a long time both worrisome and ill understood. It is therefore not surprising that Marx's systematic critique of them—in the name of the traditional values of freedom, equality, and fulfillment—might have seemed compelling.

Second, although the claim that Marx correctly identified scientific laws governing social, economic, and historical change was incorrect, the idea that there *are* (some) impersonal laws governing these domains is plausible; it certainly has not been disproved. Whatever else one may say about him, Marx did champion this embryonic social-scientific idea, while generating suggestive hypotheses about the role of social classes. Finally, his system—which was closer to Hegel's philosophical humanism than to any scientific theory—provided a comforting replacement for traditional religion, complete with a historically guiding purpose, an eventual heaven on earth, and a cause to which one could be devoted. All in all, Marx's system was, for many, a guide to the perplexed with the authority of science and the comforts of religion; of course it inspired devoted followers.

It was, nevertheless, too good to be true, which should have inspired more skepticism at the outset. Marxist thought did, of course, have dedicated critics. But it also attracted much respectful attention among European cultural and intellectual elites, as well as a fervent following among political agitators, some of whom interpreted it as a blueprint for seizing power. Did it really offer such a blueprint? The most insightful brief discussion of this question I know of is the final section, "Marxism as a Source of Leninism," of volume 1 of Kołakowski's *Main Currents of Marxism.*

Kołakowski's verdict is mixed. He recognizes that Marx's philosophy doesn't contain anything like the level of detail needed for concrete political action. For example, after his death, Marx's followers had to decide what, if anything, they could do to hasten the inevitable revolution. Nothing in Marx's writing definitively settled the matter.

> The debate between necessity and freedom could be resolved in theory, but at a certain point it had to be decided whether revolutionary movement must wait for capitalism to mature economically or whether it should seize power as soon as the political situation permitted. . . . Those who relied on the gradual and automatic development of capitalism into communism, and those who stressed the creative historical role of revolutionary initiative, could both find support in Marxist writings.[58]

Because Marx's descriptions of the communist society that was to follow the revolution were also stated abstractly, they too required interpretation before specific policies could be extracted. The problem wasn't that Marx explicitly advocated tyranny, but that many of his formulations, especially in *Capital,* invited it—or, at least made tyrannical interpretations plausible. Kołakowski illustrates this difficulty as follows.

> It was possible to argue as follows: according to Marx all social antagonisms were based on class conflicts. When private ownership of the means of production was abolished, there would be no more classes and no social conflict except that due to lingering resistance of the possessing classes. Marx envisioned that there would be no "mediacy" in the socialist state: this meant, in practical terms, the abolition of the liberal bourgeois separation of powers and the unification of the legislature, executive, and judiciary. . . . Marx had declared that the state and civil society would become identical. . . . Marx had

said that the negative freedom of the liberal bourgeois
tradition [freedom of speech, thought, assembly, etc.]
would have no place in a socialist society. As, by definition, the proletariat's aspirations were embodied in
the proletarian state, those who failed in any way to conform to the new unity deserved destruction as survivals
of bourgeois society. . . . By arguing on these lines, the
whole Marxist-Romantic theory of unity, classes, and
the class struggle could be used (which does not mean
this was historically inevitable) to justify the establishment of an extreme despotism which professedly embodied the maximum possible freedom. . . . In short, the
Leninist-Stalinist version of socialism was a possible interpretation, though certainly not the only possible one,
of Marx's doctrine.[59]

Does this tyrannical interpretation conflict with significant parts of Marx's corpus? Yes, especially the earlier
parts. But the works of systematic philosophers always
contain conflicts. Some reflect changes of mind, while
some reflect tensions that are never resolved. This seems
to have been true of Marx. Recognizing this, Kołakowski
declares Marx neither wholly guilty nor wholly innocent of
advocating the most problematic aspects of the Leninist-
Stalinist state. His final verdict, as I read him, is *complicit,*
which strikes me as correct.

Having stated how naturally the tyrannical interpretation
arises from some of Marx's words, Kołakowski closes with
this more nuanced judgment.

It is easy to reply to objections such as these [stated in
the above cited passage] that Marx (except perhaps for
a short time after the revolutions of 1848) not only did
not question the principles of representative democracy
but regarded them as a necessary part of popular rule,

and that although on two occasions he used the term "dictatorship of the proletariat" . . . he had in mind the class content of the power system and not, as Lenin did, the liquidation of democratic institutions. It follows that the despotic socialism of history is not socialism as Marx intended it: *the question, however, is how far it represents the logical outcome of his doctrine. To this it may be answered that the doctrine is not wholly innocent, though it would be absurd to say that the despotic forms of socialism were a direct outcome of the ideology itself.*[60]

The Leninist-Stalinist version of Marxism was . . . one attempt to put into practice the ideas that Marx expressed in a philosophical form. . . . The view that freedom is measured . . . by the degree of unity of society, and that class interests are the only source of social conflict, is one component of the theory. *If we consider that there can be a technique of establishing social unity, then despotism is a natural solution to the problem inasmuch as it is the only known technique for the purpose.* Perfect unity takes the form of abolishing all institutions of mediation, including representative democracy and the rule of law as an independent instrument for settling conflicts. The concept of negative freedom presupposes a society in conflict. If this is the same as a class society, and if a class society means a society based on private property, then there is nothing reprehensible in the idea that an act of violence which abolishes private property at the same time does away with the need for negative freedom *tout court.*[61]

CHAPTER 12

LAWS, CONSTITUTIONS, AND THE STATE

The nature of a system of laws: H.L.A. Hart's The Concept of Law; *the role of a constitution in a legal system; a philosophical approach to constitutional interpretation; extra-constitutional change: the administrative state.*

The aim of this chapter is to illuminate what laws and legal systems are in a way that sheds light on two related problems facing modern, democratic societies. One involves a gradual, unmandated transfer of power from democratically elected legislatures to unelected members of the judiciary. The other involves a massive increase in executive power at the expense of both the legislature and the judiciary. The role of philosophy in examining these problems is not to quantify their extent, or to offer detailed solutions, but to articulate conceptual frameworks within which the problems can be assessed and practical solutions can be found.

WHAT IS LAW?

The first question in the philosophy of law is *What is a law?* or, more generally, *What is a legal system?* We all know that laws are rules of a certain sort, often backed by force, which, when violated, may render one liable to punishment. Thanks to H.L.A Hart, who is widely recognized as the leading philosopher of law in the last century, we now understand that there is considerably more to a legal system than that. In *The Concept of Law,* he identifies the *authority of law* as existing between two poles, one deriving from coercion and one deriving from moral and nonmoral value.[1] Legal systems do, of course, typically include rules backed by force specifying punishments for violations. But, as Hart points out, they also include rules granting powers to agents satisfying various requirements—powers to make contracts, perform marriages, arbitrate disputes, practice certain vocations, etc. Hart also emphasized that even the criminal code of a legal system amounts to more than a set of commands that are not to be violated. Unlike laws, commands backed by force alone don't generate obligations. A robber who demands "Your money or your life" may force you to comply. You might say that, having no choice, you were *obliged* to do so, despite the fact that you had no *obligation* to obey. By contrast, something in law, beyond its threat of force, does generate *legal obligations.*

This leads Hart to morality. Both legal and moral rules classify actions as required, forbidden, or permissible. Often, what is morally forbidden is legally forbidden too. Thus, it's not surprising that law and morality both generate duties or obligations. But there are differences between the two. Legal obligations arise from a specific type of *social* rule, which may vary from one jurisdiction to another. By contrast, moral obligations seem to be unconditional, and so based on something more than social convention. Whereas some acts that are legally required in one place might be forbidden in another, the claim that the same act (in comparable circumstances) may be morally right here and morally wrong there (rather than simply thought to be so) is rightly viewed with suspicion.

As Hart emphasizes, social rules aren't mere regularities. One may say, "As a rule, American adults drink coffee in the morning," but this merely reports a *habit*; there is no *rule* mandating morning coffee. Genuine rules—of law, morality, etiquette, or of social institutions generally—require sanctions (criticism or worse) for violations. They are also internalized action-guiding rules that many agents recognize as providing reasons for acting. Legal systems contain primary action-guiding rules of this sort that are identified by what Hart calls *social rules of recognition*, which invest certain institutions with authority to make, to change, and to adjudicate disputes involving the action-guiding rules. In the United States the basic rule of recognition is that laws passed by institutions set up by, and operating in accord with, the U.S. Constitution, and the constitutions of the several states, are to be obeyed unless they have been overturned by recognized constitutional processes. Laws that have this authority are typically seen by many people as providing them with legitimate, even if not always conclusive, reasons for action.[2]

What kinds of reasons? Since legal systems specify punishments for violations of criminal laws, one reason to obey them is to avoid punishment. But, according to Hart, this can't be *the sole source of obedience* in any genuine legal system. In order to count as a legal system, the authority issuing action-guiding rules must be legitimate, which requires a presumption on the part of a substantial portion of the populace that there are *prima facie* reasons for obeying the rules, independent of fear of likely punishment for not doing so. Naturally, a system doesn't cease to be legitimate simply because some people regard some of its rules to be pointless; nor does it lose that status because large numbers find many of its rules to be nonoptimal. Its status as a legal system would be threatened if most of its action-guiding rules either regulated actions widely regarded not to require regulation, or regulated actions understood to require regulation but did so in ways widely seen to be seriously inferior to easily identifiable and easily enactable practical alternatives.

Conversely, if most action-guiding rules of a putative legal system regulate actions that are widely agreed to require regulation, and the regulations imposed are not widely taken to be seriously inferior to easily imagined alternatives, a substantial portion of the citizens will take themselves to have some reason (perhaps among many) independent of fear of likely punishment for obeying the law. They needn't have detailed knowledge of the law, nor must their *main* reason for obeying it be more than fear of punishment. But there must be some influential group, including officials of the system, who do have substantial legal knowledge and who do take themselves to have substantial reasons, not related to punishment, to obey the laws.

What might such a reason be? One reason for obeying some laws is derived from the mere fact that most other members of the society do. This is obvious when laws codify social conventions to which one conforms because the pattern created by the conformity of others makes it easier, safer, or more advantageous for one to similarly conform. For example, in the United States drivers are, unless otherwise instructed, legally required to drive on the right-hand side of the road. In the UK driving on the left is mandated. In these cases, the fact that others conform provides one with a reason to conform, independent of the threat of legal punishment for doing otherwise (which, though relevant, is secondary). Because the value of coordinated behavior so outstrips the chaos of uncoordinated behavior, most are happy to conform.

In these cases, different rules would be equally good, if they were obeyed. In other cases, different rules might all be better than having no social rules, even though having certain rules is much better than having others. Consider a rule stipulating that disputes arising from alleged defamation of character be sanctioned by legally regulated dueling rather than by making defamation an adjudicable tort. Presumably both are superior to treating retaliation for perceived defamation to be a purely private matter in which the legal system has no interest. Still, a rule that articulates standards for defamation and impartial trials for adjudicating claims is superior to one that merely regulates the forms of allowable duels. Because of this, a system incorporating adjudication has a greater claim to one's allegiance than a system incorporating regulated duels. Thus, the authority of a legal system typically depends on more than the mere fact that its way of coordinating behavior is better than having no system of coordination.

There are at least three sources of support that may play important roles in elevating social rules backed by force to the status of an authoritative legal system. One is *prudential*: many citizens may judge the system to be as effective as might reasonably be expected in enhancing their welfare and that of those they care about. Another source of legal authority is *moral*: many may believe (i) that the legal system enhances the general welfare, relative to other achievable schemes, (ii) that the burdens and benefits it imposes are not grossly unfair, and (iii) that the natural rights of all are protected in some important ways. A third source of authority is *participatory*: a widespread belief that the rule-making process is reasonably representative, and so capable of being influenced by the governed.

Perfection along any of these dimensions isn't required. Legal systems vary in the extent to which their authority is dependent on them. When a system ranks high in all dimensions, citizens typically take themselves to have a strong *prima facie* obligation to obey its laws. However, social rules need not have this level of authority to qualify as a genuine legal system. It is enough that the populace accords some authority to the system's directives, and believes itself to have some reasons, over and above fear of punishment, to obey them.[3]

This aspect of Hart's view, making it a form of *legal positivism*, provoked considerable controversy throughout the second half of the twentieth century, and beyond. As a positivist, he insisted that law, like most systems of social rules, can be described and studied without endorsing or repudiating the values the rules encode. In calling certain things *laws*, one is committed to the nonevaluative claim that some portion of the society endorses values supporting them. Nevertheless, as Hart clearly recognized, there can be individual laws, and even entire legal systems, that are, on balance, evil.

This didn't interfere with his recognition that there are deep connections between law and morality. The central purpose of legal systems is to articulate and enforce a code of conduct that allows people to live together. He says:

> [T]he social morality of societies which have reached the stage where this [the morality of a society] can be distinguished from its law, always includes certain obligations and duties, requiring the sacrifice of private inclination or interest which is essential to the survival of any society. . . . Among such rules obviously required for social life are those forbidding, or at least restricting, the free use of violence, rules requiring certain forms of honesty and truthfulness in dealings with others, and rules forbidding the destruction of tangible things or their seizure from others. If conformity with these most elementary rules were not thought a matter of course among any group of individuals, living in close proximity to each other, we should be doubtful of the description of the group as a society, and certain that it could not endure for long. Moral and legal rules of obligation and duty have therefore certain striking similarities. . . .

[B]oth make demands which must obviously be satisfied by any group of human beings who are to succeed in living together.[4]

Hart maintains that legal systems must promote the survival and welfare of the population in order to establish and maintain themselves. Since he insists that the authority of any such system depends in part on the uncoerced acceptance of it as a guide to conduct by many of its members, we may draw two conclusions. First, legal systems promote the survival and, to some extent, the welfare of the governed. Second, they are voluntarily accepted by many in large part because of the perceived good they do.

Nevertheless, legal systems can suffer from shortcomings that render them evil. For example, they may oppress subgroups.

Coercive power . . . established on the basis of authority . . . may be used to subdue and maintain in a position of permanent inferiority, a subject group whose size, relative to the master group, may be large or small depending on the means of coercion. . . . For those thus oppressed there may be nothing in the system to command their loyalty, but only things to fear. They are its victims, not its beneficiaries.[5]

In addition, even the beneficiaries of a legal system who accept it voluntarily may do so, in part, for nonmoral or immoral reasons.

[I]t is true that the coercive power of law presupposes its accepted authority [by some]. But the dichotomy of "law based merely on power" [which Hart takes to be a contradiction in terms] and "law which is accepted as morally binding" is not exhaustive. Not only may vast numbers be coerced by laws which they do not regard as morally binding, but it is not even true that those who accept the system voluntarily, must conceive of themselves as morally bound to do so, though the system will be most stable when they do. In fact, their allegiance to the system may be based on many different considerations.[6]

Hart's view of the relationship between law and morality may be summarized as follows. (i) Human welfare is greatly advanced by the ability of human beings to live together in communities. Law is necessary for such communities to survive and improve the conditions of their members. Since all legal systems allow us to escape a Hobbesian war of all against all, there is something necessary and good about them. (ii) As a rule, laws governing conduct are general (rather than directed at specific, or even named, individuals); they proscribe or prescribe actions of certain general sorts in conditions of specified types. However, because even immoral or unjust provisions can be stated in these terms, there is no guarantee that a legal system will, on the whole, be morally acceptable. (iii) Even when generally and objectively stated laws are morally good, or at any rate acceptable, an unjust pattern of enforcement—routinely ignoring some specified conditions in some cases, or adding unspecified conditions in others—may lead to serious injustice.

SEPARATION OF LEGAL POWERS

In societies with functioning legal systems, behavior is regulated by law. This requires some person or group to be responsible for making the laws, some person or group to be responsible for administering and enforcing them, and some person or group to be responsible for adjudicating disputes about what the law requires, determining the guilt or innocence of those accused of violations, and deciding punishment for those found guilty. In many modern states, these functions are performed by separate and largely independent institutions, typically to prevent too great a concentration of power in one body. Although the ways in which the powers are separated vary in different legal systems, in democracies the legislature, elected by citizens, typically makes the laws, the executive (sometimes elected, sometimes chosen by the legislature) administers and enforces the law, and the judiciary, often appointed rather than elected, adjudicates legal disputes, tries accused violators, and decides punishment (within ranges typically set by the legislature). Since institutional actors naturally try to maximize their own power, each branch of government sometimes encroaches on the others. Hence, the health of a legal system often depends on its ability to minimize such encroachments and maintain the proper distribution of powers.

In what follows, we will look at two current dramas, one involving a struggle between the judiciary and the other two branches, the other pitting the executive against the other two. I will, for concreteness, focus on the forms the struggles are taking in the United States.

JUDGE-MADE LAW: NECESSARY BUT LIMITED

The first problem to be investigated is often discussed in terms of the distinction between *judicial activism* and *judicial restraint*. Thinking of the problem in this way invites one to imagine that the issue is how much the nondemocratic judiciary encroaches on the democratic legislature. The issue has arisen because recent decades have seen many important issues about which large proportions of the population hold strong opinions removed from the normal give-and-take of democratic politics by Supreme Court decisions—prayer in school, sexually and racially integrated education, racial, gender, and ethic preferences, abortion, definitions of and legal requirements on marriage, religious symbols on public property, the presence or absence of restrictions on various forms of free speech, including contributions to political campaigns, and many other matters.

This "activism" has now reached the point at which certain instances it are criticized by the political left, while others are criticized by the political right. This is one sign of something we should have known all along. The real question is not how active the Court is in striking down legislative acts. The question is, *On what basis does the Court have the right to do so, and what general principles should guide it when it does?* Our first task in answering that question is to articulate a conceptual framework for understanding the proper role of the American judiciary in interpreting the law and applying it to the facts of cases brought before it.

Section 1 of Article I of the Constitution of the United States says, *"All legislative powers herein granted shall be vested in a Congress of the United States. . . ."* To take this seriously is to recognize that neither the courts, the executive, nor the regulatory agencies are authorized to make laws. This implies that the first task in judicial interpretation is to determine what a law says, asserts, or stipulates. *Saying, asserting,* and *stipulating* are speech acts. Each involves taking a certain stance toward the content expressed by a use of language. To *say* or *assert* something is to commit oneself to that content's being true. To *stipulate* is to make it true by asserting it. For a proper authority to stipulate that the speed limit on highways is 60 miles per hour is for the authority to state that the speed limit is 60, and for the act of making that statement to be a, or the, crucial factor in making what is asserted true.

To discover what the law asserts or stipulates is to discover what the lawmakers asserted or stipulated in adopting a text. As with ordinary speech, this is sometimes *not* a function of linguistic meaning alone, which is sometimes contextually incomplete. Consider, for example, the sentence 'I am finished'. Although grammatically complete, it lacks a constituent identifying what was finished. Since it is semantically incomplete, it must be completed by the nonlinguistic situation of use, the larger discourse, or the presuppositions of speaker-hearers. 'She is going to a nearby restaurant' is similar. Nearby what? Our present location? Her present location? A location she, or we, will be visiting next week? It depends on context. Since there is no end to the possible completions of utterances like these, to think of these sentences as ambiguous is to think of them as having indefinitely many meanings, arising from indefinitely many preestablished linguistic conventions. But there is no such multiplicity. These sentences have single under-specified meanings that require contextual completion.

The verb 'use' is similar. Whenever one uses something, one uses it to do something. When we say "Fred used a hammer," we often have in mind what he used it for. When the purpose isn't known to our audience, we say more, e.g., "Fred used a hammer to break the window." When the purpose is obvious—to pound in a nail—we leave it implicit, knowing others will understand. Sometimes we may say, having found a hammer on the floor, "I know Fred used it for something, but I don't know what." This is just one possible completion of the meaning of 'Fred used a hammer'. Lacking a purpose-constituent, the sentence is silent about purpose, just as the linguistic meaning of 'I am finished' is silent about what was finished.

What an ordinary speaker uses a sentence S to assert in a given context is, roughly, what an ordinarily reasonable and attentive hearer or reader who knows the linguistic meaning of S, and is aware of all relevant intersubjectively available features of the context of the utterance, would rationally take the speaker's use of S to be intended to convey and commit the speaker to. In standard communication, all parties know the linguistic meanings of the words, the purpose of the communication, the questions currently at issue, and the relevant facts about what previously has been asserted and accepted. Because speakers and hearers typically know this, what is asserted by a given utterance can usually be identified with *what the speaker means* and *what the hearers take the speaker to mean* by the words on that occasion. Applying this to legal interpretation, we look for what the lawmakers meant, and what an ordinarily reasonable and attentive person who understood the linguistic meanings of their words, the publicly available facts, the recent history in the lawmaking context, and the background of existing law into which the new provision is expected to fit, would take them to have meant. That is the content of the law.

There are, of course, complications due, in part, to the frequently collective character of the language users and their audience. Sometimes the lawmaker is a legislative body, sometimes it is an administrative agency, sometimes it is the chief executive issuing an order, and sometimes it is a judge, or court majority, whose written opinion modifies a previous version of the law. What gives the speech acts of these institutional actors the force of law is their position in the constitutionally based legal system that their institutional audiences and the populace as a whole acknowledge as authoritative.

The task of discovering asserted or stipulated legal content is illustrated by Justice Scalia's dissent in the 1993 case *Smith v. United States*. The relevant statutory text is:

[A]ny person who . . . uses or carries a firearm [in the course of committing a crime of violence or drug trafficking] shall, in addition to the punishment provided for such [a] crime . . . be sentenced to a term of imprisonment of not less than five years.[7]

The defendant, Smith, *traded a gun for illegal drugs*, thereby committing a crime of drug trafficking. Did this constitute *using a firearm in the commission of such a crime* in the sense of the statute? A lower court said it did, Smith appealed, and the Supreme Court upheld the lower court's ruling, finding the ordinary meaning of *"uses a firearm"* to cover uses of any sort.

Scalia disagreed.

In the search for statutory meaning, we give nontechnical words and phrases their ordinary meaning. . . . To use an instrumentality ordinarily means to use it for its intended purpose. *When someone asks, "Do you use a cane?,"* he is not inquiring whether you have your grandfather's silver-handled walking stick on display in the hall; he wants to know whether you walk with a cane. Similarly, to speak of "using a firearm" is to speak of using it for its distinctive purpose, i.e., as a weapon. To be sure, "one can use a firearm in a number of ways," . . . including as an article of exchange . . . but that is not the ordinary meaning of "using" the one or the other.[8]

The Court asserts that the "significant flaw" in this argument is that "to say that the ordinary meaning of 'uses a firearm' includes using a firearm as a weapon" is quite different from saying that the ordinary meaning "also excludes any other use." The two are indeed different—but it is precisely the latter that I assert to be true. The ordinary meaning of "uses a firearm" does not include using it as an article of commerce. *I think it perfectly obvious, for example, that the objective falsity requirement for a perjury conviction would not be satisfied if a witness answered "no" to a prosecutor's inquiry whether he had ever "used a firearm," even though he had once sold his grandfather's Enfield rifle to a collector.*[9]

In the first passage, Scalia correctly identifies *what question is asked* by one who says "Do you use a cane?" In the second, he correctly identifies *what is asserted* when his hypothetical agent answers "No" to the prosecutor's question "Have you ever used a firearm?" Applying the lesson to the Smith case, Scalia concludes that in adopting the statutory text, *Congress asserted* that the *use of a firearm as a weapon* (or carrying it for that purpose) is subject to additional punishment. Regrettably, he misstated his conclusion, claiming that the *ordinary meaning* of "anyone who uses a firearm" pertains only to uses of a firearm as a weapon. The Court majority pointed out that this was false:

When a word is not defined by statute, we normally construe it in accord with *its ordinary or natural meaning*. . . . Surely petitioner's treatment of his [gun] *can be described* as "use" [of the firearm] *within the everyday meaning of that term*. Petitioner "used" his [gun] in an attempt to obtain drugs by offering to trade it for cocaine.[10]

Of course, Smith's action *can be so described*, and, of course, the text employs "uses a firearm" with its ordinary meaning. The linguistic meaning of "uses an N" is *silent* about how N is used. So, when "uses a firearm" occurs in a sentence, the assertion must be *completed*, either by adding a qualifying phrase (e.g., "as a weapon," or "as an item of barter") or by extracting the needed content from the presuppositions of the language users—in this case the shared

presuppositions of Congress and its audience, which included judges and justices, prosecutors, police, lawyers,
members of the press, informed members of the public,
others who might fall within the scope of the law, and citizen jurors called in cases in which the law is invoked. If,
as seems natural, Congress would, rationally, have been
understood as asserting that *uses of a firearm as a weapon* are
subject to additional punishment, that was the content of
the law.

This example illustrates what I take to be the first principle of a proper theory of judicial interpretation.[11]

(i) The content of a legal provision is what was asserted or
stipulated by lawmakers and/or ratifiers in approving
it. Although the linguistic meaning of the text is one
component in determining that content, it isn't the
only component.

The second principle identifies exceptional cases in which
applying the asserted or stipulated content of a legal provision to the facts of the case in a court proceeding doesn't
yield a proper verdict.[12]

(ii) In applying the law to the facts of a case, the legal
duty of a judge is to reach the verdict determined
by the asserted content, unless (a) that content is
vague and so doesn't, when combined with the facts
presented in the case, determine a definite verdict, or
(b) the content, the surrounding law, and the facts of
the case determine inconsistent verdicts, or (c) the
content plus new facts that couldn't reasonably have
been anticipated by the lawmakers are patently and
importantly inconsistent with the intended purpose of
the law, which is the publicly stated purpose that supporters advanced to justify it.

This principle covers cases in which judges have no choice but to modify existing legal content in some way. The job of the courts is to mediate between the immense and unforeseeable variety of possible behaviors that may occur, and the legally codified general principles designed to regulate that behavior. Often this requires judges to *precisify* legal provisions in order to reach determinate decisions. This happens when the antecedent contents of the relevant laws neither determinately apply, nor determinately fail to apply, to the facts of a case. Inconsistency is also a concern. Since the body of laws in modern society is enormously complex, the task of maintaining consistency is never-ending. Typically, the inconsistency is not generated by two laws that flatly contradict each other, so that no possible pattern of behavior could conform to both. Instead, it is generated by the combination of two or more laws with some possible, but unanticipated, behavior. Since the range of such behavior—which, if it occurred, would generate inconsistency—is without foreseeable bounds, no legislative process, no matter how careful, precludes the need for judicial resolutions of inconsistencies. The same is true of inconsistencies between a law's content and its rationale or purpose that arise from unanticipated situations following its passage.

To get a hint of what judges should do in these cases, it is best to begin by reviewing how we treat analogous cases in ordinary life in which we are given vague, contradictory, or self-defeating instructions. Suppose A's wife says to A, "Please pick up a large, inexpensive hat for me from the shop. I need it to keep the sun off my face when we go out later." This request is *vague*, because it isn't precise what counts as *large* or what counts as *inexpensive*. When A reaches the shop, he finds that no hats are clearly small or clearly large. Although they vary in price, none are clearly inexpensive, either. Knowing the purpose of his wife's request, A selects one that will keep the sun off her face reasonably well, without costing more than any that would do just as well. Although A can't claim to have done *exactly* what she literally asked him to do, he minimized the degree to which he failed to do so, while maximizing the degree to which her purpose could be fulfilled. When he reports back, she is pleased. This sheds light on the situation faced by the judge when asked, in a case of type (iia), to apply a law that is vague about a crucial fact to which it must be applied.

For a situation analogous to (iib), imagine that A's wife says, "I am dying for a soda. Please bring me the largest bottle of soda in the fridge." On reaching the fridge, A sees it contains two bottles of soda identical in size. Since the request presupposed there would a bottle of soda larger than any other, the request was *inconsistent with the relevant facts,* making it impossible for A to do precisely what was asked. Nevertheless, he has no trouble. Noticing that one bottle is open, causing the soda to lose its fizz, A brings the other to his wife, thereby fulfilling the purpose of her request, while minimizing the degree to which he fails to do what was requested—i.e., bring the one bottle of soda larger than any other bottle of soda there.

The analogy with (iic) is a slight variant of the previous case. In the new case, A's wife makes the same request as before, but the fridge contains only the large, open bottle of soda that has lost its fizz plus two smaller, unopened bottles, one larger than the other. Knowing his wife can't stand soda that has gone flat, A realizes that although he could do what was literally asked, doing that would defeat the purpose of his wife's request. To avoid this, he brings her the larger of the unopened bottles, fulfilling her purpose to the maximum degree possible, while minimizing the degree to which he failed to do what he was asked to do.

These examples illustrate a fact about the use of words to guide action that applies both in ordinary life and in the law. When words guide us, we calculate the asserted (or stipulated) content of the use of the words and the evident purpose of that assertion (or stipulation). These, together with relevant nonlinguistic facts, determine our action. In the cases we have examined, A discharges the obligations imposed by his wife's request, despite either being unable to do what was literally requested because the request is vague or inconsistent, or being able to do what was asked only at the cost of making it self-defeating. In each case, A minimizes the degree to which his action deviates from the content of his wife's request while maximizing the degree to which he fulfills its intended purpose.

Applying this lesson to judges gives us rule (iii), governing the cases mentioned in (ii).[13]

(iii) In cases of type (iia–c), the judicial authority is authorized to make new law by adopting a minimum change in the asserted or stipulated content of the law that maximizes the fulfillment of the lawmaker's discernable intended purpose in making that assertion or stipulation.

The logic supporting (iii) is transparent. Everyone agrees that the job of the courts is to *interpret* the law by applying it to the facts presented in cases brought before it. In difficult cases—in which (a) the legal content is vague and so doesn't, when combined with the facts, determine a definite verdict, or (b) the content, the surrounding law, and the facts determine inconsistent verdicts, or (c) the content plus new facts which could not have been anticipated are patently and importantly inconsistent with the discernable intended purpose of the law—the judges are authorized by principle (iii) to do what all of us routinely do in ordinary life to fulfill our obligations when given instructions that require minimum modifications in order to maximize the satisfaction of their intended purpose.

Adopting (i)–(iii) as principles guiding legal interpretation involves recognizing two different aspects of interpretation. The first, which might be called *mere interpretation,* requires judges to articulate the asserted or stipulated content of legal texts plus the lawmaker's intended purpose in stipulating or asserting that content. Nothing else is needed to faithfully apply the law in unproblematic cases. The second aspect of interpretation, which might be called *rectification,* involves minimally modifying that content to maximize the lawmaker's intended purpose in cases in which it is necessary to do so. To think of the legal obligations of judges in this way is to recognize that although judges are, in a limited sense, lawmakers who sometimes change the content of the law, their legal duty—in countries, like the United States, in which legislation is reserved for the other (democratically elected) branches of government—requires them to be maximally *deferential* to the original lawmakers.[14]

A THEORY OF CONSTITUTIONAL INTERPRETATION

The American Constitution and Bill of Rights were fully ratified by 1791. A compromise between two groups of states with different social institutions and economic systems, already deeply divided over slavery, it was also a philosophical document, drawing on Locke, Hume, and others. Presented as a contract between "we the people" and those we select as our agents, the Constitution is the law that binds the national government.

It begins with this preamble:

We the people of the United States, in order to form a more perfect union, establish justice, insure domestic tranquility, provide for the common defense, promote the general welfare, and secure the blessings of liberty to ourselves and our posterity, do ordain and establish this Constitution for the United States of America.

The Constitution then specifies the structure of government, the governmental offices, terms of office, methods of appointment or election, the legal responsibilities of the different branches and of those filling offices, as well as the scope and limits of government power. No institution or group of officeholders is identified as the sovereign or supreme ruler. Still, if you ask *Who is sovereign?*, there is an answer. We, the citizens, are sovereign. Originally the citizens of the thirteen ratifying states were; today, the citizens of 50 states are. We, collectively, choose the leaders and provide the government with its legitimacy by taking fidelity to the Constitution to be our supreme Hartian *rule of recognition*.

The trope—*We the people of the United States . . . do ordain and establish*—in which the Constitution fictionally presents itself as if it were written by all the people, is, in fact, a contract between its author-sovereigns and the government officials who are authorized to act on their behalf. Writing in this way to a broad and indeterminate population which they hoped would endorse their product, the real authors of the document—Gouverneur Morris, the drafting committee at the Philadelphia Convention, James Madison (who wrote the original amendments), and others—were inviting their audience to buy into their vision, thereby turning it into a reality. Because the issues were hotly contested, it was not obvious that they would. But once the Constitution was ratified, the factions largely disappeared as winners and losers of different constitutional arguments came together to support the fledgling republic. A fascinating case of a fiction struggling to become a reality, and succeeding, the Constitution is authoritative because we, its putative authors, take it to be.

Important amendments subsequent to the Bill of Rights have changed the Constitution over the years. Although the Constitution itself changes in no other ways, *constitutional law* does. One source of change, implicit in the Constitution, involves changes wrought by Supreme Court decisions in which the Court applies constitutional text to facts brought before it. The Court's first interpretive task is to derive the originally asserted or stipulated content of the constitutional provision. When applying this content to the facts of the case logically determines a unique result, it is the duty of the Court to return that verdict.

Sometimes, however, it is indeterminate whether unanticipated facts of a new case, do, or don't, fall under the original content of a constitutional text. The Court must then resolve the indeterminacy by making the minimum modification of the originally asserted constitutional content that maximizes fulfillment of the original intended constitutional purpose. Since this involves an imprecise balancing of two values, the result may be a restricted range of outcomes any of which would be legally justified. When judges select an outcome and that decision becomes an established precedent, they modify the constitutional law that existed prior to their construction—*whether or not the selected outcome falls within the objectively authorized range.* But the Constitution doesn't change. Its original contents and purposes continue as touchstones against which new, judge-made constructions can be tested, sometimes leading to their revision or invalidation, if a later Court shows them to be inferior to constructions more in harmony with original constitutional contents and purposes.

Constitutional law also changes when constitutional provisions are quietly ignored and replaced by extra-constitutional practices that go unchallenged. For example, Article I, Section 8 of the Constitution gives Congress alone the power to declare war. Nevertheless, that power was compromised by the Korean War, the Vietnam War, and the First and Second Gulf Wars. Congress never declared war in Korea, though the Korean War left 36,000 American soldiers dead. Although the other wars were sanctioned by congressional resolutions, they weren't declarations of war, and in Vietnam the resolution followed military involvement rather than initiating it. This result has, arguably, shifted American constitutional law.

Barack Obama's "Iran deal" is another example. Although it was clearly a treaty with a foreign nation, the president didn't submit it to the Senate, the approval of which by a two-thirds majority was constitutionally required. As with limited wars, a congressional fig leaf was offered instead. As I write, Obama's deal has now been repudiated by a new president, Donald Trump. But if Obama's practice is repeated with impunity, the clause concerning foreign treaties might also become a dead letter.

This new factor—*de facto* constitutional change—plus the power of the Supreme Court to change constitutional law while still being responsible to the original Constitution, requires small, but significant, additions to the theory of judicial interpretation, which I sketched in the previous section. The theory, which I call "deferentialism," is my own version of a broad family of related theories known as "originalism."[15]

CONSTITUTIONAL DEFERENTIALISM

C1. The original content of a constitutional provision is what was asserted or stipulated by lawmakers and/or ratifiers in approving it. This, along with the originally intended purpose of that assertion, is that to which the Court must be faithful.

C2. When dealing with cases in which the original content of a constitutional provision CP has been ignored and replaced by an extralegal practice, the Court must first articulate the content of the practice, incorporating past precedents (if any), and then either replace it with the original asserted content and intended purpose of CP or revise it by bringing it as close as possible to that content and purpose, without undermining important and well-founded expectations created by the practice (and precedents) on which those subject to the law have invested valuable resources that are not easily recovered.

C3. In applying existing constitutional law—whether original content of a constitutional clause or a modification of it resulting from an earlier precedent—to the facts of a case, the legal duty of the Court is to reach the verdict determined by that content, unless (a) it is vague and so doesn't, when combined with the facts of the case, determine a definite verdict, or (b) it plus other constitutional provisions and facts of the case determine inconsistent verdicts, or (c) the content plus new facts that could not have reasonably been anticipated at the time the constitutional provision was adopted are patently and importantly inconsistent with the intended purpose of the provision, or (d) the earlier precedent is found to be insufficiently faithful to original constitutional content and purpose.

C4. In cases of type (C3a–c), the Court is authorized to make new constitutional law by articulating a minimum change in existing law that maximizes the fulfillment of its intended purpose. In cases of type (C3d), the Court is authorized either to replace it with the original asserted content and intended purpose of a constitutional provision, or to revise it by bringing it as close as possible to that content and purpose, without undermining important and legitimate expectations that have grown up on which relevant agents are relying.

This theory updates the theory of judicial interpretation outlined earlier, accommodating the facts—(i) that the Constitution contains sweeping principles, the contents of which encompass both a clearly determinate core and an indeterminate periphery, (ii) that applying that content to new circumstances requires periodic adjustments, (iii) that making the adjustments is primarily the job of the Supreme Court, and (iv) that because the Court does *not* have the authority to act as an independent political body, its authorized adjustments must preserve core contents of constitutional provisions to the maximum extent possible, while making only those changes that further the fulfillment of their original intended purposes.[16]

This theory is descriptive in the sense that H.L.A. Hart's account of legal systems is descriptive. It is a fact about the American system that the interpretation of legal texts by judges is governed by rules that determine their judicial responsibilities. Although these rules have normative consequences, the claim that a given set of norms is taken by citizens to be authoritative is descriptive. Deferentialism purports to articulate the content of those norms. Whether or not it does is a controversial matter.

It does conform to what Supreme Court justices standardly *say* in justifying their decisions—always purporting to find reasons for them in constitutional texts or authoritative precedents.[17] Still, a substantial number of their decisions over the last century do seem to have violated the tenets of deferentialism. Although this raises questions about whether deferentialism enjoys sufficient support among prominent members of the legal profession, it doesn't by itself show that American law isn't deferentialist. After all, deferentialism doesn't espouse Supreme Court infallibility.

Rather, it stipulates that the originally asserted contents of laws passed by institutions set up by, and operating in accord with, the original content of the Constitution remain legally valid, *unless they have been overturned by constitutional processes*. It further recognizes the Supreme Court as the highest authority in these matters. Thus, Americans' acceptance of its decisions as genuine law, *whether or not they have believed the cases to have been rightly decided*, is consistent with deferentialism.

Still, deferentialism is controversial. One leading argument against it goes like this: (i) The country has often been faced with serious problems the elected branches of government were unable to solve. (ii) Since deferentialism, and originalism more generally, would not have allowed the needed results, the Court had to solve the problems in another way. (iii) Thus deferentialism (and originalism) can't give a correct account of the legal responsibility of justices in interpreting the Constitution.

There are two problems with this argument. First, as I argue elsewhere, (ii) is false, since deferentialism can reach results validating the positive aspects of important cases like *Brown v. Board of Education,* while avoiding damaging missteps in the reasoning found in those decisions.[18] Second, even if (i) and (ii) were true, it wouldn't falsify the deferentialist *description* of what the Court is *legally authorized* to do. After all, every official position, short of that of an absolute ruler, carries limitations on one's authority. Hence, no matter what one imagines the limits of the legal authority of judges to be, it will always be possible for circumstances to arise in which the morally best policy outcome in a given case can't be judicially achieved without exceeding that authority.

So, is the deferentialist account of the legitimate limits of judicial authority correct or not? On the plus side, deferentialism is a version of a broad category of easily understood, increasingly well-worked-out theories, known as *originalist,* which reflect Americans' continuing reverence for the Constitution, their respect for its separation of powers, and their awareness of its delegation of legislative authority to Congress alone. Although it is widely recognized that justices sometimes must adjust constitutional content to new circumstances, they are widely expected to be maximally deferential to the Constitution when doing so. On the minus side, large numbers of politicians, law professors, and members of the legal profession reject originalism. This might be decisive, if they were united behind a well-articulated and widely accepted positive alternative to it, but they are not.

These considerations raise a normative question: *Whatever the current social norms determining the scope and limits of legitimate judicial authority in the United States currently are, what should they be?* In fact, a version of this question is already implicit in deferentialism itself. In acknowledging that judges are sometimes authorized to make the minimum change in existing legal content that maximizes fulfillment of the law's original intended purpose, deferentialism directs them to perform a task that can often be done more or less equally well in several ways. What should guide judges in choosing among them? There is no current consensus on this matter.

At this point, the question is straightforwardly normative. Would we do better authorizing judges

(i) to exercise their own moral judgment in selecting the best of the remaining deferentially acceptable policy alternatives,

(ii) to decide the individual case at hand, while refusing to provide a general rationale favoring any of the remaining, equally deferential, alternatives, thus eschewing the precedential status of the decision and leaving the policy choice to the democratic branches, to voters, or, in constitutional cases, to the amendment process, or

(iii) to exercise their own discretion, treating it as precedential, when the issues raised by the alternatives are minor, while leaving broadly consequential policy issues to the people or the democratic branches?

The question is ripe for debate.

An interesting argument for (ii) or (iii) is given by John McGinnis and Michael Rappaport in *Originalism and the Good Constitution.*[19] Their guiding premise is that the form of democratic government that produces the best consequences for its citizens—securing liberty, stability, consensus, and well-being—is one that relies on supermajoritarian rules and processes (as exemplified in the United States by the ratification of the original Constitution, the amendment process, and the supermajoritarian features of federalism, the separation of powers, and a bicameral legislature). Nothing could be further from this ideal than the ability of a bare majority of nine unelected judges with lifetime tenure to remove important constitutional matters from the normal give-and-take of democratic politics.

One of their most interesting points concerns the process of amending the Constitution, which, on the face of it, would seem to be the best way of updating a governing document that is more than 200 years old. Today that process is often regarded too difficult. But is it? The Constitution has been amended 17 times since the ratification of the Bill of Rights in 1791, including twelve amendments in the twentieth century (all but one before 1972). Why the current dearth of amendments? McGinnis and Rappaport argue that the rampant judicial activism starting in the mid-1930s has been an important, but unfortunate, cause. Although the vast changes in the economy in the twentieth century may well have justified greater governmental oversight than had previously existed, they argue that this would have been better achieved by hammering out informed and efficient constitutional amendments. After all, the hegemony of New Deal Democrats then was very likely sufficient to allow them to play the leading role in drafting and ratifying amendments that were arguably needed. Unfortunately, the path taken relied on piecemeal adjustments of an unrepresentative and economically unsophisticated Supreme Court, whose peremptory rulings preempted what might have been achieved by a more consensual process.[20] Worse, once the tide of judicial activism gained momentum, it began to produce divisive, partisan results that undermined public faith that the Court could be trusted not to subvert constitutional content, old or new.[21]

EXTRA-CONSTITUTIONAL CHANGE: THE ADMINISTRATIVE STATE

In addressing our next constitutional issue, we continue to follow Hart in taking law to be a system of internalized social rules obeyed not only because they are backed by force, but also because they are perceived to advance individual and general welfare, protect liberty, punish vice, and distribute benefits and burdens in morally acceptable ways, while being reasonably responsive to the views of the governed. Legal rules regulating behavior are identified by *rules of recognition* that invest institutions with authority to make action-guiding rules. As noted, the key element determining the authority of American law is fidelity to the U.S. Constitution.

Two key features of the Constitution are its separation of powers between the legislative, executive, and judicial branches, and its explicit guarantees of individual rights, which historically have been protected by the Supreme Court. Both are now threatened by the rise of the administrative state, composed of executive departments plus regulatory agencies. The former include the departments of Health and Human Services, Housing and Urban Development, Agriculture, Commerce, Interior, Justice, Labor, Education, Energy, Treasury, Transportation, State, Defense, Homeland Security, and more. The latter—regulatory agencies—include the SEC (Securities and Exchange Commission), NLRB (National Labor Relations Board), EPA (Environmental Protection Agency), FCC (Federal Communications Commission), OSHA (Occupational Safety and Health Administration), FTC (Federal Trade Commission), FDA (Food and Drug Administration), ICC (Interstate Commerce Commission), and more.

Professor Gary Lawson of Boston University Law School describes the characteristic feature of these agencies. As he puts it,

[T]he destruction of the principle of separation of powers is perhaps the crowning jewel of the modern administrative revolution. Administrative agencies routinely combine all three governmental functions [executive, legislative, and judicial] in the same body.[22]

His example is the FTC.

The Commission promulgates substantive rules of conduct. The Commission then considers whether to authorize investigations into whether the Commission's rules have been violated. If the Commission authorizes an investigation, the investigation is conducted by the Commission, which reports its findings to the Commission. If the Commission thinks that the Commission's findings warrant an enforcement action, the Commission issues a complaint. The Commission's complaint that a Commission rule has been violated is then prosecuted by the Commission and adjudicated by the Commission. The Commission's adjudication can either take place before the full Commission or before a semi-autonomous administrative law judge [employed by the Commission]. If the Commission chooses to adjudicate before an administrative law judge rather than before the Commission and the decision is adverse to the Commission, the Commission can appeal to the Commission.[23]

In these agencies, a single body legislates, investigates, charges, and prosecutes accused violators. It also adjudicates, often convicting and passing sentence without giving the accused his or her constitutional rights to a trial by an independent judge or jury, to immunity from self-incrimination, or to challenge the constitutionality of the administrative process. Only after conviction and often payment of a fine is the accused allowed to challenge in federal court.

As Philip Hamburger of Columbia Law School shows in *Is Administrative Law Unlawful?*, today's administrative law is a greatly expanded version of earlier undemocratic rule, arising from the British Crown's attempt to escape limitations on royal power arising from the Magna Carta in 1215 and the Petition of Right in 1628.[24] The framers of the U.S. Constitution were aware of the Crown's use of the Star Chamber and High Commission to achieve results outside the legal structure of Parliament and common law. Wishing to avoid this end-run around the law, the framers separated legislative, judicial, and executive power. As Hamburger explains, the rise of the administrative state is a return to what they took to be an evil they were determined to avoid.

The Fourth Amendment to the U.S. Constitution was one means of doing so. It outlawed *general warrants* allowing search and seizure without convincing an independent judge there was *probable cause* for thinking an individual had committed a crime.

> The right of the people to be secure in their persons, houses, papers, and effects against unreasonable searches and seizures shall not be violated, and no Warrants shall issue, but on probable cause, supported by Oath or affirmation, and particularly describing the place to be searched, and the persons or things to be seized.

General warrants were ruled unconstitutional in England in 1763. But the Crown continued to use certain versions of them, called *writs of assistance,* in some settings. In 1761 this type of general warrant became an issue in the Superior Court of Massachusetts. An American lawyer, James Otis, challenged the writs, likening them to the Crown's use of special *prerogative warrants* that bypassed Parliament and common-law courts. Otis argued that the law in colonial Massachusetts had long required writs that could be granted only "on oath and probable suspicion." He concluded, "It is the business of this court to demolish this monster of oppression, and tear into rags this remnant of Star Chamber tyranny."[25] Though Otis didn't win in court, he won in the press, helping fuel the drive for independence and the elimination of search and seizure without a judicial finding of probable cause. Hamburger argues that when administrative agencies today compel people to disclose all personal or business material relevant to agency investigations, they are eviscerating the Fourth Amendment, while reviving an ancient system of government outside the law that was known and rejected at the American founding.

The Fifth Amendment is also threatened.

No person shall be held to answer for a capital, or otherwise infamous crime, unless on presentment or indict-
ment of a Grand Jury . . . nor shall any person be subject for the same offence to be twice put in jeopardy of
life or limb, nor shall be compelled in any criminal case
to be a witness against himself, nor be deprived of life,
liberty, or property, *without due process of law*; nor shall
private property be taken for public use without just
compensation.

By the late eighteenth century, *due process of law* was a legal
term of art deriving ultimately from clause 39 of the Magna
Carta:

No free man shall be seized or imprisoned, or stripped
of his rights or possessions, or outlawed or exiled, or
deprived of his standing in any other way, nor will we
proceed with force against him, or send others to do so,
except by the lawful judgment of his equals or by the law
of the land.

The Seventh Amendment to the U.S. Constitution extends
the right to trial by jury to civil cases and protects facts in
a civil case from being reversed by another court. Nevertheless, today federal agencies make rules, conduct investigations into possible violations, demand private records
without a warrant, compel one to testify against oneself,
and impose fines, wielding executive, legislative, and judicial power, without constitutional limitations.

   This state of affairs is largely due to questionable congressional delegations of power. Does the Constitution give
Congress the legal authority to so delegate? Hamburger
and Lawson say *no*. The Constitution separates legislative,

executive, and judicial power into different branches of government, ensuring that no institution combines them. Since Congress doesn't have executive or judicial power, it can't delegate them. Its legislative powers are enumerated in the Constitution, along with those that are *necessary and proper* for executing those powers. Since there is no *delegation clause* in the Constitution, *the power to delegate its legislative power* is not an enumerated power.

Is it an implied power that is necessary and proper for the execution of its enumerated powers? It is, only if Congress couldn't produce the legislation it is empowered to enact without further delegating some of its power to other agencies. An argument can be made that administrative expertise is sometimes needed to achieve wise, or even only moderately tolerable, results. The question then becomes, *Could these results be gotten in another way*—e.g., by asking agencies for a range of possible rules and advice on how to evaluate them? The burden of proof to show this wouldn't work is on proponents of the administrative state.

In addition to being *necessary,* implied powers must also be *proper.* Is it *proper* for Congress to sub-delegate part of its legislative power? Hamburger thinks not. The argument begins with Section 1 of Article I: "All legislative powers herein granted shall be vested in a Congress of the United States, which shall consist of a House of Representatives and a Senate." Can an agent, Congress, which has been vested with powers by others, then sub-delegate some of those powers to others? For Hamburger and a growing number of legal theorists, the entire Constitution is a delegation of specific powers from those in whom the powers originate—*we the people*—to specific branches of the government, which are our agents. We authorize them to manage specific portions of our business.[26]

Next we ask, *How were legal instruments authorizing some to have the power to act on behalf of others understood in the late eighteenth century?* According to Lawson, guardians, executors, and others acting under power of attorney functioned as fiduciaries authorized by *agency instruments*. Hamburger and others maintain that the Constitution is a *grand agency instrument*. The American founding father James Iredell, who was first a member of the North Carolina convention ratifying the Constitution and later a justice of the Supreme Court of the United States, called the Constitution *"a great power of attorney."*[27]

A recent book by that title develops the argument in more detail.[28] It finds a rich set of legal rules for interpreting agency instruments in Britain and the colonial United States. According to these rules, agents exercising delegated powers generally *could not sub-delegate* without an explicit authorization in the agency instrument itself. Robert Natelson puts it this way:

> When not authorized in the instrument creating the relationship, fiduciary duties were nondelegable. The applicable rule was *delegatus non potest delegare*—the delegate cannot delegate. As Mathew Bacon phrased it in his *A New Abridgment of the Law,* "One who has an Authority to do an Act for another, must execute it himself, and cannot transfer it to another, for this being a Trust and Confidence reposed in the Party, cannot be assigned to a Stranger."[29]

If the U.S. Constitution was understood to be an agency instrument, it would have been assumed that powers delegated to one institution of government cannot be sub-delegated to another institution.

Hamburger makes a similar argument, tracing the prohibition of legislative sub-delegation from Locke through Whig and Tory history, into pre-constitutional America.

If the principal selects his agent for her knowledge, skill, trustworthiness, or other personal qualities, he presumably gave the power to her, not anyone else. Of course, a principal could expressly authorize subdelegation, but he could not otherwise be understood to have intended this. . . . On such reasoning the principle of delegation bars any subdelegation of legislative power. In the Constitution, the people delegate legislative powers to Congress. The people, moreover, specify that they grant the legislative powers to a Congress, "consisting of a Senate and House of Representatives," with members chosen in specified ways. *The delegation to Congress thus is to a body chosen for its institutional qualities, including members chosen by their constituents for their personal qualities. Congress and its members therefore cannot sub delegate their power.*[30]

Given all this, one does well to note the many clauses in the Constitution dealing with the selection, structure, and operation of Congress. As Lawson remarks, "No agency instrument would contain such detailed selection procedures and then implicitly allow an end-run around them."[31] In short, it would have been clear in 1788 that Congress can't sub-delegate its legislative authority to others.

What should we think about this today? When Congress passes a law, it is unrealistic to suppose that every concept employed in it can be rigorously defined there. Nor is every detail for implementing the law spelled out. Some of these tasks must be left for administrative departments or agencies. How, then, are we to distinguish between true legislative content and the practical details of implementation? The answer must, it seems, come by extending the distinction between *interpretation* and *rectification,* needed by any plausible theory of the interpretation of legal texts.[32]

Consider a judge applying a statute to facts of a case. The first task is to determine what the lawmakers said or stipulated in adopting the statute. This is interpretation proper. As we have seen, sometimes, but not always, that is the end of the story. More must be done when the asserted content is vague in a way that fails to decide between relevant alternatives. The same is true if it conflicts with other assertions, or if it transparently doesn't advance the communicative purposes at hand. When analogs of such vagueness, inconsistency, or evident impracticality occur in a court case, the judges or justices must sometimes *rectify* the law the legislators enacted in adopting the legal text. Their legal duty in doing so is not to strike out on their own, but to make the minimal change in the law's content that maximizes fulfillment of the lawmakers' rationale (legislative purpose) in passing it.

Being prescribed in judicial review, this process can be expanded to implementation by administrative agencies. When an administrative agency is tasked with implementing an act of Congress, it should articulate both the asserted content of the law and the intended purpose of Congress in making that assertion. Confronted with different means of implementation, the agency should select, from those that are fully consistent with the asserted content of the law, the one that best satisfies Congress's intended purpose, to the extent to which those can be discerned with reasonable specificity. When they can't be so discerned, the agency should take no action on the matter without further clarifying legislation. When relevant asserted content and intended purpose are sufficiently specific, deviations from them are authorized only when no system of implementation consistent with asserted content minimally satisfies that purpose. In such cases the system of implementation that deviates least from asserted content while maximally satisfying intended purpose should be adopted. The agency should then be required to submit its results to Congress for final approval.

Finally, this new conception of agency-Congress interaction must be subject to judicial review, without the now customary extreme deference to the agencies. This will require existing doctrines of judicial deference to the presumed legality of agency rules and the agency's factual record of enforcement to be revised. For the court to accept the agency's factual record is, in effect, to deprive the individual or institution targeted by the agency to a trial by jury, because in such trials *a jury is the judge of fact*. While in a normal trial the judge is the arbiter of legal questions, in appeals of administrative penalties federal courts typically treat earlier actions of an agency as if they were the actions of a lower court. Federal district courts can, of course, rule that the agency acted improperly, but in practice they typically defer to its legal interpretations. Even when an appeal is successful, the federal court often merely sends the case back to the agency for reconsideration. None of this conforms to the Constitution.

This abandonment of the Constitution raises a troubling question. *Has administrative power become so central to modern government that there is no practical way of doing without it?* Hamburger thinks not. He reports that outside of the Social Security Administration, agencies employ only 257 special administrative law judges. These could, in principle, be replaced by new federal district judges, independent of the agencies. What about administrative rule making? Since the agencies fall under the executive branch, the president could order them to send major rules that impose binding legal obligations on citizens to Congress for approval, thereby injecting political accountability into the process. Other agency rules, merely defining benefit levels for programs and implementing the delivery of benefits, could be left with the agencies.

These actions could bring the administrative state more in line with the Constitution, to which earlier philosophers—e.g., Locke, Hume, and Witherspoon—indirectly contributed by insisting on strict separation of powers, political accountability of major policy makers, and enforcement of natural rights (see chapter 4). Today the challenge is for philosophers, historians, legal theorists, and social scientists to spotlight the issue and articulate alternatives to current practices, thereby shaping the future of free societies.

CHAPTER 13

THE OBJECTIVITY
OF MORALITY

*The challenge to autonomous (nonreligious) ethics inherited
from Hume and Kant; deriving moral and nonmoral* ought
from factual is; *the empirical search for factual, morally
relevant premises; the social and psychobiological content
of the moral sense in human nature; the biological basis
of social affiliation; the limits of the moral sense versus its
historically expanding reach; the role of socioeconomic
institutions in expanding our biologically based morality.*

THE CHALLENGE

For much of the twentieth century moral philosophy remained in the shadow of David Hume and Immanuel
Kant. Although Hume argued that the source of morality is a sentiment of benevolence toward others embedded in our common human nature, he also announced
an unbridgeable chasm between fact and value, famously
expressed in the slogan that one cannot derive *ought* from
is. Kant agreed that morality is rooted in human nature,
but denied it sprang from desire, sentiment, or any human
passion. Since the demands of morality are unconditional,
he reasoned, moral imperatives must be categorical, rather
than hypothetical. When one says to a student "You ought
to study," one presumes that the student has an interest
in learning, or at least in passing the course. Because of
this, the prudential *ought* has the force of a hypothetical

imperative—*if you want to learn, or pass the course, you ought to study.* By contrast, the moral *ought—You ought never lie—*is, Kant thought, never conditioned on any contingent desire or aim of the agent. Since all our aims—including our desire to continue to live—seem, in principle, to be renounceable, it might appear that no moral obligation—*You ought to do X—*can be grounded in any desire or aim of ours. In short, no such *ought* can be derived from any such *is.*

That wasn't the end of Kant's story. Agreeing that human nature is the source of morality, he took the crucial element to be our rationality, which, he thought, directs us to act only on rules we can rationally will to be universally followed. Noting that universal lying and promise-breaking would destroy the trust that makes them possible, he rightly concluded that one cannot rationally will them to be universally performed. However, he wrongly concluded that this showed it to be irrational to lie or break a promise. It didn't; moreover, sometimes it's not wrong to lie. Even when it is wrong, there need be nothing irrational about it. One cannot prove that one ought not lie, or break a promise, by deriving that conclusion from the premise that the agent is rational.

These results challenge the integrity of moral inquiry. If one cannot establish claims about what we ought to do by deriving them from claims about any aspects—rational or nonrational—of human nature, then it is tempting to conclude that there is no moral knowledge, and perhaps no objective moral facts. That was the burden under which much of the moral philosophy of the twentieth century labored, and from which it has only recently begun to extricate itself.

DERIVING NONMORAL *OUGHT* FROM FACTUAL *IS*

The first step in doing so is to look more closely at the slogan "One cannot derive *ought* from *is.*" Although it is standardly taken to mean that no evaluative conclusion is a *logical consequence* of a factual conclusion, that can't be right. In formal logic, whether or not one sentence is a logical consequence of another never depends on the specific meanings, or interpretations, of any *nonlogical words*— words other than 'all', 'some', 'and', 'or', 'not', 'if, then', and '='. Thus 'Mary ought to study ' fails to be a *logical* consequence of 'Mary promised to study' for the same trivial reason that 'The ball is red' fails to be a *logical* consequence of 'The ball is crimson' and that 'John won't win' fails to be a *logical* consequence of 'John doesn't realize that he won't win'. In each case, the inference is, arguably, valid, even though it doesn't count as *logical* because it depends on the interpretation of nonlogical words in the premise or the conclusion.

For the slogan to have its intended force, the consequence relation must be conceptual, not merely logical—e.g., the relation must be *necessary* or *a priori consequence*. A proposition Q (expressed by a sentence) is a *necessary consequence* of a proposition P if and only if it is *impossible* for P to be true without Q being true—if and only if for any state w that it is possible for the world to be in, if P would be true were the world in state w, then Q would also be true were the world in w. Proposition Q is an *a priori consequence* of proposition P if and only if it is possible to determine that Q is true, if P is true by deductive reasoning alone, without appealing to empirical evidence to justify one's conclusion. Presumably those who say that one cannot derive *ought* from *is* mean that no claim about what one ought to do is both a *necessary* and an *a priori* consequence of any factual claims.

This way of understanding the alleged impossibility of deriving *ought* from *is* is more interesting. To see why, we need to say more about the truth conditions of a statement that *A ought to do X*. To make things easier, let's begin with cases in which the *ought* statement expresses, not a judgment about what is morally required, but a prudential judgment about what is best for A, understood as what contributes most to A's welfare (from a range of relevant acts). What is welfare? It is natural to think of it as consisting of the advancement of one's most basic interests and the development of one's most important capacities, which contribute most to one's flourishing and well-functioning as a human being. These, in turn, depend on human nature. According to the view of human beings as intensely social animals to be advocated here, the basic constituents of our welfare may be said to be: health, safety, companionship, membership in a community, freedom of action, development of our physical and intellectual capacities, satisfaction of our native curiosity, enjoyment of sensual pleasures, opportunities for excitement and the pursuit of difficult goals in concert with others, the ability to contribute to the welfare of others we care about and to benefit from those who care about us, and the knowledge that we are contributing to a larger human enterprise that will outlast us.

Welfare, so understood, comes in degrees. Normal human beings usually care about their own welfare and wish to advance it, while differing on how much significance they attach to the various components that go into it. They also care about other things, for which they are sometimes willing, quite properly, to sacrifice their welfare. In addition, they are often either ignorant of, or mistaken about, what their welfare consists in and what will advance it. Though they typically want to be better off—to increase their welfare—they not infrequently want or desire things that are inconsistent with that goal.

What, then, is the connection between one's welfare and one's reasons for action? First, the fact that performing a given action X would—objectively—increase one's welfare provides one with a reason for action—the greater the increase the stronger the reason—whether or not one recognizes that X would do so. Second, recognizing the fact that performing X would increase one's welfare nearly always provides one with some desire or motivation to perform X, even though (a) the intensity of one's desire need not be proportionate to the strength of the reason, and (b) even when it is, one may have stronger reasons or more intense desires to do something else. What, in light of this, are the truth conditions of prudential *ought* claims? Putting aside both moral reasons and reasons stemming entirely from a concern for the welfare of others, we may take a prudential use of *A ought to do X* to be true if and only if A has more reason to do X than A has to do anything else (from a range of relevant alternative acts), in short, if and only if A's doing X would most advance A's welfare.

In assessing what it is for A to have *more reason* to do X than to do Y, there are two confusions to avoid. First, when we ask, at a given time, which actions A has most (prudential) reason to perform, we are *not* asking which of A's desires or interests are currently most intensely or urgently felt; we are asking what, on balance, would maximize A's welfare, considered as a state that has its ups and downs over time. It is perfectly possible for agents who are otherwise rational, but who have not developed necessary self-discipline, to allow the intensity of immediate desire to lead to actions they know to be contrary to their larger interests. Second, we must not, harkening back to chapter 8, identify maximizing A's welfare with maximizing *the expected utility (from A's point of view) of A's choice of one action from a range of alternative actions* (which is a product of A's utilities plus A's subjective probabilities that performing certain actions would produce desired outcomes). If I know that A is ignorant of relevant facts, or that some of A's beliefs are false, I may know that some of A's subjective probabilities are unrealistic, and, for that reason, I may be better able to evaluate the benefits to A of a given course of action than A is. If so, my remark "You ought (or ought not) do A" may be true, even if it doesn't match A's own ranking of expected utilities. My remark will be true if and only if A's performing X will maximize A's total welfare when compared with other relevant acts.

Finally we ask, "What true factual premises are needed to derive prudential conclusions about what A ought to do that are necessary and *a priori* consequences of those premises?" The answer should be clear. We need truths about what A's welfare consists in plus truths about what outcomes would be produced were A to perform various actions. In many situations, there may be considerable ignorance, uncertainty, and even error, about these matters. Because of this, we often won't know which factual truths would allow us to derive truths about what, prudentially, A ought to do. But sometimes we will, and even when we don't, our ignorance is no reason to doubt that there are such factual truths. Thus there is no compelling reason to doubt that, often, some prudential claims about what A ought, or ought not, do will be both necessary and *a priori* consequences of factual truths about A, and A's situation.

Nevertheless, this result is limited, even if we continue to put distinctively moral reasons aside. To see this, consider a case in which A contemplates an action X that would benefit someone B whom A cares about a great deal, even though performing X would diminish A's welfare. This situation will arise when A's knowledge of (or belief in) B's benefit increases A's welfare less than the cost to A's welfare of performing X, which could be avoided by doing something else. Because of this, A *ought not*, prudentially, do X because A's purely prudential reasons for doing X outweigh all his prudential reasons for doing anything else.

However, it's not obvious that this means that A *ought not* do X, all things considered—even if we continue to bracket moral reasons. If A cares more about B's welfare than A's own, A may think *"I ought to do X"* while being fully aware of what doing X would involve for both of them. A need not be thinking that benefiting B is morally required; in some cases it may not be. A may simply recognize that since A wants to benefit B more than A wants anything else, doing X will bring about the result that A most desires. Surely, we can't say, in all such cases, that it would be wrong (morality aside) for A to do X, or that *A ought not, all things considered, do X*. This suggests that the *ought* statements we have been considering may be equivalent to different maximizing statements. The prudential statement is equivalent to the claim that doing X would be more beneficial to A's welfare than performing any relevant alternative act, while the "all things considered" statement (in the circumstance we are imagining) is equivalent to the claim that doing X will satisfy A's deepest desire. Presumably, these *oughts* can be derived from factual statements about A, the actions under consideration, and the targets of those actions.

DERIVING MORAL *OUGHT* FROM FACTUAL PREMISES

Why should statements about what one morally ought to do be different? The challenge is to find facts about normal human agents and their relations with others that are capable (i) of supporting the truth of the statements to the effect that they *morally ought* to do certain things and (ii) of providing them with what they can, in principle, recognize to be *reasons*—facts with the potential of moving them—to perform the required actions. In looking for such facts, we look for *other people* an agent cares about plus *relationships and activities* that the agent values in which he or she is, in one way or another, involved with others. The others whom the one cares about (to widely varying degrees) may be family, friends, loved ones, associates, coworkers, members of the same profession, fellow citizens, and even all of humanity, including the unborn. They may include any on whose welfare one places some positive value (large or small) whom one imagines might in some way be affected by one's actions. The relationships and activities with others that one values encompass any reciprocal or coordinated action from which the participants derive value that wouldn't be available if they couldn't, in general, count on others to play their expected parts. These include personal relationships, promises and commitments, participation in business and professional practices, common market-based economic activities, truthful linguistic communication, and many more activities.

Moral reasons for one's actions are facts about the impact of those actions on the welfare and legitimate activity-based or relationship-based expectations of others. The fact that an action one is capable of performing would have a positive effect on the welfare of those one cares about is a broadly moral reason for performing it—the stronger the effect, the stronger the reason. In a different sort of case, the fact that an action conforms to the legitimate activity-based expectations of those with whom one voluntarily interacts in an activity providing benefits for all is also a moral reason for performing the act. To understand this sort of reason, imagine yourself participating in a voluntary group activity that benefits all if each plays his or her part, but which may fail to be beneficial if one or more participants opt out. Realizing this, and wishing not to incur the anger and negative consequences that would result from discovery that one is shirking, one has a self-interested reason not to opt out. This, in turn, may, and very often does, provide the basis of a moral reason for conforming to the legitimate expectations of others. This occurs either when one cares, to some degree, for the other participants, or when one doesn't want to be the kind of person who would let others down—e.g., the kind of person one would condemn oneself if were to view one's action from the perspective of another participant. The strength of this second sort of moral reason is proportionate to the importance of one's role in the activity, the benefits produced by it for the participants on the particular occasion in question, and the centrality of that general type of activity in the social life of which one is a part. Summing up, we may say that, *in general, the acts one morally ought to perform are those one has the strongest moral reasons to perform, provided that they don't require one to make sacrifices out of proportion with the nature of the benefits for others they achieve.*

Which moral reasons are stronger than which others, how they combine to produce an act's overall moral stringency, as well as how and when that stringency is discounted, in determining what one morally ought to do, by the sacrifices to one's welfare entailed by performing it, are complex matters studied by normative ethical theorists. I don't, and I am not sure anyone does, know how to reduce these to any precise formula. But the foundational point remains. All the determinants of these moral calculations—one's own welfare, the effects of the action on one's welfare and that of others, and the relation of the action to the relation- and activity-based expectations of others with whom one is involved—are factual matters. If, in addition, the relative strengths of these matters and their manner of combination are also ordinary factual matters, then it may, in principle, be possible to derive *moral oughts* from factual premises about what *is*. Although I haven't demonstrated this to be so, it's not obvious that we should take for granted that it isn't. If we don't do that, we should be open to the idea that moral facts, like other facts, are capable of being investigated and known, even if that knowledge is sometimes very hard to achieve.

There is, however, another worry to be confronted. Although the idea of moral objectivity is welcome, one might worry that it comes at the price of an objectionable moral relativity. In grounding moral reasons for action in the interests and values of the agent, one must give up the Kantian idea that moral obligations are binding on all rational agents, who could, in principle, entirely lack fellow feeling with, or compassion for, others. The point is illustrated by the reaction of a class of possible rational agents to three facts that would, in ordinary life, be regarded as relevant to establishing the truth of claims about moral obligation: (i) the fact that lying or breaking a promise subverts the trust that makes one's lie or promise possible (which, all other things being equal, would be morally objectionable), (ii) the fact that one who avoids sharing the burden of a collective effort from which one benefits asks others to do what one refuses to do oneself, and (iii) the fact that benefiting oneself will, in certain situations, seriously harm innocent others. It is natural to think that facts such as these support the truth of moral claims about what one ought, or ought not, do only if they provide reasons for *all agents* to act in the morally required way.

Do they? Imagine a rational being who lacks any concern for others, who coldly calculates benefits for himself alone, and always acts accordingly. Because facts (i)–(iii) are unconnected to his interests, they won't count as reasons for him. To be sure, a race of relentless interest-maximizers might sometimes coordinate their actions to achieve mutually beneficial ends. They may then behave in a way that appears to be cooperative. But they won't, thereby, behave morally, because they will opt out whenever they can enjoy the benefits without incurring the costs of participation, and because genuine affection, loyalty, trust, and reciprocity will be absent.

This scenario suggests that some facts we commonly take to support moral conclusions don't provide reasons for *all conceivable rational agents* to act. How, then, do they provide *us* with binding reasons? How do facts that *can, in principle, be known,* without one's taking any special motivational stance toward them, facts with no *conceptual connection* to the values and interests of the knower, count as genuinely moral? Couldn't you and I know those facts, while understanding our own interests perfectly, without taking them to provide *us* with reasons to act? If so, then the idea that we have other-regarding duties that *can't* be shirked by adopting different motivating ends is a fairy tale.

This is a powerful challenge to moral objectivity. Surely, reasons for action do depend on potentially motivating values and interests. If these can, in principle, vary without limit from one rational agent to another, no mere *facts* can provide *all such agents* with reasons to perform other-regarding acts. Thus, there is no objective morality that binds all possible rational agents. This conclusion has, plausibly, been taken to be a conceptual truth by many philosophers and social scientists for decades. If it is such a truth, nothing can override it.

The way out of this intellectual cul-de-sac is to recognize that we do not seek the impossible—an objective morality for *all possible rational beings*. We seek an objective morality grounded in human nature, governing all normal *human beings*. This is what the tradition in moral philosophy stemming from Aristotle, Hume, Hutcheson, and Smith, through the logical positivist Moritz Schlick, tried to provide. However, as Schlick emphasized, the task can no longer be left to philosophers alone.[1] If objective morality is to be grounded in sociological, psychological, and biological facts of human nature, philosophers, natural scientists, and social scientists must join forces in ways that are only beginning to be explored.

THE EMPIRICAL SEARCH FOR FACTUAL, MORALLY RELEVANT PREMISES

One of the most promising steps in this direction was taken by the renowned social scientist James Q. Wilson (1931–2012), in *The Moral Sense.*[2] Its central philosophical thesis is that there is such a thing as empirical knowledge of moral facts, which can be advanced and made more systematic by social scientific research. Its central social-scientific thesis is that we have a moral sense consisting of a complex set of social and biological dispositions relating us to our fellows, which is the product of our innate endowment and our early family experience. Although the moral sense doesn't by itself yield a comprehensive set of universal moral rules, it can, Wilson argues, provide a factual basis relevant to the moral assessment of agents, their acts, and their policies in widely different circumstances.

Because his theses are empirical, it follows that, for him, moral truths grounded in human nature are not knowable *a priori*. Whether or not they are necessary truths (in the philosophical sense) depends on whether or not the parts of our innate endowment on which the moral sense depends are necessary to being human (in the sense that loss of them in any possible future evolution would result in new, nonhuman organisms). No matter how that turns out, his theses are directly relevant to the question of whether it is possible to derive moral claims about what one ought, or ought not, do as *a priori* and necessary consequences of true factual premises. If Wilson is right, this may be possible—provided our premises include, not only a full description of our inherent human nature, but also a complete specification of circumstances giving rise to the moral questions facing the agent.

Since both sets of factual premises are needed, Wilson doesn't attempt such derivation. However, he does argue that statements about the innate moral sense of human agents provide *evidential support* for statements about what, in the main, normal human agents should, or shouldn't, do. The sources of this support are *other-regarding* ends and interests that are inextricably linked in normal human agents with self-regarding concerns, and so beyond their power to renounce at will. These other-regarding motivators provide us with moral reasons for action in various situations. It is not required that they be the only reasons bearing on an act; often they aren't. Because we typically have many, often conflicting, reasons, it is not required—in order for something to count as a moral reason for acting in a certain way—that we actually do act in that way. Nor is it required that we consciously recognize or acknowledge each reason we have. It is enough that our fundamental interests would, to some substantial degree, be furthered by performing the act.

What, then, does it mean to say that A *morally ought* to do X? To answer this question, we must distinguish moral reasons from purely self-interested reasons. Suppose we take our moral reasons to do X to be a subset of potentially motivating reasons arising from our concern for the well-being of others, and for our cooperative relationships with them (broadly construed). Recognizing that these other-regarding interests arise from our social attachments, we note that they are often intertwined with our self-conceptions, and are, therefore, central to our own well-being. These are distinguished from our purely self-interested concerns for food, leisure, comfort, health, and a long life. Given all this, we might take the claim that *A morally ought to do X* to be true if and only if (i) A has some moral reason to do X, (ii) A's *moral reasons* for doing X outweigh A's moral reasons for doing anything else, and (iii) doing X would not require A to sacrifice A's own welfare to an unreasonable degree.

Given this, one can see how it might turn out to be conceptually possible to derive *moral oughts* from a rich set of *factual* premises about what is. Whether or not one takes this to be a realistic possibility depends on one's conception of human nature. This is where Wilson makes his contribution. If he is right, our genetic endowment, our early family experience, and the unalterable circumstances of the human condition provide us with a motivational base that ties us by bonds of affection, social affiliation, and mutual interest to others.

In making his case, Wilson repudiates Freud and embraces Darwin. Because cooperation promotes survival, we have been bred by natural selection to be social animals. We don't simply need what others can provide, and so are moved by self-interest to depend on them. We are also disposed to form powerful cognitive and emotional *attachments* to them. Parents are innately disposed to protect, nurture, and love their babies. Children naturally bond with parents, while imitating and emulating those with whom they are intimate. In their early years they form reciprocal bonds of affection and trust in which their well-being and self-conception is intertwined with others. Entering into games and collective activities, they learn fairness, which involves adhering to common rules and earning rewards proportional to the value of their efforts.

This fusion of natural sentiment with rational principle gives birth to morality. Sentiment infuses our participation in games and collective activities with those we like and admire, and who we hope will like and admire us in return. Often our companions are models of the people we wish to become. The rules governing our activities with them are typically impersonal principles that apply to anyone who occupies a given role in the effort. Because these rules define the commonly accepted terms of participation in a mutually beneficial undertaking, it is in the self-interest of each participant to obey them. But they are more than prudential rules of thumb. Because the parties are often comrades bound by ties of social affiliation, rule violations carry psychic risks beyond the loss of the purely self-interested benefits secured by participation. Violations of rules governing interaction with one's socially affiliated fellows are *affronts* to them, to one's friendship with them, to one's image in their eyes, and to the person one wants, with their help, to be. With this, instrumentally useful rules obeyed to secure the benefits of group action become principles to be honored even when no one is looking. This is the point at which sentiment, social affiliation, and recognition of mutual interest are incorporated into the binding commitments and broad principles that, at least partially, constitute morality.

That is Wilson's basic picture. Further progress can be made by recognizing (i) that we are beings that construct our own identities in relation to others, (ii) that in doing this we often must rely on others for guidance about *who we are* and *whom we wish to become*, (iii) that the most successful way to secure this guidance requires being open to and caring about others, while trusting them to feel similarly about us, and (iv) that to build the relationships we need we must internalize impersonal rules that encompass not only the ancient principle *Do unto others as you would have them do unto you,* but also its corollary, *Be the kind of person you want and expect others to be.*

THE SOCIAL AND PSYCHOLOGICAL CONTENT
OF THE MORAL SENSE IN HUMAN NATURE

Wilson divides the content of the moral sense into four virtues: sympathy, fairness, self-control, and duty. *Sympathy* is our sensitivity to, and concern for, the well-being of valued others. *Fairness* is a disposition to engage in rule-governed conduct based on reciprocity, equal or proportionate rewards for equal or proportionate contributions, and impartiality (including a willingness to have disputes settled by disinterested third parties in accord with rules known in advance). *Self-control* is the ability to resist temptations, not only in order to advance one's own self-interest, but also to keep promises. *Duty* is the disposition to honor commitments and obligations even when it is not in one's narrow self-interest to do so.

The interaction between virtue and self-interest is complex. If the virtues weren't distinct from self-interest, they wouldn't be virtues; if they weren't intertwined with self-interest, we wouldn't acquire them. Because most people admire other-regarding behavior, it is generally in one's interest to develop a reputation for being sympathetic, honest, fair, and reliable. Because we are always observing and judging others, the best way to acquire such a reputation is to cultivate the virtues we want others to believe we have. Paraphrasing Robert Frank,[3] Wilson says, "people will accept your behavior as a sign of honesty or duty only when it would be costly to fake it. If it is very costly to fake it, you can't fake it; the reputation you then earn for honesty or duty corresponds exactly to reality. You *are* dutiful."[4]

The advantage one derives from the good opinion of others is one reason why it is normally in one's interest to acquire the habits of virtue. Although acting morally won't always benefit you, it very often will. Even when it doesn't—when acting morally requires real self-sacrifice—

there are compensating rewards. Because virtuous agents have cultivated their natural sociability, established committed relationships with others, and internalized duties, their ultimate goals have expanded to include contributing to the welfare of others, honoring their commitments, and living up to their idealized self-images. Thus, the degree to which their goals are realized is measured in part by the contributions they make to the welfare of those they care about, the extent to which they have honored their commitments, and the degree to which they have lived up to their conceptions of the persons they most wish to be.

These compensations are *not* a higher form of selfishness. To be selfish is to lack other-regarding ends; to be unselfish is to have such ends and to act on them. The ends that move us are things we desire, not the satisfaction we feel when we get what we aimed at. We do feel satisfied when we achieve our ends, whether those ends are other-regarding or self-regarding. But *satisfaction* isn't what we desire; it is the feeling we have when we get what we desire. Behaving morally involves desiring well-being of others and acting on that desire.

Wilson connects our natural sociability to conscience.

Conscience [the awareness of duty], like sympathy, fairness, and self-control, arises . . . out of our innate desire for attachment, and thus acquires its strongest development when those attachments are the strongest. People with the strongest conscience will be . . . those with the most powerfully developed affiliation.[5]

He uses psychopaths, who have very little social affiliation, to illustrate his point.

[T]he psychopath is the extreme case of the nonsocial personality, someone for whom the ordinary emotions

of life have no meaning. Psychopaths lie without com-
punction, injure without remorse, and cheat with little
fear of detection. Wholly self-centered and unaware of
the emotional needs of others, they are, in the fullest
sense of the term, unsocial. . . . If man were simply the
mere calculator that some economists and game theories
imagine, this is what he would be.[6]

Empirical findings suggest a neurophysiological basis for
this condition. Wilson reports that psychopaths lack certain
involuntary physiological responses—e.g., those detected
by a polygraph when normal subjects lie. Psychopaths
also lack responses associated with fear or apprehension
caused by painful shocks following a stimulus. They have
defects in role-playing ability, and they use thrill-seeking
to compensation for under-arousal.[7] The thread tying these
findings together is the evidence of a neurological basis for
striking differences in the qualities of lived experience between psychopaths and normal human beings that make
the former blind to central facts of ordinary human nature
that underlie morality.

By contrast, Wilson describes ordinary agents as

fully social beings: we have genuine emotions and can
sense the emotional state of others. We are not so
greatly in need of excitement that we are inclined to
treat others as objects designed for our amusement.
We judge others and expect to be judged by them. . . .
To . . . some degree . . . we develop a visceral reaction to
the actions that we contemplate, experiencing internally
and automatically the prospect of praise or blame. . . .
Of special importance is fear: our memory of unpleasant
consequences begins to arouse our apprehension even
when no consequences may occur. In this way our conscience is shaped.[8]

Wilson connects conscience with our earliest and strongest attachment, the bond between parent and child. Citing research on subjects ranging from gentile rescuers of Jewish Holocaust victims, to civil rights and campus activists in the 1960s, to later conservative activists, he argues that a strong sense of duty is correlated with unusually strong parent-child relationships.[9] Studying American airmen imprisoned in Hanoi during the Vietnam War, he also notes the power of social attachment in the most extreme circumstances, which called for resistance to prolonged torture.

> Duty . . . meant honoring an obligation to behave under duress in a way that signified how much the prisoners valued their comrades and how little they valued their captors. The key rule was unity over self. Fidelity arose out of a social connection . . . [kept alive by tapping coded messages to one's fellows, each in solitary confinement]. . . . A tiny and remote chance that one would be honored intangibly by one's comrades was more valuable than a high and immediate chance that one would be rewarded materially by one's enemies. . . . When guilt and fear are one's only emotions, fear can be tolerated more easily if guilt can be overcome, and that in turn requires some signs, however faint, that one is not alone and that one's comrades, however distant, share a set of rules by which guilt can be assessed.[10]

THE BIOLOGICAL BASIS OF SOCIAL AFFILIATION

Wilson points to well-documented, unlearned, pro-social behavior of infants that elicits corresponding innate, nurturing responses from parents and other adults. He attributes these to an innate disposition for attachment arising

from natural selection. Attachment is common to all species that nurture their young after birth, but it is especially
strong in humans because of the very long period in which
the human infant and growing child requires parental care.
Individuals and species willing to devote long periods to
caring for their young leave more offspring behind with
more intense, cooperative, social attachments than individuals of other species—adding up to a potent recipe for
evolutionary success. Nor is the child's disposition to form
strong affective attachments limited to parents; it generalizes to relationships formed with siblings, unrelated play-
mates, and other adults.[11]

Wilson also notes the complex relationship between attachment, moral sense, and the acquisition of language.

> What is striking about the newer findings of child psy-
> chologists is that the emergence of a moral sense occurs
> before the child has acquired much in the way of a lan-
> guage. The rudiments of moral action—a regard for the
> well-being of others and anxiety at having failed to per-
> form according to a standard—are present before any-
> thing like moral reasoning could occur. . . . Indeed, the
> acquisition of language itself, rather than a necessary
> precursor to moral action, is itself a manifestation of the
> natural sociability of mankind.[12]

Noting the innate disposition of human children to acquire
highly complex linguistic knowledge and abilities between
the ages of 18 and 28 months, Wilson analogizes the rapid
and uniform acquisition of our moral sense with our rapid
and uniform acquisition of language, concluding that in
both cases much of what is "learned" is hardwired into our
brains from the beginning.

> [T]he acquisition of language itself, rather than a neces-
> sary precursor of moral action, is itself a manifestation

of the natural sociability of mankind. . . . By the age of three a child will be using complex grammar and be able to invent new languages (play languages) that obey grammatical principles they have never heard, and they will do so in accord with certain deep grammatical structures that produce certain uniformities in language across cultures.[13]

If the essential elements of social behavior . . . had to be learned or were produced by the higher and later-to-evolve parts of the brain . . . then it would be difficult to imagine how the species could have survived. . . . [I]f somehow only the higher parts of the brain were involved in sociability, they would often be overridden by the more urgent, primitive demands of fear, hunger, sex, and anger.[14]

Many of our self-seeking impulses can be kept on a short leash by some of our more social ones because both derive from the oldest, most "primitive" part of our nervous system. . . . Sociability does not require a modern brain and may not even require . . . language. Mating, rearing a child, and defending it against predators may express some of the more "primitive"—that is more instinctive—aspects of our nature.[15]

Emphasizing his biological theme, Wilson also draws on Darwin.

This view of how a moral sense emerges was stated with utmost clarity by Charles Darwin a century before developmental psychologists began to gather data that confirmed it. The third chapter of *The Descent of Man* is about the moral sense, and the key passage is this. "Any animal whatever, endowed with well-marked social instincts, would inevitably acquire a moral sense or conscience, as soon as its intellectual powers had become as well-developed, or nearly as well-developed, as in man."

This is so, Darwin went on to say, for four reasons. First, social instincts will lead a creature to take pleasure in the company of its fellows and do certain services for them. It will even lead to what we call sympathy. . . . Second, as the mental faculties become more highly developed, man . . . can recall past actions, reflect on them and the motives for them, and as a consequence experience a sense of dissatisfaction from having failed to act when action was required. Third, with the advent of language, the wishes of others can be expressed, and there can occur discussions as to how each should act. Finally, the repetition of social acts . . . as modified by the expressed preferences of others, will lead to the development of habits that are, for most of us, the fundamental basis of the moral life.[16]

Wilson also helps fill in what Darwin took to be a lacuna in earlier accounts of morality by David Hume, Adam Smith, and others who emphasized inborn sympathy for others. Darwin objected that these accounts do not explain certain aspects of morality, such as duty and fairness, that are less dependent on empathy or compassion for others. Wilson replies that our native sociability provides a platform on which these more rule-bound parts of morality are built.[17] It does so, he argues, because sociability "animates the kind of family life in which children learn at a very early age that play requires fair play, that if help is expected, help must be offered."[18]

Given all this, one would expect to find some moral universals. Wilson maintains that we do find such tendencies in norms governing the organization of societies around *kinship*,[19] norms governing marriage as an institution in which responsibility is taken for child care and collective economic well-being,[20] prohibitions against infanticide[21] and against unjustifiable homicide and unprovoked assaults,[22] and taboos against incest,[23] plus rules requiring promises be kept and property respected, and fairness in one's dealings with others.[24] In many cases, exceptions are made for special circumstances, certain standard excuses are recognized, and the contents of admonitions or injunctions are subject to some variation. For example, the great majority of documented cases of culturally permitted infanticide (in the anthropological literature Wilson cites) involve either a scarcity of food, deformed infants, or uncertain parentage. Moreover, he reports that infanticide rarely occurs after the first few hours of life (when bonding occurs) and it almost never occurs after the first month.[25]

There are, of course, also cross-cultural differences, including the extent to which individuals internalize universalistic moral rules that extend beyond their communal group. Wilson hypothesizes that individualistic child-rearing cultures, in the United States and elsewhere, lead children to develop strong peer-defined, peer-enforced rules of fairness that result from being encouraged from an early age to play with friends and acquaintances, and to make their own decisions. The result is a greater extension of sympathy to unrelated outsiders, a more impersonal rule-based conception of fairness, and a greater deference to universalistic standards. By contrast, he thinks that cultures like Japan, in which families rather than individuals are more central, emphasize preserving family honor and avoiding shame. They also define obligations more in terms of kinship, social position in the local community, or membership in an ethnic group. Such cultures still have other-regarding morality, but not one that so readily extends to all human beings.[26] These broad generalizations about cultural differences, reflecting Wilson's impressions nearly three decades ago, must, of course, be taken with a grain of salt—not least of which because cultural interpenetration and homogenization have, presumably, progressed to a considerable degree since then. Still, his perspective may be useful in raising broad issues about cultural variability.

THE BIOLOGICAL LIMITS OF THE MORAL SENSE VERSUS ITS HISTORICALLY GROWING REACH

The contrast between the moral concerns of more versus less individualistic cultures presents a challenge. If morality arises from a universal innate moral sense, why do we find different moral conceptions in societies at different times and places, and how should we respond to the differences between them? Not all of these differences need to be resolved. The fact that two cultures solve a moral problem differently needn't mean they are motivated by different ends, or that at least one must get things wrong. Sometimes what is morally required may not be a unique action, but some action from morally comparable alternatives. Nor are all alternatives equally available in different cultures. Different levels of knowledge, different resources, different economic or social conditions, and differences in climate and geography can limit available actions and thereby determine different moral outcomes. Finally, the same action can have different consequences, and so get different evaluations, due to nonmoral differences in the circumstances in which it is performed. None of this undermines Wilson's universal moral sense.

He does, however, implicitly recognize a serious challenge.

The most remarkable change in the moral history of mankind has been the rise—and occasionally the application—of the view that all people, and not just one's own kind, are entitled to fair treatment. . . . Many [on the other hand, think that] morality governs our actions toward others in much the same way that gravity governs the motions of the planets: its strength is in inverse proportion to the square of the distance between them.[27]

Why does the existence of a universalistic moral aspiration at some places and times, but not others, constitute a challenge to Wilson? According to him, our moral sense develops out of the attachments and sympathies generated from our earliest childhood experiences with parents, siblings, relatives, close friends and companions. These are the ones with whom our interests and identities are intertwined, the ones to whom we are instinctively connected, and the ones to whom we are, in the first instance, morally committed. As we grow older, the circle is enlarged, but the difference between the moral significance of those inside the circle and those outside remains. Up to a point, this isn't a problem. Our moral duties to the near and dear are different from, and often more urgent than, our duties to arbitrary others. *What must be explained is how our duties ever manage to extend beyond our limited sphere and to encompass, at least to some degree, all human beings.*

Wilson offers an historical explanation. He tells us that about 300 CE, family and kinship structure in Europe began to diverge from an earlier pattern in which marriage partners and property inheritance were determined by heads of male-dominated clans, multiple wives were allowed, and it was easy for males to divorce their wives. Over the next several centuries that pattern changed in northern and western Europe to one in which monogamous marriages established outside the clan, by consent of the partners themselves, became increasingly common, leading to growing numbers of independent nuclear families sustaining themselves on their own plots of land. The Church ratified consensual marriage, and banned polygamy, adultery, concubinage, and remarriage after divorce. It also enforced church discipline on people as individuals rather than as clan members. This facilitated the growing recognition that a woman could share an inheritance, serve as her husband's business partner, and raise her children after his death. The result was a more child-centered family and the development of a more individualistic culture that was susceptible to more universalistic appeals in morality.

> The ground was prepared for the growth of individualism and universalism by the dramatic changes that occurred in family life during some thousand years, stretching from the end of the Roman Empire to the Renaissance. In this time, monogamous marriages triumphed over polygamy and male divorce power, and gradually shifted its focus away from parental and kinship concerns to the advantage of the conjugal couple. The family they were founding . . . consolidated its position as the basic cell of Western society.[28]

The final piece of the puzzle was the extension of private property and the codification of rules governing it. Speaking of post-thirteenth-century England, Wilson says:

> Individualism in economic and social life existed, rooted in property rights, partible inheritances, and cash markets. Land was a commodity that could be . . . bought and sold, fathers bequeathed their land to particular offspring . . . men and women hired out for cash wages. . . . Women, unmarried as well as married, could (and did) own property, make wills and contracts, and bring suit. . . . There were no insuperable barriers dividing poor farmers from rich ones, and so some who began poor ended up rich. The existence of individual property rights made England . . . a litigious society: if land could be bought and sold, inherited and bequeathed, it was in-

evitable that there would be countless disputes. . . . The courts of equity that settled these disputes inevitably decided something even more important than arguments over land; they resolved—or at least shaped—a broader set of claims about individual rights.[29]

These changes provided the soil that nourished the Enlightenment celebration of individual liberty, the rights of individuals, equality before the law, and the equitable treatment of all human beings.

THE ROLE OF SOCIOECONOMIC INSTITUTIONS IN EXTENDING OUR BIOLOGICALLY BASED MORALITY

Ironically, this story of what Wilson sees as the changing shape of human morality may also be the greatest challenge to his view of morality as founded in an innate moral sense. Human communities in every century in every inhabited region of the earth have shared the components of his moral sense—our native sociability, our prolonged dependence as infants, the bond between parent and child, the social attachments with friends, family, and neighbors, and the intertwining of our self-interest and self-conception with a concern not only for winning the good opinion of those with whom we are connected, but also for their genuine well-being. Yet despite this commonality, only a few human communities have conceived of moral obligations in semi-universalistic, post-Enlightenment terms. Why, if this aspect of morality is grounded in our biological endowment, should its appearance be so unusual, and so late in coming?

The answer, one might think, is that the moral sense is only one, and not the strongest, part of our human nature, and that moral systems that arise from it are influenced by nonmoral aspects of our nature as well as by our physical, social, and economic environments. Since Wilson recognizes all manner of historical, geographical, and other contingencies that affect what is best for particular societies at particular times, he wouldn't disagree with this. The real challenge comes from a deeper question. Why do we think that morality *ought* to include a degree of post-Enlightenment moral universalism? Why is it, all other things equal, *morally better* for us to recognize some obligations to those outside our tribe? *What, from Wilson's perspective, does this even mean?*

Consider what, following David Hume and Adam Smith, we call 'utility'—roughly, the advancement of fundamental interests, and hence of the welfare of individuals. Certain actions, habits, rules, and patterns of social organization are more likely than others to advance the welfare of humans living in societies. Ultimately, these welfare-advancing rules require individual agents to extend moral standing beyond family and friends to the tribe, beyond the tribe to the neighboring tribe, and, eventually, to all human beings. Surely, one may think, it is best for *humanity* that individuals internalize this lesson. It may also be best for *individuals* whose own moral commitments and self-conceptions have been shaped by a post-Enlightenment culture to live by it. These individuals already value the welfare of distant others. This, it may be argued, is what makes it true that they have moral obligations to such others; that they ought, or ought not, perform certain actions out of concern for them. All this can be admitted, but it doesn't touch the problem that post-Enlightenment approximations of universalism poses for Wilson.

Is it true, or not, that individuals whose cultural conceptions of morality don't incorporate post-Enlightenment universalism ought to treat outsiders with sympathy, fairness, and reciprocity? On the account I have been developing, we can't say that they morally *ought* to treat outsiders in this way unless we can show that doing so would, in the main, advance the moral and nonmoral interests they already have. Would it? One might argue that such a change in outlook would advance their culture to the overall benefit of their descendants, whom they care about. But such a historical transformation, which might, if successful, take many generations to achieve, is speculative. There is no guarantee that it will ever come, let alone that it will come quickly enough to engage the imaginations of present agents. Must we then say that these individuals have *no binding moral obligations to outsiders*, even though we take ourselves and other members of our culture to be so bound?

Not necessarily. Universalistic moral conceptions typically understand fairness as requiring reciprocity. If those from less universalistic, or even strongly tribal, cultures wish to reap the full benefits of cooperative interaction with those from more universalistic cultures, they will, at some point, have to realize that reciprocity in dealing with outsiders is expected, and so come to find it to be in their interest to reciprocate. If they do, then, over time, increased participation in mutually beneficial activities may change the attitudes of all parties, enriching and expanding the moral universe of each. It is, after all, just such reciprocity that, in one way or another, led our ancestors, and most of us at different stages of our lives, to extend empathetic moral concerns we initially felt only for the near and dear to larger groups. Thus, the proper response to the challenge posed by those with limited moral horizons is to work to expand them, not by charity, but by reciprocal social interaction, on the basis of the commonalities they already share with us.

What is true about the relationship between cultures with mismatched moral universes may also be true of similarly mismatched individuals, or groups of individuals, in any culture. All societies contain some who fail to accord significant moral status to those their neighbors recognize as morally significant others. The centrality of reciprocity to our moral lives dictates that the morally expansive neighbors of their more morally isolated fellows offer them opportunities for cooperative interaction, conditional on the willingness of all parties to engage in genuinely reciprocal behavior. If the required reciprocity is not forthcoming, such offers should be withdrawn. There is, after all, a price to be paid for opting out of practices of mutually beneficial concern. If there weren't, moral virtues would never be acquired.

Our view of those with restricted moral universes should, of course, not be confused with those who inhabit no moral universe. Consider the following thought experiment raised by a philosopher in response to the perspective offered here.[30]

> Suppose that a pharmaceutical company developed a drug that would change our nature in such a way that we became asocial; in particular, we would stop caring about other people's welfare. The good news, they tell us, is that we won't care about what other people think of us; so when they disapprove of our asocial behavior, it won't matter to us. Obviously, it would be wrong for *us*, with our current nature, to take such a drug—because we are obliged to care about other people, and to try to continue caring. But the question is: what if somebody accidentally put the drug into the water supply, so that we all woke up tomorrow morning not caring about other people? Would this mean that we had suddenly lost any obligation to act in an altruistic fashion?

The answer to these questions is that those who consumed the drug would cease to be moral agents, and so would have no more moral obligations than nonhuman animals do. If any of us remained who had not consumed the morality-destroying drug, we would see some of the actions of those who did as bad, in the way it is bad when sharks devour a swimmer, even though sharks aren't moral agents. Nevertheless, we might continue to care about our unfortunate friends and loved ones who had been changed by the drug. We might also treat them with a degree of kindness in appreciation of the fine people they had been, and out of gratitude for what they had, before their misfortune, done for us. We might, in short, treat them in much the same way we treat, and are obligated to treat, those who, from age or injury, are now much diminished versions of their former selves. But we would no longer see them as full moral agents, and so not interact with them as before.

This is the philosophical conception of morality to which we are led by Wilson's view of an innate, biologically based moral sense. It is one in which morality is a social institution that is evolving, historically and nonbiologically, into a richer system capable of increasing human welfare by increasing the scope of human cooperation. As social cooperation increases, biologically based values are extended, creating new moral relationships that allow previously underivable *oughts* to be derived from expanded factual premises about what agents value and are able to contemplate. It is this conception—not of changing moral *opinions* but of expanding moral *reality*—the elaboration and refinement of which requires the cooperation of today's philosophers, biologists, and social scientists.

ADVANCING CIVILIZATION

The story told here about the opportunities for progress in our understanding of moral matters is, admittedly, less the celebration of an advance in human civilization to which philosophy has contributed than a sketch of how such an

advance may now be possible. Although the needed components for hastening this process exist in philosophy, biology, neuroscience, and social science, they are fragmented
and not organized into a coherent, institutionally coordinated search for the advancement of moral knowledge.
There is no such current search. If there were, it would exist
in the modern university. But, except for various pockets
of inspired investigation in a few leading philosophy departments, it doesn't.

Other than this growing philosophical interest, the pre-
vailing ethos on campus scarcely recognizes the possibility
of advances in *moral knowledge* founded on fact- and reason-
based inquiry. Instead, morality tends to be viewed by too
many students, faculty, and administrators as a domain in
which genuine knowledge is impossible and consensus can
be reached only by relying on strong feelings and unreflec-
tive opinions backed by intimidation. Unfortunately, something similar can be said about other social institutions
as well. This all-too-common contemporary conception
of morality—which runs counter to the central messages
of Socrates, Plato, and Aristotle at the dawn of western
philosophy—has become a danger to our civilization. In
order to combat it, more philosophers and their colleagues
in the natural and social sciences must step forward.

CHAPTER 14

VIRTUE, HAPPINESS, AND MEANING IN THE FACE OF DEATH

The twin aims of western philosophy: to lay the conceptual foundations of theoretical knowledge, and to chart a path to virtue, happiness, and meaning in life; the urgency of the second in an era of declining Christianity; the goal of uniting philosophical and empirical investigations of human nature; the centrality of knowledge in viable philosophical conceptions of virtue and happiness; the meaning of life, the finality of death, and the centrality of our connections to others, past, present, and future.

At the beginning of chapter 2, I pulled apart two inquiries the fusion of which by Socrates, Plato, and Aristotle generated the intellectual energy that created and continues to sustain western philosophy. One inquiry attempts to lay the conceptual foundations of reason and evidence-based explanations of the natural world. The other attempts to reveal the individual's ultimate purpose and to chart a path to happiness, virtue, and wisdom. Although I have pursued both inquiries in this book, there is more to say about the second.

Philosophers can take pride in their contributions to the quality of our education, law, politics, economics, and morality. But the resources of philosophy have not been fully utilized. Although advances in those areas are related to each individual's personal quest for happiness and virtue, they don't directly address the existential burden of guiding individual lives. That burden, which had for centuries in the west been lifted from philosophy and borne by Christianity, has returned now that Christianity is no longer the dominant intellectual force it once was. Nor can political ideology fill the void of existential emptiness, as the massive political tragedies of the last century and the destructive enthusiasms gripping significant segments of the west today vividly illustrate. This is the context in which it has become incumbent on philosophy to make its resources for advancing the individual's personal quest for meaning more evident—to make visible the contours of a life the value of which to something larger than oneself is great enough to sustain one through all setbacks unto death. In Plato's dialogue *Phaedo,* Socrates suggests that philosophers study and prepare for death, learning that it is not to be feared—a theme later taken up by the Stoics, and by Boethius. Today's philosophers should think about how they can add to this heritage.

The challenge is not to replace religious faith with any other kind of faith, but to articulate a rational approach to life that helps individuals find what they need to face their own mortality, while continuing to contribute to the reason and evidence-based project of improving human societies. The danger to be avoided is expressed in a widely cited mid-twentieth-century remark of Malcolm Muggeridge (1903–1990):

One of the peculiar sins of the twentieth century which we have developed to a very high level is the sin of credulity. It has been said that when human beings stop believing in God, they believe in nothing. The truth is much worse: they believe in anything.

Essentially the same warning, expressed in a very different style, is put in the mouth a character extolling belief in the transcendent value of racial or ethnic identity in Tom Wolfe's final novel, *Back to Blood,* in 2012.

> "Religion is dying . . . but everybody still has to believe in *something.* It would be intolerable—you couldn't stand it—to finally have to say to yourself, 'Why keep pretending? I'm nothing but a random atom inside a supercollider known as the universe.' But *believing in* by definition means *blindly*, doesn't it? So, my people, that leaves only our blood, the bloodlines that course through our very bodies, to unite us. . . . All people, everywhere, you have no choice but *Back to blood.*"[1]

The worry expressed by Muggeridge and Wolfe is real. Yes, religion may, for large classes of people, be dying. Yes, we do need beliefs to endow our lives with meaning and purpose. But no, not just any passionate beliefs will do. We need rational, evidence-based beliefs capable of providing us *knowledge* of who we are, what we most value, what we are capable of, and what we cannot escape. Only then can we confidently articulate rational life-plans that, in bringing out the best in us, lead us to the meaning we need to deal with the challenges of life and the inevitability of death. The task can no longer be delegated to others. Philosophers, armed with all we have learned from what has gone before, may now be in a position to build on, and even exceed, the contributions of their ancient predecessors.

In doing so, we must blend the old with the new. In chapter 13, I explained how prudential statements about what one ought to do may serve as a model for understanding the motivational force of statements about what one morally ought to do. Prudential guidance purports to identify actions that best advance one's welfare. Since one may sometimes be in the dark about this, one may be motivated to accept guidance from a trusted family member, friend, or authority. Since one's *moral reasons* for acting arise from one's concern for the well-being of others and one's reciprocal relationships with people of various sorts, moral reasons also have motivational force. The fact that our other-regarding interests arise from our social attachments, and so are central to our self-conceptions, magnifies that force.

Human psychobiology and the facts of the human condition provide us with a motivational base in which our intertwined self- and other-regarding interests tie us to others. The new empirical challenge for philosophically minded social scientists is to verify and precisify this conception of human nature inherited from their philosophical predecessors. The new social and political challenge is to continue the process of developing social and economic institutions that blend self-interest with reciprocal respect for others in extensive systems of social cooperation, broadening our productive contact with them. The new philosophical challenge is to reconceptualize traditional understandings of virtue and happiness to accommodate our growing scientific knowledge of human nature, and to articulate compelling conceptions of the meaning of life in an era in which the consolations of religion are vanishing and the finality of one's own death, and even the ultimate extinction of human life, appear, increasingly, to be incontrovertible.[2]

For me, this reconceptualization begins with Aristotle's belief that being human involves being naturally endowed with certain values, interests, and capacities. Taking the capacity for rational thought to be part of our essence, he rightly took the development and exercise of one's rationality to be intrinsically fulfilling. Those who develop this capacity to the fullest value knowledge for its own sake, and so seek to discover fundamental truths about themselves, humanity, and the world. Being rational, human beings are also natural problem solvers, reasoning about how to best achieve their various ends. Although Aristotle took the disinterested discovery of theoretical truth to be the highest goal, he also rightly believed that a life spent pursuing ordinary human goals relating one to family, friends, colleagues, and community can lead to great happiness. Pursuing those goals wisely requires cultivating virtues, like *self-control, generosity, ambition,* and *courage.*

Three lessons can be gleaned from this Aristotelian perspective. First, virtues—including both those that are naturally thought of as golden means between contrasting extremes and those (like honesty and kindness) that may not be—are character traits that require not only a good will and a kind heart, but also rational judgment and practice to fully develop. Second, the most basic goal of ethics is not to define which actions ought to be performed in any given set of circumstances, which may prove impossible, but to specify the kind of character one should strive for. Third, the virtuous person is one whose dispositions to act reflect a judicious mix of self-regarding and other-regarding values.

In speaking of the connection between self and others, Aristotle emphasizes the importance of companions, whom he likens to second selves—those close enough to provide one with insight about oneself, in part because one wishes to share oneself with them for the mere joy of doing so. Wisdom, as he understood it, improves the recognition of what advances one's long-term welfare and the identification of actions most likely to advance it. Thus, the path to wisdom is our best route to personal fulfillment. But wisdom is not a solitary achievement. The theoretical knowledge we need typically rests on the efforts of countless others over long periods. Even our intimate knowledge of ourselves is often heavily dependent on others.

We construct our lives by choices we make among alternatives open to us. Our lives are something like books we are writing, without ready-made endings, and sometimes without even a good plan of what should come next. To continue our books, we need coauthors who may know certain things about us better than we do. To secure their help, we must open ourselves to them and value them for who they are, trusting that they will return the favor. First and foremost, coauthors include our closest companions, but they also may include, to a lesser degree, neighbors and colleagues, indeed anyone we count on in the activities that matter most to us. Everyone knows that others can often judge how we look, and what our manner conveys, better than we can. The same is true of aspects of our character.

Our interconnectedness with others relates wisdom to virtue and happiness. Virtuous character traits are widely admired because they are important in ensuring the benefits of social cooperation. Because they are admired, being judged virtuous is very much to one's advantage. Because virtues are sometimes hard to fake, particularly in the long run, and the efforts to uncover fakery are unceasing, being virtuous is often the best strategy for being so judged. In addition, we naturally love, like, respect, admire, appreciate, emulate, and feel protective of selected others. These are people we genuinely care about, and who we hope feel similarly about us. Because of their relationship to us, the sacrifices we make of our own narrowly self-interested goals on their behalf are compensated by the high other-regarding value we place on their welfare. Since reciprocity is a given within this select sphere, we also know that either we, or those near and dear to us, may benefit from the other-regarding actions of those in our moral circle. As social institutions become more complex and encompassing, this circle arising from our natural sociability is extended, generating concern for, and graded reciprocal obligations to, others without well-defined limits. In this way, virtue and happiness often end up being complementary rather than competing pursuits.

It's not that virtue guarantees happiness; the vicissitudes of fortune can bring down the best among us. Nor does happiness always depend on virtue; it is possible for great good fortune to be lavished on the undeserving. Nevertheless, both virtue and happiness depend on satisfying one's most fundamental self- and other-regarding ends, which are normally mutually supporting. Thus, cultivating virtue is usually a good strategy for achieving happiness. Although there are cases in which sacrificing one's happiness is the price of virtue, determining the extent to which happiness is lost in those cases, and evaluating the importance of that loss, depends on understanding what happiness is.

Aristotle claimed that happiness is our ultimate goal, thereby seeming to indicate that it is the end to which all other ends are subservient. That was unfortunate, because it suggests that happiness is both the thing we most desire and that for which we desire anything else. It isn't either. He was on firmer ground in denying that happiness is a feeling of elation, a collection of intense pleasurable sensations, or, indeed, any kind or collection of feelings or sensations at all. According to Aristotle, species of animals and human beings have natural functions. Human happiness, as he conceived it, consists in performing our natural function well, which he took to involve rational and virtuous living. Although we wouldn't put it exactly as he did, we can formulate a similar idea in more modern terms.

Suppose we take happiness to be a high level of welfare, the constituents of which (as I indicated in the previous chapter) involve the satisfaction of our most basic physical, mental, and social needs, the development of our most distinctive human capacities, and the satisfaction of our most important, biologically based desires. Such a state is clearly both desirable and widely desired.

Since it encompasses the satisfaction of our social needs, which includes our commitment to valued others, it also encompasses some elements of virtuous living. It is important to note that being in this state involves the existence of events and states of affairs about which it is possible to be ignorant—e.g., whether one is really both safe and healthy, whether one has, in fact, both achieved what one has aimed at and successfully developed one's most important capacities, and whether those one cares most about are truly thriving, in part due to one's efforts. Hence, *knowing* that one is happy, in this Aristotelian sense, requires far more than knowledge of one's feelings.

To *falsely* believe that one is happy in this special sense is not to be happy. For example, one might know what the central constituents of one's welfare are, while wrongly thinking that each contingency on which it depends has been met. You might feel happy because you *believe* that, with your help, the love of your life is thriving, thereby cementing your life together—when in fact you have merely been used all along. Since you don't know this, you might *feel* great. But the feeling would be false, and of diminished value.

What would you say, if, after discovering the truth, you were asked whether you had been happy? If your conception of happiness is simply a matter of feelings, you might say, "Yes, I was happy, but my happiness was based on a lie." Many people today do seem to think of happiness in that way. But if you are one of them, you should realize that happiness, as you conceive it, is inherently transitory, often being in flux from day to day or hour to hour. On the other hand, if you identify happiness with Aristotelian well-being, you will say, in answer to the question, "I wrongly thought I was happy, but in fact I wasn't; I had merely been deceived and humiliated."

For our purposes, it doesn't matter which conception is the most prevalent; both are coherent. What is important is to recognize that, in order for what we call "happiness" to be the philosophically important and highly desirable state we often take it to be, being in that state must require one's stable state of contentment to be well founded. Understanding happiness in this way, *what we most hope for ourselves* is not simply to be in a stable state of contented good feeling about our lives, our relationships, and what we imagine ourselves to have achieved. We want to know that these feelings are well founded.

Most of us do desire a combination of the subjective good feeling with knowledge. We do, of course, desire some things, like a delicious dessert or a warm shower, merely for the feelings we have when we get them. In these cases we might—like a dieter longing for an ice cream sundae—gladly sacrifice the object of our original desire (the sundae) for artificially generated (sundae-eating) subjective sensations. But this is the exception rather than the rule. As Robert Nozick emphasizes, given the offer of entering an "experience machine" in which you would spend the rest of your life enjoying fully realistic simulations of the satisfaction of your desires, while wrongly believing the events you took to be occurring to be real, most of us would decline the offer, preferring instead to remain in touch with reality.[3] We would do this despite realizing that we will probably not fulfill many of our fondest wishes, and will fail to achieve some of our most compelling goals.

What's more, our choice would be correct. The *feeling of happiness* that the experience machine provides is *not* what we most wish for. What we desire for ourselves, far more than the quality of any particular experiences, is to have a positive relation with reality—to know it, to shape it, to improve it, and to share our lives with similarly engaged others. What I most desire for others, and what I most want to contribute, are: the happiness and fulfillment of my wife, the flourishing of my sons, the return to health

of a dear friend, the well-being of my friends and colleagues, the education of my students, the advancement
of the School of Philosophy at my university, the progress
of philosophy (and all areas it touches), the spread of free
institutions, the vitality of my country, and the revival of
the strength and vigor of the best traditions of western
civilization. In addition, I wish for continued advances in
medicine, technology, and economic well-being throughout the world plus the gradual expansion of the reach of
humane, universalistic, and mutually shared moral concerns. For myself, I most desire continued health, productivity, and longevity, plus the opportunity to do my part
(sometimes large, sometimes small) to advance my other
goals. It is a full plate, the pursuit of which has little to
do with subjective experiences of the sort generated by
Nozick's imagined experience machine. In this, I am not
unusual.

This nonsubjective conception of happiness brings us
to compelling questions about the meaning of life and the
finality of death. For one who, like me, places no credence
in a personal afterlife, the prospect of death is frighten-
ingly simple—namely, nonexistence. Why, one may ask, is
it frightening? Since the nonexistent experience nothing,
none of us will experience anything bad, unpleasant, or
even boring, after we die—just as we had no such experiences before we were conceived. It is, of course, disappointing that we won't learn about many things we wish
for. Wouldn't it be wonderful to observe, and even assist
in, the triumphs of wives, husbands, children, friends,
colleagues, and cherished institutions after we are gone?
Wouldn't it be even better to protect them from danger and
strengthen them in hard times? Yes, it would, but that isn't
in the cards. Although we may regret missing out, the realization that we will isn't why we fear death. We fear death
because we find the prospect of nonexistence dizzyingly

unfathomable and terrifying. There is no getting over it; we are simply built that way.

That being so, we must cope as best we can. It may help to achieve clarity about what awaits, while developing the courage to face what can't be avoided in a way that preserves our dignity and sets a good example for others. These are no small things, nor are they beyond our power. Strength of mind and firmness of character can be developed and made habitual, providing one with the resources to confront what comes. But these virtues aren't the whole story to our response to death. As one gets older, and death slowly approaches, one's personal future shrinks, bringing the shape of one's life as a whole into clearer focus. This raises the question of what, in the end, one's life will amount to.

In addition to foreshortening the personal future into which we can project, advancing years often diminish our ability to participate in some activities we once enjoyed. But this can be counterbalanced, not only by increased wisdom and decreased pressure to advance our careers, but also by sharpening our focus on the people, projects, and institutions we most value, including those we confidently expect to outlive us. Often this is natural enough, as parents focus on their adult children and young grandchildren, entrepreneurs pass on family businesses, scholars strike out in new directions or undertake long-delayed projects, and practitioners of all kinds enjoy training and sharing their experience with the rising generation.

The details vary for each person, but the prescription is general. Broaden and deepen your commitment to people and things you most value, and—in the best cases—to whom, or to which, you have the most to offer. Your purpose can then be found in the contribution you make to ends transcending yourself. Acting in this way ties you to the continuing stream of human life that long preceded and will, you have reason to believe, long outlast you.[4] If peace can be found in approaching death, the way to find it is through ever closer and more active involvement with highly valued aspects of the human project.

This, admittedly, is easier said than done. Just as you can't find happiness without already valuing others and pursuing goals independent of your own happiness, so you can't find meaning simply because you need to fill your own emptiness. You can't find meaning unless you are not, in fact, empty, because you already care about people, projects, and institutions beyond yourself. And if you do care, you will act in ways calculated to actually help, rather than merely to advance your reputation for trying. There is no peace in confronting your coming annihilation, if you don't genuinely care about the future you won't see. If you do care, the value you place on your reputation will be dwarfed by the good you do for others.

The final requirement is humility. Don't predicate your faith in the future on its living up to your image of it. No people, no projects, no institutions that outlast you will conform to all your most important ideas and values. Nor should they. No matter who you are, your perspective is limited. Your ability to anticipate events that will shape the future is no greater than the corresponding abilities of those who weren't alive to experience the events that shaped you and your era. So don't think of what you offer those who follow as a package deal. Don't worry about what parts of the package the future may discard. Be content that some of what you have offered will be taken up and valued, and trust that those who follow may know better than you how to sort it all out. This advice is particularly important in an era in which political ideology is all too often pursued with quasi-religious fervor. If you expect to find meaning in your commitment to the welfare of others, both now and after you are gone, you need to respect them and their perspectives, while anticipating that those perspectives will differ in some important respects from your own.

The good news is that all of this is achievable. The bad news is that it doesn't always come easily. If you are one for whom it doesn't, it may take years of effort to develop the character traits needed to give your life the meaning you now seek and will eventually need when it comes to an end. Best to start now.

THE NOBLE DEATHS OF SOCRATES AND DAVID HUME

Two of the most famous and inspirational deaths in all of philosophy illustrate how a philosophical perspective on life can contribute to a noble death. The first occurred in 399 BCE, when Socrates, then in his early seventies, was tried, found guilty, and executed for impiety and corrupting the young, which he is alleged to have done by questioning religious doctrine and pretending to wisdom he didn't have. His ingenious defense, described in Plato's *Apology,* was built around the story of a friend returning from the oracle of Delphi (a sacred place at which the god Apollo was reputed to speak through his oracle) with the message that no human being is wiser than he, Socrates.[1] Hearing this, he protests that he is isn't wise; on the contrary, he is searching for wisdom because he knows he isn't wise. Might it be, Socrates wonders, that the god is suggesting otherwise? Perhaps it is his divinely inspired duty to determine the truth or the falsity of the god's puzzling remark. Taking it to be so (ironically giving the lie to the charge of impiety), Socrates resolves to engage the wisest men he can find in order to discover what they know.

When he does so, he discovers that those reputed to be wise in fact aren't, even though they take themselves to be. Since it is better to know one's own ignorance than to confidently believe falsehoods, it turns out that Socrates may, after all, be the wisest. Unfortunately, however, his persistent questioning sometimes provokes hostility, which leads his enemies to bring charges against him. Taking the search for the truth to be the highest good, Socrates refuses to give up his quest despite the fact that doing so would allow him to avoid conviction and death. Because his relentless search for knowledge has become the meaning of his existence, he can't give it up without forsaking virtue and happiness by repudiating everything he has stood for. To some, his stubbornness may seem extreme. Surely, one may object, he can't achieve virtue or happiness, if he is dead. Wouldn't a less than stellar life without philosophical inquiry be better than no life at all?

Socrates responds by observing that one should not assume that death is a great evil. Although he didn't take himself to know what death would bring, he thought the soul might survive, and even flourish. But even if death is the dreamless sleep of nonexistence, staving it off for a few extra years would not, he believed, be worth rejecting what gave his life meaning. He tells us why it wouldn't in Plato's dialogue *Crito,* which takes place in prison early on the day of the execution.[2] His friend Crito has a plan for Socrates to escape and go into exile, using money that Crito and his friends can spare. Although the plan would be easy be to pull off, Crito can't convince Socrates to cooperate. Socrates protests that (i) to escape is to break the law, (ii) to do that, even after a miscarriage of justice, is morally wrong, and (iii) one must never do anything morally wrong. Indeed, Socrates argues, to do so would be to harm one's soul, which is always worse than to suffer harm.

But why would it be wrong to break the law by escaping? Because, Socrates maintains, we owe a debt to the state incurred by the enormous benefits that have come to us from living in an ordered society. Surely, he maintains, it would be wrong to repay this debt by undermining the laws on which this order depends. Though not without force, this argument is unconvincing. Although we do greatly benefit from living in a civilized state, we also, as citizens, contribute to it—including, in Socrates's case, serving as an Athenian soldier. It is in the nature of legal systems, even those that are relatively unjust, that the benefits of social organization vastly exceed the sum of individual efforts needed to sustain them. But the fact that we benefit by cooperating with one another doesn't generate a moral obligation to obey every law in every circumstance, no matter how deficient the law, or the state, may be.

Fortunately, this unconvincing line of argument was not all Socrates had to offer. At the end of the dialogue, he emphasizes the harm his escape would do to his friends who would be found complicit in the plot, the damage it would do to his own reputation, and, most of all, the threat that his self-serving behavior would pose to the way of life he had come to represent. The debate with Crito is resolved when it becomes clear that if Socrates truly believes his message—that rigorously honest, soul-searching philosophy is the path to wisdom, virtue, and happiness—he must not undermine it.

With this, we can better understand his remarks in the *Apology*. It was, he rightly thought, worthwhile to sacrifice his few remaining years of life in order to advance, rather than destroy, the powerful message that his life and work were destined to convey to others. Human beings, who know they will die, can greatly enrich their lives—particularly in later years—by identifying with, and valuing, a reality much larger than themselves. Because Socrates valued what he could give to those who would follow more than he valued a little more time on earth, he was doing what was best for him in accepting his fate.

It is not surprising, then, that Socrates's death was tranquil. The scene is described at the end of the next dialogue, the *Phaedo*. Here are a few passages beginning just before sunset when a prison officer informs Socrates and his friends that it is time for the execution.

> Socrates, he [the officer] said . . . I shall not have to find fault with you, as I do with others, for getting angry with me and cursing when I tell them to drink the poison. . . . I have come to know during this time that you are the noblest and the gentlest and the bravest of all the men that have ever come here, and now especially I am sure that you are not angry with me. . . . So now—you know what I have come to say—good-bye, and try to bear what must be as easily as you can.[3]
>
> As he spoke, he burst into tears, and turning round, went away. Socrates looked up at him and said, Good-bye to you. . . . Then addressing us [his friends] he went on. What a charming person! All the time I have been here he has visited me, and sometimes had discussions with me, and shown me the greatest kindness, and how generous of him now to shed tears for me at parting! But come, Crito, let us do as he says.[4]
>
> But surely, Socrates, said Crito, the sun is still upon the mountains. Besides, I know that in other cases people have dinner and enjoy their wine, and sometimes the company of those whom they love, long after they receive the warning. . . . No need to hurry. There is still plenty of time.[5]
>
> It is natural that these people whom you speak of should act in that way, Crito, said Socrates, because they think that they gain by it. And it is also natural that I should not, because I believe I should gain nothing by drinking the poison a little later—I should only make

myself ridiculous in my own eyes if I clung to life and hugged it when it has no more to offer.[6]

With this Socrates took the bowl of hemlock and drank it in one breath.

Up till this time most of us had been fairly successful in keeping back our tears, but when we saw that he was drinking, that he had actually drunk it, we could do so no longer. In spite of myself the tears came pouring out, so that I covered my face and wept brokenheartedly— not for him but for my own calamity in losing such a friend. Crito had given up even before me, and had gone out when he could not restrain his tears. But Apollodorus, who had never stopped crying even before, now broke out into such a storm of passionate weeping that he made everyone in the room break down, except Socrates himself, who said, Really, my friends, what a way to behave! . . . Calm yourselves and try to be brave.[7]

As the poison gradually spread throughout Socrates's body, he covered his head, until at one point he pulled off the cover and said his last words. "Crito, we ought to offer a cock to Asclepius. See to it, and don't forget." The dialogue then ends, *"Such . . . was the end of our comrade, who was, we may fairly say, of all those whom we knew in our time, the bravest and also the wisest and most upright man."*[8]

The second famous death is that of David Hume, who died in 1776 at the age of 65. A leader of the Scottish Enlightenment, the most famous British empiricist, and one of the leading British philosophers of all time, he was also a celebrated historian of England. His contributions to metaphysics, epistemology, and the philosophy of mind were enormously influential. His naturalistic theory of moral evaluation, emphasizing other-regarding sentiments in human nature and opposing narrow egoistic theories, and his theory of justice, based on our beneficial experience with historically evolving social and economic institutions, were prescient and highly influential. Together, they fit very well with the view of morality as beginning with a psycho-biological account of human nature, aided by rationally formulated general rules of reciprocity, and expanding through the development of increasingly sophisticated systems of social cooperation.

The following excerpts are from a letter describing Hume's last days, written by his friend, the great philosopher and economist Adam Smith, to a mutual friend. Though Hume's death wasn't heroic, his remarkable equanimity was inspiring. His was the death of a man who had done all that he judged he could, who had left no work undone—including not only his great contributions to history and philosophy, but also his generous financial provision for family and friends. Having secured his legacy to the world, and to those near and dear, he could depart it in as pleasant a way as one might imagine.[9]

DEAR SIR,—It is with a real, though a very melancholy pleasure, that I sit down to give some account of the behavior of our late excellent friend, Mr. Hume, during his last illness. . . . Upon his return to Edinburgh [from a journey recounted by Smith] though he found himself much weaker, yet his cheerfulness never abated, and he continued to divert himself, as usual, with correcting his own works for a new edition, with reading books of amusement, with the conversation of his friends; and, sometimes in the evening, with a party at his favorite game of whist. His cheerfulness was so great, and his conversation and amusements ran so much in their usual strain, that, notwithstanding all bad symptoms, many people could not believe he was dying. . . . Mr. Hume's magnanimity and firmness were such, that his most affectionate friends knew that they hazarded nothing in talking or writing to him as to a dying man, and that so far from being hurt by this frankness, he was rather pleased and flattered by it. I happened to come into his room while he was reading this letter [from another friend], which he had just received, and which he immediately showed me. I told him, that though I was sensible how very much he was weakened, and that appearances were in many respects very bad, yet his cheerfulness was still so great, the spirit of life seemed still to be so very strong in him, that I could not help entertaining some faint hopes. He answered,

"Your hopes are groundless. An habitual diarrhea of more than a year's standing, would be a very bad disease at any age: at my age it is a mortal one. When I lie down in the evening, I feel myself weaker than when I rose in the morning; and when I rise in the morning, weaker than when I lay down in the evening. I am sensible, besides, that some of my vital parts are affected, so that I must soon die."

"Well," said I, "if it must be so, you have at least the satisfaction of leaving all your friends, your brother's family in particular, in great prosperity."

He said that he felt that satisfaction so sensibly, that when he was reading, a few days before, Lucian's *Dialogues of the Dead,* among all the excuses which are alleged to Charon for not entering readily into his boat, he could not find one that fitted him; he had no house to finish, *he had no daughter to provide for, he had no enemies upon whom he wished to revenge himself.*

"I could not well imagine," said he, "what excuse I could make to Charon in order to obtain a little delay. *I have done every thing of consequence which I ever meant to do; and I could at no time expect to leave my relations and friends in a better situation than that in which I am now likely to leave them. I therefore have all reason to die contented."*

But, though Mr. Hume always talked of his approaching dissolution with great cheerfulness, he never affected to make any parade of his magnanimity. He never mentioned the subject but when the conversation naturally led to it, and never dwelt longer upon it than the course of the conversation happened to require: it was a subject, indeed, which occurred pretty frequently, in consequence of the inquiries which his friends, who came to see him, naturally made concerning the state of his health. The conversation which I mentioned above, and which passed on Thursday the 8th of August, was the last, except one, that I ever had with him.

He had now become so very weak, that the company of his most intimate friends fatigued him; for his cheerfulness was still so great, his complaisance and social disposition were still so entire, that when any friend was with him, he could not help talking more, and with greater exertion, than suited the weakness of his body. At his own desire, therefore, I agreed to leave Edinburgh, where I was staying partly upon his account. . . .

[Several days later,] I received the following letter from Doctor Black.

"DEAR SIR,—Yesterday, about four o'clock, afternoon, Mr. Hume expired. The near approach of his death became evident in the night between Thursday and Friday, when his disease became excessive, and soon weakened him so much that he could no longer rise out of his bed. He continued to the last perfectly sensible, and free from much pain or feelings of distress. He never dropped the smallest expression of impatience; but when he had occasion to speak to the people about him, always did it with affection and tenderness. I thought it improper to write to bring you over, especially as I heard that he had dictated a letter to you desiring you not to come. When he became very weak, it cost him an effort to speak, and he died in such a happy composure of mind, that nothing could exceed it."

Thus died our most excellent and never to be forgotten friend; concerning whose philosophical opinions men will, no doubt, judge variously, every one approving or condemning them, according as they happen to coincide or disagree with his own; but concerning whose character and conduct there can scarce be a difference of opinion. His temper, indeed, seemed to be more happily balanced, if I may be allowed such an expression, than that perhaps of any other man I have ever known. Even in the lowest state of his fortune, his great and necessary frugality never hindered him from exercising, upon proper occasions, acts both of charity and generosity. It was a frugality founded, not upon avarice, but upon the love of independency. The extreme gentleness of his nature never weakened either the firmness of his mind or the steadiness of his resolutions. His constant pleasantry was the genuine effusion of good nature and good humor, tempered with delicacy and modesty, and without even the slightest tincture of malignity, so frequently the disagreeable source of what is called wit in other men. It never was the meaning of his raillery to mortify; and, therefore, far from offending, it seldom failed to please and delight, even those who were the objects of it. To his friends, who were frequently the objects of it, there was not perhaps any one of all his great and amiable qualities, which contributed more to endear his conversation. And that gaiety of temper, so agreeable in society, but which is so often accompanied with frivolous and superficial qualities, was in him certainly attended with the most severe application, the most extensive learning, the greatest depth of thought, and a capacity in every respect the most comprehensive. Upon the whole, I have always considered him, both in his lifetime and since his death, as approaching as nearly to the idea of a perfectly wise and virtuous man, as perhaps the nature of human frailty will permit.

BIOS OF LEADING FIGURES

ALBERTUS MAGNUS (Albert the Great) (circa 1200–1280), an amateur scientist, philosopher of nature, and theologian, was an important official in the Dominican order, professor of theology at the University of Paris, and the teacher of Thomas Aquinas.

ARISTOTLE (384–322/1 BCE), along with his teacher Plato, was one of the two greatest philosophers of the ancient world. His investigations in logic, epistemology, metaphysics, ethics, politics, physics, biology, psychology, and aesthetics set the standard for centuries.

THOMAS AQUINAS (1225–1274), one of the most influential philosophers and theologians of all time, played a central role in reviving Greek philosophy by bringing Aristotle back to life and blending his thought with Christianity in a synthesis of faith and reason.

AUGUSTINE (354–430) was a gifted writer, theologian, and powerful figure in the early Church. His version of Christianity, infused with elements of Platonism, was a dominant force in Christian thought from the fifth through the thirteenth centuries.

FRANCIS BACON (1561–1626) was a British philosopher of science who stressed the practical value of technological innovations and their power to change the world. His writings helped create a climate of opinion favorable to scientific progress.

ROGER BACON (1212–1292) was a British monk with far-reaching interests in science, natural philosophy, mathematics, and astronomy, in addition to theology. He wrote on light, eclipses, tides, the structure of the eye, vision, and scientific method.

GARY BECKER (1930–2014) was a Nobel Prize–winning economist whose work extended rational decision theory with agent-relative probabilities and utilities beyond economic behavior, measured in dollars and cents, to utility-maximizing behavior in broader settings.

GEORGE BERKELEY (1685–1753), a bishop in the Anglican Church, was an empiricist who pursued scientific interests and developed a theory of vision.

The scientist and natural philosopher ROBERT BOYLE (1627–1691) discovered Boyle's law of gases. He was also John Locke's scientific mentor at Oxford and a founding member of the Royal Society of London, which published Newton's *Principia*.

Nobel laureate JAMES BUCHANAN (1919–2013) is widely known as the father of public choice theory, applying the principles of cost-benefit analysis and rational decision theory to governments and political institutions.

NOAM CHOMSKY (1928–) revolutionized linguistics, laying the groundwork for the scientific study of natural human languages, conceived of as integrated cognitive systems relating sound and meaning. This work, in turn, became a pillar modern cognitive science.

A leading philosopher, logician, and mathematician, ALONZO CHURCH (1903–1995) was, together with his Ph.D. student Alan Turing, responsible for important advances in philosophical logic and the mathematical theory of computation leading to the digital age.

NICOLAUS COPERNICUS (1473–1543) developed the first systematic geocentric conception of the solar system, showing how heretofore apparent "retrograde" movements of planets could be explained if the earth and other planets orbited the sun.

A world-renowned philosopher whose *cogito ergo sum* set the epistemological agenda for philosophy for centuries, RENÉ DESCARTES (1596–1650) also discovered the sine law of the refraction of light and laid the conceptual foundations for analytic geometry.

The special and general theories of relativity of the philosophically minded theoretical physicist ALBERT EINSTEIN (1879–1955) transformed modern physics, making him the modern counterpart of Isaac Newton.

JERRY FODOR (1935–) is a leading philosopher of psychology who played a key role in moving psychology away from behaviorism and laying the foundations of the modern computational-representational concept of mind.

The philosopher-mathematician GOTTLOB FREGE (1848–1925) invented modern symbolic logic, advanced the philosophy of mathematics, and provided the conceptual basis for understanding linguistic meaning in both natural and mathematical languages.

GALILEO GALILEI (1564–1642) was a mathematician and natural philosopher, as well as one of the fathers of modern physics and the most advanced astronomer of his day. His observations provided conclusive proof of the geocentric conception of the solar system.

Arguably the leading philosopher of logic of all time, KURT GÖDEL (1906–1978) proved revolutionary theorems about the scope and limits of contemporary logical systems.

PAUL GRICE (1913–1988) demonstrated how rational communicative strategies combine with linguistic meanings to contribute information conveyed by uses of sentences, advancing linguistics and the philosophy of language.

H.L.A. HART (1907–1992) was the foremost philosopher of law of the twentieth century. His leading work, *The Concept of Law,* is widely taken to be the defining statement of the school of thought known as legal positivism.

A Nobel laureate in economics and defender of classical liberalism, FRIEDRICH HAYEK (1899–1992) stressed the role of political and economic liberty in generating the knowledge required for social and economic progress.

A precursor of Marx, GEORG WILHELM FRIEDRICH HEGEL (1770–1831) believed reality to be a single divine mind, evolving through internal conflict to unified self-consciousness. He saw human minds as evolving toward unification of individual interests in the general will represented by an authoritative governing state.

THOMAS HOBBES (1588–1679) was the first great political philosopher of the early modern era. His justification of government as arising from a hypothetical social contract rationally adopted in the state of nature became the starting point for subsequent views.

DAVID HUME (1711–1776) was a great British empiricist and a distinguished historian of England. His analyses of causation, associationist psychology, naturalistic morality, and incrementalist political and social philosophy were enormously influential.

The teacher of Adam Smith, FRANCIS HUTCHESON (1694–1745) was a Scottish "moral-sense" philosopher who influenced John Witherspoon and David Hume.

The German philosopher IMMANUEL KANT (1724–1804) was among the most systematic thinkers of all time. In addition to transforming ethics, Kant developed theories of space, time, number, perception, and knowledge that set the agendas for later philosophers.

JOHANNES KEPLER (1571–1630) was the mathematician, natural philosopher, and astronomer who discovered the elliptical form of planetary orbits and the mathematical properties of gravity, illuminating its perplexing nature.

A child prodigy, SAUL KRIPKE (1941–) emerged as the greatest philosopher of the second half of the twentieth century, transforming our philosophical understanding of necessity and possibility, and providing the mathematical structure to study them. His applications of these ideas to the study of language have proved particularly important.

GOTTFRIED WILHELM LEIBNIZ (1646–1716) was a mathematician whose invention of calculus was independent of Newton's. He was also a philosophical logician, the author of an ingenious metaphysical system, and a critic of Newton's conception of absolute space.

JOHN LOCKE (1632–1704) developed an empiricist psychology and theory of knowledge. His theory of limited, democratic government protecting natural rights was a major influence on the American Revolution and the Constitution of the United States.

In addition to inventing calculus, ISAAC NEWTON (1642–1727) developed a model of the universe, based on his celebrated laws of motion, that explained a dazzling array of diverse empirical observations and dominated physics for nearly 200 years.

ROBERT NOZICK (1938–2002) defended limited government and argued that liberty subverts all redistributionist patterns. His work *Anarchy, State, and Utopia* became a libertarian classic.

WILLIAM OF OCKHAM (1287–1349) was a logician, philosopher, and critic of importing Greek metaphysics into Christian thought. Known for "Ockham's Razor," warning against positing hypothetical entities beyond those needed to explain evident truths, he was a leader in the growing scientific outlook of his time.

PLATO (427–347 BCE) was the father of western philosophy, the founder of the first European university (Plato's Academy), the teacher of Aristotle, and the author whose Dialogues immortalized Socrates. His work transformed western culture.

Despite his early death, FRANK P. RAMSEY (1903–1930) made brilliant contributions to philosophy, mathematical logic, and economics, chief of which was his groundbreaking work on subjective probability and agent-relative utility theory.

Regarded by many as the leading political philosopher of the twentieth century, JOHN RAWLS (1921–2002) provided a widely influential justification of the liberal welfare state that revived normative theorizing in the analytic tradition.

BERTRAND RUSSELL (1872–1970) was a leading philosophical logician and philosopher of language and mathematics. His distinction between logical and grammatical form and his conception of the role of logic in philosophy became cornerstones of the analytic tradition.

A critic of aspects of the Thomistic synthesis of Aristotelian philosophy with Christian theology, JOHN DUNS SCOTUS (1266–1308) was one of the most important philosopher-theologians of the High Middle Ages.

ADAM SMITH (1723–1790) was a leading founder of modern economics. A close friend of David Hume, he succeeded his teacher, Francis Hutcheson, in the Chair in Moral Philosophy at Glasgow University, where he wrote an important book on human nature as the source of morality.

GEORGE STIGLER (1911–1991) was a Nobel Prize–winning economist in the public choice school, which used rational choice theory to extend economic thinking to include public policy and public institutions in addition to traditional economic actors.

Along with Kurt Gödel and Alonzo Church, ALFRED TARSKI (1901–1983) established foundations of symbolic logic that transformed it into a mature discipline. He is best known for his theory of truth, on which the analysis of *logical consequence* is now based.

The father of digital computation, ALAN TURING (1912–1954) was a mathematician and logician whose work provided the theoretical foundation for modern computer science. In World War II he broke the German codes based on Germany's famous Enigma machine.

JOHN WITHERSPOON (1723–1794) arrived in America in 1768 to become president of Princeton, and head of its departments of Philosophy, English, and History. A member of the Continental Congress, signer of the Declaration of Independence, and a devotee of the Scottish Philosophical Enlightenment, he was the revered teacher of scores of America's founding fathers.

A leading figure in twentieth-century philosophy, LUDWIG WITTGENSTEIN (1889–1951) stressed the importance of understanding logic and language in the service of transforming philosophy and revealing the nature of representational thought.

ACKNOWLEDGMENTS

In preparing this manuscript I profited greatly from the comments of two anonymous referees provided by Princeton University Press, as well as from friends and colleagues including Jing He, Ed McCann, Frank Price, Kevin Robb, Jake Ross, and Porter Williams. The perspective of my wife Martha, who read the entire manuscript and offered many insights and comments, was invaluable.

NOTES

CHAPTER 1

1. Metaphysics 980a21, tr. W. D. Ross. In Aristotle (1941).
2. The orality and limited literacy of Greek culture in the fifth century BCE (and beyond) is defended in Harris (1989) and Thomas (1992). An informative overview is given in the Introduction to Robb (1994). For further discussion, see Yunis (2003).
3. Burkert (1985), p. 120.
4. Havelock (1967), pp. 198–99.
5. Chapter 6 of Robb (1994) explicates Plato's criticism, in the early dialogues *Ion* and *Euthyphro,* of the role of oral epic poetry in education and moral instruction, and his determination to replace it with rigorous, Socratic reasoning. Chapter 7 explains that the growing literacy of the aristocratic and business classes in late-fifth-century Athens preceded the union of literacy and formal education in the fourth century.
6. In chapter 1 of his book *Reading Thucydides* (2006), James V. Morrison divides the transition in ancient Greece from an oral to a literate alphabetic culture into three stages: (i) the era of primary orality between 1200 to 750 BCE, prior to the introduction of writing, (ii) the various stages of proto-literacy from 750 to 400 BCE, when the Greek alphabet was introduced and writing for special ceremonies and commerce coexisted with a culture in which the primary medium of education, politics, poetry, and the like was still the spoken word, and (iii) the period of alphabetic literacy, in which poets and thinkers produced works that were intended to be read by their audiences rather than heard.
7. See Havelock (1983), especially pages 29, 40–41, for relevant discussion of the transition from Anaxagoras (500–428 BCE) to Plato and Aristotle on motion and related concepts.
8. See pp. 130–33 of Heath (1981) for details.
9. Ibid., pp. 139–62.
10. Ibid., pp. 176–80.
11. Ibid., p. 202.
12. Ibid., pp. 162–65.
13. Ibid., p. 217.
14. Ibid., p. 284.
15. Ibid., p. 3.

16. An early pathbreaking article giving evidence that most Greeks prior to Socrates would not have thought of the soul as an autonomous personality, or a self-governing being, is Burnet (1916).

17. Havelock (1967), p. 197. The first post-Homeric uses of the word 'psyche' (roughly, soul) are found in Heraclitus. See Robb (1968), Furley (1956), Robinson (1968), Claus (1983), and Bremmer (1983).

18. Ibid., p. 30.

19. Aristotle's school derived its name from the Greek word for walking, and in particular from an area of a temple to Apollo which housed the school, where Aristotle was in the habit of teaching philosophy while walking around a colonnaded space.

20. See the early works *Eudemus* and *Protrepticus,* cited on pp. 12, 13 of Copleston (1962a) and in *The Encyclopedia Britannica* at https://www.britannica.com/biography/Aristotle. In those works, Aristotle accepts Plato's doctrine of recollection, in which the Ideas, or Forms, are apprehended before birth. He also argues for the immortality of the soul.

21. Perishable substances in the natural world, which are combinations of form and matter, are made to be what they are by their essential forms. Although these forms are immaterial, they have no existence apart from inhering in the perishable things of which they are forms. Thus, they are not independent and eternal. Aristotle does admit the existence of some nonperishable (eternal) things which, in the *Categories,* he calls secondary substances. This opens the door for some eternal forms, but not those that make up the natural world.

22. If Socrates were merely the combination of the form *humanity* (which is common to all humans) and a particular bit of prime matter pm_S, then all differences between Socrates and every other human would have to be the result of the particular properties of pm_S (which is not supposed to have any properties). Moreover, if (as it seems) it is *necessarily true that Socrates ≠ Plato,* then pm_S *could not* have made up Plato, since if it had, then Socrates would have been Plato. In other words, it would have to be an essential property of pm_S that it made up Socrates, if it made up anything. Although it is hard to read the full Aristotelian corpus as entirely consistent with any one interpretation, it is particularly hard to read it as supporting this view. Thus, it seems, we need to take the soul of Socrates to be an individuating form.

23. At one point in *De Anima,* Aristotle does say that rationality, the highest power of the human soul, is eternal. But it is unclear what he meant. For one thing, Socrates, who was a combination of matter and form, was not identical with his Aristotelian soul, still less with one of its several powers. For another, Aristotle says that all memory, all loving, and all hating perish with death, leaving only pure rationality. Finally, it seems possible that in saying that the rational power of the soul is eternal he was really stating in a somewhat misleading way that the rationality we exhibit is the essence of God, and so is eternal for that reason. For discussion see pp. 70–73 of Copleston (1962a).

24. Copleston (1962a), pp. 58–59.

25. Aristotle sketched two different forms of the good life, one of contemplation pursing theoretical knowledge for its own sake (the path of theoretical philosophy) and one a life of action in the world based on practical wisdom provided

by practical philosophy (particularly ethics and political philosophy). See chapter 3 of Cooper (2012).

26. See Plato's *Apology, Crito,* and *Phaedo* in Plato (1961).

27. See Cooper (2012), p. 146 (including fns. 2 and 4), also n. 19 on pp. 410–11, and sections 5–7 of chapter 5.

28. See chapter 4 of Cooper (2012) for a nuanced discussion of stoicism, and sections 2–4 of chapter 5 for a discussion of epicureanism.

CHAPTER 2

1. See chapter 1, section 2 of D'Arcy (1930).

2. Ibid.

3. Chapter 1, section 3 of D'Arcy (1930) discusses the fragmentary knowledge of Aristotle in Christian Europe up to the middle of the 12th century, as well as the more complete knowledge of Aristotle attained by Arabs and Jews in Syria, Egypt, and Spain during the period.

4. See chapters 30, 41, 42, and 51 of Copleston (1962b).

5. Ibid., pp. 12–13.

6. Ibid., p. 21.

7. Although Aristotle's "unmoved mover" was called 'God', it bore little relation to the Christian god. "The First Mover's . . . activity must be purely spiritual, and so intellectual. . . . Aristotle . . . defines God as 'Thought of Thought.' . . . God is subsistent thought, which eternally thinks itself. . . . God, therefore, knows only Himself." Copleston (1962a), pp. 58–59.

8. In giving this brief summary of related arguments of the two philosophers, I set aside the interesting and complex historical and philosophical issues raised by them. For informed discussion, see Weisheipl (1965).

9. See Wippel (1981), Weisheipl (1983), and Dales (1990).

10. One might, of course, doubt the premises. Even if one grants them and accepts that each contingent thing or change depends on some necessary being or fact, one still hasn't shown there is a *unique* such being or fact on which *everything* depends. Perhaps different contingent things or changes depend on different necessary beings or facts. Nor has one established the existence of any sort of god, let alone the Christian god. Finally, the retreat to necessity that is intended to stop the regress of explanations might, if not circumscribed, eliminate contingency altogether. *If everything is as it is because of something that couldn't have been otherwise, then it is hard to see how anything could have been otherwise.* A key question for the Christian proponent of the argument is whether the necessary being, God, could have acted other than he did act. If necessarily he always acts for the best, one may wonder not only whether this is this the best of all possible worlds, but also whether it is the only one.

11. Aquinas thought there are many human souls, which there wouldn't be if the soul of each human being were the property *being human*, which is common to all humans. Thus when Copleston says it is matter "which marks off one corporeal thing from other members of the same species" and that "what makes human souls different from one another is their union with different bodies," he can't be denying that different human beings differ in both form and matter

(Copleston 1955, pp. 95–96). See Book 2, chapter 81 of Aquinas (1975), *Summa Contra Gentiles,* where he says, "So this soul is commensurate with that body, that soul with that body, and so on with all of them." For an informative discussion of the problem, see pp. 121–47 of Pegis (1934).

12. Aquinas (1947), *Summa Theologica,* Ia. 75.IC.
13. Aquinas (1947), Ia. 75.IC, and (1975), *Summa Contra Gentiles,* II. 65.
14. Aquinas (1947), Ia. 75.2C.
15. Ibid., Ia. 75.2C.
16. The argument for this is discussed on pp. 303–4 of McCabe (1969). This argument is also discussed on pp. 173–74 of Copleston (1955).
17. Kretzmann (1993), p. 132.
18. Ibid., p. 133.
19. Copleston (1962b), pp. 94–98, and Kretzmann (1993), p. 136.
20. Aquinas (1949), *Disputed Questions on the Soul* IC, my emphasis.
21. Aquinas (1947), *Summa Theologica,* Ia.3.1, 93.2C, 93.6C.
22. Aquinas (1975), 4.79.
23. See p. 136 of Kretzmann (1993).
24. One of Aquinas's important early critics was St. Bonaventure, who thought Aquinas had overintellectualized Christianity. More other-worldly and mystical than Aquinas, he once remarked: "[A]mong philosophers the word of wisdom was given to Plato, to Aristotle the word knowledge. The one looked principally to what is higher, the other to what is lower. . . . But the word both of knowledge and of wisdom was given by the Holy Ghost to Augustine." (Quoted on p. 15 of D'Arcy 1930).

 Apparently seeing no need for a systematic philosophical approach for acquiring worldly knowledge (which would have to be reconciled with Christianity's inspirational message), Bonaventure offered a kind of Augustinian mystical synthesis, and so saw no need for the Thomistic synthesis. Many others, however, felt the need to engage with Aquinas more directly. See Gilson (1955).
25. Copleston (1962b), p. 151.
26. See ibid., pp. 289–90.
27. See ibid., pp. 56–57.
28. This was Ockham's general form of argument involving the razor. He says the following (Ockham 1952, p. 37): "Nouns which are derived from verbs and also nouns which derive from adverbs . . . have been introduced only for the sake of brevity in speaking or as ornaments of speech . . . and so they do not signify any things in addition to those from which they derive." The translation is from Copleston (1993), p. 76.
29. Passage from Ockham, *Quodlibeta septem,* 1, 12, Paris, 1487, translated by Copleston (1993), p. 96.
30. See chapters 1, 9, 10, 18, and section 4 of chapter 24 of Copleston (1993).

CHAPTER 3

1. Although the work, *De Revolutionibus Orbium Coelestium Libri IV,* in which Copernicus presented his system wasn't published until 1543, its main ideas were developed around 1512 or shortly thereafter.

2. Preface to Kepler ([1609] 1858–71).
3. Newton's not dissimilar reaction will be discussed below.
4. Letter to Herwart, Feb. 10, 1605.
5. Galileo was Professor of Mathematics at Pisa from 1589 to 1592 and at Padua from 1592 to 1610, when he was brought by Cosimo II de' Medici, Grand Duke of Tuscany, to Florence, where he was free to pursue his mathematical, philosophical, and scientific work. It was about that time that he constructed his improved telescope.
6. The impetus that prompted Galileo to conduct his famous experiment at the Tower of Pisa was a paper published by Stevin in 1586 in which he reported the results of his own experiment with lead balls of different weights.
7. Galileo had been an outspoken supporter of the Copernican system—as established truth rather than merely well-supported theory—since at least 1613. This led to decades of tension with papal authorities that culminated in his condemnation by the Inquisition in 1633, resulting in a sentence of what amounted to house arrest—first in the house of his friend the archbishop of Siena and then in his own villa near Florence. During that time he continued to work until going blind in 1637, when he sent a new treatise on physics to Holland that was published in 1638.
8. A strong contemporary case for a physicalist conception of color is given by the articles authored by Alex Byrne and David Hilbert in the volume Byrne and Hilbert (1997).
9. Letter to Mersenne (1:70). See the entry in *Stanford Encyclopedia of Philosophy*, https://plato.stanford.edu/entries/descartes/.
10. Descartes ([1641] 1991).
11. Descartes ([1644] 1983).
12. The passage is from "The Author's Letter" (9B:14), of the French translation, in 1647, of Descartes's ([1644] 1983) (which originally appeared in Latin).
13. The implicit premise here, that what one can coherently conceive must be genuinely possible, is, for good reason, now widely (though still not universally) recognized to be questionable.
14. There are two potential problems with this argument: (i) the idea that which states are possible is independent of which state turns out to be actual, and (ii) the idea that if something is coherently conceivable, then it is genuinely possible. The most promising current explanation of why (ii) is false will be discussed in chapter 9.
15. Newton ([1687] 1934, 1999).
16. Newton's work is explained in a little more detail in chapter 10, where it is used to introduce the philosophical underpinnings of 20th-century physics.
17. Third letter to Bentley, 1692, in Newton (1959–84).
18. Newton (1999), p. 943, from "General Scholium," an essay by Newton appended to the second edition of *Principia*.
19. Newton ([1687] 1934), vol. 1, p. 6.
20. Ibid., p. 11.
21. Could the water's position relative to some body other than the bucket explain what we observe? This seems unlikely, since we can easily imagine the experiment taking place in an empty universe with the same result. Newton himself invokes this kind of thought experiment not with a bucket of water but with

an empty universe consisting of two globes linked by a cord revolving around their common center (Newton [1687] 1934), vol. 1, p. 12).

22. Boyle (1692).

23. Seventh page of "Epistle to the Reader," in Locke ([1689] 1975).

24. Principle (iii) is sometimes taken to be a consequence of the truth (sometimes called "Leibniz's Law"): *Necessarily, if x = y, then any property of x is a property of y.* From this it follows *that necessarily, if x has property P, then anything that does not have P isn't identical with x.* However, what is needed to derive (iii) is not that, but rather: *If x has property P, then necessarily (i.e., it is a necessary truth that) anything that doesn't have P isn't x.* This needed principle doesn't follow without assuming the very thing one is trying to prove. Thus, the case for (iii) fails. See Soames (2014b), pp. 417–19, for an explanation.

25. This point is explicitly endorsed in a letter to Volder, on p. 226 of volume 2 of Leibniz (1875–1890).

26. For Leibniz, these truths are contingent in the sense that we finite beings can't provide complete analyses that show their subjects to contain the properties predicated of them.

27. See the third, fourth, and fifth letters to S. Clarke in volume 7 of Leibniz (1875–1890), pp. 363, 373, and 400. See also p. 183 of vol. 2. In chapter 10, I return to the dispute between Leibniz and Newton, indicating its relation to developments in modern physics.

28. Hume (1964), vol. 2, page 419.

29. Ibid., pages 428–29.

30. Ibid., page 436.

31. Ibid., page 440.

CHAPTER 4

1. Hobbes ([1651] 1994), p. 113.

2. Second Treatise, Chapter 2, Article 6, in Locke (1987).

3. Ibid., 8, 95.

4. Ibid., 9, 131.

5. Ibid., 11, 138.

6. Copleston (1964), p. 151.

7. Hume's *A Treatise of Human Nature*, book III, part I, section 2 (Hume 1964, vol. 2, p. 246).

8. Hume's *Treatise*, book III, part II, section 2 (ibid., pp. 262–63).

9. Ibid., p. 263.

10. Hume's *Treatise*, book III, part II, sections 3, 4, and 5 (Hume 1964, vol. 2).

11. Hume's *Treatise*, book III, part II, section 1 (ibid., p. 258).

12. Hume's *Treatise*, book III, part II, section 2 (ibid., pp. 269–71).

13. Hume's *Treatise*, book III, part II, section 2 (ibid., p. 271).

14. See Adair (1957).

15. Herman (2001), p. 173.

16. Smith ([1776] 1997), book IV, chapter 7, part 3. A thorough account of Adam Smith's far-reaching influence on American founders, including Madison and Jefferson, is presented in Fleischacker (2002).

17. A nod should also be given to two other philosophers—to Jeremy Bentham (1748–1832), who evaluated the rightness or wrongness of individual actions on the basis of the total value of their consequences (for human happiness), and to John Stuart Mill (1806–1873), some of whose writings can be read as suggesting evaluating the rightness or wrongness of actions in terms of the consequences (for human happiness) not of individual actions themselves but of the universal adoption of rules mandating or prohibiting such actions.

CHAPTER 5

1. Also prominent among these philosophers was Charles Sanders Peirce, an American contemporary of Frege who independently developed a system of logic comparable to Frege's, which, though not without influence, did not have the historical impact that Frege's did.

2. Frege ([1879] 1967).

3. The definitions of *model*, of *truth in a model*, and of *logical consequence* in terms of truth in a model were not made explicit until they arose from the work of Alfred Tarski in the 1930s. Nevertheless, for the most part, Frege's logical and semantic principles implicitly tracked them, in part, perhaps, because his logical and semantic ideas gave birth to the practices from which the later definitions were abstracted. This point is taken up in more detail in chapter 6.

4. Frege ([1884] 1950).

5. Frege ([1893, 1903] 1964).

6. Although for Frege concepts are associated with predicates, they are neither ideas in the mind, nor anything psychological. Rather, they are functions that map objects of which the predicates are true onto *truth,* and those of which the predicates are not true onto *falsity.* In this way they are more like sets, of which there are infinitely many, than they are like the finitely many ideas present in any human mind.

7. The system, popularized in Giuseppe Peano (1889), is standardly attributed to Richard Dedekind, who is said to have come up with it in 1888, though Frege also seems to have come up with it independently.

8. The discovery of the contradiction, its application to the systems of Frege and Russell, and the lessons to be drawn from the contradiction are discussed in Soames (2014b), pp. 120–29.

9. Bertrand Russell and Alfred North Whitehead (1910, 1912, 1913), *Principia Mathematica.* Simplified explanations are given in Soames (2014b), pp. 474–88, 500–11.

10. See Soames (2014b), pp. 488–91, 494.

11. There are two versions of Russell's theory of types—the original ramified theory used in *Principia Mathematica* and the simple theory in Ramsey (1925). The axiom of reducibility is required by the former but not the latter. As Kamareddine, Laan, and Nederpelt (2002) report, that axiom was "questioned from the moment it was introduced." (See also Gödel 1944). Although the replacement of the ramified theory by the simple theory, and the resulting elimination of reducibility, was a mathematical step forward, it highlighted a philosophical worry that Russell had managed to blur. Using a theory of logical types to block his 1903 contradiction requires a questionable theory of intelligibility. Just as it

is impossible for a set to be a member of itself, so Russell maintained, a proper logical analysis would show it to be *meaningless*, not just false, to say that a set is a member of itself. But that's not obvious. To say that no set is identical with any of its members *seems true*; if so, its negation should be false, not meaningless. It is also virtually impossible to explain simple type theory involving real sets without saying things which, once one has the theory, are declared to be meaningless. Surely there is something wrong with any theory the strictures of which pronounce the best descriptions of the theory to be incoherent. Although this doesn't undercut the claims the theory makes about sets, and the identification of the natural numbers with some of them, it does undercut the idea that the type theory is nothing more than a system encoding logical principles needed to reason about any subject.

Landini (1998) and Klement (2004) plausibly argue that in adopting his type theory Russell had come to think there is no more reason to suppose that one who says "Some sets are so and so, while others are such and such" is committed to the real existence of sets than there is to think that one who says "The average man has 1.7 children" is committed to there being some really existing person who is the average man. The issue involves what is now called the *substitutional* analysis of the quantification into predicate position employed in *Principia Mathematica*. On this analysis, Russell's type-theoretic constraints on intelligibility are, arguably, justified, but—as shown in Hodes (2015), Soames (2014b), pp. 511–31, and Soames (2015a)—the reduction of mathematics to logic, along with other aspects of Russell's philosophical logic, are threatened. The reduction of mathematics to set theory, which posits the real existence of sets, isn't threatened, but set theory isn't logic.

12. Zermelo (1904, 1908a, 1908b), Fraenkel ([1922] 1967).
13. These essentially are the arguments given in two classic articles in recent philosophy of mathematics, Benacerraf (1965, 1973).
14. This way of thinking of natural numbers grows out of two pathbreaking articles—one, Boolos (1984), by my former teacher, George Boolos, and the other, "Arabic Numerals and the Problem of Mathematical Sophistication," forthcoming by my former Ph.D. student Mario Gomez-Torrente.
15. Page 2, section 1 of Wittgenstein (1953).
16. Ibid., pp. 2–3.
17. Thanks to Jing He for helpful discussion of this point.
18. See pp. 435–436 of Boolos (1984) for a fuller discussion.
19. For more detail, see Gomez-Torrente (forthcoming).

CHAPTER 6

1. See chapter 1 of Soames (2014b).
2. Tarski ([1935] 1983) and ([1936] 1983). Although the contemporary notion of *truth in a model* is based on these papers, it is an abstraction from the concepts explicitly defined there.
3. Gödel had already proven results relating *provable sentence (of a given logical system)* to *logical truth* and *logical consequence,* using informal understandings of those concepts. Even Frege had an implicit grasp of them. According to him,

the truths of logic were entirely general, and did not depend on any special subject matter. This suggests that any sentence that counts as a logical truth should remain such no matter how its names, function signs and predicates are interpreted. Since a model is a formalization of the idea of such an interpretation, it shouldn't be seen as entirely foreign to Frege.

4. Gödel (1930).

5. Section 4 of chapter 1 of Soames (2014b) explains the difference between first and higher-order quantification in Frege.

6. Hahn, Carnap, and Neurath (1929).

7. The theorem is formally proved in Tarski ([1935] 1983). It is often called the *Gödel-Tarski theorem* because it is an obvious corollary of Gödel's first incompleteness theorem, presented in Gödel (1931).

8. A free occurrence of a variable in a formula is one that is not bound (i.e., governed) by a quantifier containing that variable. For example, the three occurrences of 'x' within the parentheses in the formula *every x (x = x & x ≠ y)* are bound by 'every x', while the occurrence of 'y' is free.

9. A more detailed explanation is given in section 3.3 of chapter 8 of Soames (2018).

10. Here, 'P' is a predicate variable, occupying predicate positions in sentences, that ranges over of sets of objects.

11. See section 3.4 of chapter 8 of Soames (2018), and the references cited there.

12. Gödel (1932).

13. This theorem is discussed in section 4 of chapter 8 of Soames (2018).

14. Church (1936b).

15. Church (1936a).

16. See A fuller discussion is found in section 5.1 of chapter 8 of Soames (2018).

17. Turing (1936/37).

18. Church (1937).

19. A more extensive explanation is found in sections 5.2 and 5.3 of chapter 8 of Soames (2018).

CHAPTER 7

1. *The Logical Structure of Linguistic Theory*—Chomsky ([1955] 1975)—was written when Chomsky was at the Harvard Society of Fellows, but it wasn't published until 1975. *Syntactic Structures*—Chomsky (1957)—is a much shortened summary of the main themes of that work. *Aspects of a Theory of Syntax*—Chomsky (1965)—revises his original conception of the organization of a grammar while articulating an explicitly mentalistic conception of the nature of linguistic theories, of which there had merely been some hints in Chomsky ([1955] 1975). Although his leading ideas about syntax, and its relation to semantics, have undergone many changes since then, this mentalistic philosophy of language has remained central to his thought. His entire professional life, after the Harvard Society, has been spent as a professor at MIT.

2. Pages 146–47 of Miller, Galanter, and Pribram (1960).

3. See Soames (1984) for an alternative to Chomsky's heavily psychological conception of linguistics that nevertheless preserves the significance of linguistics for psychology, and conversely.

4. See Soames (2016a) and chapter 2 of Soames (2010b).
5. The placeholder view is examined and rejected in chapter 5 of Soames (2010b).
6. Russell's conception of our passive awareness of propositions is stated on p. 60 of Russell (1904). Its significance is discussed on pp. 71–72 of Soames (2014c). See also Soames (2016a, chapter 2 of 2010b).
7. See sections 3, 4, and 5 of chapter 9 of Soames (2014b).
8. For discussion, see Soames (2016b), and chapter 2 of Soames (2018).
9. For discussion, see Soames (2008a).
10. Soames (1987, 2008b).
11. King (2007), Soames (2010a, 2013a, 2015b), Jesperson (2010, 2012), King, Soames, and Speaks (2014), Hanks (2015), and Moltmann (2017).
12. How a proposition represents things is read off the acts with which it is identified, from which we derive its truth conditions. A proposition p is true at world-state w if and only if, were the world actually in state w, things would be as p represents them—where *what p represents* is what any conceivable agent who entertains p would represent. No one has to entertain p for p to be true.
13. Nevertheless, one who says "it is a necessary truth that Hesperus is Phosphorus" does not assert that it is a necessary truth that the body in question is seen both in the morning and the evening. For explanation and discussion of the significance of this fact, see Soames (2015b), pp. 85–93.
14. See chapters 3–6 and chapter 9 of Soames (2015b).
15. Kaplan (1979, 1989).
16. Chapter 7 of Soames (2010a).
17. Soames (2008c).
18. Paul Grice, "Logic and Conversation," given as The William James Lecture in 1967 at Harvard University, first published in Grice (1989).

CHAPTER 8

1. Tautologies—like *Either I roll a 7 or ~ I roll a 7*—are assigned probability 1. Their negations are assigned 0.
2. Kolmogorov ([1933] 1950).
3. A countable infinity is one the members of which can be uniquely and exhaustively paired with the natural numbers without remainder.
4. In such a case the agent believes each of the following: There are exactly n tickets; ticket 1 won't win, ticket 2 won't win . . . ticket n won't win; one of the tickets will win.
5. Ramsey ([1926] 1990).
6. Ibid., p. 78.
7. Skyrms (1994).
8. Kemeny (1955).
9. P. 67 of Ramsey (1926 [1990]).
10. Ibid., p. 69.
11. Ibid., p. 70.
12. Ibid., p. 70.
13. Ibid., pp. 72–73.
14. Von Neumann and Morgenstern (1944), Savage (1954), Jeffrey (1965, 2004).

15. Becker ([1964] 1993, 1965, 1969, 1971,1973, 1974a, 1974b, [1981] 1991, 1985, 1992).
16. Becker (1992), p. 39.
17. The short but fascinating life of Ramsey is discussed at length in a book written by his sister (Paul 2012), which in turn is reviewed in Monk (2016).
18. Butler (2012), pp. 21–22.
19. Stigler and Friedland (1962) and Stigler (1971).
20. In contrast to his negative results concerning public choice, Arrow achieved an important positive result by showing that if a government (rightly or wrongly) wishes to redistribute wealth generated by a free, competitive economy, efficiency can be maximized by using taxes to accomplish redistribution, instead of controlling prices to redistribute income. Ever since, most economists have found this result compelling.
21. Buchanan (1986).
22. Ibid. Knute Wicksell, mentioned in the passage, was an important predecessor on whom Buchanan based much of his own approach.

CHAPTER 9

1. See chapter 7.
2. See Kripke (1980), chapters 14 and 17 of Soames (2003), and Soames (2007).
3. Soames (1989).
4. Place (1956), Smart (1963), Lewis (1966), and Armstrong (1968).
5. Kripke (1959).
6. Kripke (1971), pp. 152–53.
7. See Putnam (1967).
8. Kripke (1980), pp. 150–51.
9. Fodor (1981), p. 183.
10. As argued in Soames ([1990] 2009b), Fodor's own discussion is ambiguous between a thesis with this force vs. other, stronger but more doubtful theses.
11. Fodor (1981), pp. 189–90.
12. Ibid., p. 183.
13. See Kripke (1980), Putnam (1975a), Kaplan (1989), and chapter 4 of Soames (2010a).
14. For further discussion, see Soames ([1990] 2009b).

CHAPTER 10

1. The passage quoted is from the sixth page of "Notes for an Autobiography," published in *The Saturday Review of Literature* on November 26, 1949, which is a shortened version of the autobiographical statement in Einstein (1948).
2. Letter to Schlick in Einstein (1998), p. 220. For a brief discussion of Ernst Mach's influence on the logical empiricist school of philosophy of which Schlick was a part, see Soames (2018), pp. 109–12; for Einstein's influence on Schlick, see pp. 114–22.
3. See Norton (2010).

4. Here I follow the illuminating discussion of chapter 3 of Maudlin (2012), which the reader should consult for details.
5. Einstein ([1905] 1989).
6. The example is explained on p. 134 of Grünbaum (1967).
7. Ibid., pp. 134–35.
8. Ibid., p. 136.
9. Einstein ([1920] 2002).
10. See Norton (2010).
11. Chapter 4 of Maudlin (2012) discusses these points, including the fact that the law of inertia also covers bodies outside the light-cone plus the fact that in special relativity the paths of two physical entities not subject to external forces can't intersect more than once.
12. Maudlin (2012), pp. 77–79.
13. Ibid., p. 78.
14. Ibid., p. 71. See pp. 72–74 for discussion of the physical interpretation of what these calculations are.
15. Ibid., p. 76. See also pp. 79–83 for widespread, and seemingly authoritative, but nevertheless misleading, confusions to be avoided.
16. See Maudlin (2012), pp. 89–94, for an explanation of how we could set up and calibrate accurate clocks and relate them to one another on parallel trajectories through space-time. Although one can calibrate some chosen pair of such co-moving clocks and thereby assign simultaneous relations to arbitrarily distant space-time events, the assignment is conventional rather than objective, since selecting a pair of co-moving clocks on a different trajectory would result in a different simultaneity assignment. Simultaneity is not an objective physical notion in relativity theory. The point is extended to speed on pp. 95–96. How the twins A and B would look to each other during A's journey is described on pp. 103–5.
17. For Einstein in 1905, speed was roughly *speed as measured in a given "inertial reference frame"*—a system of space-time points the coordinates of which, with respect to which bodies are not acted on by forces, move in a straight line at a constant rate. He imagined an observer in such a frame who sees a second observer moving past him at what the first observer measures to be a constant rate. Einstein's principles—(i) that the speed of light in a reference frame doesn't depend on the motion of the light source and (ii) that the same physical laws apply in all reference frames—led him to predict that a clock stationary in the second reference frame (moving relative to the first observer) will be measured by the clock in the first frame to be ticking slowly, and, similarly, that the first observer's clock will be measured by the second observer's clock to be running slowly. He also predicted that a rigid rod in the second reference frame will have shrunk when measured by rigid rods in the first reference frame, and similarly for rods in the first frame measured by rods in the second.
18. Maudlin (2012), chapter 5.
19. The nature of rigid rods and the contractions (and expansions) they undergo when subjected to trajectory changing forces in space-time are explained by the philosophically minded physicist John Bell, in "How to Teach Special Relativity," which is chapter 9 of Bell (2008). See also pp. 116–20 of Maudlin (2012).
20. This is a version of the Michelson-Morley experiment in 1887, which Einstein was aware of, and accommodated in his theory of special relativity.

21. EarthSky (2011).
22. Feynman, Leighton, and Sands (1975), vol. 2.
23. Maudlin (2012), p. 138.
24. For discussion of a range of similar examples, see chapter 1 of Albert (1992).
25. Even this is a bit strange, at least terminologically, since normal *functions* are thought only to have mathematical, rather than physical, existence. Some contemporary physicists and philosophers of physics think of the wave function as a "nomological entity"—something like a law that "tells" the full-fledged physically existing things how to move through space-time. This too is, of course, hard to get one's head around. (Thanks to Porter Williams for informing me of this.)
26. Thanks again to Porter Williams for helpful discussion.
27. For a fuller discussion, see chapter 11 of Carroll (2010).
28. Bohm (1951, 1952).
29. See, e.g., Everett (1973).
30. Deutsch (1997), Wallace (2012), and Carroll (2010).

CHAPTER 11

1. Hayek (1960), Rawls (1971), and Gauss (2016).
2. Hayek (1960), p. 42.
3. Ibid., p. 44.
4. Ibid., pp. 44–45.
5. Ibid., p. 93.
6. Ibid., p. 94.
7. Ibid., p. 97.
8. Ibid., p. 98.
9. Ibid., p. 96.
10. Ibid., p. 96.
11. Thanks to Jake Ross for bringing this to my attention.
12. See chapter 7 of Robert Nozick (1974).
13. Ibid., p. 157.
14. There is reason to think he would welcome this. On p. 87 of Hayek (1960) he says, "Our objection is against all attempts to impress upon society a deliberately chosen pattern of distribution." What he may not have seen was that this prohibition applies to his own conclusion that in a free society distribution will roughly correspond to the value society perceives in a person's actions.
15. Nozick (1974), p. 161.
16. The decades-long eclipse of normative inquiry is discussed in chapters 12 and 13 of Soames (2018).
17. On page 19 Rawls (1971) justifies the exclusion of agents' "undeserved" personal characteristics from a fair decision procedure for choosing rules governing social cooperation on the grounds that such characteristics set people at odds and allow them "to be guided by their *prejudices*" (my emphasis). On page 74 he says that because natural assets are the outcome of a "natural lottery," the possession of those assets is "arbitrary from a moral perspective." He adds that "there is no more reason to permit the distribution of income and wealth by

natural assets than by historical and social fortune. . . . *Even the willingness to make an effort, to try, and so to be deserving in the ordinary sense is itself dependent upon happy family and social circumstances"* (my emphasis).

18. Rawls (1971), p. 141 (my emphasis).
19. Ibid., pp. 136–37.
20. Ibid., pp. 143–44.
21. Ibid., 148 (my emphasis).
22. Ibid., p. 144.
23. Ibid., p. 145.
24. Ibid., p. 145.
25. Ibid., section 28.
26. Ibid., p. 169.
27. Ibid., p. 169.
28. See ibid., section 26.
29. Ibid., p. 176.
30. Again, thanks to Jake Ross for articulating this possibility.
31. See pages 74 and 101–2 of Rawls (1971).
32. Ibid., p. 100.
33. Ibid., 90–91.
34. If one asks what property of societies Gaus attempts to model—overall goodness or overall justice—one doesn't get a clear answer. He tends to follow Rawls's terminology, often speaking of overall justice. However, his conception seems not to be fundamentally focused on fairness, but rather on overall goodness, which includes justice or fairness along with other things.
35. See section 2.1 of chapter 2 of Gaus (2016).
36. Ibid., p. 68.
37. Ibid., p. 73.
38. Ibid., pp. 76–77.
39. Ibid., p. 81, my emphasis.
40. Ibid., p. 82.
41. Ibid., pp. 142–43.
42. Thanks to Jake Ross for bringing this to my attention.
43. Gaus (2016), chapter 4, sections 1.3–1.4.
44. Ibid., chapter 4, section 2.2.
45. Ibid., chapter 4, sections 3.1–3.3.
46. Ibid., all of chapter 4.
47. Ibid., pp. 215–220.
48. Ibid., pp. 217–18.
49. See section 3, "Marxism as a source of Leninism," of chapter 16, book 1, volume 1 of Kołakowski ([1978] 2005).
50. Quoted in Kołakowski ([1978] 2005) at page 43.
51. Ibid., p. 223.
52. For useful discussion, see pp. 227–30 of Kołakowski ([1978] 2005).
53. Marx (1970), vol. 1, chapter 14, section 5.
54. Ibid., chapter 15, section 4.
55. Ibid., chapter 25, section 4.
56. Kołakowski ([1978] 2005), p. 252.
57. Ibid., pp. 255–56.

58. Ibid., p. 341.
59. Ibid., pp. 342–43.
60. Ibid., p. 343, my emphasis.
61. Ibid. pp. 343–44, my emphasis.

CHAPTER 12

1. Hart ([1961] 2012).
2. According to Hart, it is a necessary condition for a system of social rules to have this authority in order to count as a legal system. He does not, as far as I can see, assert that it is both necessary and sufficient.
3. It is enough to satisfy the Hartian necessary condition for being a legal system noted in the previous note.
4. Ibid., pp. 171–72.
5. Ibid., p. 210.
6. Ibid., p. 203.
7. 18 U.S. code section 924(c)(1) (2006).
8. Ibid., p. 242, my emphasis.
9. Ibid., p. 242, n. 1, my emphasis.
10. Ibid., p. 228.
11. See Soames (2013b).
12. Ibid.
13. Ibid.
14. Ibid.
15. Leading originalist sources include Barnett (2014, 2016), Barnett and Bernick (2018), Baude (2015), Harrison (1992), Lawson and Seidman (2017), McGinnis and Rappaport (2013), Rappaport (2013), Solum (2011, 2013, 2018), and Upham (2015).
16. The updated theory is presented and explained in Soames (forthcoming).
17. For a recent partial endorsement of deferentialist jurisprudence, see the remarks of Justice Elena Kagan at the Chicago-Kent School of Law on October 16, 2007: "Pretty much all of us now look at the text first and the text is what matters most. And if you can find clarity in the text that's pretty much the end of the ballgame."
18. See Soames (forthcoming).
19. McGinnis and Rappaport (2013).
20. Ibid., chapter 5.
21. See their discussion of the Equal Rights Amendment proposed in 1972, which, they argued failed to be ratified because of the loss of broad confidence caused by the Court's excessively activist and undemocratic rulings.
22. Lawson (1994), p. 1248.
23. Ibid., p. 1248.
24. Hamburger (2014).
25. Quoted on p. 188 of Hamburger (2014) in an illuminating section on the role of American opposition to general warrants and writs of assistance in the run-up to the Revolution, in the writing of state constitutions, and, ultimately, in the U.S. Constitution, with its vigorous insistence on *due process of law*.

26. Hamburger (2014), pp. 337–402.
27. Cited by Lawson (2015), p. 1535.
28. Lawson and Seidman (2017).
29. Natelson (2010), pp. 58–59.
30. Hamburger (2014), p. 386, my emphasis.
31. Lawson (2015), p. 1538.
32. Soames (2013b).

CHAPTER 13

1. Schlick ([1930] 1939). See also chapter 12 of Soames (2018).
2. Wilson (1993).
3. Frank (1988).
4. Wilson (1993), p. 102.
5. Ibid., p. 105.
6. Ibid., p. 107.
7. Ibid., pp. 106–8.
8. Ibid., p. 108.
9. Ibid., p. 109.
10. Ibid., p. 113.
11. Ibid., pp. 123–33.
12. Ibid., p. 130.
13. Ibid., p. 130.
14. Ibid., pp. 132–33.
15. Ibid., p. 133.
16. Ibid., pp. 130–31.
17. So did Hume, whose an account of justice, discussed in chapter 4, stresses the interaction between other-regarding sentiment, self-interest, and past experience of benefits in functioning social institutions.
18. Wilson (1993), p. 132.
19. Ibid., pp. 15–16, 19, 158.
20. Ibid., pp. 15–16, 158–59.
21. Ibid., pp. 20–23.
22. Ibid., pp. 17, 141–42.
23. Ibid., pp. 17–18.
24. Ibid., pp. 141–42.
25. It is important not to overinterpret Wilson on this or other "universals." His point is that there are certain tendencies inherent in human nature, not that the tendencies give rise to exceptionless moral rules, or even to the nonexistence of substantial human groupings in human history in which the "exceptions" were frequent.
26. Ibid., pp. 154–55.
27. Ibid., p. 191.
28. Ibid., p. 205.
29. Ibid., p. 213.
30. Thanks to one of the readers of the manuscript for the Princeton University Press.

CHAPTER 14

1. Wolfe (2012), pp. 23–24.
2. Notable recent works addressing these issues include Nagel (1979, 1987), Feldman (1992), Kagan (2012), and Scheffler (2016).
3. Nozick (1974), pp. 42–45. See also the chapter on happiness in Nozick (1989).
4. Surprisingly perhaps, it is not necessary to believe that although you are not immortal, the human race is. One can find meaning even if one is convinced that the duration of the human race, the solar system, and even our galaxy is finite. Fortunately, the time periods so far surpass the human ability to vividly imagine them that we limited creatures can scarcely take them into account.

APPENDIX

1. Plato 20e, 21.
2. Plato 43 through 54.
3. Plato 116c.
4. Plato 116d.
5. Plato 116e.
6. Plato 117.
7. Plato 117d, e.
8. Plato 118.
9. The letter is reprinted in Hume (1964), vol. 3, pp. 9–14. The italics are mine, emphasizing the importance in Hume's last days of what he had contributed to those he would leave behind.

REFERENCES

Adair, Douglass (1957). "That Politics May Be Reduced to a Science: David Hume, James Madison, and the Tenth Federalist." *Huntington Library Quarterly* 20:343–60.

Albert, David (1992). *Quantum Mechanics and Experience.* Cambridge, MA: Harvard University Press.

Aquinas, Thomas (1947). *Summa Theologica.* New York: Benzinger Brothers.

—— (1949). *Disputed Questions on the Soul.* St. Louis and London: B. Herder Book Co.

—— (1975). *Summa Contra Gentiles.* Book 1 trans. Anton C. Pegis, Book 2 trans. James Anderson, Book 3 trans. Vernon Bourke; Book 4 trans. Charles J. O'Neil. Notre Dame, IN: University of Notre Dame Press.

Aristotle (1941). *The Basic Works of Aristotle,* ed. Richard McKeon, translated under the general editorship of W. D. Ross. New York: Random House.

Armstrong, David (1968). *A Materialist Theory of Mind.* London and New York: Routledge and Kegan Paul.

Arrow, Kenneth (1951). *Social Choice and Individual Values.* New York: Wiley.

Barnett, Randy E. (2014). *Restoring the Lost Constitution.* Revised ed. Princeton, NJ, and Oxford: Princeton University Press.

—— (2016). *Our Republican Constitution.* New York: Broadside Books (of Harper Collins).

Barnett, Randy E., and Evan D. Bernick (2018). "The Letter and the Spirit: A Unified Theory of Originalism." *Georgetown Law Journal* 107, 1:1–55.

Baude, William (2015). "Is Originalism Our Law?" *Columbia Law Review* 115:2349.

Becker, Gary ([1964] 1993). *Human Capital,* 3rd ed. Chicago: University of Chicago Press.

—— (1965). "A Theory of the Allocation of Time." *The Economic Journal* 75:493–517.

—— (1969). "An Economic Analysis of Fertility." In *National Bureau of Economic Research: Demographic and Economic Change in Developed Countries,* 209–40. New York: Columbia University Press.

—— (1971). *The Economics of Discrimination.* Chicago: University of Chicago Press.

—— (1973). "A Theory of Marriage: Part 1." *Journal of Political Economy* 81:813–46.

—— (1974a). "A Theory of Marriage: Part 2." *Journal of Political Economy* 82:11–26.

—— (1974b). *Essays in the Economics of Crime and Punishment.* New York: National Bureau of Economic Research Columbia University Press.

—— (1985). "Human Capital, Effort, and the Sexual Division of Labor." *Journal of Labor Economics* 3:33–58.

—— ([1981] 1991). *A Treatise on the Family*. Cambridge, MA: Harvard University Press;

—— (1992). "The Economic Way of Looking at Life." *https://www.nobelprize.org /prizes/economic-sciences/1992/becker/lecture/*. Nobel Media AB.

Bell, John Stewart (2008). *Speakable and Unspeakable in Quantum Mechanics*. Cambridge: Cambridge University Press.

Benacerraf, Paul (1965). "What Numbers Could Not Be." *Philosophical Review* 74:47–73.

—— (1973). "Mathematical Truth." *Journal of Philosophy* 70:661–79.

Bohm, David (1951). *Quantum Theory*. New York: Prentice-Hall.

—— (1952). "A Suggested Theory of Quantum Mechanics." *Physical Review* 83:166–79.

Boolos, G. (1984). "To Be Is to Be the Value of a Variable (or to Be Some Values of Some Variables)." *Journal of Philosophy* 81:430–49.

Boolos, G., and R. Jeffrey (1974). *Computability and Logic*. Cambridge: Cambridge University Press.

Boyle, Robert (1692). *The General History of the Air,* ed. John Locke. London: Awnsham and John Churchill.

Braithwaite, R. B., ed. (1931). *Foundations of Mathematics and Other Logical Essays*. London: Kegan Paul.

Bremmer, J., ed. (1983). *The Early Greek Concept of the Soul*. Princeton, NJ: Princeton University Press.

Buchanan, James M., Jr. (1986). "The Constitution of Economic Policy." *https:// www.nobelprize.org/prizes/economic-sciences/1986/buchanan/lecture/*. Nobel Media AB.

Burkert, W. (1985). *Greek Religion*. Cambridge, MA: Harvard University Press.

Burnet, John (1916). "The Socratic Doctrine of the Soul." *Proceedings of the British Academy*, vol. 7.

Butler, Eamonn (2012). *Public Choice: A Primer*. London: The Institute of Economic Affairs.

Byrne, Alex, and David Hilbert (1997). *The Philosophy of Color,* vol. 1. Cambridge, MA: MIT Press.

Carroll, Sean (2010). *From Eternity to Here*. New York: Dutton.

Chomsky, Noam ([1955] 1975). *The Logical Structure of Linguistic Theory*. New York: Plenum Press; unpublished ms. available 1955.

—— (1957). *Syntactic Structure*. The Hague: Mouton.

—— (1965). *Aspects of a Theory of Syntax*. Cambridge, MA: MIT Press.

Church, Alonzo (1936a). "A Note on the Entscheidungsproblem." *Journal of Symbolic Logic* 1:40–41.

—— (1936b). "An Unsolvable Problem of Elementary Number Theory." *American Journal of Mathematics* 58:345–63.

—— (1937). "Review: A. M. Turing, On Computable Numbers, with an Application to the Entscheidungsproblem." *Journal of Symbolic Logic* 2:42–43.

Claus, D. (1983). *Toward the Soul*. New Haven, CT: Yale University Press.

Cooper, John M. (2012). *Pursuits of Wisdom*. Princeton, NJ: Princeton University Press.

Copernicus, Nicolaus. (1543). *De Revolutionibus Orbium Coelestium Libri IV.* Nuremberg: Johann Petreius.

Copleston, Frederick (1955). *Aquinas*. Baltimore: Penguin.

—— (1962a). *A History of Philosophy*, vol. 1, part 2. Image edition. New York: Doubleday.

—— (1962b). *A History of Philosophy*, vol. 2, part 2. Image edition. New York: Doubleday.

—— (1964). *A History of Philosophy*, vol. 5, part 1. Image edition. New York: Doubleday.

—— (1993). *A History of Philosophy*, vol. 3. Image edition. New York: Doubleday.

Dales, Richard C. (1990). *Medieval Discussions of the Eternity of the World*. New York: E. J. Brill.

D'Arcy, M. C. (1930). *Thomas Aquinas*. London: Ernest Benn Limited.

Descartes, René ([1641] 1991). *Meditations on First Philosophy*, trans. George Heffer-man. Notre Dame, IN: Notre Dame University Press. Originally published as *Meditationes de primo philosophia*.

—— ([1644] 1983). *Principles of Philosophy*, trans. V. R. Miller and R. P. Miller. Dordrecht: Reidel.

Deutsch, David. (1997). *The Fabric of Reality*. London: Penguin.

Downs, Anthony (1957). *An Economic Theory of Democracy*. New York: Harper.

EarthSky (2011). "Epic Study Confirms Einstein on Space-Time Vortex around Earth." http://earthsky.org/space/epic-study-confirms-einstein-on-space -time.

Einstein, Albert ([1905] 1989). "On the Electrodynamics of Moving Bodies," trans. Anna Beck. In *The Collected Papers of Albert Einstein*, vol. 2, 275–310. Princeton, NJ: Princeton University Press. Originally published as "Zur Elektrodynamik bewegter Körper." *Annalen der Physik* 17:275.

—— ([1916] 1997). "The Foundation of the General Theory Of Relativity," trans. Alfred Engel. In *The Collected Papers of Albert Einstein*, vol. 6, 146–200. Prince-ton, NJ: Princeton University Press. Originally published as "Die Grundlagen der allgemeinen Relativitätstheorie," *Annalen der Physik* 49:769–822.

—— ([1920] 2002). "Fundamental Ideas and Methods in the Theory of Relativity, Presented in Their Development." In *The Collected Papers of Albert Einstein*, vol. 7, 113–50. Princeton, NJ: Princeton University Press. Originally published as "Grundgedanken und Methoden der Relativitätstheorie in ihrer Entwicklung dargestellt."

—— (1948). "Autobiography." In *Einstein: Philosopher-Scientist*, ed. P. A. Schilpp. Evanston, IL: Library of the Living Philosophers.

—— (1949). "Notes for an Autobiography." *The Saturday Review of Literature*, November 26.

—— (1998). *The Collected Papers of Albert Einstein*, vol. 8A. Princeton, NJ: Prince-ton University Press.

Everett, Hugh (1973). *The Many Worlds Interpretation of Quantum Mechanics*. Prince-ton Series in Physics. Princeton, NJ: Princeton University Press.

Feldman, Fred (1992). *Confrontations with the Reaper*. Oxford: Oxford University Press.

Feynman, Richard, Robert Leighton, and Matthew Sands (1975). *The Feynman Lec-tures on Physics*, vol. 2. Reading, MA: Addison-Wesley.

Fleischacker, Samuel (2002). "Adam Smith's Reception among the American Found-ers, 1776–1790." *William and Mary Quarterly* 59:897–924.

Fodor, Jerry A. (1968). *Psychological Explanation: An Introduction to the Philosophy of Psychology.* New York: Random House.

—— (1981). *Representations.* Cambridge, MA: M.I.T. Press.

Fodor, Jerry, T. G. Bever, and M. F. Garrett (1974). *The Psychology of Language: An Introduction to Psycholinguistics and Generative Grammar.* New York: McGraw-Hill.

Fraenkel, Abraham ([1922] 1967). "The Notion 'Definite' and the Independence of the Axiom of Choice," trans. Beverly Woodward. In Van Heijenoort (1967), 284–89.

Frank, Robert H. (1988). *Passion within Reason.* New York: Norton.

Frege, Gottlob ([1879] 1967). *Begriffsschrift,* trans. S. Bauer-Mengelberg. In Van Heijenoort (1967), 1–82.

——([1884] 1950). *The Foundations of Arithmetic,* trans. J. L. Austin. Oxford: Blackwell. Originally published as *Die Grundlagen der Arithmetik,* Breslau: Verlag von Wilhelm Koebner.

—— ([1893, 1903] 1964). *The Basic Laws of Arithmetic,* ed. and trans. M. Furth. Berkeley and Los Angeles: University of California Press, 1964. Originally published as *Grundgesetze der Arithmetik,* 2 vols., Jena.

Furley, D. J. (1956). "The Early History of the Concept of Soul." *Bulletin of the Institute of Classical Studies* 3:1–18.

Gaus, Gerald (2016). *The Tyranny of the Ideal.* Princeton, NJ: Princeton University Press.

Gilson, E. (1955). *Christian Philosophy in the Middle Ages.* New York: Random House.

Gödel, Kurt (1930). "Die Vollständigkeit der Axiome des logischen Funktionenkalkuls." *Monatshefte für Mathematik und Physik* 37:349–60; trans. as "The Completeness of the Axioms of the Functional Calculus of Logic," by S. Bauer-Mengelberg, in Van Heijenoort (1967), 582–91; reprinted in Gödel (1986), 102–23.

—— (1931). "Über formal unentscheidbare Sätze der Principia Mathematica und verwandter Systeme I." *Monatshefte für Mathematik und Physik* 38:173–98; trans. as "On Formally Undecidable Propositions of 'Principia Mathematica' and Related Systems I," by Jean Van Heijenoort, in Van Heijenoort (1967), 596–616; reprinted in Gödel (1986), 144–95.

—— (1932). "Über Vollständigkeit und Widerspruchsfreiheit." *Ergebnisse eines mathematischen Kolloquiums* 3:12–13. English translation "On Completeness and Consistency" in Gödel (1986), 235–37.

—— (1944). "Russell's Mathematical Logic." In *The Philosophy of Bertrand Russell,* ed. P. A. Schilpp, 125–53. La Salle, IL: Open Court.

—— (1986). *Collected Works. I: Publications 1929–1936,* ed. S. Feferman, S. Kleene, G. Moore, R. Solovay, and J. van Heijenoort. Oxford: Oxford University Press.

Gomez-Torrente, Mario (forthcoming). "Arabic Numerals and the Problem of Mathematical Sophistication."

Grice, Paul (1989). *Studies in the Way of Words.* Cambridge, MA: Harvard University Press.

Grünbaum, Adolf (1967). "The Philosophical Significance of Relativity Theory." In *The Encyclopedia of Philosophy,* ed. Paul Edwards, vol. 7, 133–40. New York and London: Collier Macmillan.

Hahn, H., R. Carnap, and O. Neurath (1929). "The Scientific Conception of the World." Pamphlet, translated and reprinted in Sarkar (1996a), 321–41.

Hamburger, Philip (2014). *Is Administrative Law Unlawful?* Chicago: University of Chicago Press.

Hanks, Peter (2015). *Propositional Content.* Oxford: Oxford University Press.

Harris, W. V. (1989). *Ancient Literacy.* Cambridge, MA: Harvard University Press.

Harrison, John (1992). "Reconstructing the Privileges or Immunities Clause." *Yale Law Journal* 101:1385–1474.

Hart, H.L.A. ([1961] 2012). *The Concept of Law.* Oxford: Oxford University Press.

Havelock, E. (1967). *Preface to Plato.* Cambridge, MA: Harvard University Press.

—— (1983). "The Linguistic Task of the Presocratics." in *Language and Thought in Early Greek Philosophy*, ed. K. Robb, 7–82. La Salle, IL: The Hegeler Institute.

Hayek, Friedrich A. (1960). *The Constitution of Liberty.* Chicago: University of Chicago Press.

Heath, Thomas Little (1981). *A History of Greek Mathematics*, vol. 1. New York: Dover; corrected version of original Oxford edition published in 1921.

Herman, Arthur (2001). *How the Scots Invented the Modern World.* New York: Crown Publishers.

Hobbes, Thomas ([1651] 1994). *Leviathan*, ed. E. Curley. Indianapolis, IN: Hackett.

Hodes, Harold (2015). Why Ramify? *Notre Dame Journal of Formal Logic* 56:379–415.

Hume, David (1964). *Philosophical Works*, ed. T. H. Green and T. H. Grose. 4 vols. Darmstadt: Scientia Verlag Aalen. Reprint of original publication, London: Longmans, Green and Co.

Jeffrey, Richard (1965). *The Logic of Decision.* Chicago: University of Chicago Press.

—— (2004). *Subjective Probability.* Cambridge: Cambridge University Press.

Jesperson, Bjorn (2010). "How Hyper Are Hyper Propositions?" *Language and Linguistics Compass* 39:296–30.

—— (2012). "Recent Work on Structured Meaning and Propositional Unity." *Philosophy Compass* 7:620–30.

Johnson-Laird, P. N. (1983). *Mental Models: Towards a Cognitive Science of Language, Reference, and Consciousness.* Cambridge: Cambridge University Press.

Johnson-Laird, P. N., and P. C. Watson (1977). *Thinking: Readings in Cognitive Science.* Cambridge: Cambridge University Press.

Kagan, Shelly (2012). *Death.* New Haven, CT: Yale University Press.

Kamareddine, Fairouz, Twan Laan, and Rob Nederpelt (2002). "Types in Logic and Mathematics before 1940." *Bulletin of Symbolic Logic* 8:185–245.

Kaplan, David (1979). "On the Logic of Demonstratives." *Journal of Philosophical Logic* 8:81:98.

—— (1989). "Demonstratives: An Essay on the Semantics, Logic, Metaphysics, and Epistemology of Demonstratives and Other Indexicals." In *Themes from Kaplan*, ed. Joseph Almog, John Perry, and Howard Wettstein, 481–563. New York: Oxford University Press.

Kemeny, J. (1955). "Fair Bets and Inductive Probabilities." *Journal of Symbolic Logic* 20:263–73.

Kepler, Johannes ([1609] 1858–71). *Astronomia Nova,* ed. C. Frisch. 8 vols. Frankfurt and Erlangen.

King, Jeffrey C. (2007). *The Nature and Structure of Content.* Oxford: Oxford University Press.

King, Jeff, Scott Soames, and Jeff Speaks (2014). *New Thinking about Propositions.* Oxford: Oxford University Press.

Klement, Kevin (2004). "Putting Form before Function: Logical Grammar in Frege, Russell, and Wittgenstein." *Philosophers' Imprint*, (www.philosophersimprint.org /004002/) 4, 2: 1–47.

Kołakowski, Leszek ([1978] 2005). *Main Currents of Marxism*. New York: Norton.

Kolmogorov, A. N. (1950). *Foundations of Probability*. New York: Chelsea Publishing.

Kretzmann, Norman (1993). "Philosophy of Mind." in *The Cambridge Companion to Aquinas,* ed. Norman Kretzmann and Eleonore Stump. Cambridge: Cambridge University Press.

Kripke, Saul (1959). "A Completeness Theorem in Modal Logic." *Journal of Symbolic Logic* 24:1–14.

—— (1971). "Identity and Necessity." In *Identity and Individuation,* ed. Milton Munitz. New York: NYU Press.

—— (1980). *Naming and Necessity*. Cambridge, MA: Harvard University Press.

Landini, Gregory (1998). *Russell's Hidden Substitutional Theory*. Oxford: Oxford University Press.

Lawson, Gary (1994). "The Rise and Rise of the Administrative State." *Harvard Law Review* 107:1231–1254.

—— (2015). "The Return of the King: The Unsavory Origins of Administrative Law." *Texas Law Review* 93:1521–45.

Lawson, Gary, and Guy Seidman (2017). *A Great Power of Attorney: Understanding the Fiduciary Constitution*. Lawrence: University of Kansas Press.

Leibniz, G. W. (1875–1890). *Die mathematischen Schriften von G. W. Leibniz,* ed. C. I. Gerhardt. 7 vols. Berlin.

Lewis, David (1966). "An Argument for the Identity Theory." *Journal of Philosophy* 63:17–25.

Locke, John ([1689] 1975). *An Essay Concerning the Human Understanding*, ed. Peter H. Niddich. Oxford: Clarendon Press.

—— (1987). *Locke's Two Treatises on Civil Government*. Richard Ashcraft, ed. London: Routledge.

Marx, Karl (1970). *Capital*. Three volumes, trans. Samuel Moore and Edward Aveling. London: Lawrence and Wishart, and Moscow: Progress Publishers.

Maudlin, Tim (2012). *The Philosophy of Physics: Space and Time*. Princeton, NJ: Princeton University Press.

McCabe, Herbert (1969). "The Immortality of the Soul." in *Aquinas,* Anthony Kenny ed., Garden City, NY: Doubleday.

McGinnis, John, and Michael Rappaport (2013). *Originalism and the Good Constitution*. Cambridge, MA: Harvard.

Miller, G. A., E. Galanter, and K. H. Pribram (1960). *Plans and the Structure of Behavior.* New York: Holt, Reinhart and Winston.

Moller, Dan (2014). "Justice and the Wealth of Nations." *Public Affairs Quarterly* 28, 2 (April): 95–114.

Moltmann, Friederike (2017). *Act-Based Conceptions of Propositional Content*. Oxford: Oxford University Press.

Monk, Ray (2016). "One of the Great Intellects of His Time." *New York Review of Books,* December 22.

Morrison, James V. (2006). *Reading Thucydides*. Columbus: Ohio State University Press.

Nagel, Thomas (1979). "Death." In *Mortal Questions*, 1–10. Cambridge: Cambridge University Press.

—— (1987). *What Does It All Mean?* Oxford: Oxford University Press.

Natelson, Robert G. (2010). "The Legal Origins of the Necessary and Proper Clause." In *The Origins of the Necessary and Proper Clause*, ed. G. Lawson, G. P. Millar, R. G. Natelson, and G. I. Seidman, 52–83. Cambridge: Cambridge University Press, 2010.

Newton, Isaac ([1687] 1934). *Principia*, trans. Andrew Motte, rev. by Florian Cajoli, 2 vols. Berkeley: University of California Press.

—— (1959–84). *The Correspondence of Isaac Newton*, ed. H. W. Turnbull, J. F. Scott, A. R. Hall, and L. Tilling. 7 vols. Cambridge: Cambridge University Press.

—— (1999). *The Principia: Mathematical Principles of Natural Philosophy: A New Translation*, trans. I. B. Cohen and Anne Whitman. Berkeley: University of California Press.

Norton, John (2010). "How Hume and Mach Helped Einstein Find Special Relativity." In *Discourse on a New Method: Reinvigorating the Marriage of History and Philosophy of Science*, ed. M. Dickson and M. Domski, 359–86. Chicago and La Salle, IL: Open Court.

Nozick, Robert (1974). *Anarchy, State, and Utopia*. New York: Basic Books.

—— (1989). *The Examined Life*. New York: Simon and Schuster.

Ockham, William (1952). *Tractatus de successivis*. In *Ockham: Selected Philosophical Writings*, ed. P. Boehner. London: O.F.M. (Order of Friars Minor).

Paul, Margaret (2012). *Frank Ramsey (1903–1930): A Sister's Memoir*. London: Smith-Gordon.

Peano, Giuseppe (1889). *Arithmetices principia, novo methodo exposita* (The Principles of Arithmetic, Presented by a New Method). Turin: Bocco; reprinted in Van Heijenoort (1967), 83–97.

Pegis, Anton C. (1934). *St. Thomas and the Problem of the Soul in the Thirteenth Century*. Toronto: Pontifical Institute of Mediaeval Studies.

Place, U. T. (1956). "Is Consciousness a Brain Process?" *British Journal of Psychology* 47:44–50.

Plato (1961). *Collected Dialogues*, ed. Edith Hamilton and Huntington Cairns. New York: Pantheon Books 1961.

Putnam, Hilary (1967). "The Nature of Mental States." In *Art, Mind, and Religion*, ed. W. H. Capitan and D. D. Merrill. Pittsburgh: Pittsburgh University Press; reprinted in Putnam (1975b).

—— (1975a). "The Meaning of 'Meaning.'" In Putnam (1975b), pp. 215–71.

—— (1975b). *Philosophical Papers*, vol. 2: *Mind, Language, and Reality*. Cambridge: Cambridge University Press, 1975.

Ramsey, F. P. (1925). "The Foundations of Mathematics." *Proceedings of the London Mathematical Society* 25:338–84; reprinted in Braithwaite (1931).

—— ([1926] 1990). "Truth and Probability." In *Philosophical Papers*, D. H. Mellor, ed., Cambridge: Cambridge University Press, 1990, 52–94; also in Braithwaite (1931).

Rappaport, Michael (2013). "Originalism and the Colorblind Constitution." *Notre Dame Law Review* 89:71–132.

Rawls, John (1971). *A Theory of Justice*. Cambridge, MA: Harvard University Press.

Robb, K. (1968). "Psyche and Logos in the Fragments of Heraclitus: The Origins of the Concept of Soul." *The Monist* 69:315–51.

—— (1994). *Literacy and Paideia in Ancient Greece.* Oxford: Oxford University Press.

Robinson, T. M. (1968). "Heraclitus on Soul." *The Monist* 69:305–14.

Rosser, J. Barkley (1937). "Gödel Theorems for Non-Constructive Logics." *Journal of Symbolic Logic* 2:129–37.

Russell, Bertrand (1904). "Meinong's Theory of Complexes and Assumptions." *Mind* 13:204–19, 336–34, 509–24; reprinted in *Essay's in Analysis,* ed. Douglas Lackey, New York: George Braziller 1973, 21–76.

Russell, Bertrand, and Alfred North Whitehead (1910). *Principia Mathematica,* vol. 1. Cambridge: Cambridge University Press.

—— (1912). *Principia Mathematica,* vol. 2. Cambridge: Cambridge University Press.

—— (1913). *Principia Mathematica,* vol. 3. Cambridge: Cambridge University Press.

Sarkar, Sahotra (1996). *The Emergence of Logical Empiricism: From 1900 to the Vienna Circle,* vol. 1. New York: Garland Publishing.

Savage, Leonard (1954). *The Foundations of Statistics.* New York: Dover.

Scheffler, Samuel (2016). *Death and the Afterlife.* Oxford: Oxford University Press.

Schlick, Moritz (1915). "Die philosophische Bedeutung des Relativsatsprinzips." *Zeitschrift für Philosophie und philosophische Kritik* 159:129–75. Published as "The Philosophical Significance of the Principle of Relativity," trans. P. Heath, in Schlick (1979), vol. 1, 153–89.

—— (1920). *Space and Time in Contemporary Physics,* trans. H. Brose. New York: Oxford University Press. Originally published as *Raum und Zeit in der gegenwartigen Physik,* Berlin: Springer.

—— ([1930] 1939). *Problems of Ethics,* trans. David Rynin. New York: Prentice Hall. Originally published as *Fragen der Ethik.* Vienna: Springer.

—— (1979). *Philosophical Papers,* vols. 1 and 2. Ed. B. van de Velde-Schlick and H. Mulder. Dordrecht: Reidel.

Skyrms, Brian (1994). *Pragmatism and Empiricism.* New Haven, CT: Yale University Press.

Smart, J. J. C. (1963). *Philosophy and Scientific Realism.* New York: Humanities Press.

Smith, Adam ([1759] 2002). *The Theory of the Moral Sentiments.* Cambridge: Cambridge University Press. Originally published London: A Millar.

—— ([1776] 1997). *The Wealth of Nations.* London: Penguin. London: W. Strahan.

Soames, Scott (1984). "Linguistics and Psychology." *Linguistics and Philosophy* 7:155–79; reprinted in Soames (2009a), 133–58.

—— (1987). "Direct Reference, Propositional Attitudes, and Semantic Content." *Philosophical Topics* 15:47–87; reprinted in Soames (2009b), 33–71.

—— (1989). "Semantics and Semantic Competence." *Philosophical Perspectives* 3:575–96; reprinted in Soames (2009a), 182–201.

—— ([1990] 2009). "Belief and Mental Representation." In *Information, Language and Cognition,* ed. Philip P. Hanson, 217–46. Vancouver: University of British Columbia Press. Reprinted in Soames (2009b), 81–110.

—— (2003). *Philosophical Analysis in the Twentieth Century,* vol. 2. Princeton, NJ, and Oxford: Princeton University Press.

—— (2007). "What Are Natural Kinds?" *Philosophical Topics* 35:329–42; reprinted in Soames (2014a).

—— (2008a). "Truth and Meaning—in Perspective." *Midwest Studies in Philosophy* 32:1–19; reprinted in Soames (2009a).

—— (2008b). "Why Propositions Can't Be Sets of Truth-Supporting Circumstances." *Journal of Philosophical Logic* 37:267–76; reprinted in Soames (2009b), 72–80.

—— (2008c). "Drawing the Line between Meaning and Implicature—and Relating Both to Assertion." *Noûs* 42:529–54; reprinted in Soames (2009a), 298–325.

—— (2009a). *Philosophical Essays*, vol. 1. Princeton, NJ: Princeton University Press.

—— (2009b). *Philosophical Essays*, vol. 2. Princeton, NJ: Princeton University Press.

—— (2010a). *Philosophy of Language.* Princeton, NJ: Princeton University Press.

—— (2010b). *What Is Meaning?* Princeton, NJ: Princeton University Press.

—— (2013a). "Cognitive Propositions." *Philosophical Perspectives: Philosophy of Language* 27:479–501.

—— (2013b). "Deferentialism." *Fordham Law Review* 82:101–22; reprinted in Soames (2014a).

—— (2014a). *Analytic Philosophy in America.* Princeton, NJ: Princeton University Press.

—— (2014b). *The Analytic Tradition in Philosophy,* vol. 1. Princeton, NJ: Princeton University Press.

—— (2014c). "For Want of Cognitive Propositions." In Soames (2014a).

—— (2015a). "Reply to Critics of the *Analytic Tradition in Philosophy*, Volume 1." *Philosophical Studies* 172:1681–96.

—— (2015b). *Rethinking Language, Mind, and Meaning.* Princeton, NJ, and Oxford: Princeton University Press.

—— (2016a). "Yes, the Search for Explanation Is All We Have." *Philosophical Studies* 173, 9: 2565–73.

—— (2016b). "Propositions, the *Tractatus*, and 'The Single Great Problem of Philosophy.'" *Critica* 48, 143:3–19.

—— (2017). "Deferentialism, Living Originalism, and the Constitution." In *The Nature of Legal Interpretation*, ed. Brian Slocum, 218–40. Chicago: University of Chicago Press.

—— (2018). *The Analytic Tradition in Philosophy,* vol. 2. Princeton, NJ: Princeton University Press.

—— (forthcoming). "Originalism and Legitimacy." *Georgetown Journal of Law and Public Policy.*

Solum, Lawrence B. (2011). "What Is Originalism?" http://dx.doi.org/10.2139/ssrn.1825543.

—— (2013). "Originalism and Constitutional Construction." *Fordham Law Review* 82: 453.

—— (2018). "Surprising Originalism." The Regula Lecture, *ConlawNOW* 9:235.

Stigler, George (1971). "The Theory of Economic Regulation." *Bell Journal of Economics and Management Science* 3:3–18.

Stigler, George, and Friedland, Claire (1962). "What Can Regulators Regulate? The Case of Electricity." *Journal of Law and Economics* 5:1–16.

Tarski, Alfred ([1935] 1983). "The Concept of Truth in Formalized Languages," trans. J. H. Woodger. In Tarski (1983), 152–278. Originally published as "Der Wahrheitsbegriff in den formalisierten Sprachen." *Studia Philosophica* 1:261–405.

—— ([1936] 1983). "On the Concept of Logical Consequence," trans. J. H. Woodger. In Tarski (1983), 409–20. Originally published as "Über den Begriff der logischen Folgerung," *Acts du Congres International de Philosophie Scientifique* 7 (Actualités Scientifiques et Industrielles, vol. 394), 1–11. Paris: Hermann et Cie.

—— (1983). *Logic, Semantics, Metamathematics*, 2nd ed., ed. J. Corcoran. Indianapolis: Hackett.

Thomas, R. (1992). *Literacy and Orality in Ancient Greece.* Cambridge: Cambridge University Press.

Tullock, Gordon (1967). "The Welfare Costs of Tariffs, Monopolies, and Theft." *Western Economic Journal* 5:224–32.

Turing, Alan (1936/37). "On Computable Numbers with an Application to the Entscheidungsproblem." *Proceedings of the London Mathematical Society*, series 2, 42:230–65.

—— (1950). "Computing Machinery and Intelligence." *Mind* 49:433–60.

Upham, David R. (2015). "Interracial Marriage and the Original Understanding of the Privileges or Immunities Clause." *Hastings Constitutional Law Quarterly* 42:213–86.

Van Heijenoort, Jean, ed. (1967). *From Frege to Gödel.* Cambridge, MA: Harvard University Press.

von Neumann, John, and Oskar Morgenstern (1944). *The Theory of Games and Economic Behavior.* Princeton, NJ: Princeton University Press.

Wallace, David (2012). *The Emergent Multiverse.* Oxford: Oxford University Press.

Weisheipl, James A. (1965). "The Principle *Omne quod movetur ab alio movetur* in Medieval Physics." *Isis* 56:26–45.

—— (1983). "The Date and Context of Aquinas's *De aeternitate mundi."* in *Graceful Reason: Essays in Ancient and Medieval Philosophy Presented to Joseph Owens,* ed. Lloyd P. Gerson. Toronto: Papers in Mediaeval Philosophy.

Wilson, James Q. (1993). *The Moral Sense.* New York: Free Press.

Wippel, John F. (1981). "Did Thomas Aquinas Defend the Possibility of an Eternally Created World?" *Journal of the History of Philosophy* 19:21–37.

Wittgenstein, Ludwig ([1922] 1961). *Tractatus Logico-Philosophicus,* trans. D. Pears and B. McGuinness. London: Routledge, 1961.

——. (1953). *Philosophical Investigations,* trans. G.E.M. Anscombe. N. p.: Macmillan.

Wolfe, Tom (2012). *Back to Blood.* New York: Little Brown.

Yunis, H., ed. (2003). *Written Texts and the Rise of Literate Culture in Ancient Greece.* Cambridge: Cambridge University Press.

Zermelo, Ernst (1904). "Proof That Every Set Can Be Well Ordered," trans. S. Bauer-Mengelberg. In Van Heijenoort (1967), 139–41.

—— (1908a). "A New Proof of the Possibility of a Well-Ordering," trans. S. Bauer-Mengelberg. In Van Heijenoort (1967), 183–98.

—— (1908b). "Investigations of the Foundations of Set Theory I," trans. S. Bauer-Mengelberg. In Van Heijenoort (1967), 199–215.

INDEX

a posteriori knowledge, 199
a priori knowledge, 63, 68–69, 80,
    197–200, 229, 352; consequence,
    343, 346, 352
Anaxagoras, 5
Anselm, 53
Aquinas, Thomas, 22–33, 397, 409–410
Aristotle (Aristotelian), 1–4, 10–19,
    21–25, 28–29, 32, 38, 45–46, 49,
    55, 93, 220–221, 249, 351, 372–373,
    376–377, 379, 408nn20–23,
    408n25, 409n7
Armstrong, David, 193
Arrow, Kenneth, 179, 184, 417n20
assertoric content, 136, 150–155,
    312–327, 338
astronomy, 4–6, 31, 41, 45–46, 55, 398,
    400–401
atomism (metaphysical), 4, 47–48,
    54, 63
Augustine (Augustinian), 20–22, 32,
    104, 397, 410n24
Averroes, 22
Avicenna, 22

Bacon, Francis, 49, 60, 397
Bacon, Matthew, 336
Bacon, Roger, 31–32, 40, 49, 221, 398
Becker, Gary, 179–180, 398
Beeckman, Isaac, 50
Benacerraf, Paul, 414n13
Bentham, Jeremy, 413n17
Berkeley, George, 61, 65–66, 69, 70, 398
Bever, T. G., 213
Black, Duncan, 179
Boethius, 374
Bohm, David, 247

Bohr, Niels, 242
Bonaventure, 32, 410n24
Boolos, George, 414n14
Born, Max, 242
Boyle, Robert, 60, 69, 89, 398
Brown v. Board of Education, 327
Buchanan, James, 179, 185–187, 398
Buridan, John, 40, 221
Burkert, Walter, 2
Burr, Aaron, 86
Butler, Eamonn, 181

cardinality properties, 104–111
Carnap, Rudolf, 92, 195
Carroll, Sean, 249
categorical imperative, 89–91
causation, 37, 61, 65, 67–69
Chomsky, Noam, 134–136
Christianity, 19, 20–24, 28, 30–34,
    38–39, 374
Church, Alonzo, 113, 115, 125, 129–132
Clarke, Samuel, 225–226
cognitive acts, 107, 144–150, 191, 214
completeness, 120–130
computability, 113–114, 129–132
consent (of the governed), 76–79
consequence (logical), 95–96, 100,
    114, 116–120, 127–128, 130–131,
    342–343, 404, 413n3, 414n3
Cooper, John, 409nn25–28
Copernicus, Nicolaus, 41–43, 46, 69,
    221
Copleston, Frederick, 23, 30, 409n7,
    409n11

Darwin, Charles, 70–72, 354, 361–362
decidability, 114–124, 127, 129–131

decision theory, 157–187
deferentialism, 311–321, 324–330
definition, 6–7, 10, 68, 95–101, 110,
    175, 177, 197, 229, 295
degrees of belief (credences), 158–160,
    165–169, 174–178
democracy, 79–80, 184–187, 291,
    301–303, 311–312, 321–340
Descartes, René, 44, 49–55, 60, 62, 66,
    69, 73, 89, 188–191, 221
Deutsch, David, 249
Dirac, Paul, 242
Downs, Anthony, 179, 184–185
dualism (mind-body), 49, 52–53,
    188–191
Dutch Book, 167–168

economics, 73, 87–89, 178–187,
    250–302, 329–330
Eddington, Arthur, 239–240
Einstein, Albert, 221–224, 227–242,
    418n17
Elbourne, Paul, 143
empiricism, 61, 65–68, 85; logical, 121
Epicurus (Epicureanism), 1, 18
Euclid (Euclidian), 5, 57, 68–69,
    225–226
Eudoxus, 5
Everett, Hugh, III, 247–249
Everitt, Francis, 240

fairness, 83, 263–274, 288, 354,
    356–357, 362–364, 368–369, 419n17
Feynman, Richard, 240–241
Fichte, Johann Gottlieb, 289–290
Freud, Sigmund, 354
Friedland, Claire, 183
Fodor, Jerry, 213–218
forms, 7–15, 21, 23–29, 33–35, 38,
    408n20, 408n21
Frank, Robert, 356
Frege, Gottlob, 92–104, 110–112,
    113–120, 139–141, 144, 413n3,
    413n6, 415n6
functionalism (mental), 201–203,
    207–211

Galilei, Galileo, 44–49, 55, 62, 69, 73,
    221, 240–241, 411n5, 411n6, 411n7

Garrett, M. F., 213
Gaus, Gerald, 250–251, 277–288
geometry, 5–8, 42–43, 50, 57–60, 72,
    100, 229–235, 239
God, 10, 14–15, 21, 24, 29–38, 43,
    50–51, 53–54, 62–65, 374, 408n23,
    409n7, 409n10
Gödel, Kurt, 113–115, 119–130, 414n3,
    415n7
Gomez-Torrente, Mario, 107, 414n14
government failure, 181–187
gravity, 43–44, 54–56, 65, 72, 239–241
Grice, Paul, 155
guises (ways of cognizing), 146–150,
    214–215

Hamburger, Philip, 332–337, 339
happiness, 15–18, 20, 373–385,
    387–388
Hart, H.L.A., 303–310, 322, 326,
    330
Havelock, Eric, 2, 8, 407n7, 408n17
Hayek, Friedrich, 250–262, 273–276,
    288, 419n14
Heath, Thomas, 5–6
Hegel, Georg Wilhelm Friedrich, x,
    289–293, 298–299
Heim, Irene, 143
Heisenberg, Werner, 242
Heraclitus, 3, 408n17
Hippocrates, 5
Hobbes, Thomas (Hobbesian), 73–75,
    262, 310
Homer, 2–3, 15, 73
Hume, David, 61, 66–72, 80–91, 103,
    222–223, 321, 340, 341, 351, 362,
    368, 390–395
Husserl, Edmund, 92
Hutcheson, Francis, 86–89, 351

identities, theoretical, 193–201,
    202–208
incompleteness (linguistic), 150–155,
    313–317
Incompleteness Theorems (Gödel):
    First Theorem, 120–125; Second
    Theorem, 128–129
Inquisition, 411n7
Iredell, James, 336

Johnson-Laird, Philip, 213, 217
justice, 83–85, 250–302, 391, 420n34, 422n17

Kagan, Elena, 421n17
Kant, Immanuel, x, 40, 65, 68–70, 89–91, 222, 264, 289–290, 341–342, 350
Kaplan, David, 150
Kepler, Johannes, 42–46, 49, 55, 62, 69, 221
Klement, Kevin, 414n11
Kołakowski, Leszek, 299–302
Kolmogorov, A. N., 161–162
Kratzer, Angelika, 143
Kretzmann, Norman, 26
Kripke, Saul, 195–201, 203–208

Landini, Gregory, 414n11
Langford, C. H., 195
law (positive): constitutional, 155, 305, 312, 321–340, 402, 421n25; interpretation of, 152–155, 311–340; nature of, 303–310; obedience to, 74–80, 303–310, 386–388
laws of nature, 1, 56, 70, 75, 83
Lawson, Gary, 331–332, 334–337
legal positivism, 307–310
Leibniz, G. W., 62–65, 69, 89, 198, 225, 412n24
Leninism, 280, 299–302
Lewis, C. I., 195
Lewis, David, 193
liberty, 75–80, 85–86, 88, 90, 251–252, 255–256, 260–263, 269–270, 273, 275, 278, 288, 329–330, 367
linguistics, 96, 112, 133–150
Locke, John, 60–61, 65–66, 70, 75–80, 85, 88, 262, 321, 336, 340
logic, 1, 10–11, 15, 21, 30, 40, 55, 62–63, 92–112, 113–132, 133, 136–137, 141–143, 161–162, 164–165, 212, 244, 343; higher-order, 120, 125–128
logical positivism, 222–223, 351

Mach, Ernst, 222–223, 417n2 (chapter 10)
Magna Carta, 332–334
Magnus, Albertus, 22–23, 32

Manichaeism, 21
Marcus, Ruth Barcan, 195
market failure, 181–182
Marx, Karl, 250–251, 280, 289–302
mathematics, 1, 3–8, 10, 15, 30–31, 40–41, 43, 45, 48–50, 54–55, 62, 69–72, 88–89, 92–112, 113–117, 126–127, 129–130, 132, 155–156, 161, 169, 231, 234, 242–243, 246, 249
matter, 1, 3, 12–13, 15, 23–29, 33, 46, 48, 54, 60, 63, 65, 70–71, 220, 225, 239–240, 409n11; prime matter, 12–13, 33, 408n22
Maudlin, Tim, 228, 234–237, 418n16, 418n19
Maxwell, James Clerk, 232–233
McGinnis, John, 329–330, 421n21
meaning (linguistic), 6, 34–37, 96, 100–101, 104–106, 134–156, 191–193, 313–317, 414n11; and understanding, 147–148
meaning of life, 15, 18, 22, 30, 39, 373–387, 423n4 (chapter 14)
measured v. unmeasured particles, 243–248
Mill, John Stuart, 413n17
modal logic, 141–144
model, 95–96, 118–119, 126, 130, 141, 142–143, 158, 277–286, 415n3; truth in a, 118–119, 141, 413n3
Montesquieu, 85
morality, 75–76, 81–91, 250–302, 304–310, 341–372, 376–382, 388–391; "moral constitution," 287; moral knowledge, 288, 342, 349, 351, 353–354, 372; moral merit, 257–258, 264, 270–271; moral motivation, 345, 352, 353–354; moral objectivity, 349–371, 422n25; moral reasons, 307, 344–354, 376; moral responsibility, 9, 15, 257; moral sense, 81, 83–85, 86, 352–371; moral worth/dignity, 256, 258, 271, 369–370
Morrison, James, 407n6
motion, 1, 3, 8, 15, 40–42, 45–48, 54–65, 72, 220, 223–227, 231–233, 238, 241
Muggeridge, Malcolm, 374–375

Natelson, Robert, 336
necessity/possibility, 12, 23, 35–38, 53, 62–63, 67–68, 116, 141–144, 195–208, 343; conceptual, 90, 195–201, 342, 351, 354, 411n13
Newton, Isaac, 54–69, 83, 88–89, 220–221, 225–227, 232, 239–241, 411n21
Nietzsche, Friedrich, x
Niskanen, William, 179
Nozick, Robert, 260–262, 276–277, 381–382

Ockham, William of, 34–38, 40, 221, 410n28
Olson, Mancur, 179
ontological argument, 53–54, 62
Oresme, Nicholas, 40, 221
original position, 264–273, 278
Otis, James, 333
ought from *is*, 342–355

Parmenides, 3–4
Partee, Barbara, 143
Peano arithmetic, 100, 110–111, 128–129, 413n7
physics, 11, 15, 40–41, 44–51, 54–55, 60, 62, 73, 88–89, 193, 200, 218, 220–249; micro, 242–249
Pierce, Charles Sanders, 413n1
Place, U. T., 193
Plato, 1–12, 15–19, 20–21, 33, 146, 372–374, 386–387, 407n5, 410n24
predicate calculus, 93, 113, 116–128
pre-Socratic, 3–4
probability: conditional/unconditional, 162–166; laws of (Kolmogorov's), 161–166; objective, 243–247; subjective, 16, 157–187
proof, 93–94, 114, 116–120, 123–125, 129–132, 211–212
properties, 62–63, 103–111, 138, 144–146, 148, 192–193, 198, 243–244; accidental, 12–13, 196–197; essential, 12–13, 23–24, 62, 196–198, 206, 408n22, 412n24; primary v. secondary, 48, 61, 65

propositional calculus, 116
propositions, 8, 62–63, 138–155, 189–193, 416; attitudes to, 139, 143, 213–218, 416n6; as cognitive act types, 144–155, 416n12; cognitively distinct, representationally identical, 146–149; Frege-Russellian, 139–140, 144; as meanings, 146–155, 191
public choice theory, 180–187
Pullum, Geoffrey, 143
Pythagoras, 4–5

quantification, 120, 142–143, 151–152, 414n11, 415n8
quantum mechanics, 242–249

Ramsey, F. P., 157, 166–181, 413n11, 417n17
Rappaport, Michael, 329–330, 421n21
Rawls, John, 250–251, 262–278, 286, 288, 403, 419n17
relativity: general, 239–241; special, 227–238, 418n16, 418n17
representation, mental, 61, 65–66, 139–149, 188–193, 209–218, 416n12
rights, 74–90, 307, 330–334, 336–337, 340
Roberts, Craige, 143
Robb, Kevin, 407n5
Ross, Jake, 419n11, 420n30, 420n42
Rousseau, Jean-Jacques, 85
Russell, Bertrand, 92, 100–104, 111–112, 139–141, 144, 403, 413n11, 416n6

Scalia, Antonin, 314–316
Scheiner, Christoph, 46
Schlick, Moritz, 222–223, 351–352, 417n2
Schrödinger, Erwin, 242
Scotus, John Duns, 33
self-interest, 83–85, 87, 180, 263–267, 272, 278, 348, 353–356, 367, 376, 378, 422n17
semantics, study of, 137–155

separation of powers, 80, 300,
310–311, 328–340
simultaneity, 222, 223, 226–231,
418n16
Smart, J.J.C., 193
Smith, Adam, 86–89, 181–182, 351,
362, 368, 391
Smith v. United States, 314–317
Socrates, 1–19, 20, 23, 25, 27–29, 33,
120, 372–374, 386–390
soul, 9, 13, 15, 19, 21, 24–30, 33–34,
38, 50, 387, 408n16, 408n17,
408n20, 408n22, 408n23, 409n11
space (absolute v. relative), 57–60,
64–65, 225–241
state of nature, 74–81, 262–263
Stevin, Simon, 46
Stigler, George, 179, 183–184, 403
Stoics (Stoicism), 1, 18–21, 93, 116, 374
Supreme Court (of the United
States), 152–153, 311–337
syntax, study of, 134–136, 415n1

Tarski, Alfred, 113, 119, 121–123, 141,
413n3, 415n7
Thales, 3–4
truth, 15, 95–97, 114, 116–119, 141–146,
404, 413–416, in a model, 118–119,
141, 413n3; at a world-state, 416n12
Tullock, Gordon, 179, 183

Turing, Alan, 113, 115, 129–132, 210
Turing machine, 130–132

U.S. Constitution, 152, 154, 305, 312,
321–340, 421n25
utility: agent-relative, 168–178; expected, 168–172, 176, 186

virtue(s), 17–18, 356–359, 373–385,
387–388
voting, 184–185

Wallace, David, 249
Watson, P. C., 213
wave function, 243–245, 419n25
welfare, 179–180, 251, 269–272, 274,
344–349, 368, 377–380
Whitehead, Alfred North, 101
Wicksell, Knut, 187, 417
Williams, Porter, 419n25, 419n26
Wilson, James Q., 352–371, 422n25
Witherspoon, John, 86, 340
Wittgenstein, Ludwig, 92, 104–106,
140–141
Wolfe, Tom, 375
world-states, 142–144, 198–200,
416n12

Zeno, 18, 25
Zermelo-Fraenkel set theory, 102